THE POEMS AND
SONGS OF
Robert Burns

ROBERT BURNS

From the portrait by Alexander Nasmyth in the Scottish National Portrait Gallery

THE POEMS AND SONGS OF

Robert Burns

Edited by

JAMES KINSLEY

Professor of English Studies in the
University of Nottingham

Volume I
TEXT

OXFORD
AT THE CLARENDON PRESS
1968

Oxford University Press, Ely House, London W. 1

GLASGOW NEW YORK TORONTO MELBOURNE WELLINGTON
CAPE TOWN SALISBURY IBADAN NAIROBI LUSAKA ADDIS ABABA
BOMBAY CALCUTTA MADRAS KARACHI LAHORE DACCA
KUALA LUMPUR HONG KONG TOKYO

PRINTED IN GREAT BRITAIN

PREFACE

In 1930 Robert Dewar, then professor of English literature in the University of Reading, began work on a new Oxford edition of Burns's poems. He was finely equipped for this task. Raised in rural Ayrshire, in a community like that in which Burns grew up, and far more at his ease in the dialect of the west country than any younger scholar is likely to be, he had made a long study of the Scottish vernacular tradition. He began his work, too, at a time when many of the Burns manuscripts that had been dispersed during the nineteenth century were passing back through the salerooms into great public collections; and when Professor J. De Lancey Ferguson was completing his edition of Burns's letters. Dewar's progress was slow under the strains of the war years, and of university office; but by the late 1940s he had collated a mass of manuscript material and had begun to establish his text. Failing health forced him to abandon work in 1955, and—at his own request—I succeeded him as editor. He generously passed on his transcripts to me, with a number of his books; and although I decided to begin again on different editorial principles, his papers were invaluable. They gave me an immediate conspectus of the whole range of manuscripts and textual problems; accurate descriptions and collations of a number of manuscripts which were again inaccessible, or could not be traced; and a continuous check on my own work. But I owe even more to Dewar's critical approach; to his engrossing talk about a poet whom he understood as much by instinct and spiritual kinship as by study; and to the friendship of a man who was, like Burns's John Rankine, 'rough, rude, ready-witted . . . The wale o' cocks for fun an' drinkin'—a 'ram-stam boy' in the midst of a decorous profession.

My first concern has been to provide a complete text of Burns's original poems, and of songs and ballads which he recovered and reshaped from oral tradition, based on a critical review of all the accessible manuscripts and the early printings. This material, and the principles on which it has been edited, are described in my Textual Introduction.

The canon of Burns's work will probably never be fully established. The core is firm enough: it consists mainly of the Kilmarnock and Edinburgh editions, the signed contributions Burns made to the four volumes of *The Scots Musical Museum* which appeared in his lifetime, and original poems which were unpublished when he died but survive in holograph. Outside this core is a mass of lyric verse in manuscript, which is in some degree traditional; and the deliberate impersonality with which Burns reshaped Scottish folk-song in the traditional styles often throws his editor back on provisional, subjective judgements. Such decisions, based on fragmentary evidence—and sometimes only on intuition—will probably irritate readers who are used to discussing problems of authorship in the work of poets with distinctive styles and themes; and some of my judgements may, through chance discoveries in chapbooks and manuscript gatherings of folk-song, turn out to be wrong. But an editor of Burns who is rigorously exclusive will, more certainly, omit much that his author had a hand in. Burns worked to recover and consolidate the native lyric tradition; and an edition of his songs is inevitably, to some extent, another 'Museum' of that tradition. Where there is no present certainty, I have thought it right to be cautiously liberal in admitting to the canon songs which survive in holograph, and to confine my judgements to the Commentary. There is a third category of poems—numerous though intrinsically less important—which were published by nineteenth-century editors, apparently from manuscripts, but for which no manuscript authority can now be found. The methods of some of these editors are known to have ranged from an uncritical acceptance of local tradition to downright fabrication, and many of the poems in this group are epigrams and short occasional pieces which do not give an editor much internal evidence to work on. Where the source of a poem is uncertain, but I have been unable to reject it on stylistic grounds, I have accepted the early attribution—though sometimes with reluctance.

I have reverted to the practice of Chambers and Scott

Douglas in arranging the poems and songs, as far as possible, in the order in which they were written; and, where I could not argue for a precise date, in the years in which they were probably written. When I have been able to relate a song to a letter or an occasion with fair assurance, I have withdrawn it from the *Musical Museum* or other collection in which it appeared. Otherwise, the songs are placed in sequence at the point where they were first published. There are some disadvantages to the student in an arrangement by date instead of by genre. But much of Burns's work is intimately related to his life, and his poems to his letters; and my own understanding of him has been greatly enriched by working in a biographical framework. Moreover, the reader who wants to study genres will find that even in a chronological sequence many of the epistles, songs, and epigrams fall together in groups.

I do not offer systematic critical or biographical comment. General assessment of Burns is now, I believe, more scholarly and sophisticated than it has ever been, and the modern student has a number of good critical studies at his hand— by F. B. Snyder (1932), J. De L. Ferguson (1939), Hans Hecht (1950), David Daiches (1952), Robert Dewar (1955), Kurt Wittig (1958), Thomas Crawford (1960), and David Craig (1961). I have, however, provided biographical notes at the head of each section of the Commentary, and I have allowed myself some comment on the major poems and the best of the songs.

Less space is given to 'sources' and analogues than in Henley and Henderson's discursive commentary (1896). I have provided selective references for the airs; but the reader with a special interest in Burns's music will continue to use J. C. Dick's elaborate—though not always accurate— edition (1903), which has recently been reprinted. I have, however, attempted a more comprehensive literary commentary than those of my predecessors. The introductory note to each poem gives some account, where it is appropriate, of the occasion and date, manuscripts and printings, genre, verse-form, and style. The main purpose of the subsidiary notes is explanatory; but I have been as generous as the scale of my edition allowed with illustrative quotation, both literary and social, and with cross-reference. Burns's poems and songs have been given a variety of titles by himself and by his editors; I have used numbers, additionally, to simplify reference.

The Glossary includes all Scots words and 'terms of art' peculiar to Scotland, with etymological notes; Scottish forms and spellings of English words, where these may cause difficulty or misunderstanding; English words which are obsolete, or are used in senses now obsolete; colloquialisms and cant terms. For common words which Burns uses in their primary senses, a few selected references are given; for words with variable meaning, reference is fuller.

This is the first collected edition to include all the identifiable airs for the songs in their eighteenth-century form. I have as far as possible copied those versions of the airs which Burns specifically recommended to James Johnson or George Thomson. But the versions in all the main songbooks and music-books have been collated, and (where we have no directions from Burns) selected on two principles: melodic simplicity, and close correspondence with the songs. J. C. Dick edited the airs, altering keys and otherwise accommodating the singer. I have, however, made conservative copies, removing only instrumental flourishes: there is an obvious—and I hope acceptable—propriety in giving direct transcripts from eighteenth-century music-books to accompany an old-spelling text. Most of my transcripts, moreover, are from *The Scots Musical Museum*, in which the airs had already been adapted to the songs by Johnson's musical collaborator, Stephen Clarke, or in a few instances by Burns himself. The transcripts do not, of course, include all the minor variations that may be needed in working through complete songs; the singer must make his own accommodations. It is advisable to follow Burns's own practice, and assimilate the air before trying to fit words to it.

I owe heavy general debts to my predecessors, Robert Chambers, William Wallace, W. Scott Douglas, T. F. Henderson, and J. C. Dick; and to Professor J. De Lancey Ferguson, the editor of Burns's letters. Two great Scottish scholars, the late Sir William Craigie and the late David Nichol Smith, reconciled me by example to the difficulties of working on Burns 'furth of the kingdom', and gave me invaluable advice at the outset on editorial and linguistic problems. Mr. David Murison and the staff of the Scottish National Dictionary have been ready and patient with lexicographical aid. Dr. Thomas Parry and the Senate of the University College of Wales, by electing me Gregynog Lecturer at Aberystwyth in 1963, enabled me to get Burns's songs in historical perspective. The President and Fellows of the British Academy, and the President and executive committee of the Burns Federation, made generous grants towards the cost of photographing manuscripts in Scotland and the United States.

Robert Dewar would have wished me to offer acknowledgement of his debt to the following—though some are no longer alive to receive it—for help in locating manuscripts and for permission to use them: Mr. Oliver R. Barrett, Chicago; Mr. Frank B. Bemis, Boston; Capt. Victor Cazalet, M.P.; Dr. R. W. Chapman; Mr. Davidson Cook; Mr. Charles R. Cowie; Mr. R. P. Esty, Ardmore, Pennsylvania; Mr. J. C. Ewing; Mrs. J. W. Falconer, Minneapolis; Professor J. De L. Ferguson; Dr. R. T. Fitzhugh; Mr. L. V. Lester Garland; Mr. John S. Gribbel, Philadelphia; the Hon. Charles S. Hamlin and the Librarian, Library of Congress, Washington; Mr. Walter M. Hill, Chicago; Mr. Herbert G. Jones, Portland, Maine; Lady Lawrence; the Librarian, the Historical Society of Pennsylvania; the Librarian, the Pierpont Morgan Library, New York; Dr. Henry Meikle, late Librarian of the National Library of Scotland; Mr. John McBurnie, formerly Sheriff-Clerk of Dumfriesshire; Mr. Frederick T. Page; the Earl of Rosebery; the Rosenbach Company, New York; Dr. J. C. Smith; Mr. Gabriel Wells, New York; and Mr. Owen D. Young, New York.

I owe similar debts of gratitude to Dr. William Beattie, the Trustees, and the staff of the National Library of Scotland; the staff of the School of Scottish Studies, Edinburgh; and the Trustees, Librarians, and library staff of the following: Arbroath Public Library; Ayr County Library; the Bodleian Library, Oxford; the British Museum; the Carnegie Library, Ayr; the City Libraries of Edinburgh,

Glasgow, and Liverpool; the Henry E. Huntington Library at San Marino, California; the Pierpont Morgan Library, New York; the John Rylands Library, Manchester; the Scottish Rite Temple, Washington; and the Universities of Edinburgh, Glasgow, Leeds, Nottingham, and Reading. Scholars, collectors, and societies who have traced manuscripts or made them accessible to me are: Mr. David Clark, Thornhill; Mr. Paul Fenimore Cooper, New York; Admiral Sir Frederick Dalrymple-Hamilton of Bargany; Mr. A. M. Donaldson, Vancouver; the late Sir Charles Dunlop and the trustees of the Burns Cottage, Alloway, and Mr. W. H. Dunlop; Dr. J. W. Egerer, New York; Sir James Fergusson of Kilkerran; Mr. Clark Hunter, Paisley; the Irvine Burns Club; the Kilmarnock Burns Club; Mr. G. Legman, Valbonne; Mr. Alexander Macmillan, the Royal Academy, Ayr; the late John McVie, Edinburgh; Mr. Otto Manley, New York; the Paisley Burns Club; Professor W. L. Renwick; the Earl of Rosebery; Herr J. A. Stargardt, Marburg; Mr. A. E. Truckell, curator of Dumfries Burgh Museum; Signore Mario Uzielli, Liestal. I gratefully acknowledge the help I have had with specific editorial problems from Mr. Thomas Crawford, Aberdeen; Mr. Cedric Thorpe Davie, St. Andrews; the late Mr. J. B. Leishman; Mr. Ian Ross, University of Texas; Professor John C. Weston, University of Massachusetts; and from my colleagues at Nottingham, Miss H. A. Beecham, Professors J. T. Boulton, W. R. Fryer, and Ivor Keys, Dr. A. E. Rodway, and Professor Alastair Smart. Francis C. Inglis & Son, Edinburgh, conducted an elaborate photographic campaign in Edinburgh and Ayrshire on my behalf. It is again a pleasure to acknowledge the courtesy and resourcefulness of the Secretary and staff of the Clarendon Press, Oxford.

My final debt is to my wife, who has endured ten years of obsessed monologue on an alien poet with tolerance and salutary scepticism.

JAMES KINSLEY

School of English Studies
The University
Nottingham

CONTENTS

VOLUME I

VOLUME II

CONTENTS

VOLUME III

CONTENTS

I

EARLY POEMS
1774–1784

LOCHLIE AND
MOUNT OLIPHANT

1. O once I lov'd

O ONCE I lov'd a bonnie lass,
   An' aye I love her still,
An' whilst that virtue warms my breast
I'll love my handsome Nell.

As bonnie lasses I hae seen,   5
   And mony full as braw,
But for a modest gracefu' mein
The like I never saw.

A bonny lass I will confess,
   Is pleasant to the e'e,   10
But without some better qualities
She's no a lass for me.

But Nelly's looks are blythe and sweet,
   And what is best of a',
Her reputation is compleat,   15
   And fair without a flaw;

She dresses ay sae clean and neat,
   Both decent and genteel;
And then there's something in her gait
Gars ony dress look weel.   20

O once I lov'd. *Text from SMM, 1803 (551; unsigned), collated with the* First
Commonplace Book (*1CPB; dated August 1783*), *the Stair MS (1786), and the Adam
MS. Title from SMM; in 1CPB and Stair* Song—Tune, I am a man unmarried—.
Head-note in Stair The following Song is only valuable to those who would wish to
see the Author's first production in verse.—It was composed when he was a few
months more than his sixteenth year.—
   2 An' aye] Ay and *1CPB Stair Adam*   3 virtue] *corrected to* honor *in 1CPB
at a later date*: Honor *Stair Adam*   4 I'll] I *Stair*   4 *chorus* Fal lal de dal
&c. *in 1CPB Stair Adam*   14–16 And . . . flaw] *Adam and Stair have*
               Good-humor'd, frank an' free;
             An' still the more I view them o'er,
               The more they captive me
17–20 *om. Stair Adam*

A gaudy dress and gentle air
    May slightly touch the heart,
But it's innocence and modesty
    That polishes the dart.

'Tis this in Nelly pleases me,   25
    'Tis this enchants my soul;
For absolutely in my breast
    She reigns without controul.

2. Song, composed in August

Tune, I had a horse, I had nae mair

Very slow

I

Now westlin winds, and slaught'ring guns
    Bring Autumn's pleasant weather;
The moorcock springs, on whirring wings,
    Amang the blooming heather:

24 polishes] polisses *1CPB*

Song, composed in August. *Text from the edition of 1786, collated with the* First
Commonplace Book *(1CPB; lines 1–8 only), the Hastie MS (Ha), SMM, 1792 (351),
SC, 1799 (93), and the editions of 1787, 1793, 1794. SC has lines 1–8, 25–40, with
additions not by Burns. Title in 1CPB* Har'ste—A Fragment; *first-line title in SMM
and SC. Ha lacks title and tune. Tune in SMM* Come kiss wi' me, come clap wi' me;
in SC Ally Croaker
    1 westlin] breezy *1CPB*   slaught'ring] sportsmen's *SC*   2 Bring] Brings
SMM   3 The *87–94 SMM SC*: And the *1CPB 86* moorcock] gor-cock *SMM*

Now waving grain, wide o'er the plain,   5
   Delights the weary Farmer;
The moon shines bright, as I rove at night,
   To muse upon my Charmer.

II

The Pairtrick lo'es the fruitfu' fells;
   The Plover lo'es the mountains;   10
The Woodcock haunts the lanely dells;
   The soaring Hern the fountains:
Thro' lofty groves, the Cushat roves,
   The path o' man to shun it;
The hazel bush o'erhangs the Thrush,   15
   The spreading thorn the Linnet.

III

Thus ev'ry kind their pleasure find,
   The savage and the tender;
Some social join, and leagues combine;
   Some solitary wander: 20
Avaunt, away! the cruel sway,
   Tyrannic man's dominion;
The Sportsman's joy, the murd'ring cry,
   The flutt'ring, gory pinion!

IV

But PEGGY dear, the ev'ning's clear,   25
   Thick flies the skimming Swallow;
The sky is blue, the fields in view,
   All fading-green and yellow:
Come let us stray our gladsome way,
   And view the charms o' Nature;   30
The rustling corn, the fruited thorn,
   And ilka happy creature.

5 grain . . . plain] crops, with yellow tops *1CPB*   6 Delights] Delight
1CPB   7 The] An' the *1CPB 86* as *Ha SMM*: when *1CPB 86–94 SC* at] by
SMM   8 upon my Charmer] on (*overwriting?* upon) *followed by cipher (? for
Jeany Armour) 1CPB. See Commentary*   9 Pairtrick lo'es the fruitfu' *Ha SMM*:
Partridge loves the fruitful *86–94*   10 lo'es *Ha SMM*: loves *86–94*   11
lanely *Ha SMM*: lonely *86–94*   14 o' *Ha SMM*: of *86–94*   25 But] Come
SC   30 o' *Ha SMM*: of *86–94*   32 ilka *Ha SMM*: ev'ry *86–94 SC*

V

We'll gently walk, and sweetly talk,
   While the silent moon shines clearly;
I'll clasp thy waist, and fondly prest,   35
   Swear how I lo'e thee dearly:
Not vernal show'rs to budding flow'rs,
   Not Autumn to the Farmer,
So dear can be, as thou to me,
   My fair, my lovely Charmer!   40

3. I dream'd I lay, &c.

Very slow

I DREAM'D I lay where flowers were springing
   Gaily in the sunny beam,
List'ning to the wild birds singing,
   By a falling, chrystal stream;

34 While . . . shines *Ha SMM*: Till . . . shine *86–94 SC*   35 clasp *Ha SMM*: grasp *86–94 SC*   36 lo'e *Ha SMM*: love *86–94 SC*

I dream'd I lay. *Text from the Hastie MS, f. 32, collated with SMM, 1788 (146; signed X). Title from SMM*
    3 List'ning *SMM*: Listening *MS*

Streight the sky grew black and daring,   5
    Thro' the woods the whirlwinds rave;
Trees with aged arms were warring,
    O'er the swelling, drumlie wave.

Such was my life's deceitful morning,
    Such the pleasures I enjoy'd;   10
But lang or noon, loud tempests storming
    A' my flowery bliss destroy'd.
Tho' fickle Fortune has deceiv'd me,
    She promis'd fair, and perform'd but ill;
Of mony a joy and hope bereav'd me,   15
    I bear a heart shall support me still.

4. Song

Tune, My Nanie, O

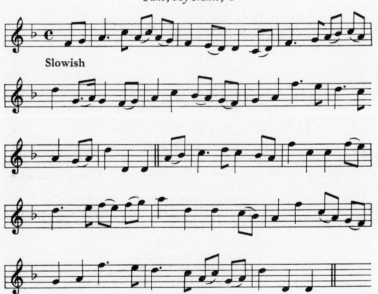

Slowish

6 whirlwinds rave *SMM*: whirlwind drave *partly corrected in MS*   12 bliss]
correcting hopes *in MS*

Song. *Text from the Edinburgh edition, 1787, collated with the* First Commonplace
Book (*1CPB; dated April 1784*), *the Stair MS* (S), *the Dalhousie MS* (*Dal; letter to
Thomson, 26–27 October 1792*), *SC, 1793* (*4*), *SMM, 1803* (*580*), *and the editions*

I

Behind yon hills where Lugar flows,
    'Mang moors an' mosses many, O,
The wintry sun the day has clos'd,
    And I'll awa to Nanie, O.

II

The westlin wind blaws loud an' shill;   5
    The night's baith mirk and rainy, O;
But I'll get my plaid an' out I'll steal,
    An' owre the hill to Nanie, O.

III

My Nanie's charming, sweet an' young;
    Nae artfu' wiles to win ye, O: 10
May ill befa' the flattering tongue
    That wad beguile my Nanie, O.

IV

Her face is fair, her heart is true,
    As spotless as she's bonie, O;
The op'ning gowan, wat wi' dew,   15
    Nae purer is than Nanie, O.

of 1793, 1794. See Commentary. Title in 1CPB Song—(Tune As I came in by London
O); *in SMM* My Nannie O; *first-line title in SC*
    1 Lugar] Stincher *1CPB*: Stinsiar *S*: Stinchar 87–94: Lugar *Dal*: riv'lets *SMM*
flows] row *SMM*   2 'Mang] Are *SMM*   3 The wintry sun the day] The weary
sun the day *1CPB*: The Sun the wintry day *S*   4 *Chorus added in 1CPB*:

> And O my bonny Nannie O,
> My young, my handsome Nannie O
> Tho' I had the world all at my will,
> I would give it all for Nanie, O

5 The] Tho' *SC*   wind blaws] winds blaws *SMM*: winds blaw *SC*   shill]
shrill *SMM*   6 The night's] And its *SC*   mirk] dark *1CPB S*   7 But]
om. *SMM SC*   8 *chorus added (after first eight-line stanza) in SMM*:

> To Nannie O, to Nannie O;
> I'll get my plaid, an' out I'll steal,
> An' o'er the hill to Nannie O.

V

A country lad is my degree,
  An' few there be that ken me, O;
But what care I how few they be,
  I'm welcome ay to Nanie, O.   20

VI

My riches a's my penny-fee,
  An' I maun guide it cannie, O;
But warl's gear ne'er troubles me,
  My thoughts are a', my Nanie, O.

VII

Our auld Guidman delights to view   25
  His sheep an' kye thrive bonie, O;
But I'm as blythe that hauds his pleugh,
  An' has nae care but Nanie, O.

VIII

Come weel come woe, I care na by,
  I'll tak what Heav'n will sen' me, O;   30
Nae ither care in life have I,
  But live, an' love my Nanie, O.

5. A Penitential thought, in the hour of Remorse —Intended for a tragedy

In my early years nothing less would serve me than courting
the tragic Muse.—I was, I think, about eighteen or nineteen
when I sketched the outlines of a Tragedy forsooth; but the
bursting of a cloud of family Misfortunes, which had for
some time threatened us, prevented my farther progress.—In   [5]

24 a', my] a' about *1CPB*   25 auld] *not in 1CPB S*   26 an' kye] & his
ky *1CPB*   29 weel] well *SMM*: weal *SC*   32 *chorus added in 1CPB as
before (l. 4, note), ending* to Nanie O.

A Penitential thought. *Text from B.M. MS Egerton 1656 (ff. 14ᵛ–15ʳ), collated with
the* First Commonplace Book (*1CPB; dated* March—84), *the MS at Lady Stair's
House, Edinburgh* (LSH), *the Glenriddell MS* (Glen; Letters, *pp. 35–36, a transcript
of 1CPB), and Cromek,* Reliques, *1808 (p. 405). Title from 1CPB* (Intended for a

those days I never wrote down anything; so, except a speech
or two, the whole has escaped my memory.—The following,
which I most distinctly remember, was an exclamation from
a great character—great in occasional instance[s] of generosity,
and daring at times in villainies.—He is supposed to meet with   [10]
a child of misery, and exclaims to himself——

ALL devil as I am, a damned wretch,
 A harden'd, stubborn, unrepenting villain,
Still my heart melts at human wretchedness;
And with sincere tho' unavailing sighs
I view the helpless children of Distress.   5
With tears indignant I behold th' Oppressor,
Rejoicing in the honest man's destruction,
Whose unsubmitting heart was all his crime.

Even you, ye hapless crew, I pity you;
Ye, whom the Seeming good think sin to pity;   10
Ye poor, despis'd, abandon'd vagabonds,
Whom Vice, as usual, has turn'd o'er to Ruin.
O, but for kind, tho' ill-requited friends,
I had been driven forth like you forlorn,
The most detested, worthless wretch among you!   15

O injur'd God! Thy goodness has endow'd me
With talents passing most of my compeers,
Which I in just proportion have abus'd;
As far surpassing other common villains
As Thou in natural parts hadst given me more—   20

tragedy *added by Burns later*). *Title in LSH* A Fragment, in the hour of remorse, on
seeing a fellow creature in misery whom I had once known in better days; *in Glen*
Intended for a character in a tragedy I was projecting—. *Head-note in Egerton only*
 1 devil] villain *LSH* damned] *correcting* hardened *LSH* 2 villain] sinner
LSH 4 tho'] but *LSH* 9 hapless] helpless *Cromek* 13 kind . . . friends]
friends, and interposing Heaven *LSH* 15 you] ye *1CPB* 16–20 O . . .
more] *om. Cromek* 20 hadst] hast *1CPB:* has *LSH*

6. Song—

Tune, Invercald's reel—Strathspey

Slowish

Chorus

TIBBY I hae seen the day
Ye wadna been sae shy
For laik o' gear ye lightly me
But trowth I care na by—

Yestreen I met you on the Moor   5
Ye spak'na but gaed by like stoor
Ye geck at me because I'm poor
But fien' a hair care I.—

[When comin' hame on Sunday last
Upon the road as I cam' past   10
Ye snufft an' gae your head a cast
But trouth I caretna by.—]

I doubt na lass, but ye may think
Because ye hae the name o' clink
That ye can please me at a wink   15
Whene'er ye like to try—

Song. *Text from the* First Commonplace Book (*1CPB; dated September 1784*), *collated with the Hastie MS, f. 50, Currie (iv. 286–7), and SMM, 1788 (196; signed X). First-line title in MS and SMM*

  1 Tibby] O Tibbie, *SMM*   3 For *MS SMM*: An' for *1CPB*   4 trowth
. . . by *MS SMM*: fien' a hair care I *1CPB*   7 geck at] *MS SMM*: lightly
1CPB   9–12 *om. in MS SMM Currie*   12 caretna] *correcting* carena *in 1CPB*

But sorrow tak' him that's sae mean
Altho' his pouch o' coin were clean
Wha follows ony saucy Quean
    That looks sae proud and high——   20

Altho' a lad were e'er sae smart
If that he want the yellow dirt
Ye'll cast your head anither airt
    An' answer him fu' dry——

But if he hae the name o' gear   25
Ye'll fasten to him like a breer
Tho' hardly he for sense or lear
    Be better than the ky——

But Tibby lass tak' my advice
Your daddie's gear mak's you sae nice   30
The de'il a ane wad speir your price
    Were ye as poor as I——

[There lives a lass beside yon park
I'd rather hae her in her sark
Than you wi' a' your thousand mark   35
    That gars you look sae high——

An' Tibby I hae seen the day
Ye wadna been sae shy
An' for laik o' gear ye lightly me
    But fien' a hair care I.]   40

19 Wha *MS* (*earlier word over-written*) *SMM*: That *1CPB*   26 to *MS*
SMM: till *1CPB*   30 daddie's *MS SMM*: father's *1CPB*   33–40 *om. in*
MS SMM   33 beside yon] in yonder *Currie*   34 I'd rather hae] I would
na gie *Currie*   35 Than you . . . your] For thee . . . thy *Currie*   36 That
gars you] Ye need na *Currie*

7. A Fragment—

Tune, John Anderson, my jo—

ONE night as I did wander,
    When corn begins to shoot,
I sat me down to ponder
    Upon an auld tree root:
Auld Aire ran by before me,   5
    And bicker'd to the seas;
A cushat crouded o'er me
    That echoed thro' the braes.

A Fragment. *Text from Cromek*, Reliques, *1808 (p. 341)*

8. Song

Tune, Corn rigs are bonie

Lively

I

IT was upon a Lammas night,
    When corn rigs are bonie,
Beneath the moon's unclouded light,
    I held awa to Annie:

Song. *Text from the edition of 1786, collated with those of 1787, 1793, 1794*

The time flew by, wi' tentless heed,   5
   Till 'tween the late and early;
Wi' sma' persuasion she agreed,
   To see me thro' the barley.

II

The sky was blue, the wind was still,
   The moon was shining clearly;   10
I set her down, wi' right good will,
   Amang the rigs o' barley:
I ken't her heart was a' my ain;
   I lov'd her most sincerely;
I kiss'd her owre and owre again,   15
   Amang the rigs o' barley.

III

I lock'd her in my fond embrace;
   Her heart was beating rarely:
My blessings on that happy place,
   Amang the rigs o' barley!   20
But by the moon and stars so bright,
   That shone that hour so clearly!
She ay shall bless that happy night,
   Amang the rigs o' barley.

IV

I hae been blythe wi' Comrades dear;   25
   I hae been merry drinking;
I hae been joyfu' gath'rin gear;
   I hae been happy thinking:
But a' the pleasures e'er I saw,
   Tho' three times doubl'd fairly,   30
That happy night was worth them a',
   Amang the rigs o' barley.

CHORUS

Corn rigs, an' barley rigs,
   An' corn rigs are bonie:
I'll ne'er forget that happy night,   35
   Amang the rigs wi' Annie.

5 heed *93 94*: head *86 87*   22 hour *87-94*: night *86*

9. Song

Tune, Gilderoy

Slow

I

F<small>ROM</small> thee, E<small>LIZA</small>, I must go,
   And from my native shore:
The cruel fates between us throw
   A boundless ocean's roar;
But boundless oceans, roaring wide,   5
   Between my Love and me,
They never, never can divide
   My heart and soul from thee.

II

Farewell, farewell, E<small>LIZA</small> dear,
   The maid that I adore!   10
A boding voice is in mine ear,
   We part to meet no more!

Song. *Text from the edition of 1786, collated with SC, 1793 (15), and the editions of
1787, 1793, 1794. Title in SC: From thee, Eliza, I must go—Air, Donald.*

But the latest throb that leaves my heart,
    While Death stands victor by,
That throb, ELIZA, is thy part,   15
    And thine that latest sigh!

10. Winter, A Dirge

I

THE Wintry West extends his blast,
    And hail and rain does blaw;
Or, the stormy North sends driving forth,
    The blinding sleet and snaw:
While, tumbling brown, the Burn comes down,   5
    And roars frae bank to brae;
And bird and beast, in covert, rest,
    And pass the heartless day.

II

'The sweeping blast, the sky o'ercast,'*
    The joyless *winter-day*,   10
Let others fear, to me more dear,
    Than all the pride of May:
The Tempest's howl, it *soothes* my soul,
    My *griefs* it seems to join;
The leafless trees my fancy please,   15
    Their *fate* resembles mine!

III

Thou Pow'r SUPREME, whose mighty Scheme,
    These *woes* of mine fulfil;
Here, firm, I rest, they *must* be best,
    Because they are *Thy* Will!   20

* Dr. Young.

13 latest] last *SC 87 (London)* 94

Winter, A Dirge. *Text from the edition of 1786, collated with the First Commonplace
Book (1CPB; dated April 1784) and the Kilmarnock MS (Kil), and the editions of 1787,
1793, 1794. Title in 1CPB* Song— (Tune MᶜPherson's Farewel); *in Kil* A Dirge—
Composed in Winter *corrected to* Winter, A Dirge— Tune—MᶜPherson
    5 While, tumbling] *corrected to* Wild tumbling, *in Kil*: And tumbling *1CPB*
7 And] While *Kil*   8 heartless] weary *1CPB*   16 Their] There *1CPB*
19 be] *om. 1CPB*

Then all I want (Oh, do thou grant
This one request of mine!)
Since to *enjoy* Thou dost deny,
Assist me to *resign!*

11. Song—

Tune, If he be a Butcher neat an' trim

The Butcher boy

O<small>N</small> Cessnock banks a lassie dwells;
Could I describe her shape and mien;
Our lassies a' she far excels,
An' she has twa sparkling, rogueish een.

She's sweeter than the morning dawn   5
When rising Phœbus first is seen
And dew-drops twinkle o'er the lawn;
An' she has twa sparkling, rogueish een.

24 Assist] O help *Kil*

Song. *Text from the Law MS (Davidson Cook's transcript in the* Burns Chronicle,
1927, pp. 23–24), collated with Cromek, Reliques, *1808 (p. 442; oral communication).
Sequence in Cromek ll. 1–28, 45–48, 37–40, 33–36 (variant), 41–44, 49–52 (29–32
omitted)*

1 a lassie dwells] there lives a lass *Cromek*   3 Our . . . excels] The graces of
her weelfar'd face *Cromek*   4 she . . . rogueish] the glancin' of her sparklin'
Cromek   5 sweeter] fresher *Cromek*   7 And] When *Cromek*   8 *et passim*
she . . . rogueish] she's twa glancin' sparklin' *Cromek*

She's stately, like yon youthful ash
    That grows the cowslips braes between   10
And drinks the stream with vigour fresh;
    An' she has twa sparkling, rogueish een.

She's spotless, like the flow'ring thorn
    With flow'rs so white and leaves so green
When purest in the dewy morn;   15
    An' she has twa sparkling, rogueish een.

Her looks are like the vernal May
    When ev'ning Phœbus shines serene,
While birds rejoice on ev'ry spray;
    An' she has twa sparkling, rogueish een.   20

Her hair is like the curling mist
    That climbs the mountain sides at e'en,
When flow'r-reviving rains are past;
    An' she has twa sparkling, rogueish een.

Her forehead's like the show'ry bow   25
    When gleaming sun-beams intervene
And gild the distant mountain's brow;
    An' she has twa sparkling, rogueish een.

Her cheeks are like yon crimson gem,
    The pride of all the flowery scene,   30
Just opening on its thorny stem;
    An' she has twa sparkling, rogueish een.

Her teeth are like the nightly snow
    When pale the morning rises keen,
While hid the murmuring streamlets flow;   35
    An' she has twa sparkling, rogueish een.

10 cowslips] cowslip *Cromek*   11 drinks . . . fresh] shoots its head above
each bush *Cromek*   13 like] as *Cromek*   17 vernal May] sportive lamb *Cromek*
18 ev'ning . . . serene] flow'ry May adorns the scene *Cromek*   19 While . . .
spray] That wantons round its bleating dam *Cromek*   22 climbs . . . sides]
shades . . . side *Cromek*   26 gleaming] shining *Cromek*   29–32 *om. Cromek*
33–35 Her teeth . . . flow;] *Cromek has*

    Her teeth are like a flock of sheep,
        With fleeces newly washen clean,
    That slowly mount the rising steep;

Her lips are like yon cherries ripe
   Which sunny walls from Boreas screen;
They tempt the taste and charm the sight;
   An' she has twa sparkling, rogueish een.   40

Her breath is like the fragrant breeze
   That gently stirs the blossom'd bean,
When Phœbus sinks behind the seas;
   An' she has twa sparkling, rogueish een.

Her voice is like the ev'ning thrush   45
   That sings on Cessnock banks unseen,
While his mate sits nestling in the bush;
   An' she has twa sparkling, rogueish een.

But it's not her air, her form, her face,
   Though matching beauty's fabled Queen;   50
'Tis the mind that shines in ev'ry grace,
   An' chiefly in her rogueish een.

12. To Ruin

I

A<small>LL</small> hail! inexorable lord!
   At whose destruction-breathing word,
     The mightiest empires fall!
Thy cruel, woe-delighted train,
The ministers of Grief and Pain,   5
     A sullen welcome, all!
With stern-resolv'd, despairing eye,
   I see each aimed dart;
For one has cut my *dearest tye*,
   And quivers in my heart.   10
     Then low'ring, and pouring,
      The *Storm* no more I dread;
     Tho' thick'ning, and black'ning,
      Round my devoted head.

37 yon] the *Cromek*   38 Which] That *Cromek*   43 seas *Cromek*: sea *MS*
46 on] in *Cromek*   51 'Tis] But *Cromek*   52 rogueish] sparklin' *Cromek*

To Ruin. *Text from the edition of 1786, collated with those of 1787, 1793, 1794*

II

And thou grim Pow'r, by Life abhorr'd,   15
While Life a *pleasure* can afford,
    Oh! hear a wretch's pray'r!
No more I shrink appall'd, afraid;
I court, I beg thy friendly aid,
    To close this scene of care!   20
When shall my soul, in silent peace,
    Resign Life's *joyless* day?
My weary heart it's throbbings cease,
    Cold-mould'ring in the clay?
      No fear more, no tear more,   25
      To stain my lifeless face,
     Enclasped, and grasped,
      Within thy cold embrace!

13. A Prayer, in the Prospect of Death

I

O THOU unknown, Almighty Cause
    Of all my hope and fear!
In whose dread Presence, ere an hour,
    Perhaps I must appear!

II

If I have wander'd in those paths   5
    Of life I ought to shun;
As *Something*, loudly, in my breast,
    Remonstrates I have done;

III

Thou know'st that Thou hast formed me,
    With Passions wild and strong;   10
And list'ning to their witching voice
    Has often led me wrong.

A Prayer. *Text from the edition of 1786, collated with the* First Commonplace Book
(*1CPB; dated August 1784) and the editions of 1787, 1793, 1794*
    Title in 1CPB: A prayer, when fainting fits, and other alarming symptoms of a
Pleurisy or some other dangerous disorder, which indeed still threaten me, first put
Nature on the alarm.—

IV

Where human *weakness* has come short,
  Or *frailty* stept aside,
Do Thou, ALL-GOOD, for such Thou art,   15
  In shades of darkness hide.

V

Where with *intention* I have err'd,
  No other plea I have,
But, *Thou art good*; and Goodness still
  Delighteth to forgive.   20

14. Stanzas on the same Occasion

WHY am I loth to leave this earthly scene?
  Have I so found it full of pleasing charms?
Some drops of joy with draughts of ill between;
  Some gleams of sunshine mid renewing storms:
Is it departing pangs my soul alarms?   5
  Or Death's unlovely, dreary, dark abode?
For guilt, for guilt, my terrors are in arms;
  I tremble to approach an angry GOD,
And justly smart beneath his sin-avenging rod.

Fain would I say, 'Forgive my foul offence!'   10
  Fain promise never more to disobey;
But, should my Author health again dispense,
  Again I might desert fair Virtue's way;

Stanzas. *Text from the Edinburgh edition, 1787, collated with the* First Commonplace Book (*1CPB; pp. 19, 33*), *the Stair (S) and Edinburgh (Edin) MSS, a holograph version in a British Museum copy of 86 (BM), and the editions of 1793, 1794. Title in 1CPB* Misgivings in the hour of Despondency—and prospect of Death*; in S* Misgivings of Despondency on the approach of the gloomy Monarch of the Grave*; in Edin* Stanzas on the same occasion, in the manner of Beattie's Minstrel*; in BM* Reflections on a Sickbed
    4 mid] midst *1CPB Edin*   5 soul] heart *1CPB*   11 Fain . . . disobey] Forgive where I so oft have gone astray *1CPB*   13 might] would *1CPB S Edin*

Again in Folly's path might go astray;
   Again exalt the brute and sink the man;   15
Then how should I for Heavenly Mercy pray,
   Who act so counter Heavenly Mercy's plan?
Who sin so oft have mourn'd, yet to temptation ran?

O Thou, Great Governor of all below!
   If I may dare a lifted eye to thee,   20
Thy nod can make the tempest cease to blow,
   Or still the tumult of the raging sea:
With that controuling pow'r assist ev'n me,
   Those headlong, furious passions to confine;
For all unfit I feel my powers to be,   25
   To rule their torrent in th' allowed line;
O, aid me with Thy help, *Omnipotence Divine!*

15. A Prayer, Under the Pressure of violent Anguish

O Thou great Being! what Thou art,
   Surpasses me to know:
Yet sure I am, that known to Thee
   Are all Thy works below.

Thy creature here before Thee stands,   5
   All wretched and distrest;
Yet sure those ills that wring my soul
   Obey Thy high behest.

14 in . . . astray] to passions I would fall a prey *1CPB*: by Passion would be led
astray *S BM*: with passions would be led astray *Edin*   16 should] can *1CPB S*
18 yet] then *1CPB*   19–27 O Thou . . . *Divine!*] *om. here in 1CPB; given later*
20 I . . . to] one so black with crimes dare call on *MSS*   21 nod] breath *1CPB*
22 Or] And *1CPB BM*   24 headlong, furious] rapid headlong *BM*   25 I feel
my powers to 94: my native powers *MSS*: I feel my powers 87 93

A Prayer. *Text from the Edinburgh edition, 1787, collated with the* First Commonplace book (*1CPB*) *and the editions of 1793, 1794. A holograph version collated by
H.–H. from the Rosebery copy of Fergusson's Poems (1782) follows 1CPB at lines 4, 15*
  2 Surpasses] *corrected from* Surpassest *in 1CPB, perhaps not by Burns*   4 Thy
works] affairs *1CPB*   7 wring] press *1CPB*

Sure Thou, Almighty, canst not act
   From cruelty or wrath!   10
O, free my weary eyes from tears,
   Or close them fast in death!

But if I must afflicted be,
   To suit some wise design;
Then, man my soul with firm resolves   15
   To bear and not repine!

16. [Though fickle Fortune has deceiv'd me]

THOUGH fickle Fortune has deceiv'd me,
   She promis'd fair and perform'd but ill;
Of mistress, friends, and wealth bereav'd me,
   Yet I bear a heart shall support me still.—

I'll act with prudence as far 's I'm able,   5
   But if success I must never find,
Then come Misfortune, I bid thee welcome,
   I'll meet thee with an undaunted mind.—

17. [O raging Fortune's withering blast]

O RAGING Fortune's withering blast
   Has laid my leaf full low! O
O raging Fortune's withering blast
   Has laid my leaf full low! O

9 Almighty] All Perfect *1CPB*   15 Then,] O! *1CPB*

Though fickle Fortune has deceiv'd me. *Text from the* First Commonplace Book,
p. 41 (dated September 1785)
  5 far 's] *correcting* lang's *in 1CPB*

O raging Fortune's withering blast. *Text from the* First Commonplace Book, *p. 42
(dated September 1785), collated with Cromek,* Reliques, *1808 (p. 353). Notes in MS:*
. . . I set about composing an air in the old Scotch style.—I am not Musical Scholar
enough to prick down my tune properly, so it can never see the light, and perhaps
'tis no great matter, but the following were the verses I composed to suit it.—
   The tune consisted of three parts so that the above verses just went through the
whole Air.—

My stem was fair my bud was green   5
    My blossom sweet did blow; O
The dew fell fresh, the sun rose mild,
    And made my branches grow; O
But luckless Fortune's northern storms
    Laid a' my blossoms low, O   10
But luckless Fortune's northern storms
    Laid a' my blossoms low, O.

18. Extempore

O WHY the deuce should I repine,
    And be an ill foreboder;
I'm twenty-three, and five feet nine,
    I'll go and be a sodger.

I gat some gear wi' meikle care,   5
    I held it weel thegither;
But now its gane, and something mair,
    I'll go and be a sodger.

19. The First Psalm

THE man, in life where-ever plac'd,
    Hath happiness in store,
Who walks not in the wicked's way,
    Nor learns their guilty lore!

Nor from the seat of scornful Pride   5
    Casts forth his eyes abroad,
But with humility and awe
    Still walks before his GOD.

That man shall flourish like the trees
    Which by the streamlets grow;   10
The fruitful top is spread on high,
    And firm the root below.

Extempore. *Text from Currie (i. 354), dated* April, 1782

The First Psalm. *Text from the Edinburgh edition, 1787, collated with those of 1793, 1794*

But he whose blossom buds in guilt
  Shall to the ground be cast,
And like the rootless stubble tost,   15
  Before the sweeping blast.

For why? that GOD the good adore
  Hath giv'n them peace and rest,
But hath decreed that wicked men
  Shall ne'er be truly blest.   20

20. The *First Six Verses* of the Ninetieth Psalm

O Thou, the first, the greatest friend
  Of all the human race!
Whose strong right hand has ever been
  Their stay and dwelling-place!

Before the mountains heav'd their heads   5
  Beneath Thy forming hand,
Before this ponderous globe itself
  Arose at Thy command:

That Pow'r which rais'd and still upholds
  This universal frame,   10
From countless, unbeginning time
  Was ever still the same.

Those mighty periods of years
  Which seem to us so vast,
Appear no more before Thy sight   15
  Than yesterday that's past.

Thou giv'st the word; Thy creature, man,
  Is to existence brought;
Again Thou say'st, 'Ye sons of men,
  'Return ye into nought!'   20

The First Six Verses. *Text from the Edinburgh edition, 1787, collated (Dewar) with
the Edinburgh MS and the editions of 1793, 1794*
  7 ponderous] mighty *MS*   18 to existence] *correcting* into being *in MS*

Thou layest them with all their cares
  In everlasting sleep;
As with a flood Thou tak'st them off
  With overwhelming sweep.

They flourish like the morning flow'r,   25
  In beauty's pride array'd;
But long ere night cut down it lies
  All wither'd and decay'd.

21. Song

Tune, The Weaver and his shuttle O

MY father was a farmer upon the Carrick border O
  And carefully he bred me, in decency and order O
He bade me act a manly part, though I had ne'er a
    farthing O
For without an honest manly heart, no man was worth
    regarding. O
    Chorus Row de dow &c.

Then out into the world my course I did determine. O   5
Tho' to be rich was not my wish, yet to be great was
    charming. O
My talents they were not the worst; nor yet my educa-
    tion: O
Resolv'd was I, at least to try, to mend my situation. O

In many a way, and vain essay, I courted fortune's favor; O
Some cause unseen, still stept between, and frustrate each
    endeavor; O   10
Some times by foes I was o'erpower'd; sometimes by
    friends forsaken; O
And when my hope was at the top, I still was worst mis-
    taken. O

21 with] and *MS*   22 everlasting] never ending *MS*

Song. *Text from the* First Commonplace Book (*1CPB; pp. 10–11), collated with
Cromek*, Reliques, *1808 (p. 330). Note in 1CPB (dated April 1784):* The following
Song is a wild Rhapsody, miserably defficient in Versification, but as the sentiments
are the genuine feelings of my heart, for that reason I have a particular pleasure in
conning it over.
    10 and] to *Cromek*

Then sore harass'd, and tir'd at last, with fortune's vain
  delusion; O
I dropt my schemes, like idle dreams; and came to this
  conclusion; O
The past was bad, and the future hid; its good or ill
  untryed; O   15
But the present hour was in my pow'r, and so I would
  enjoy it, O

No help, nor hope, nor view had I; nor person to befriend
  me; O
So I must toil, and sweat and moil, and labor to sustain
  me, O
To plough and sow, to reap and mow, my father bred me
  early, O
For one, he said, to labor bred, was a match for fortune
  fairly, O   20

Thus all obscure, unknown, and poor, thro' life I'm
  doom'd to wander, O
Till down my weary bones I lay in everlasting slumber; O
No view nor care, but shun whate'er might breed me
  pain or sorrow; O
I live today as well 's I may, regardless of tomorrow, O

But chearful still, I am as well as a Monarch in a
  palace; O   25
Tho' fortune's frown still hunts me down with all her
  wonted malice: O
I make indeed, my daily bread, but ne'er can make it
  farther; O
But as daily bread is all I heed, I do not much regard
  her. O

When sometimes by my labor I earn a little money, O
Some unforeseen misfortune comes generally upon me; O   30
Mischance, mistake, or by neglect, or my good-natur'd
  folly; O
But come what will I've sworn it still, I'll ne'er be
  melancholy, O

18 moil] broil *Cromek*

All you who follow wealth and power with unremitting
    ardor, O
The more in this you look for bliss, you leave your view
    the farther; O
Had you the wealth Potosi boasts, or nations to adore
    you, O   35
A chearful honest-hearted clown I will prefer before
    you. O

22. Fragment—

Tune—Galla water—

Altho' my bed were in yon muir,
    Amang the heather, in my plaidie,
Yet happy, happy would I be
    Had I my dear Montgomerie's Peggy.—

When o'er the hill beat surly storms,   5
    And winter nights were dark and rainy;
I'd seek some dell, and in my arms
    I'd shelter dear Montgomerie's Peggy.—

Were I a Baron proud and high,
    And horse and servants waiting ready,   10
Then a' 'twad gie o' joy to me,
    The sharin't with Montgomerie's Peggy.—

Fragment. *Text from the* First Commonplace Book, *p. 40, collated with Cromek,*
Reliques, *1808 (p. 350)*

23. John Barleycorn*. A Ballad

I

THERE was three kings into the east,
   Three kings both great and high,
And they hae sworn a solemn oath
John Barleycorn should die.

II

They took a plough and plough'd him down, 5
   Put clods upon his head,
And they hae sworn a solemn oath
John Barleycorn was dead.

III

But the chearful Spring came kindly on,
   And show'rs began to fall;   10
John Barleycorn got up again,
   And sore surpris'd them all.

IV

The sultry suns of Summer came,
   And he grew thick and strong,
His head weel arm'd wi' pointed spears, 15
   That no one should him wrong.

* This is partly composed on the plan of an old song known by the same name.

John Barleycorn. *Text from the Edinburgh edition, 1787, collated with the Kilmarnock MS (Kil), the* First Commonplace Book *(1CPB; dated June 1785), and the editions of 1793, 1794*
   Title in 1CPB: John Barleycorn.—A Song, to its own Tune. / I once heard the old song, that goes by this name, sung; and being very fond of it, and remembering only two or three verses of it viz. the 1st, 2d and 3d, with some scraps which I have interwoven here and there in the following piece.—
   Title followed by a note in Kil: There is an old Scotch song known by that name whose first two verses begin the following, and the general idea of it runs thro the whole.
   4 John] That John *1CPB*   5 They took] They've taen *1CPB Kil*   8 John] That John *1CPB*   9 But . . . on] But the spring time it came on *1CPB:* The Spring-time came with kindly warmth *Kil*   13 The . . . came] The Summer it came on *1CPB:* The Summer came with sultry heat *Kil*   16 That no] That not no *1CPB*

V

The sober Autumn enter'd mild,
  When he grew wan and pale;
His bending joints and drooping head
  Show'd he began to fail.   20

VI

His colour sicken'd more and more,
  He faded into age;
And then his enemies began
  To show their deadly rage.

VII

They've taen a weapon, long and sharp,   25
  And cut him by the knee;
Then ty'd him fast upon a cart,
  Like a rogue for forgerie.

VIII

They laid him down upon his back,
  And cudgell'd him full sore;
They hung him up before the storm,   30
  And turn'd him o'er and o'er.

IX

They filled up a darksome pit
  With water to the brim,
They heaved in John Barleycorn,   35
  There let him sink or swim.

X

They laid him out upon the floor,
  To work him farther woe,
And still, as signs of life appear'd,
  They toss'd him to and fro.   40

17 The . . . mild] The Autumn it came on *1CPB*: The Autumn came with
fresh'ning breeze *Kil*   18 When] And *1CPB Kil*   25 They've taen a
weapon] They took a hook was *1CPB*: They took a weapon *Kil*   26 by the]
down at *1CPB*   35 They] They've *1CPB*   37 They laid] They've thrown
1CPB

XI

They wasted, o'er a scorching flame,
   The marrow of his bones;
But a Miller us'd him worst of all,
   For he crush'd him between two stones.

XII

And they hae taen his very heart's blood,   45
   And drank it round and round;
And still the more and more they drank,
   Their joy did more abound.

XIII

John Barleycorn was a hero bold,
   Of noble enterprise,   50
For if you do but taste his blood,
   'Twill make your courage rise.

XIV

'Twill make a man forget his woe;
   'Twill heighten all his joy:
'Twill make the widow's heart to sing,   55
   Tho' the tear were in her eye.

XV

Then let us toast John Barleycorn,
   Each man a glass in hand;
And may his great posterity
   Ne'er fail in old Scotland!   60

43 a] the *1CPB*   44 crush'd] *correcting* ground *in 1CPB*   52 your] *correcting* his *in 1CPB*   54 'Twill] And *1CPB*   58 man] one *Kil*   57–60 *om. here in 1CPB; given on a later page*

24. The Death and Dying Words of Poor Mailie, The Author's only Pet Yowe, An Unco Mournfu' Tale

As Mailie, an' her lambs thegither,
Was ae day nibbling on the tether,
Upon her cloot she coost a hitch,
An' owre she warsl'd in the ditch:
There, groaning, dying, she did ly,   5
When *Hughoc* he cam doytan by.

Wi' glowrin een, an' lifted han's,
Poor *Hughoc* like a statue stan's;
He saw her days were near hand ended,
But, waes my heart! he could na mend it!   10
He gaped wide, but naething spak,
At length poor *Mailie* silence brak.

'O thou, whase lamentable face
Appears to mourn my woefu' case!
My *dying words* attentive hear,   15
An' bear them to my *Master* dear.

Tell him, if e'er again he keep
As muckle gear as buy a *sheep*,
O, bid him never tye them mair,
Wi' wicked strings o' hemp or hair!   20
But ca' them out to park or hill,
An' let them wander at their will:
So, may his flock increase an' grow
To *scores* o' lambs, an' *packs* of woo'!

* A neibor herd-callan.

The Death . . . of Poor Mailie. *Text from the edition of 1786, collated with the* First Commonplace Book (*1CPB*), *the Kilmarnock MS* (*Kil*), *and the editions of 1787, 1793, 1794*
   Title The Author's only] my ain *1CPB Kil*   2 Was] Were *1CPB*   6 *Note in 86–94*

Tell him, he was a Master kin',   25
An' ay was guid to me an' mine;
An' now my *dying* charge I gie him,
My helpless *lambs*, I trust them wi' him.

O, bid him save their harmless lives,
Frae dogs an' tods, an' butchers' knives!   30
But gie them guid *cow-milk* their fill,
Till they be fit to fend themsel;
An' tent them duely, e'en an' morn,
Wi' taets o' *hay* an' ripps o' *corn*.

An' may they never learn the gaets,   35
Of ither vile, wanrestfu' *Pets*!
To slink thro' slaps, an' reave an' steal,
At stacks o' pease, or stocks o' kail.
So may they, like their great *forbears*,
For monie a year come thro' the sheers: 40
So *wives* will gie them bits o' bread,
An' *bairns* greet for them when they're dead.

My poor *toop-lamb*, my son an' heir,
O, bid him breed him up wi' care!
An' if he live to be a beast,   45
To pit some havins in his breast!
An' warn him, what I winna name,
To stay content wi' *yowes* at hame;
An' no to rin an' wear his cloots,
Like ither menseless, graceless brutes.   50

An' niest my *yowie*, silly thing,
Gude keep thee frae a *tether string*!
O, may thou ne'er forgather up,
Wi' onie blastet, moorlan *toop*;
But ay keep mind to moop an' mell,   55
Wi' sheep o' credit like thysel!

30 butchers'] butcher's *Kil*   31 *cow-milk*] het milk *1CPB*   36 wanrestfu']
unrestfu' *1CPB*   39 great] auld *1CPB*   41 *wives* will] wives 'll
1CPB Kil   47 him, what I winna name 87-94: him ay at ridin time *1CPB*
Kil 86   54 blastet, moorlan] blastiet moorla *Kil*

And now, *my bairns*, wi' my last breath,
I lea'e my blessin wi' you baith:
An' when ye think upo' your Mither,
Mind to be kind to ane anither.   60

Now, honest *Hughoc*, dinna fail,
To tell my Master a' my tale;
An' bid him burn this cursed *tether*,
An' for thy pains thou 'se get my blather.'

This said, poor *Mailie* turn'd her head,   65
An' clos'd her een amang the dead!

25. Poor Mailie's Elegy

LAMENT in rhyme, lament in prose,
   Wi' saut tears trickling down your nose;
Our *Bardie*'s fate is at a close,
     Past a' remead!
The last, sad cape-stane of his woes;   5
     Poor Mailie's dead!

58 *Followed in 1CPB by a cancelled verse* As lang 's ye can keep ay the gither
59 ye] you 87–94   think upo'] ever mind *1CPB*

Poor Mailie's Elegy. *Text from the edition of 1786, collated with the Kilmarnock MS*
(Kil) *and the editions of 1787, 1793, 1794. An early draft, complete in six stanzas, is as*
follows (facsimile in the Burns Chronicle, *1932, pp. 25–27):*

           Elegy
      Lament in rhyme, a' ye wha dow,
      Your elbuck rub an' claw your pow,
      Poor Robin's ruin'd stick an' stow
           Past a' remead:
      His only, darlin, AIN PET YOWE   5
           Poor Mailie 's dead!

      Ochon, alais, his luckles lot!
      In losin her he lost a NOTE;
      He sell'd her lambs to buy a coat
           A mournin weed;   10
      He 's saxpence poorer than a groat
           Sin' Mailie 's dead!

3 Our *Bardie*'s] Poor Robin's *Kil*

It's no the loss o' warl's gear,
That could sae bitter draw the tear,
Or make our *Bardie*, dowie, wear
    The mourning weed: 10
He's lost a friend and neebor dear,
    In *Mailie* dead.

Thro' a' the town she trotted by him;
A lang half-mile she could descry him;
Wi' kindly bleat, when she did spy him,   15
    She ran wi' speed:
A friend mair faithfu' ne'er came nigh him,
    Than *Mailie* dead.

    She was nae get o' runted rams
    Wi' woo' like gaits, an' legs like trams;
    She was the flow'r o' Fairlie lambs   15
        A famous breed!
    Now Robin greetan chows the hams
        O' Mailie dead!

    O Fortune, how thou does us mock!
    He thought in her he saw a stock: 20
    Would heave him up, wi' hyvie folk
        To cock his head;
    Now a' his hopes are gane like smoke
        For Mailie's dead!

    Wae worth the man wha first did shape   25
    That wyle, wunchancy thing, a rape,
    It maks good fellows girn an' gape
        Wi' choakin dread,
    An' Robin's bonnet wave wi' crape
        For Mailie dead!   30

    Ye BARDIES a', in cantie KYLE,
    Wi' saut tears tricklin down like oil;
    Come join the melancholious style
        O' ROBIN's reed;
    For never, never mair he'll smile   35
        Sin' MAILIE'S DEAD.

There are two versions in Kil. The sequence of the first is lines 1–12, 19–24, a cancelled
version of 31–36, 37–48, followed by a rule to mark the end of the poem. The second
version, immediately below, is in the sequence followed in 1786–94: lines 1–12
repeated, 13–18, the opening and close of 19–24, 25–36, and the first words of l. 37.
See Commentary

  9 make our *Bardie*] gar poor Robin *Kil*   13 Thro' a' the town] Ay whare
he gaed, *Kil*   14 him] *om. Kil*

I wat she was a *sheep* o' sense,
An' could behave hersel wi' mense: 20
I'll say 't, she never brak a fence,
    Thro' thievish greed.
Our *Bardie*, lanely, keeps the spence
    Sin' *Mailie*'s dead.

Or, if he wanders up the howe,   25
Her living image in *her yowe*,
Comes bleating to him, owre the knowe,
    For bits o' bread;
An' down the briny pearls rowe
    For *Mailie* dead.   30

She was nae get o' moorlan tips,
Wi' tauted ket, an' hairy hips;
For her forbears were brought in ships,
    Frae 'yont the TWEED:
A bonier *fleesh* ne'er cross'd the clips   35
    Than *Mailie*'s dead.

Wae worth that man wha first did shape,
That vile, wanchancie thing—*a raep*!
It maks guid fellows girn an' gape,
    Wi' chokin dread;
An' *Robin*'s bonnet wave wi' crape   40
    For *Mailie* dead.

O, a' ye *Bards* on bonie DOON!
An' wha on AIRE your chanters tune!
Come, join the melancholious croon   45
    O' *Robin*'s reed!
His heart will never get aboon!
    His *Mailie*'s dead!

---

19 *sheep*] yowe *Kil*   23 Our *Bardie*] Now Robin *Kil*   25 Or, if] At
times *Kil*   27 to 87–94: till *Kil* 86   31–36 She was . . . dead.] *Kil has
(cancelled) ll. 13–18 of the draft* Elegy   37 that] the *Kil*   38 vile]
wile *Kil*   39 maks] gars *Kil*   44 An'] Or *Kil*   47 heart will] heart 'll
Kil

26. [Remorse]

I intirely agree with that judicious Philosopher Mr Smith in
his excellent Theory of Moral Sentiments, that Remorse is the
most painful sentiment that can embitter the human bosom.
Any ordinary pitch of fortitude may bear up tolerably well,
under those calamities, in the procurement of which, we our-   [5]
selves have had no hand; but when our own follies or crimes,
have made us miserable and wretched, to bear it up with
manly firmness, and at the same time have a proper penitential
sense of our misconduct,—is a glorious effort of Self-com-
mand.—   [10]

O F all the numerous ills that hurt our peace;
   That press the soul, or wring the mind with
    anguish;
Beyond comparison the worst are those
That to our Folly, or our Guilt we owe.
In ev'ry other circumstance the mind   5
Has this to say, it was no deed of mine:
But, when to all the evil of misfortune
This sting is added, blame thy foolish self;
Or worser far, the pangs of keen remorse:
The tort'ring, gnawing consciousness of guilt—   10
Of guilt, perhaps, where we've involved others;
The young, the innocent, who fondly lov'd us:
Nay more, that very love their cause of ruin—
O! burning Hell! in all thy store of torments
There's not a keener LASH—   15
Lives there a man so firm who, while his heart
Feels all the bitter horrors of his crime,
Can reason down its agonizing throbs,
And, after proper purpose of amendment,
Can firmly force his jarring thoughts to peace?   20
O happy, happy, enviable man!
O glorious magnanimity of soul!

Remorse. Text from the First Commonplace Book (*1CPB; pp. 5–6, September 1783*),
collated with Burns's copy of 1CPB in the Glenriddell MSS (Glen) and Currie (ii. 8–9)
  4 That . . . owe *Glen Currie*: By our own folly, or our guilt brought on *1CPB*
18 its *Glen*: it's *1CPB*   20 peace? *Glen*] peace, *1CPB*

27. Song

Tune, Prepare, my dear Brethren, to the tavern let's fly, &c.

I

N^o Churchman am I for to rail and to write,
No Statesman nor Soldier to plot or to fight,
No sly Man of business contriving a snare,
For a big-belly'd bottle's the whole of my care.

II

The Peer I don't envy, I give him his bow;   5
I scorn not the Peasant, tho' ever so low;
But a club of good fellows, like those that are here,
And a bottle like this, are my glory and care.

III

Here passes the Squire on his brother—his horse;
There Centum per Centum, the Cit with his purse;   10
But see you the Crown how it waves in the air,
There a big-belly'd bottle still eases my care.

Song. *Text from the Edinburgh edition, 1787, collated with the Huntington Library
MS, SMM 1803 (587), and the editions of 1793, 1794. Title in SMM* No Churchman
am I

3 sly . . . snare] plodding, dull, mercantile HOMME DES AFFAIRES *MS*
5 don't envy] envy not *MS*   7 But] *not in MS*   those] these *MS*   here *94
SMM*: there *MS 87 93*   8 are] is *MS*   8 *additional stanza in MS:*

> Sir PIT at his FINANCE may set him to work,
> And HASTINGS be libell'd a robber by BURKE;
> Till the NABOB admits in the TEAGUE for a share,
> While a big belly'd bottle's the chief of my care.

11 the Crown] "*D'en haut" *MS, with a note:* *D'en haut) the motto of Sir J.
Whiteford's arms, hung in Mauchline, as a tavern-sign to J. Dow, of bibipotent
fame.

IV

The wife of my bosom, alas! she did die;
For sweet consolation to church I did fly;
I found that old Solomon proved it fair,   15
That a big-belly'd bottle's a cure for all care.

V

I once was persuaded a venture to make;
A letter inform'd me that all was to wreck;
But the pursy old landlord just waddl'd up stairs,
With a glorious bottle that ended my cares.   20

VI

'Life's cares they are comforts*'—a maxim laid down
By the Bard, what d'ye call him, that wore the black
      gown;
And faith I agree with th' old prig to a hair;
For a big-belly'd bottle's a heav'n of care.

A Stanza added in a Mason Lodge:

Then fill up a bumper and make it o'erflow,   25
And honours masonic prepare for to throw;
May ev'ry true Brother of th' Compass and Square
Have a big-belly'd bottle when harass'd with care.

28. On Ja⁵ Grieve, Laird of Boghead, Tarbolton

Here lies Boghead amang the dead,
      In hopes to get salvation;
But if such as he, in Heav'n may be,
      Then welcome, hail! damnation.—

* Young's Night Thoughts.

21 *note in MS:* D⁵ Young   24 of care *93 94 SMM:* of a care *MS 87*   25 *A
Stanza . . . Lodge:*] *not in MS*   26 And honours masonic] Your highest of
honours *MS*   28 harass'd *93 94 SMM:* press *MS:* pressed *87*

On Ja⁵ Grieve. *Text from the* First Commonplace Book, *p. 14 (dated April 1784).
Holograph in a copy of* Poems *1787 subtitled* A sanctimonious rascal of the first water
(cf. 28A)

28A. On an Innkeeper in Tarbolton—

HERE lies 'mang ither useless matters,
A. Manson wi' his endless clatters.—

29. Song.—In the character of a ruined Farmer—

Tune, Go from my window, Love, do!—

1

THE sun he is sunk in the west;
  All creatures retired to rest,
While here I sit, all sore beset,
  With sorrow, grief, and woe:
And it's O, fickle Fortune, O!   5

2

The prosperous man is asleep,
Nor hears how the whirlwinds sweep;
But Misery and I must watch
  The surly tempest blow:
And it's O, fickle, &c.   10

On an Innkeeper. Transcript by J. W. Egerer from a holograph in a copy of Poems
1787 (sold in New York 1962)

Song. Text from the Stair MS, f. 9

3

There lies the dear Partner of my breast;
Her cares for a moment at rest:
Must I see thee, my youthful pride,
   Thus brought so very low!
And it's O, fickle &c.   15

4

There lie my sweet babies in her arms;
No anxious fear their little hearts alarms;
But for their sake my heart does ache,
   With many a bitter throe:
And it's O, fickle &c.   20

5

I once was by Fortune carest;
I once could relieve the distrest:
Now life's poor support, hardly earn'd,
   My fate will scarce bestow:
And it's O, fickle &c.   25

6

No comfort, no comfort I have!
How welcome to me were the grave!
But then my wife and children dear—
   O, whither would they go!
And it's O, fickle &c.   30

7

O whither, O whither shall I turn!
All friendless, forsaken, forlorn!
For in this world, Rest or Peace,
   I never more shall know!
And it's O, fickle Fortune, O!   35

30. Mary Morison

Tune, Duncan Davison

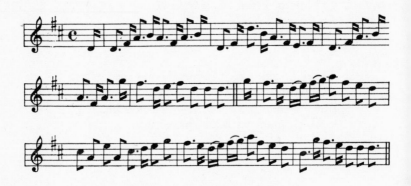

O MARY, at thy window be,
    It is the wish'd, the trysted hour;
Those smiles and glances let me see,
    That make the miser's treasure poor:
How blythely wad I bide the stoure,   5
    A weary slave frae sun to sun;
Could I the rich reward secure,
    The lovely Mary Morison!

Yestreen when to the trembling string
    The dance gaed through the lighted ha',   10
To thee my fancy took its wing,
    I sat, but neither heard, nor saw:
Though this was fair, and that was braw,
    And yon the toast of a' the town,
I sigh'd, and said amang them a',   15
    'Ye are na Mary Morison.'

Mary Morison. *Text from the Dalhousie MS (letter to Thomson, 20 March 1793),*
collated with SC, 1818 (219). First-line title in SC; set to the air The Glasgow Lasses.
After Duncan Davison *Thomson adds in the MS* Or, Bide ye yet
   2 wish'd, the] *correcting* wished, *in MS*   5, 18 wad] wou'd *SC*   6 frae]
from *SC*

O Mary, canst thou wreck his peace,
    Wha for thy sake wad gladly die!
Or canst thou break that heart of his,
    Whase only faute is loving thee!   20
If love for love thou wilt na gie,
    At least be pity to me shown;
A thought ungentle canna be
    The thought o' Mary Morison.

20 faute] fault *SC*

II

POEMS
1784–1785

MOSSGIEL

31. Epitaph on my own friend, and my father's friend, Wᵐ Muir in Tarbolton Miln—

Aɴ honest man here lies at rest
As e'er God with his image blest.
The friend of man, the friend of truth;
The friend of Age, and guide of Youth:
Few hearts like his with virtue warm'd,   5
Few heads with knowledge so inform'd:
If there's another world, he lives in bliss;
If there is none, he made the best of this.—

32–37. Epitaphs

32. On a Celebrated Ruling Elder

Here Sowter **** in Death does sleep;
To H–ll, if he's gane thither,
Satan, gie him thy gear to keep,
He'll haud it weel thegither.

33. On a Noisy Polemic

Below thir stanes lie Jamie's banes;
O Death, it's my opinion,
Thou ne'er took such a bleth'ran b–tch,
Into thy dark dominion!

Epitaph on my own friend. *Text from the Alloway MS (Al), collated with the* First Commonplace Book, *p. 14 (1CPB), the Huntington Library MS (Geddes's copy of 87), the Glenriddell MS, p. 66 (Glen; transcript), and Currie, 1800 (iv. 402). Title from 1CPB; title in Al Geddes Glen Currie* Epitaph—On a Friend—
 1 An . . . rest] Here lies a chearful, honest breast, *1CPB*

Epitaphs. *Text from the edition of 1786, collated with the* First Commonplace Book *(1CPB; 32 and 35 only) and the editions of 1787, 1793, 1794.*

On a Celebrated Ruling Elder. *Title in 1CPB* Epitaph on Wᵐ Hood Senʳ in Tarbolton
 1 ****] Hood *1CPB*

34. On Wee Johnie

Hic jacet wee *Johnie*

Whoe'er thou art, O reader, know,
    That Death has murder'd Johnie;
An' here his *body* lies fu' low—
    For *saul* he ne'er had ony.

35. For the Author's Father

O ye whose cheek the tear of pity stains,
    Draw near with pious rev'rence and attend!
Here lie the loving Husband's dear remains,
    The tender Father, and the gen'rous Friend.

The pitying Heart that felt for human Woe;   5
    The dauntless heart that fear'd no human Pride;
The Friend of Man, to vice alone a foe;
    'For ev'n his failings lean'd to Virtue's side.*'

36. For R. A. Esq;

Know thou, O stranger to the fame
Of this much lov'd, much honor'd name!
(For none that knew him need be told)
A warmer heart Death ne'er made cold.

37. For G. H. Esq;

The poor man weeps—here G——n sleeps,
    Whom canting wretches blam'd:
But with *such as he*, where'er he be,
    May I be *sav'd* or *d*——'d!

* Goldsmith.

For the Author's Father. *Title in 1CPB* Epitaph on my ever honor'd Father
    1 whose . . . stains,] who sympathise with Virtue's pains: *1CPB*   8 'For ev'n]
For 'even *correcting* And 'even *in 1CPB*

38. A Fragment

The Earl of Glencairn's

I

WHEN *Guilford* good our Pilot stood,
    An' did our hellim thraw, man,
Ae night, at tea, began a plea,
    Within *America*, man:
Then up they gat the maskin-pat,   5
    And in the sea did jaw, man;
An' did nae less, in full Congress,
    Than quite refuse our law, man.

II

Then thro' the lakes *Montgomery* takes,
    I wat he was na slaw, man;   10
Down *Lowrie's burn* he took a turn,
    And *C–rl–t–n* did ca', man:
But yet, whatreck, he, at *Quebec*,
    Montgomery-like did fa', man,
Wi' sword in hand, before his band,   15
    Amang his en'mies a', man.

A Fragment. *Text from the Edinburgh edition, 1787, collated with the Alloway MS, SMM, 1788 (101), SC, 1801 (127), and the editions of 1793, 1794. First-line title in SMM and SC. Tune in 87 Killiecrankie, in SMM M. freicedan*

III

Poor *Tammy G–ge* within a cage
   Was kept at *Boston-ha'*, man;
Till *Willie H––e* took o'er the knowe
   For *Philadelphia*, man: 20
Wi' sword an' gun he thought a sin
   Guid Christian bluid to draw, man;
But at *New-York*, wi' knife an' fork,
   Sir Loin he hacked sma', man.

IV

B–rg––ne gaed up, like spur an' whip,   25
   Till *Fraser* brave did fa', man;
Then lost his way, ae misty day,
   In *Saratoga* shaw, man.
C–rnw–ll–s fought as lang's he dought,
   An' did the Buckskins claw, man;   30
But *Cl–nt–n's* glaive frae rust to save
   He hung it to the wa', man.

V

Then *M–nt–gue*, an' *Guilford* too,
   Began to fear a fa', man;
And *S–ckv–lle* doure, wha stood the stoure,   35
   The German Chief to thraw, man:
For Paddy *B–rke*, like ony Turk,
   Nae mercy had at a', man;
An' *Charlie F–x* threw by the box,
   An' lows'd his tinkler jaw, man.   40

VI

Then *R–ck–ngh–m* took up the game;
   Till Death did on him ca', man;
When *Sh–lb–rne* meek held up his cheek,
   Conform to Gospel law, man:

35–36 And . . . man] *marginal revision in MS, replacing deleted lines*
       An' bauld G––ne whom Minden's plain
       To fame will ever blaw, man

Saint Stephen's boys, wi' jarring noise,   45
  They did his measures thraw, man,
For *N–rth* an' *F–x* united stocks,
  An' bore him to the wa', man.

VII

Then Clubs an' Hearts were *Charlie*'s cartes,
  He swept the stakes awa', man,   50
Till the Diamond's Ace, of *Indian* race,
  Led him a sair *faux pas*, man:
The Saxon lads, wi' loud placads,
  On *Chatham's Boy* did ca', man;
An' Scotland drew her pipe an' blew,   55
  'Up, Willie, waur them a', man!'

VIII

Behind the throne then *Gr–nv–lle*'s gone,
  A secret word or twa, man;
While slee *D–nd–s* arous'd the class
  Be-north the Roman wa', man: 60
An' *Chatham*'s wraith, in heav'nly graith,
  (Inspired Bardies saw, man)
Wi' kindling eyes cry'd, '*Willie*, rise!
  'Would I hae fear'd them a', man!'

IX

But, word an' blow, *N–rth*, *F–x*, and *Co*.   65
  Gowff'd *Willie* like a ba', man,
Till *Suthron* raise, an' coost their claise
  Behind him in a raw, man:
An' *Caledon* threw by the drone,
  An' did her whittle draw, man;   70
An' swoor fu' rude, thro' dirt an' blood,
  To mak it guid in law, man.

*   *   *   *   *   *   *

65–72 *not in MS*   67 *Suthron*] Suthrons *SMM*

39. Address to the Unco Guid, or the Rigidly Righteous

My Son, these maxims make a rule,
And lump them ay thegither;
The Rigid Righteous *is a fool,*
The Rigid Wise *anither:*
The cleanest corn that e'er was dight
May hae some pyles o' caff in;
So ne'er a fellow-creature slight
For random fits o' daffin.
SOLOMON.—Eccles. ch. vii. vers. 16.

I

O YE wha are sae guid yoursel,
 Sae pious and sae holy,
Ye've nought to do but mark and tell
 Your Neebours' fauts and folly!
Whase life is like a weel-gaun mill, 5
 Supply'd wi' store o' water,
The heaped happer's ebbing still,
 And still the clap plays clatter.

II

Hear me, ye venerable Core,
 As counsel for poor mortals, 10
That frequent pass douce Wisdom's door
 For glaikit Folly's portals;
I, for their thoughtless, careless sakes
 Would here propone defences,
Their donsie tricks, their black mistakes, 15
 Their failings and mischances.

III

Ye see your state wi' theirs compar'd,
 And shudder at the niffer,
But cast a moment's fair regard
 What maks the mighty differ; 20

Address to the Unco Guid. *Text from the Edinburgh edition, 1787, collated with those of 1793, 1794*

Discount what scant occasion gave,
   That purity ye pride in,
And (what's aft mair than a' the lave)
   Your better art o' hiding.

IV

Think, when your castigated pulse   25
   Gies now and then a wallop,
What ragings must his veins convulse,
   That still eternal gallop:
Wi' wind and tide fair i' your tail,
   Right on ye scud your sea-way;   30
But, in the teeth o' baith to sail,
   It maks an unco leeway.

V

See Social-life and Glee sit down,
   All joyous and unthinking,
Till, quite transmugrify'd, they're grown   35
   Debauchery and Drinking:
O would they stay to calculate
   Th' eternal consequences;
Or your more dreaded h—ll to state,
   D—mnation of expences!   40

VI

Ye high, exalted, virtuous Dames,
   Ty'd up in godly laces,
Before ye gie poor *Frailty* names,
   Suppose a change o' cases;
A dear-lov'd lad, convenience snug,   45
   A treacherous inclination—
But, let me whisper i' your lug,
   Ye're aiblins nae temptation.

VII

Then gently scan your brother Man,
   Still gentler sister Woman;   50
Tho' they may gang a kennin wrang,
   To step aside is human:

48 aiblins] ablins *87* (*st*)

One point must still be greatly dark,
    The moving *Why* they do it;
And just as lamely can ye mark,   55
    How far perhaps they rue it.

VIII

Who made the heart, 'tis *He* alone
    Decidedly can try us,
He knows each chord its various tone,
    Each spring its various bias: 60
Then at the balance let's be mute,
    We never can adjust it;
What's *done* we partly may compute,
    But know not what's *resisted*.

40. The Ronalds of the Bennals

IN Tarbolton, ye ken, there are proper young men,
    And proper young lasses and a', man:
But ken ye the Ronalds that live in the Bennals,
    They carry the gree frae them a', man.

Their father's a laird, and weel he can spare't,   5
    Braid money to tocher them a', man,
To proper young men, he'll clink in the hand
    Gowd guineas a hunder or twa, man.

There's ane they ca' Jean, I'll warrant ye've seen
    As bonie a lass or as braw, man,   10
But for sense and guid taste she'll vie wi' the best,
    And a conduct that beautifies a', man.

The charms o' the min', the langer they shine,
    The mair admiration they draw, man;
While peaches and cherries, and roses and lilies,   15
    They fade and they wither awa, man.

The Ronalds of the Bennals. *Text from Chambers, 1851 (i. 46–47)*

If ye be for Miss Jean, tak this frae a frien',
    A hint o' a rival or twa, man,
The Laird o' Blackbyre wad gang through the fire,
    If that wad entice her awa, man.   20

The Laird o' Braehead has been on his speed,
    For mair than a towmond or twa, man;
The Laird o' the Ford will straught on a board,
    If he canna get her at a', man.

Then Anna comes in, the pride o' her kin,   25
    The boast of our bachelors a', man:
Sae sonsy and sweet, sae fully complete,
    She steals our affections awa, man.

If I should detail the pick and the wale
    O' lasses that live here awa, man,   30
The faut wad be mine, if she didna shine
    The sweetest and best o' them a', man.

I lo'e her mysel, but darena weel tell,
    My poverty keeps me in awe, man,
For making o' rhymes, and working at times,   35
    Does little or naething at a', man.

Yet I wadna choose to let her refuse,
    Nor hae't in her power to say na, man,
For though I be poor, unnoticed, obscure,
    My stomach's as proud as them a', man.   40

Though I canna ride in weel-booted pride,
    And flee o'er the hills like a craw, man,
I can haud up my head wi' the best o' the breed,
    Though fluttering ever so braw, man.

My coat and my vest, they are Scotch o' the best,   45
    O' pairs o' guid breeks I hae twa, man:
And stockings and pumps to put on my stumps,
    And ne'er a wrang steek in them a', man.

My sarks they are few, but five o' them new,
    Twal'-hundred, as white as the snaw, man,   50
A ten-shillings hat, a Holland cravat;
    There are no mony poets sae braw, man.

I never had freens weel stockit in means,
    To leave me a hundred or twa, man,
Nae weel-tocher'd aunts, to wait on their drants   55
    And wish them in hell for it a', man.

I never was cannie for hoarding o' money,
    Or claughtin't together at a', man,
I've little to spend and naething to lend,
    But devil a shilling I awe, man.   60

41. The Tarbolton Lasses

IF ye gae up to yon hill-tap,
    Ye'll there see bonie Peggy:
She kens her father is a laird,
    And she forsooth's a leddy.

There's Sophy tight, a lassie bright,   5
    Besides a handsome fortune:
Wha canna win her in a night
    Has little art in courtin.

Gae down by Faile, and taste the ale,
    And tak a look o' Mysie;   10
She's dour and din, a deil within,
    But ablins she may please ye.

If she be shy, her sister try,
    Ye'll may be fancy Jenny:
If ye'll dispense wi' want o' sense—   15
    She kens hersel she's bonnie.

As ye gae up by yon hillside,
    Spier in for bonnie Bessy:
She'll gie ye a beck, and bid ye light,
    And handsomely address ye.   20

The Tarbolton Lasses. *Text from Chambers, 1851 (i. 45)*

There's few sae bonny, nane sae guid
    In a' King George' dominion;
If ye should doubt the truth o' this—
    It's Bessy's ain opinion.

42. Song—

Tune—Bonie Dundee—

IN Mauchline there dwells six proper young Belles,
    The pride of the place and its neighbourhood a',
Their carriage and dress a stranger would guess,
    In Lon'on or Paris they'd gotten it a':
Miss Miller is fine, Miss Murkland's divine,   5
    Miss Smith she has wit and Miss Betty is braw;
There's beauty and fortune to get wi' Miss Morton,
    But ARMOUR's the jewel for me o' them a'.—

43. O leave novels &c.

Lively

Song. *Text from the Glenriddell MS (p. 1). Burns adds:* Note, Miss Armour is now known by the designation of Mrs Burns——

O leave novels &c. *Text from SMM, 1803 (573; unsigned)*

O LEAVE novels, ye Mauchline belles,
　　Ye're safer at your spinning wheel;
Such witching books, are baited hooks
　　For rakish rooks like Rob Mossgiel.
Your fine Tom Jones and Grandisons   5
　　They make your youthful fancies reel;
They heat your brains, and fire your veins,
　　And then you're prey for Rob Mossgiel.

Beware a tongue that's smoothly hung;
　　A heart that warmly seems to feel;   10
That feelin heart but acks a part,
　　'Tis rakish art in Rob Mossgiel.
The frank address, the soft caress,
　　Are worse than poisoned darts of steel,
The frank address, and politesse,   15
　　Are all finesse in Rob Mossgiel.

44. A Fragment—

Tune, I had a horse and I had nae mair—

W HEN first I came to Stewart Kyle
　　My mind it was nae steady,
Where e'er I gaed, where e'er I rade,
　　A Mistress still I had ay:
But when I came roun' by Mauchlin town,   5
　　Not dreadin' any body,
My heart was caught before I thought
　　And by a Mauchlin Lady—

A Fragment. *Text from the* First Commonplace Book, *p. 37 (dated August 1785),
collated with Cromek,* Reliques, *1808 (p. 346)*

45. Green grow the Rashes. A Fragment

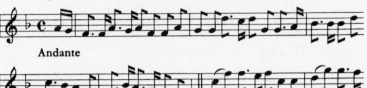

Andante

CHORUS

Green grow the rashes, O;
Green grow the rashes, O;
The sweetest hours that e'er I spend,
Are spent among the lasses, O.

I

T HERE's nought but care on ev'ry han',
   In ev'ry hour that passes, O:
What signifies the life o' man,
   An' 'twere na for the lasses, O.
         Green grow, &c.

II

The warly race may riches chase,   5
   An' riches still may fly them, O;
An' tho' at last they catch them fast,
   Their hearts can ne'er enjoy them, O.
         Green grow, &c.

III

But gie me a canny hour at e'en,
   My arms about my Dearie, O;   10
An' warly cares, an' warly men,
   May a' gae tapsalteerie, O!
         Green grow, &c.

Green grow the Rashes. *Text from the Edinburgh edition, 1787, collated with the*
First Commonplace Book (*1CPB; dated August 1784*), SMM, 1787 (77), *and the*
editions of 1793, 1794
   Title. grow] grows *SMM*   *Chorus.* 3 *spend*] spent 93 94   4 na] not *SMM*

IV

For you sae douse, ye sneer at this,
   Ye're nought but senseless asses, O:
The wisest Man the warl' saw,   15
   He dearly lov'd the lasses, O.
               Green grow, &c.

V

Auld Nature swears, the lovely Dears
   Her noblest work she classes, O:
Her prentice han' she try'd on man,
   An' then she made the lasses, O.   20
               Green grow, &c.

46. Song—

Tune: Black Joke—

M<small>Y</small> girl she's airy, she's buxom and gay,
   Her breath is as sweet as the blossoms in
     May;
A touch of her lips it ravishes quite.

13 sae douse, ye sneer] that's douse, an' sneers *1CPB*   15 warl' saw] warl'
e'er saw *87 (London) 94*   17–20 *not in 1CPB*

Song. *Text from letter to Ainslie, 29 July 1787 (transcript from Messrs Maggs),
collated with the* First Commonplace Book (*1CPB; dated September 1784*). *Title from*
1CPB

She's always good natur'd, good humor'd and free;
She dances, she glances, she smiles with a glee;   5
  Her eyes are the lightenings of joy and delight:
Her slender neck, her handsome waist,
Her hair well buckl'd, her stays well lac'd,
Her taper white leg with an et, and a, c,
For her a, b, e, d, and her c, u, n, t,   10
  And Oh, for the joys of a long winter night!!!

47. Epistle to J. R******, Enclosing some Poems

O ROUGH, rude, ready-witted R******,
  The wale o' cocks for fun an' drinkin!
There's monie godly folks are thinkin,
        Your *dreams** an' tricks
Will send you, Korah-like, a sinkin,   5
        Straught to auld Nick's.

Ye hae sae monie cracks an' cants,
And in your wicked, druken rants,
Ye mak a devil o' the *Saunts*,
        An' fill them fou;   10
And then their failings, flaws an' wants,
        Are a' seen thro'.

Hypocrisy, in mercy spare it!
That *holy robe*, O dinna tear it!
Spare't for their sakes wha aften wear it,   15
        The lads in *black*;
But your curst wit, when it comes near it,
        Rives't aff their back.

* A certain humorous *dream* of his was then making a noise in the country-side.

5 with a glee] upon me *1CPB*   6 Her . . . delight:] I never am happy when out of her sight. *1CPB*   8 buckl'd] *a correction in MS*: curl'd *1CPB*   10 a, b, e, d,] a, b, c, *1CPB*   10 c . . . t] *cipher in 1CPB*

Epistle to J. R******. *Text from the edition of 1786, collated with those of 1787, 1793, 1794*
  4 *note* country-side 87-94: world 86

Think, wicked Sinner, wha ye're skaithing:
It's just the *Blue-gown* badge an' claithing,   20
O' Saunts; tak that, ye lea'e them naething,
   To ken them by,
Frae ony unregenerate Heathen,
   Like you or I.

I've sent you here, some rhymin ware,   25
A' that I bargain'd for, an' mair;
Sae when ye hae an hour to spare,
   I will expect,
Yon *Sang*† ye'll sen't, wi' cannie care,
   And no neglect.   30

Tho' faith, sma' heart hae I to sing!
My Muse dow scarcely spread her wing:
I've play'd mysel a bonie *spring*,
   An' *danc'd* my fill!
I'd better gaen an' sair't the king,   35
   At Bunker's hill.

'Twas ae night lately, in my fun,
I gaed a rovin wi' the gun,
An' brought a *Paitrick* to the *grun'*,
   A bonie *hen*,   40
And, as the twilight was begun,
   Thought nane wad ken.

The poor, wee thing was *little hurt*;
I *straiket* it a wee for sport,
Ne'er thinkan they wad fash me for't;   45
   But, Deil-ma-care!
Somebody tells the *Poacher-Court*,
   The hale affair.

Some auld, us'd hands had taen a note,
That *sic a hen* had got a *shot*;   50
I was suspected for the plot;
   I scorn'd to lie;
So gat the whissle o' my groat,
   An' pay't the *fee*.

† A *Song* he had promised the Author.

But by my *gun*, o' guns the wale,   55
An' by my *pouther* an' my *hail*,
An' by my *hen*, an' by her *tail*,
      I vow an' swear!
The *Game* shall Pay, owre moor an' *dail*,
      For this, niest year.   60

As soon's the *clockin-time* is by,
An' the *wee powts* begun to cry,
L—d, I'se hae sportin by an' by,
      For my *gowd guinea*;
Tho' I should herd the *buckskin* kye   65
      For't, in Virginia!

Trowth, they had muckle for to blame!
'Twas neither broken wing nor limb,
But twa-three *draps* about the *wame*
      Scarce thro' the *feathers*;   70
An' baith a *yellow George* to claim,
      An' *thole* their *blethers*!

It pits me ay as mad's a hare;
So I can rhyme nor write nae mair;
But *pennyworths* again is fair,   75
      When time's expedient:
Meanwhile I am, respected Sir,
      Your most obedient.

48. Lines Addressed to Mr. John Ranken

AE day, as Death, that grusome carl,
  Was driving to the tither warl',
A mixie-maxie motely squad,
And mony a guilt-bespotted lad;
Black gowns of each denomination,   5
And thieves of every rank and station,

Lines . . . Verses. *Text from Stewart, 1801 (pp. 81–83). Sub-title of* Lines: The person
to whom his Poem on shooting the Partridge is addressed, while he occupied the
Farm of Adamhill in Ayrshire.

From him that wears the star and garter
To him that wintles in a halter:
Asham'd himself to see the wretches,
He mutters, glow'ring at the bitches,   10
'By G—d I'll not be seen behint them,
'Nor 'mang the sp'ritual core present them,
'Without, at least, ae honest man,
'To grace this damn'd infernal clan.'
By Adamhill a glance he threw,   15
'L—d, G—d!' quoth he, 'I have it now,
'There's just the man I want, in faith,'
And quickly stopped Ranken's breath.

49. Verses

*Addressed to the above J. Ranken, on his writing to the Poet, that a girl
in that part of the country was with child by him.*

I AM a keeper of the law
    In some sma' points, altho' not a';
Some people tell me gin I fa',
        Ae way or ither,
The breaking of ae point, tho' sma',   5
        Breaks a' thegither.

I hae been in for't ance or twice,
And winna say o'er far for thrice,
Yet never met with that surprise
        That broke my rest,   10
But now a rumour's like to rise,
        A whaup's i' the nest.

50. Lines

*Wrote by Burns, while on his death-bed, to J—n R—k—n, Ayrshire,
and forwarded to him immediately after the Poet's death.*

HE who of R—k—n sang, lies stiff and dead,
    And a green grassy hillock hides his head;
Alas! Alas! a devilish change indeed.

Verses. *See note to 48*
Lines. *Text from Stewart, 1801 (p. 60)*

51. Epistle to Davie, a Brother Poet

January—

I

WHILE winds frae off BEN-LOMOND blaw,
  And bar the doors wi' driving snaw,
And hing us owre the ingle,
I set me down, to pass the time,
And spin a verse or twa o' rhyme,   5
  In hamely, *westlin* jingle.
While frosty winds blaw in the drift,
  Ben to the chimla lug,
I grudge a wee the *Great-folk*'s gift,
  That live sae bien an' snug: 10
    I tent less, and want less
      Their roomy fire-side;
    But hanker, and canker,
      To see their cursed pride.

II

It's hardly in a body's pow'r,   15
To keep, at times, frae being sour,
  To see how things are shar'd;
How *best o' chiels* are whyles in want,
While *Coofs* on countless thousands rant,
  And ken na how to wair't: 20
But DAVIE lad, ne'er fash your head,
  Tho' we hae little gear,
We're fit to win our daily bread,
  As lang's we're hale and fier:

Epistle to Davie. Text from the edition of 1786, collated with the Adam and Kil-marnock (Kil) MSS, and the editions of 1787, 1793, 1794. Title in Adam An Epistle to Davy, a brother Poet, Lover, Ploughman and Fiddler. Jan: 1785; *in Kil* An Epistle to Davy: a brother Poet. Jan:—1785. *H-H. record a MS (not traced) with these variants:* 93 make] let *MS*   143 Amaist . . . ken] Without a claw or rug *MS*   146 Were . . . pen] Were harkin in my lug *MS*
  11 I tent less, and want] I want less, an' tent *Adam*   19 *Coofs*] fools *Adam*
20 And ken] An' kens *Adam Kil*

'Mair spier na, nor fear na,'*   25
  Auld age ne'er mind a feg;
The last o't, the warst o't,
  Is only but to beg.

III

To lye in kilns and barns at e'en,
When banes are craz'd, and bluid is thin,   30
  Is, doubtless, great distress!
Yet then *content* could make us blest;
Ev'n then, sometimes we'd snatch a taste
  Of truest happiness.
The honest heart that's free frae a'   35
  Intended fraud or guile,
However Fortune kick the ba',
  Has ay some cause to smile:
    And mind still, you'll find still,
      A comfort this nae sma';   40
    Nae mair then, we'll care then,
      Nae *farther* we can *fa'*.

IV

What tho', like Commoners of air,
We wander out, we know not where,
  But either house or hal'?   45
Yet *Nature*'s charms, the hills and woods,
The sweeping vales, and foaming floods,
  Are free alike to all.
In days when Daisies deck the ground,
  And Blackbirds whistle clear,   50
With honest joy, our hearts will bound,
  To see the *coming* year:
    On braes when we please then,
      We'll sit and *sowth* a tune;
    Syne *rhyme* till't, we'll time till't,   55
      And sing't when we hae done.

---

* Ramsay.

25 *MSS lack quotation marks and footnote*   39 you'll] ye'll *Kil*   55 we'll
MSS: well 86-93

V

It's no in titles nor in rank;
It's no in wealth like *Lon'on Bank*,
   To purchase peace and rest;
It's no in makin muckle, *mair*:   60
It's no in books; it's no in Lear,
   To make us truly blest:
If Happiness hae not her seat
   And center in the breast,
We may be *wise*, or *rich*, or *great*,   65
   But never can be *blest*:
     Nae treasures, nor pleasures
       Could make us happy lang;
     The *heart* ay's the part ay,
       That makes us right or wrang.   70

VI

Think ye, that sic as *you* and *I*,
Wha drudge and drive thro' wet and dry,
   Wi' never-ceasing toil;
Think ye, are we less blest than they,
Wha scarcely tent us in their way,   75
   As hardly worth their while?
Alas! how aft, in haughty mood,
   GOD's creatures they oppress!
Or else, neglecting a' that's guid,
   They riot in excess!   80
     Baith careless, and fearless,
       Of either Heaven or Hell;
     Esteeming, and deeming,
       It a' an idle tale!

VII

Then let us chearfu' acquiesce;   85
Nor make our scanty Pleasures less,
   By pining at our state:
And, ev'n should Misfortunes come,
I, here wha sit, hae met wi' some,
   An's thankfu' for them yet.   90

84 It] It's *87 (st, London) 94*   87 By] Wi' *Adam Kil*   89 I . . . sit]
correcting Yet here I sit *in Kil*: Yet here I sit *Adam*   hae] has *Adam Kil*

They gie the wit of *Age* to *Youth*;
  They let us ken oursel;
They make us see the naked truth,
  The *real* guid and ill.
    Tho' losses, and crosses,   95
      Be lessons right severe,
    There's *wit* there, ye'll get there,
      Ye'll find nae other where.

VIII

But tent me, DAVIE, *Ace o' Hearts!*
(To say aught less wad wrang the *cartes*,   100
  And flatt'ry I detest)
This life has joys for you and I;
And joys that riches ne'er could buy;
  And joys the very best.
There's a' the *Pleasures o' the Heart*,   105
  The *Lover* and the *Frien'*;
Ye hae your MEG, your dearest part,
  And I my darling JEAN!
    It warms me, it charms me,
      To mention but her *name*:   110
    It heats me, it beets me,
      And sets me a' on flame!

IX

O, all ye *Pow'rs* who rule above!
O THOU, whose very self art *love*!
  THOU know'st my words sincere!   115
The *life blood* streaming thro' my heart,
Or my more dear *Immortal part*,
  Is not more fondly dear!
When heart-corroding care and grief
  Deprive my soul of rest,   120
Her dear idea brings relief,
  And solace to my breast.

93 make] let *Adam*   118 Is] Are *Adam*   119–22 When . . . breast.]
Adam has   In all my share of care an' grief,
                    Which Fate has largely given,
                My hope, my comfort an' relief
                    Are thoughts of HER in HEAVEN.
119–22 *Corrected in Kil from Adam version*

Thou BEING, Allseeing,
  O hear my fervent pray'r!
Still take her, and make her,   125
  THY most peculiar care!

X

All hail! ye tender feelings dear!
The smile of love, the friendly tear,
  The sympathetic glow!
Long since, this world's thorny ways   130
Had number'd out my weary days,
  Had it not been for you!
Fate still has blest me with a friend,
  In ev'ry care and ill;
And oft a more *endearing* band,   135
  A *tye* more tender still.
    It lightens, it brightens,
      The tenebrific scene,
    To meet with, and greet with,
      My DAVIE or my JEAN!   140

XI

O, how that *name* inspires my style!
The words come skelpan, rank and file,
  Amaist before I ken!
The ready measure rins as fine,
As *Phœbus* and the famous *Nine*   145
  Were glowran owre my pen.
My spavet *Pegasus* will limp,
  Till ance he's fairly het;
And then he'll hilch, and stilt, and jimp,
  And rin an unco fit: 150
    But least then, the beast then,
      Should rue this hasty ride,
    I'll light now, and dight now,
      His sweaty, wizen'd hide.

124 *Adam ends*   127 feelings] feeling *Kil*   137 it] an' *Kil*   147 *Pegasus*
will] *Pegasus* 'll *Kil*   149 jimp] jump *Kil*   151 least] lest 94

52. The Holy Tulzie—

Blockheads with reason wicked Wits abhor,
But Fool with Fool is barbarous civil war.—

POPE—

O A' ye pious, godly Flocks
  Weel fed in pastures orthodox,
Wha now will keep you frae the fox,
   Or worryin tykes?
Or wha will tent the waifs and crocks   5
   About the dykes?

The twa best Herds in a' the west
That e'er gae gospel horns a blast
This five and fifty simmers past,
   O dool to tell!   10
Hae had a bitter, black outcast
   Atween themsel.—

O Moodie man, and wordy Russel,
How could ye breed sae vile a bustle?
Ye'll see how New-light Herds will whistle,   15
   And think it fine!
The L—d's cause gat na sic a twissle
   Since I hae min'.—

O Sirs! wha ever wad expeckit
Your duty ye wad sae negleckit?   20

The Holy Tulzie. Text from B.M. MS Egerton 1656, ff. 12ʳ–14ʳ (Eg), collated with the Alloway MS (Al; ll. 29–66, 85–96 only), An Unco Mournfu' Tale, 1796 (UMT), ?1799 (HT), and Stewart, 1801 (pp. 34–38). See Commentary. Title in Stewart The Twa Herds (without the epigraph). Note in Eg: The following was the first of my poetical productions that saw the light.—I gave a Copy of it to a particular friend of mine who was very fond of these things, and told him—'I did not know who was the Author, but that I had got a Copy of it by accident.'—The occasion was a bitter and shameless quarrel between two Revᵈ Gentlemen—Mʳ Moodie of Riccarton and Mʳ Russel of Kilmarnock.—It was at the time when the hue and cry against Patronage was at the worst.
 7 west] wast *Stewart* 8 horns] horn *Stewart* 9 This . . . fifty] These . . . twenty *Stewart* 12 Atween] Between *UMT HT* 14 ye breed sae] you raise so *UMT HT Stewart* 17 gat na] ne'er gat *Stewart* 19 wha ever wad] wha wad hae e'er *UMT HT*: whae'er wad ha'e *Stewart*

You wha was ne'er by Lairds respeckit,
  To wear the Plaid;
But by the vera Brutes eleckit
  To be their Guide.—

What Flock wi' Moodie's Flock could rank, 25
Sae hale and hearty every shank?
Nae poison'd Ariminian stank
  He loot them taste;
But Calvin's fountain-head they drank,
  That was a feast! 30

The Fulmart, Wil-cat, Brock and Tod
Weel kend his voice thro' a' the wood;
He knew their ilka hole and road,
  Baith out and in:
And liked weel to shed their blood, 35
  And sell their skin.—

And wha like Russel tell'd his tale;
His voice was heard o'er moor and dale:
He kend the L——d's sheep ilka tail,
  O'er a' the height; 40
And tell'd gin they were sick or hale
  At the first sight.—

He fine a maingie sheep could scrub,
And nobly swing the Gospel-club;
Or New-light Herds could nicely drub, 45
  And pay their skin;
Or hing them o'er the burning dub,
  Or shute them in.—

21 was ne'er] were no *UMT HT*: were ne'er *Stewart* 23 vera Brutes] brutes themselves *UMT HT Stewart* 27 Ariminian] soor Arminian *UMT HT Stewart* 28 loot] let *UMT HT Stewart* 29 But . . . fountain-head] Frae Calvin's well, ay clear *UMT HT Stewart* 30 That was] O, sic *UMT HT Stewart* 31 Fulmart] thummart *UMT HT Stewart* 33 knew] smell'd *UMT HT Stewart* 35 liked weel] weel he lik'd *UMT HT Stewart* 37 And wha] What herd *UMT HT Stewart* 38 o'er] thro' *UMT HT Stewart* 39 ilka] every *Al* 41 tell'd gin] tald if *Al*: saw gin *Stewart* 43 maingie] mangy'd *UMT HT* 44–46 And . . . Or . . . And] Or . . . And . . . Or *UMT HT Stewart* 44 nobly] sturdy *Al* swing] fling *Stewart* 45 Or . . . could nicely] The . . . he nice could *Al* 47 Or hing] Could shake *UMT HT Stewart* the *Al: om. Eg* dub] tub *UMT HT* 48 shute] fling *Al*: heave *UMT HT Stewart*

Sic twa——O, do I live to see't,
Sic famous twa sud disagree't!   50
And names like, 'Villain, Hypocrite,'
                    Each other giein;
While enemies wi' laughin spite
                    Say, 'Neither's liein.'——

O ye wha tent the Gospel-fauld,   55
Thee, Duncan deep, and Peebles shaul,
And chiefly great Apostle Auld,
                    We trust in thee,
That thou wilt work them het and cauld
                    To gar them gree.——   60

Consider, Sirs, how we're beset;
There's scarce a new Herd that we get
But comes frae 'mang that cursed Set,
                    I winna name:
I trust in Heaven, to see them het   65
                    Yet in a flame.——

There's D'rymple has been lang our fae;
M^cgill has wrought us meikle wae;
And that curst rascal ca'd M^cquhey;
                    And baith the Shaws,   70
Wha aft hae made us black and blae
                    Wi' vengefu' paws.——

Auld Wodrow lang has wrought mischief,
We trusted death wad bring relief;

52 Each] Ilk *UMT HT Stewart*   53 enemies] new-light herds *UMT HT Stewart*   wi' laughin spite] will laugh and say't *UMT*   54 Say . . . liein] That neither's clean *UMT*   55 O] A' *UMT HT Stewart*   56 Thee,] There's *UMT HT Stewart*   57 And . . . great] But . . . thou, *UMT HT Stewart* 60 To . . . gree] Till they agree *UMT HT Stewart*   65–66 I trust in . . . flame.] I hope frae . . . flame. *UMT HT. Stewart has*

                I hope frae heav'n to see them yet
                    In fiery flame.

  65 Heaven] G–d *Al*   67–84 There's . . . fin'.] *om. Al*   67 There's] *om. UMT HT Stewart*   our] a *UMT HT*   71 Wha] That *UMT HT Stewart* 73 wrought] hatch'd *UMT HT Stewart*   74 trusted] thought ay *UMT HT Stewart*

But he has gotten, to our grief,   75
      Ane to succeed him;
A chap will soundly buff our beef
      I meikle dread him.—

And mony mae that I could tell
Wha fair and openly rebel;   80
Forby Turn-coats amang oursel,
      There's Smith for ane;
I doubt he's but a Gray-neck still
      And that ye'll fin'.—

O a' ye flocks o'er a' the hills,   85
By mosses, meadows, moors and fells,
Come join your counsels and your skills
      To cowe the Lairds,
And get the Brutes the power themsels
      To chuse their Herds.—   90

Then Orthodoxy yet may prance,
And Learning in a woody dance;
And that curst cur ca'd Common Sense
      Wha bites sae sair,
Be banish'd o'er the seas to France,   95
      Let him bark there.—

[Then Shaw's and Dalrymple's eloquence,
M'—ll's close nervous excellence,
M'Q——e's pathetic manly sense,
      And guid M'——h,   100
Wi' S—th wha thro' the heart can glance,
      May a' pack aff.]

77 chap will] chield wha'll *UMT HT Stewart*   78 meikle] muckle *UMT HT*
79 mae] a ane *UMT HT Stewart*   80 fair and] fain would *Stewart*   83 Gray-
neck still] grey nick quill *UMT HT Stewart*   87 counsels] counsel *Stewart*
91 may] might *Al*   93 curst] fell *UMT HT Stewart*   94 Wha] That *UMT
HT Stewart*   95 seas] sea *UMT HT Stewart*   97–102 Then . . . aff.] *not
in the MSS. Text from Stewart*   101 Wi' . . . can] Wha thro' the heart can
brawly *UMT HT*

53. Holy Willie's Prayer—

And send the Godly in a pet to pray—
POPE.

Argument.

Holy Willie was a rather oldish batchelor Elder in the parish of
Mauchline, and much and justly famed for that polemical chattering
which ends in tippling Orthodoxy, and for that Spiritualized Bawdry
which refines to Liquorish Devotion.——In a Sessional process with
a gentleman in Mauchline, a M<u>r</u> Gavin Hamilton, Holy Willie, and
his priest, father Auld, after full hearing in the Presbytry of Ayr,
came off but second best; owing partly to the oratorical powers of
M<u>r</u> Rob<u>t</u> Aiken, M<u>r</u> Hamilton's Counsel; but chiefly to M<u>r</u>
Hamilton's being one of the most irreproachable and truly respectable
characters in the country.——On losing his Process, the Muse overheard
him at his devotions as follows—

O THOU that in the heavens does dwell!
   Wha, as it pleases best thysel,
Sends ane to heaven and ten to h–ll,
     A' for thy glory!
And no for ony gude or ill   5
     They've done before thee.—

Holy Willie's Prayer. *Text from the Glenriddell MS (Glen; pp. 21-25), collated with
MSS Kilmarnock (Kil), Alloway (Al), Esty (ll. 1-46 only), the Dumfries MS (Dum;
ll. 47-102, completing Esty), Dewar's transcript of a MS endorsed . . . given me by
Lord Glencairn, at Minto, 26 August, 1787 (D; offered for sale at Sotheby's, 30
June 1938), the Don MS (endorsed Enclosed in letter to Earl of Glencairn 1 August
1788), and Stewart (1801, pp. 41-45; 1802, pp. 236-9). Epigraph not in Stewart;
Argument in Glen, Esty and D only.*
   Esty has Gavin Hamilton was what the world calls, a good, moral man, but a
stranger to 'Effectual Calling' or 'the Newbirth;' so was very properly summonsed
before the kirk session by the Rev<u>d</u> M<u>r</u> Will<u>m</u> Auld, a worthy trumpeter of
the Lord; for his irregularities of walk and conversation.—The affair went to the
Presbytry, where the uncircumcised Philistines overcame the people of G—; and
the Priest of the Lord, and Holy Willy, the Lord's servant, were put to shame and
derided by the children of Belial.—Holy Willy had been called to be Presbytry
Elder; and his righteous Spirit being grieved at the triumph of the wicked ones, he
prayed unto the Lord saying—
   D has The occasion of this Prayer was a personal pique with which M<u>r</u> Auld, the
Clergyman of the place, was pleased to honor M<u>r</u> Gavin Hamilton, a gentleman of
the first worth in the country.—The quarrel ran so high that M<u>r</u> Hamilton was

   1 that] *correcting* wha *in D*: wha *Stewart* does] dost *Stewart* 6, 9 before] afore
Stewart

I bless and praise thy matchless might,
When thousands thou has left in night,
That I am here before thy sight,
    For gifts and grace,   10
A burning and a shining light
    To a' this place.——

What was I, or my generation,
That I should get such exaltation?
I, wha deserv'd most just damnation,   15
    For broken laws
Sax thousand years ere my creation,
    Thro' Adam's cause!

When from my mother's womb I fell,
Thou might hae plunged me deep in hell,   20
To gnash my gooms, and weep, and wail,
    In burning lakes,
Where damned devils roar and yell
    Chain'd to their stakes.——

Yet I am here, a chosen sample,   25
To shew thy grace is great and ample:
I'm here, a pillar o' thy temple
    Strong as a rock,
A guide, a ruler and example
    To a' thy flock.——   30

[O L——d thou kens what zeal I bear,
When drinkers drink, and swearers swear,

oblidged to appeal to the Presbytry of Ayr for vindication of his character, and employed Mr Robt Aiken Writer in Ayr, to appear for him and plead his cause.—— He did that so effectually as got an unanimous verdict in favor of his Client; and lashed Holy Willie, an old bachelor, and at that time Presbytry Elder for the Parish, so severely that on his return home he went *ben to the Spence*, and without admitting Meg as usual, he kneeled down before Heaven and burst out as follows:

15 deserv'd] deserve *Stewart*   17 Sax . . . ere] Five . . . 'fore *Stewart*
19–24 When . . . stakes.] *not in Kil*   19 from my mother's] frae my mither's
Stewart   20 deep] *om. Stewart*   21 and weep,] to weep *Stewart*
22–24 lakes . . . their stakes] lake . . . a stake *Stewart*   26 great] grace *Al*
27 o'] in *Stewart*   29 ruler] buckler, *Stewart*   31–36 O L——d . . . a'.]
Added in Stewart (1802). See Commentary

And singin' there, and dancin' here,
    Wi' great an' sma';
For I am keepet by thy fear,   35
    Free frae them a'.—]

But yet—O L—d—confess I must—
At times I'm fash'd wi' fleshly lust;
And sometimes too, in warldly trust
    Vile Self gets in;   40
But thou remembers we are dust,
    Defil'd wi' sin.—

O L—d—yestreen—thou kens—wi' Meg—
Thy pardon I sincerely beg!
O may't ne'er be a living plague,   45
    To my dishonor!
And I'll ne'er lift a lawless leg
    Again upon her.—

Besides, I farther maun avow,
Wi' Leezie's lass, three times—I trow—   50
But L—d, that friday I was fou
    When I cam near her;
Or else, thou kens, thy servant true
    Wad never steer her.—

Maybe thou lets this fleshly thorn   55
Buffet thy servant e'en and morn,
Lest he o'er proud and high should turn,
    That he's sae gifted;
If sae, thy hand maun e'en be borne
    Untill thou lift it.—   60

---

39 in] wi' *Stewart*   39 *Note in D:* Holy Willie was what is called, a Birlie-man of the place; to proof stacks, prize corn, &c.   42 wi'] in *Stewart*   51 *Note in D:* Friday—the Market day   54 never steer] ne'er ha'e steer'd *Stewart* 56 Buffet] Beset *Stewart*   57 proud and high] high and proud *Stewart* 58 That] 'Cause *Stewart*

L—d bless thy Chosen in this place,
For here thou has a chosen race:
But G—d, confound their stubborn face,
      And blast their name,
Wha bring thy rulers to disgrace   65
      And open shame.—

L—d mind Gaun Hamilton's deserts!
He drinks, and swears, and plays at cartes,
Yet has sae mony taking arts
      Wi' Great and Sma',   70
Frae G—d's ain priest the people's hearts
      He steals awa.—

And when we chasten'd him therefore,
Thou kens how he bred sic a splore,
And set the warld in a roar   75
      O' laughin at us:
Curse thou his basket and his store,
      Kail and potatoes.—

L—d hear my earnest cry and prayer
Against that Presbytry of Ayr!   80
Thy strong right hand, L—d, make it bare
      Upon their heads!
L—d visit them, and dinna spare,
      For their misdeeds!

O L—d my G—d, that glib-tongu'd Aiken!   85
My very heart and flesh are quaking
To think how I sat, sweating, shaking,
      And p—ss'd wi' dread,
While Auld wi' hingin lip gaed sneaking
      And hid his head!   90

62 has] hast *Stewart*   65 thy rulers] their rulers *Kil Al D*: thy elders
Stewart   66 open] public *Kil Al Dum D Don Stewart*   75 And] As *Stewart*
83 visit them] weigh it down *Stewart*   85 *Note in Dum:* A malignant Lawyer
who pled the unrighteous cause of G. Hamilton.   86 flesh] saul *Stewart*
87 I sat,] we stood *Stewart (1801)*   89 Auld . . . lip gaed sneaking] he . . .
lips and snakin', *Stewart (1801)*: Auld . . . lip gaed snakin' *Stewart (1802)*. *See
Commentary*   90 And hid] Held up *Stewart (1801)*

L—d, in thy day o' vengeance try him!
L—d visit him that did employ him!
And pass not in thy mercy by them,
   Nor hear their prayer;
But for thy people's sake destroy them,   95
   And dinna spare!

But L—d, remember me and mine
Wi' mercies temporal and divine!
That I for grace and gear may shine,
   Excell'd by nane!   100
And a' the glory shall be thine!
   Amen! Amen!

54. Epitaph on Holy Willie

Here Holy Willie's sair worn clay
  Taks up its last abode;
His saul has ta'en some other way,
  I fear, the left-hand road.

Stop! there he is as sure's a gun,   5
  Poor silly body see him;
Nae wonder he's as black's the grun,
  Observe wha's standing wi' him.

Your brunstane devilship I see
  Has got him there before ye;   10
But ha'd your nine-tail cat a wee,
  Till ance you've heard my story.

Your pity I will not implore,
  For pity ye have nane;
Justice, alas! has gi'en him o'er,   15
  And mercy's day is gaen.

91 thy] the *Stewart* 92 that] wha *Kil Al Dum D Don Stewart* 93–95
them] 'em *Stewart* 99 grace and gear] gear and grace *Stewart*

Epitaph on Holy Willie. *Text from Stewart, 1801 (p. 68)*

But hear me, Sir, de'il as ye are,
　　Look something to your credit;
A coof like him wou'd stain your name,
　　If it were kent ye did it.   20

55. Death and Doctor Hornbook. A True Story

Some books are lies frae end to end,
　And some great lies were never penn'd:
Ev'n Ministers they hae been kenn'd,
　　　　In holy rapture,
A rousing whid, at times, to vend,   5
　　　　And nail't wi' Scripture.

But this that I am gaun to tell,
Which lately on a night befel,
Is just as true's the Deil's in h–ll,
　　　　Or Dublin city: 10
That e'er he nearer comes oursel
　　　　'S a muckle pity.

The Clachan yill had made me canty,
I was na fou, but just had plenty;
I stacher'd whyles, but yet took tent ay   15
　　　　To free the ditches;
An' hillocks, stanes, an' bushes kenn'd ay
　　　　Frae ghaists an' witches.

The rising Moon began to glowr
The distant *Cumnock* hills out-owre;   20
To count her horns, wi' a' my pow'r,
　　　　I set mysel,
But whether she had three or four,
　　　　I cou'd na tell.

Death and Doctor Hornbook. *Text from the Edinburgh edition, 1787, collated with the editions of 1793 (HL: copy with holograph corrections in the Huntington Library), 1794*
　5 A . . . times, HL 94: Great lies and nonsense baith 87 93

I was come round about the hill,   25
And todlin down on *Willie's mill*,
Setting my staff wi' a' my skill,
        To keep me sicker;
Tho' leeward whyles, against my will,
        I took a bicker.   30

I there wi' *Something* does forgather,
That pat me in an eerie swither;
An awfu' scythe, out-owre ae shouther,
        Clear-dangling, hang;
A three-tae'd leister on the ither   35
        Lay, large an' lang.

Its stature seem'd lang Scotch ells twa,
The queerest shape that e'er I saw,
For fient a wame it had ava,
        And then its shanks,   40
They were as thin, as sharp an' sma'
        As cheeks o' branks.

'Guid-een,' quo' I; 'Friend! hae ye been mawin,
'When ither folk are busy sawin*?'
It seem'd to mak a kind o' stan',   45
        But naething spak;
At length, says I, 'Friend, whare ye gaun,
        'Will ye go back?'

It spak right howe—'My name is *Death*,
'But be na' fley'd.'—Quoth I, 'Guid faith,   50
'Ye're maybe come to stap my breath;
        'But tent me, billie;
'I red ye weel, tak care o' skaith,
        'See, there's a gully!'

'Gudeman,' quo' he, 'put up your whittle,   55
'I'm no design'd to try its mettle;
'But if I did, I wad be kittle
        'To be mislear'd,
'I wad na' mind it, no that spittle
        'Out-owre my beard.'   60

---

* This rencounter happened in seed-time 1785.

'Weel, weel!' says I, 'a bargain be't;
'Come, gies your hand, an' sae we're gree't;
'We'll ease our shanks an' tak a seat,
   'Come, gies your news!
'This while* ye hae been mony a gate,   65
   'At mony a house.'

'Ay, ay!' quo' he, an' shook his head,
'It's e'en a lang, lang time indeed
'Sin' I began to nick the thread,
   'An' choke the breath: 70
'Folk maun do something for their bread,
   'An' sae maun *Death*.

'Sax thousand years are near hand fled
'Sin' I was to the butching bred,
'And mony a scheme in vain's been laid,   75
   'To stap or scar me;
'Till ane Hornbook's† ta'en up the trade,
   'And faith, he'll waur me.

'Ye ken *Jock Hornbook* i' the Clachan,
'Deil mak his king's-hood in a spleuchan!   80
'He's grown sae weel acquaint wi' *Buchan*‡,
   'And ither chaps,
'The weans haud out their fingers laughin,
   'And pouk my hips.

'See, here's a scythe, and there's a dart,   85
'They hae pierc'd mony a gallant heart;
'But Doctor *Hornbook*, wi' his art
   'And cursed skill,
'Has made them baith no worth a f—t,
   'D—n'd haet they'll kill!   90

---

* An epidemical fever was then raging in that country.

 † This gentleman, Dr Hornbook, is, professionally, a brother of the sovereign Order of the Ferula; but, by intuition and inspiration, is at once an Apothecary, Surgeon, and Physician.

 ‡ Buchan's Domestic Medicine.

---

69 Sin'] Sin *87–94*

'Twas but yestreen, nae farther gaen,
'I threw a noble throw at ane;
'Wi' less, I'm sure, I've hundreds slain;
          'But deil-ma-care!
'It just play'd dirl on the bane,   95
          'But did nae mair.

'*Hornbook* was by, wi' ready art,
'And had sae fortify'd the part,
'That when I looked to my dart,
          'It was sae blunt,   100
'Fient haet o't wad hae pierc'd the heart
          'Of a kail-runt.

'I drew my scythe in sic a fury,
'I nearhand cowpit wi' my hurry,
'But yet the bauld *Apothecary*   105
          'Withstood the shock;
'I might as weel hae try'd a quarry
          'O' hard whin-rock.

'Ev'n them he canna get attended,
'Altho' their face he ne'er had kend it,   110
'Just sh— in a kail-blade and send it,
          'As soon's he smells 't,
'Baith their disease, and what will mend it,
          'At once he tells 't.

'And then a' doctor's saws and whittles,   115
'Of a' dimensions, shapes, an' mettles,
'A' kinds o' boxes, mugs, an' bottles,
          'He's sure to hae;
'Their Latin names as fast he rattles
          'As A B C.   120

'Calces o' fossils, earths, and trees;
'True Sal-marinum o' the seas;
'The Farina of beans and pease,
          'He has't in plenty;
'Aqua-fontis, what you please,   125
          'He can content ye.

'Forbye some new, uncommon weapons,
'Urinus Spiritus of capons;
'Or Mite-horn shavings, filings, scrapings,
   'Distill'd *per se*;   130
'Sal-alkali o' Midge-tail clippings,
   'And mony mae.'

'Waes me for *Johnny Ged's-Hole** now,'
Quoth I, 'if that thae news be true!
'His braw calf-ward whare gowans grew, 135
   'Sae white an' bonie,
'Nae doubt they'll rive it wi' the plew;
   'They'll ruin *Johnie*!'

The creature grain'd an eldritch laugh,
And says, 'Ye needna yoke the pleugh, 140
'Kirk-yards will soon be till'd eneugh,
   'Tak ye nae fear:
'They'll a' be trench'd wi' mony a sheugh,
   'In twa-three year.

'Whare I kill'd ane, a fair strae-death, 145
'By loss o' blood, or want o' breath,
'This night I'm free to tak my aith,
   'That *Hornbook*'s skill
'Has clad a score i' their last claith,
   'By drap and pill.   150

'An honest Wabster to his trade,
'Whase wife's twa nieves were scarce weel-bred,
'Gat tippence-worth to mend her head,
   'When it was sair;
'The wife slade cannie to her bed, 155
   'But ne'er spak mair.

'A countra Laird had ta'en the batts,
'Or some curmurring in his guts,
'His only son for *Hornbook* sets,
   'And pays him well, 160
'The lad, for twa guid gimmer-pets,
   'Was Laird himsel.

* The grave-digger.

'A bonie lass, ye kend her name,
'Some ill-brewn drink had hov'd her wame,
'She trusts hersel, to hide the shame,   165
       'In *Hornbook*'s care;
'*Horn* sent her aff to her lang hame,
       'To hide it there.

'That's just a swatch o' *Hornbook*'s way,
'Thus goes he on from day to day,   170
'Thus does he poison, kill, an' slay,
       'An's weel pay'd for 't;
'Yet stops me o' my lawfu' prey,
       'Wi' his d—mn'd dirt!

'But hark! I'll tell you of a plot,   175
'Tho' dinna ye be speakin o't;
'I'll nail the self-conceited Sot,
       'As dead's a herrin:
'Niest time we meet, I'll wad a groat,
       'He gets his fairin!'   180

But just as he began to tell,
The auld kirk-hammer strak the bell
Some wee, short hour ayont the *twal*,
       Which rais'd us baith:
I took the way that pleas'd mysel,   185
       And sae did *Death*.

56. [On Tam the Chapman]

As Tam the chapman on a day
  Wi' Death forgather'd by the way,
Weel pleased, he greets a wight sae famous,
And Death was nae less pleas'd wi' Thomas,
Wha cheerfully lays down his pack,   5
And there blaws up a hearty crack:
His social, friendly, honest heart
Sae tickled Death, they could na part;
Sae after viewing knives and garters,
Death taks him hame to gie him quarters.   10

On Tam the Chapman. *Text from the Aldine edition, 1839 (ii. 140)*

57. Epistle to J. L*****k, An Old Scotch Bard

April 1st, 1785.

WHILE briers an' woodbines budding green,
  An' Paitricks scraichan loud at e'en,
And morning Poossie whiddan seen,
      Inspire my Muse,
This freedom, in an *unknown* frien',
      I pray excuse.

On Fasteneen we had a rockin,
To ca' the crack and weave our stockin;
And there was muckle fun and jokin,
      Ye need na doubt;   10
At length we had a hearty yokin,
      At *sang about.*

There was ae *sang*, amang the rest,
Aboon them a' it pleas'd me best,
That some kind husband had addrest,   15
      To some sweet wife:
It thirl'd the heart-strings thro' the breast,
      A' to the life.

I've scarce heard ought describ'd sae weel,
What gen'rous, manly bosoms feel;   20
Thought I, 'Can this be *Pope*, or *Steele*,
      Or *Beattie*'s wark;'
They tald me 'twas an odd kind chiel
      About *Muirkirk.*

Epistle to J. L*****k. *Text from the edition of 1786, collated with the* First Common-place Book (*1CPB*) and *the editions of 1787, 1793, 1794. Title in 1CPB* A letter sent to John Lapraik near Muirkirk, a true, genuine, Scottish Bard.——April 1st 1785.
  17 thirl'd . . . thro'] touch'd the feelings o' *1CPB*   19 describ'd] I pleas'd *1CPB*   20 What . . . feel] The style sae tastie & genteel *1CPB*

It pat me fidgean-fain to hear 't,   25
An' sae about him there I spier 't;
Then a' that kent him round declar'd,
           He had *ingine*,
That nane excell'd it, few cam near 't,
           It was sae fine.   30

That set him to a pint of ale,
An' either douse or merry tale,
Or rhymes an' sangs he'd made himsel,
           Or witty catches,
'Tween Inverness and Tiviotdale,   35
           He had few matches.

Then up I gat, an' swoor an aith,
Tho' I should pawn my pleugh an' graith,
Or die a cadger pownie's death,
           At some dyke-back,   40
A *pint* an' *gill* I'd gie them *baith*,
           To hear your crack.

But first an' foremost, I should tell,
Amaist as soon as I could spell,
I to the *crambo-jingle* fell,   45
           Tho' rude an' rough,
Yet crooning to a body's sel,
           Does weel eneugh.

I am nae *Poet*, in a sense,
But just a *Rhymer* like by chance,   50
An' hae to Learning nae pretence,
           Yet, what the matter?
Whene'er my Muse does on me glance,
           I jingle at her.

25 It pat me fidgean-fain] My heart was fidgin' fain *1CPB*   26 there] a'
1CPB   28–30 He . . . fine.] *1CPB has*

                    He was a devil
           But had a frank & friendly heart
                    Discreet & civil.——

44 as soon as] since ever *1CPB*   45 I . . . fell] I've dealt in makin' rhymes
mysel *1CPB*   47 Yet] But *1CPB*   to . . . sel] at a pleugh or flail *1CPB*
48 Does] Do *1CPB*

Your Critic-folk may cock their nose,   55
And say, 'How can you e'er propose,
'You wha ken hardly *verse* frae *prose*,
             'To mak a *sang?*'
But by your leaves, my learned foes,
             Ye're maybe wrang.   60

What's a' your jargon o' your Schools,
Your Latin names for horns an' stools;
If honest Nature made you *fools*,
             What sairs your Grammars?
Ye'd better taen up *spades* and *shools*,   65
             Or *knappin-hammers*.

A set o' dull, conceited Hashes,
Confuse their brains in *Colledge-classes*!
They *gang in* Stirks, and *come out* Asses,
             Plain truth to speak;   70
An' syne they think to climb Parnassus
             By dint o' Greek!

Gie me ae spark o' Nature's fire,
That's a' the learning I desire;
Then tho' I drudge thro' dub an' mire   75
             At pleugh or cart,
My Muse, tho' hamely in attire,
             May touch the heart.

O for a spunk o' ALLAN's glee,
Or FERGUSON's, the bauld an' slee,   80
Or bright L*****K's, my friend to be,
             If I can hit it!
That would be *lear* eneugh for me,
             If I could get it.

57 frae] by *1CPB*   61 your Schools] the schools *1CPB*   67 dull, conceited Hashes] silly senseless asses *1CPB*   70 Plain truth] Thus sae *1CPB*
71 syne] then *1CPB*   80 FERGUSON's] Ferguson *1CPB*   81 bright
L*****K's] tight Lapraik *1CPB*

Now, Sir, if ye hae friends enow,   85
Tho' *real friends* I b'lieve are few,
Yet, if your catalogue be fow,
     I'se no insist;
But gif ye want ae friend that's true,
     I'm on your list.   90

I winna blaw about *mysel*,
As ill I like my fauts to tell;
But friends an' folk that wish me well,
     They sometimes roose me;
Tho' I maun own, as monie still,   95
     As far abuse me.

There's ae *wee faut* they whiles lay to me,
I like the lasses—Gude forgie me!
For monie a Plack they wheedle frae me,
     At dance or fair: 100
Maybe some *ither thing* they gie me
     They weel can spare.

But MAUCHLINE Race or MAUCHLINE Fair,
I should be proud to meet you there;
We'se gie ae night's discharge to *care*,   105
     If we forgather,
An' hae a swap o' *rhymin-ware*,
     Wi' ane anither.

The *four-gill chap*, we'se gar him clatter,
An' kirs'n him wi' reekin water;   110
Syne we'll sit down an' tak our whitter,
     To chear our heart;
An' faith, we'se be *acquainted* better
     Before we part.

88 I'se] I'll *1CPB*   89 gif] if *1CPB*   99 frae] fae *1CPB*   103 But]
At *1CPB*   105, 109 We'se] We'll *1CPB*   111 we'll] we'se *1CPB*

Awa ye selfish, warly race,   115
Wha think that havins, sense an' grace,
Ev'n love an' friendship should give place
        To *catch-the-plack*!
I dinna like to see your face,
        Nor hear your crack.   120

But ye whom social pleasure charms,
Whose hearts the *tide of kindness* warms,
Who hold your *being* on the terms,
        'Each aid the others,'
Come to my bowl, come to my arms,   125
        My friends, my brothers!

But to conclude my lang epistle,
As my auld pen's worn to the grissle;
Twa lines frae you wad gar me fissle,
        Who am, most fervent,   130
While I can either sing, or whissle,
        Your friend and servant.

58. To the Same

April 21*st*, 1785.

WHILE new-ca'd kye rowte at the stake,
    An' pownies reek in pleugh or braik,
This hour on e'enin's edge I take,
        To own I'm debtor,
To honest-hearted, auld L*****k,   5
        For his kind *letter*.

---

115 warly] warldly *1CPB*   122 the *tide of kindness*] true generous friendship
1CPB   123 *being*] beings *1CPB*   132 Sic subscribitur—*follows in 1CPB*

To the Same. *Text from the edition of 1786, collated with the* First Commonplace
Book (*1CPB*), *and the editions of 1787, 1793, 1794*
Head-note in 1CPB: On receiving an answer to the above I wrote the following /
April 21ˢᵗ 1785
  2 in] at *1CPB*

Forjesket sair, with weary legs,
Rattlin the corn out-owre the rigs,
Or dealing thro' amang the naigs
                    Their ten-hours bite,   10
My awkart Muse sair pleads and begs,
                    I would na write.

The tapetless, ramfeezl'd hizzie,
She's saft at best an' something lazy,
Quo' she, 'Ye ken we've been sae busy   15
                    'This month an' mair,
'That trouth, my head is grown right dizzie,
                    'An' something sair.'

Her dowf excuses pat me mad;
'Conscience,' says I, 'ye thowless jad!   20
'I'll write, an' that a hearty blaud,
                    'This vera night;
'So dinna ye affront your trade,
                    'But rhyme it right.

'Shall bauld L*****K, the *king o' hearts*,   25
'Tho' mankind were a *pack o' cartes*,
'Roose you sae weel for your deserts,
                    'In terms sae friendly,
'Yet ye'll neglect to shaw your parts
                    'An' thank him kindly?'   30

Sae I gat paper in a blink,
An' down gaed *stumpie* in the ink:
Quoth I, 'Before I sleep a wink,
                    'I vow I'll close it;
'An' if ye winna mak it clink,   35
                    'By Jove I'll prose it!'

---

11 awkart] dowie *1CPB*   15 we've] I've *1CPB*   25-30 *om. here in 1CPB;
given with omission marks after ll. 37-42*   25 king] Ace *1CPB*   32 An']
An, *86*   down gaed] in went *1CPB*   33 Quoth] Says *1CPB*

Sae I've begun to scrawl, but whether
In rhyme, or prose, or baith thegither,
Or some hotch-potch that's rightly neither,
      Let time mak proof;   40
But I shall scribble down some blether
      Just clean aff-loof.

My worthy friend, ne'er grudge an' carp,
Tho' Fortune use you hard an' sharp;
Come, kittle up your *moorlan harp*   45
      Wi' gleesome touch!
Ne'er mind how Fortune *waft* an' *warp*;
      She's but a b—tch.

She's gien me monie a jirt an' fleg,
Sin' I could striddle owre a rig;   50
But by the L—d, tho' I should beg
      Wi' lyart pow,
I'll laugh, an' sing, an' shake my leg,
      As lang's I dow!

Now comes the *sax an' twentieth* simmer,   55
I've seen the bud upo' the timmer,
Still persecuted by the limmer
      Frae year to year;
But yet, despite the kittle kimmer,
      I, Rob, am here.   60

Do ye envy the *city-gent*,
Behint a kist to lie an' sklent,
Or purse-proud, big wi' cent per cent,
      An' muckle wame,
In some bit *Brugh* to represent   65
      A *Baillie*'s name?

---

37 Sae . . . but] But what my theme 's to be, or *1CPB*   50 Sin' *1CPB*: Sin
86–94   55–60 Now . . . here.] *not in 1CPB*

Or is't the paughty, feudal *Thane*,
Wi' ruffl'd sark an' glancin cane,
Wha thinks himsel nae *sheep-shank bane*,
    But lordly stalks,   70
While caps an' bonnets aff are taen,
    As by he walks?

'O *Thou* wha gies us each guid gift!
'Gie me o' *wit* an' *sense* a lift,
'Then turn me, if *Thou* please, *adrift*,   75
    'Thro' Scotland wide;
'Wi' *cits* nor *lairds* I wadna shift,
    'In a' their pride!'

Were this the *charter* of our state,
'On pain o' *hell* be rich an' great,'   80
Damnation then would be our fate,
    Beyond remead;
But, thanks to *Heav'n*, that's no the gate
    We learn our *creed*.

For thus the royal *Mandate* ran,   85
When first the human race began,
'The social, friendly, honest man,
    'Whate'er he be,
' 'Tis *he* fulfils *great Nature's plan*,
    'And none but *he*.'   90

O *Mandate*, glorious and divine!
The followers o' the ragged Nine,
Poor, thoughtless devils! yet may shine
    In glorious light,
While sordid sons o' Mammon's line   95
    Are dark as night!

67 paughty] lordly *1CPB*   71 caps] *correcting* hats *in 1CPB*   73 O *Thou*
... guid] May He ... good *1CPB*   75 turn ... please,] tho' he turn me out
1CPB   77 nor] & *1CPB*   79 this] *correcting* it *in 1CPB*   86 When]
Since *1CPB*   93 thoughtless] honest *1CPB*

Tho' here they scrape, an' squeeze, an' growl,
Their worthless nievefu' of a *soul*,
May in some *future carcase* howl,
       The forest's fright;   100
Or in some day-detesting *owl*
       May shun the light.

Then may L*****ᴋ and B**** arise,
To reach their native, kindred skies,
And *sing* their pleasures, hopes an' joys,   105
       In some mild sphere,
Still closer knit in friendship's ties
       Each passing year!

59. To W. S*****n, Ochiltree

May—1785.

I Gat your letter, winsome Willie;
  Wi' gratefu' heart I thank you brawlie;
Tho' I maun say't, I wad be silly,
       An' unco vain,
Should I believe, my coaxin billie,   5
       Your flatterin strain.

But I'se believe ye kindly meant it,
I sud be laith to think ye hinted
Ironic satire, sidelins sklented,
       On my poor Musie;   10
Tho' in sic phraisin terms ye've penn'd it,
       I scarce excuse ye.

My senses wad be in a creel,
Should I but dare a *hope* to speel,
Wi' *Allan*, or wi' *Gilbertfield*,   15
       The braes o' fame;
Or *Ferguson*, the writer-chiel,
       A deathless name.

97 scrape, an' squeeze] grunt, & scrape *1CPB*   98 worthless] silly *1CPB*
101 some] a *1CPB*   103 Then . . . arise,] LAPRAIK, & BURNESS then may rise *1CPB*   104 To] And *1CPB*

To W. S*****n, Ochiltree. *Text from the edition of 1786, collated with those of 1787, 1793, 1794*

(O *Ferguson*! thy glorious *parts*,
Ill-suited *law*'s dry, musty arts!　　　　　20
My curse upon your whunstane hearts,
　　　　　Ye Enbrugh Gentry!
The tythe o' what ye waste at *cartes*
　　　　　Wad stow'd his pantry!)

Yet when a tale comes i' my head,　　　　　25
Or lasses gie my heart a screed,
As whiles they're like to be my dead,
　　　　　(O sad disease!)
I kittle up my *rustic reed*;
　　　　　It gies me ease.　　　　　30

Auld COILA, now, may fidge fu' fain,
She's gotten *Bardies* o' her ain,
Chiels wha their chanters winna hain,
　　　　　But tune their lays,
Till echoes a' resound again　　　　　35
　　　　　Her weel-sung praise.

Nae *Poet* thought her worth his while,
To set her name in measur'd style;
She lay like some unkend-of isle
　　　　　Beside *New Holland*,　　　　　40
Or whare wild-meeting oceans *boil*
　　　　　Besouth *Magellan*.

Ramsay an' famous *Ferguson*
Gied *Forth* an' *Tay* a lift aboon;
Yarrow an' *Tweed*, to monie a tune,　　　　　45
　　　　　Owre Scotland rings,
While *Irwin*, *Lugar*, *Aire* an' *Doon*,
　　　　　Naebody sings.

Th' *Illissus*, *Tiber*, *Thames* an' *Seine*,
Glide sweet in monie a tunefu' line;　　　　　50
But *Willie* set your fit to mine,
　　　　　An' cock your crest,
We'll gar our streams an' burnies shine
　　　　　Up wi' the best.

We'll sing auld COILA's plains an' fells,   55
Her moors red-brown wi' heather bells,
Her banks an' braes, her dens an' dells,
   Where glorious WALLACE
Aft bure the gree, as story tells,
   Frae Suthron billies.   60

At WALLACE' name, what Scottish blood,
But boils up in a spring-tide flood!
Oft have our fearless fathers strode
   By WALLACE' side,
Still pressing onward, red-wat-shod,   65
   Or glorious dy'd!

O sweet are COILA's haughs an' woods,
When lintwhites chant amang the buds,
And jinkin hares, in amorous whids,
   Their loves enjoy,   70
While thro' the braes the cushat croods
   With wailfu' cry!

Ev'n winter bleak has charms to me,
When winds rave thro' the naked tree;
Or frosts on hills of *Ochiltree*   75
   Are hoary gray;
Or blinding drifts wild-furious flee,
   Dark'ning the day!

O NATURE! a' thy shews an' forms
To feeling, pensive hearts hae charms!   80
Whether the Summer kindly warms,
   Wi' life an' light,
Or Winter howls, in gusty storms,
   The lang, dark night!

The *Muse*, nae *Poet* ever fand her,   85
Till by himsel he learn'd to wander,
Adown some trottin burn's meander,
   An' no think lang;
O sweet, to stray an' pensive ponder
   A heart-felt sang!   90

The warly race may drudge an' drive,
Hog-shouther, jundie, stretch an' strive,
Let me fair NATURE's face descrive,
    And I, wi' pleasure,
Shall let the busy, grumbling hive   95
    Bum owre their treasure.

Fareweel, 'my rhyme-composing brither!'
We've been owre lang unkenn'd to ither:
Now let us lay our heads thegither,
    In love fraternal: 100
May *Envy* wallop in a tether,
    Black fiend, infernal!

While Highlandmen hate tolls an' taxes;
While moorlan herds like guid, fat braxies;
While Terra firma, on her axis,   105
    Diurnal turns,
Count on a friend, in faith an' practice,
    In ROBERT BURNS.

Postscript

My memory's no worth a preen;
I had amaist forgotten clean,   110
Ye bad me write you what they mean
    By this *new-light*,*
'Bout which our *herds* sae aft hae been
    Maist like to fight.

In days when mankind were but callans,   115
At *Grammar*, *Logic*, an' sic talents,
They took nae pains their speech to balance,
    Or rules to gie,
But spak their thoughts in plain, braid lallans,
    Like you or me.   120

---

    * A cant-term for those religious opinions, which Dr. TAYLOR of Norwich has
defended so strenuously.

---

97 'my rhyme-composing brither!' *93–94*: 'my rhyme-composing' brither! *86 87*

In thae auld times, they thought the *Moon*,
Just like a sark, or pair o' shoon,
Woor by degrees, till her last roon
      Gaed past their viewin,
An' shortly after she was done   125
      They gat a new ane.

This past for certain, undisputed;
It ne'er cam i' their heads to doubt it,
Till chiels gat up an' wad confute it,
      An' ca'd it wrang;   130
An' muckle din there was about it,
      Baith loud an' lang.

Some *herds*, weel learn'd upo' the beuk,
Wad threap auld folk the thing misteuk;
For 'twas the *auld moon* turn'd a newk   135
      An' out o' sight,
An' backlins-comin, to the leuk,
      She grew mair bright.

This was deny'd, it was affirm'd;
The *herds* an' *hissels* were alarm'd;   140
The rev'rend gray-beards rav'd an' storm'd,
      That beardless laddies
Should think they better were inform'd,
      Than their auld dadies.

Frae less to mair it gaed to sticks;   145
Frae words an' aiths to clours an' nicks;
An' monie a fallow gat his licks,
      Wi' hearty crunt;
An' some, to learn them for their tricks,
      Were hang'd an' brunt.   150

This game was play'd in monie lands,
An' *auld-light* caddies bure sic hands,
That faith, the *youngsters* took the sands
      Wi' nimble shanks,
Till *Lairds* forbad, by strict commands,   155
      Sic bluidy pranks.

But *new-light herds* gat sic a cowe,
Folk thought them ruin'd stick-an-stowe,
Till now amaist on ev'ry *knowe*
      Ye'll find ane plac'd;   160
An' some, their *New-light* fair avow,
      Just quite barefac'd.

Nae doubt the *auld-light flocks* are bleatan;
Their zealous *herds* are vex'd an' sweatan;
Mysel, I've ev'n seen them greetan   165
      Wi' girnan spite,
To hear the *Moon* sae sadly lie'd on
      By word an' write.

But shortly they will cowe the louns!
Some *auld-light herds* in neebor towns   170
Are mind't, in things they ca' *balloons*,
      To tak a flight,
An' stay ae month amang the *Moons*
      An' see them right.

Guid observation they will gie them;   175
An' when the *auld Moon*'s gaun to lea'e them,
The hindmost *shaird*, they'll fetch it wi' them,
      Just i' their pouch,
An' when the *new-light* billies see them,
      I think they'll crouch!   180

Sae, ye observe that a' this clatter
Is naething but a 'moonshine matter;'
But tho' dull *prose-folk* Latin splatter
      In logic tulzie,
I hope we, *Bardies*, ken some better   185
      Than mind sic brulzie.

183 Latin *87–94*: latin *86*

60. A Poet's Welcome to his love-begotten Daughter; the first instance that entitled him to the venerable appellation of Father—

Thou's welcome, Wean! Mischanter fa' me,
 If thoughts o' thee, or yet thy Mamie,
Shall ever daunton me or awe me,
  My bonie lady;
Or if I blush when thou shalt ca' me   5
  Tyta, or Daddie.—

Tho' now they ca' me, Fornicator,
And tease my name in kintra clatter,
The mair they talk, I'm kend the better;
  E'en let them clash!   10
An auld wife's tongue's a feckless matter
  To gie ane fash.—

Welcome! My bonie, sweet, wee Dochter!
Tho' ye come here a wee unsought for;
And tho' your comin I hae fought for,   15
  Baith Kirk and Queir;
Yet by my faith, ye're no unwrought for,
  That I shall swear!

Wee image o' my bonie Betty,
As fatherly I kiss and daut thee,   20
As dear and near my heart I set thee,
  Wi' as gude will,
As a' the Priests had seen me get thee
  That's out o' h———.—

A Poet's Welcome. *Text from the Glenriddell MS (Glen; pp. 87–88), collated with the Alloway (Al) and Rosenbach (R) MSS, and Stewart, 1801 (pp. 51–52). Title in Al* A Welcome to a bastart wean*: in R* The Poet's Welcome to His Bastart Wean*: in Stewart* Address to an Illegitimate Child. *Sequence in Al, ll. 1–18, 25–36, 19–24, 37–48: in R, 1–12, 25–36, 13–24, 37–48. Stewart has six stanzas only: ll. 1–6, 19–24, 7–12, 25–30, 43–48 and 37–42. Glen omits ll. 37–42, perhaps accidentally: text from Al*
 1 Mischanter] mishanter *Al R Stewart* 2 thoughts . . . yet] ought . . . of *Stewart* 4 bonie] sweet, wee *Al R Stewart* 7 Tho' now] What tho' *Stewart* ca' *Al R Stewart*: name *Glen* 15 fought] bought *Al* 16 Baith . . . Queir;] An' that right dear, *Al* 17 ye're] 'twas *Al* 20 As . . . I] I . . . will *Stewart* 21 dear and near] near an' dear *Al*

Sweet fruit o' monie a merry dint,
My funny toil is no a' tint;
Tho' ye come to the warld asklent,
                    Which fools may scoff at,
In my last plack your part's be in't,
                    The better half o't.——   30

Tho' I should be the waur bestead,
Thou's be as braw and bienly clad,
And thy young years as nicely bred
                    Wi' education,
As ony brat o' Wedlock's bed,   35
                    In a' thy station.——

[Lord grant that thou may ay inherit
Thy Mither's looks an' gracefu' merit;
An' thy poor, worthless Daddie's spirit,
                    Without his failins!   40
'Twad please me mair to see thee heir it
                    Than stocked mailins!]

For if thou be, what I wad hae thee,
And tak the counsel I shall gie thee,
I'll never rue my trouble wi' thee,   45
                    The cost nor shame o't,
But be a loving Father to thee,
                    And brag the name o't.——

26 no] now *Stewart*   27 Tho' ye come] Tho' thou come *R:* Sin' thou came
Stewart   29 your] thy *R Stewart*   32 braw and bienly] elegantly *Al R*
35 brat] Gett *Al R*   37 Lord] Gude *Stewart*   38 looks an' gracefu']
person, grace an' *Stewart*   41 'Twad . . . see thee heir it] 'Twill . . . hear an'
see 't *Stewart*   43 For] An' *Stewart*   45–48 I'll . . . o't.] *Stewart has*
                    A lovin' father I'll be to thee,
                         If thou be spar'd;
                    Thro' a' thy childish years I'll e'e thee,
                         An' think 't weel war'd.
46 nor] an' *Al:* or *R*

61. The Fornicator. A New Song—

Tune, Clout the Caldron

Y E jovial boys who love the joys,
　　The blissful joys of Lovers;
Yet dare avow with dauntless brow,
　　When th' bony lass discovers;
I pray draw near and lend an ear,　　　　　　5
　　And welcome in a Frater,
For I've lately been on quarantine,
　　A proven Fornicator.

Before the Congregation wide
　　I pass'd the muster fairly,　　　　　　10
My handsome Betsey by my side,
　　We gat our ditty rarely;
But my downcast eye by chance did spy
　　What made my lips to water,
Those limbs so clean where I, between,　　　　15
　　Commenc'd a Fornicator.

With rueful face and signs of grace
　　I pay'd the buttock-hire,
The night was dark and thro' the park
　　I could not but convoy her;　　　　　　20
A parting kiss, what could I less,
　　My vows began to scatter,
My Betsey fell—lal de dal lal lal,
　　I am a Fornicator.

The Fornicator. *Text from Dewar's transcript of Burns's holograph (MS not traced),
collated with MMC (pp. 3–4). MMC has lines 1–32 only*
　2 blissful] blessfu *MMC*　　　3 Yet dare avow] An' dare avow't *MMC*
4 When th' bony] Whate'er the *MMC*　　5 lend an ear] you shall hear *MMC*
7 For] om. *MMC*　　13 But] om. *MMC* 15–16 *Scott Douglas adds a variant in
his copy of MMC:*
　　　　　　Those hills of snow which wyled me so
　　　　　　　　To be a Fornicator.

16 Commenc'd a] Commenced *MMC*　　20 could not] cou'dna *MMC*　　23 lal
... lal,] fal lal de ral! *MMC*

But for her sake this vow I make,   25
   And solemnly I swear it,
That while I own a single crown,
   She's welcome for to share it;
And my roguish boy his Mother's joy,
   And the darling of his Pater,   30
For him I boast my pains and cost,
   Although a Fornicator.

Ye wenching blades whose hireling jades
   Have tipt you off blue-boram,
I tell ye plain, I do disdain   35
   To rank you in the Quorum;
But a bony lass upon the grass
   To teach her esse Mater,
And no reward but for regard,
   O that's a Fornicator.   40

Your warlike Kings and Heros bold,
   Great Captains and Commanders;
Your mighty Cèsars fam'd of old,
   And Conquering Alexanders;
In fields they fought and laurels bought   45
   And bulwarks strong did batter,
But still they grac'd our noble list
   And ranked Fornicator!!!

25-26 But . . . it] *MMC has*

       But, by the sun an' moon I swear,
       An' I'll fulfil ilk hair o't

28 for . . . it] to a share o't *MMC*   29 And] *om. MMC*   roguish . . . joy] *Scott Douglas adds a variant* sweet wee girl, her mother's pearl *in his copy of MMC, with* her *in ll. 30-31*   30 the] *om. MMC*   31-32 For . . . Fornicator.] *MMC has*

       I for his sake the name will take,
       A harden'd Fornicator.

62. The Vision. Duan First*

TH E sun had clos'd the *winter-day*,
  The Curlers quat their roaring play,
And hunger'd Maukin taen her way
      To kail-yards green,
While faithless snaws ilk step betray   5
      Whare she has been.

The Thresher's weary *flingin-tree*,
The lee-lang day had tir'd me;
And when the Day had clos'd his e'e,
      Far i' the West,   10
Ben i' the *Spence*, right pensivelie,
      I gaed to rest.

There, lanely, by the ingle-cheek,
I sat and ey'd the spewing reek,
That fill'd, wi' hoast-provoking smeek,   15
      The auld, clay biggin;
And heard the restless rattons squeak
      About the riggin.

All in this mottie, misty clime,
I backward mus'd on wasted time,   20
How I had spent my *youthfu' prime*,
      An' done nae-thing,
But stringing blethers up in rhyme
      For fools to sing.

Had I to guid advice but harket,   25
I might, by this, hae led a market,
Or strutted in a Bank and clarket
      My *Cash-Account*;
While here, half-mad, half-fed, half-sarket,
      Is a' th' amount.   30

---

* Duan, a term of Ossian's for the different divisions of a digressive Poem. See
his Cath-Loda, Vol. 2. of M'Pherson's Translation.

The Vision. *Text from the edition of 1786, collated with the Stair MS (S) and the
editions of 1787, 1793, 1794. See Commentary*
5 ilk] each *S*   9 Day had] Day-light *S*   11 Ben] But *S*

I started, mutt'ring blockhead! coof!
And heav'd on high my wauket loof,
To swear by a' yon starry roof,
      Or some rash aith,
That I, henceforth, would be *rhyme-proof*   35
      Till my last breath—

When click! the *string* the *snick* did draw;
And jee! the door gaed to the wa';
And by my ingle-lowe I saw,
      Now bleezan bright,   40
A tight, outlandish *Hizzie*, braw,
      Come full in sight.

Ye need na doubt, I held my whisht;
The infant aith, half-form'd, was crusht;
I glowr'd as eerie's I'd been dusht,   45
      In some wild glen;
When sweet, like *modest Worth*, she blusht,
      And stepped ben.

Green, slender, leaf-clad *Holly-boughs*
Were twisted, gracefu', round her brows,   50
I took her for some Scottish Muse,
      By that same token;
And come to stop those reckless vows,
      Would soon been broken.

A 'hare-brain'd, sentimental trace'   55
Was strongly marked in her face;
A wildly-witty, rustic grace
      Shone full upon her;
Her *eye*, ev'n turn'd on empty space,
      Beam'd keen with *Honor*.   60

Down flow'd her robe, a *tartan* sheen,
Till half a leg was scrimply seen;

36 Till] To *S*   43 Ye need na doubt, I] I trow I instant *S*

And such a *leg*! my bonie JEAN
   Could only peer it;
Sae straught, sae taper, tight and clean,   65
   Nane else came near it.

Her *Mantle* large, of greenish hue,
My gazing wonder chiefly drew;
Deep *lights* and *shades*, bold-mingling, threw
   A lustre grand;   70
And seem'd, to my astonish'd view,
   A *well-known* Land.

Here, rivers in the sea were lost;
There, mountains to the skies were tost:
Here, tumbling billows mark'd the coast,   75
   With surging foam;
There, distant shone, *Art*'s lofty boast,
   The lordly dome.

Here, DOON pour'd down his far-fetch'd floods;
There, well-fed IRWINE stately thuds: 80
Auld, hermit AIRE staw thro' his woods,
   On to the shore;
And many a lesser torrent scuds,
   With seeming roar.

Low, in a sandy valley spread,   85
An ancient BOROUGH rear'd her head;
Still, as in *Scottish Story* read,
   She boasts a *Race*,
To ev'ry nobler virtue bred,
   And polish'd grace.   90

By stately tow'r, or palace fair,
Or ruins pendent in the air,
Bold stems of Heroes, here and there,
   I could discern;
Some seem'd to muse, some seem'd to dare,   95
   With feature stern.

63 my bonie JEAN 87–94: my BESS, I ween, S 86 86 *marginal note* Ayr
in S 91–132 *added in 87. In 86 Duan First ends with line 90* 91 palace]
Mansion S

My heart did glowing transport feel,
To see a Race* heroic wheel,
And brandish round the deep-dy'd steel
          In sturdy blows;   100
While back-recoiling seem'd to reel
          Their Suthron foes.

His COUNTRY's SAVIOUR†, mark him well!
Bold RICHARDTON's‡ heroic swell;
The Chief on *Sark*§ who glorious fell,   105
          In high command;
And *He* whom ruthless Fates expel
          His native land.

* The Wallaces.   † William Wallace.
‡ Adam Wallace of Richardton, cousin to the immortal Preserver of Scottish
Independence.
§ Wallace Laird of Craigie, who was second in command, under Douglas Earl of
Ormond, at the famous battle on the banks of Sark, fought *anno* 1448. That
glorious victory was principally owing to the judicious conduct and intrepid valour
of the gallant Laird of Craigie, who died of his wounds after the action.

----

98 *marginal note* Wallaces *in S*   103 *marginal note* The Great Wallace *in S*
104 *foot-note* immortal . . . Independence] great Wallace, the Deliverer of Scotland *S*
105 *foot-note in S* The famous Wallace Laird of Craigie to whose valour and conduct the glorious victory that the Scots won under George Douglas, Earl of Ormond,
was owing.—Note. Wallace died of his wounds.—   107 *He*] him *S, with
marginal note* Sir Thomas   108 *additional stanzas follow in S:*

With secret throes I mark'd that earth,
That cottage witness of my birth;
And near I saw, bold issuing forth,
          In youthful pride,
A *Lindsay* race of noble worth,   5
          Fam'd far and wide.

Where, hid behind a spreading wood,
An ancient, Pict-built Mansion stood,   Sundrum
I spy'd, among an angel brood,
          A female pair;   10
Sweet shone their high maternal blood,
          And father's air.

An ancient *tow'r* to mem'ry brought,
How Dettingen's bold heroe fought;   Stair
Still far from sinking into nought,   15
          It owns a lord,
Who far in Western climates fought,
          With trusty sword.

There, where a sceptr'd *Pictish** shade
Stalk'd round his ashes lowly laid,   110
I mark'd a martial Race, pourtray'd
    In colours strong;
Bold, soldier-featur'd, undismay'd
    They strode along.

†Thro' many a wild, romantic grove,   115
Near many a hermit-fancy'd cove,
(Fit haunts for Friendship or for Love,
    In musing mood)
An *aged Judge*, I saw him rove,
    Dispensing good.   120

* Coilus King of the Picts, from whom the district of Kyle is said to take its name, lies buried, as tradition says, near the family-seat of the Montgomeries of Coilsfield, where his burial place is still shown.
† Barskimming, the seat of the Lord Justice Clerk.

109 *marginal note* Coilsfield *in S*   111 mark'd] saw *S*   113 soldier-featur'd] sodger-featur'd *S*   114 strode] stalk'd *S*   114 *additional stanza and note in S:*

    Among the rest I well could spy
    One gallant, graceful, martial boy;
    The sodger sparkl'd in his eye,
        A diamond water;
    I blest that noble *Badge* with joy,
        That own'd me frater.

One gallant { Captⁿ Jaˢ Montgomery, Master of St. James's Lodge, Tarbolton, to which the Author has the honor to belong.

117 or] and *S*   119 *marginal note* Justice Clerk *in S*   120 *additional stanzas follow in S. Text of ll. 1–8 from S, remainder from H-H. (see Commentary):*

[Nearby] arose a Mansion fine,   Auchinleck
The seat of many a Muse divine;
Not rustic Muses such as mine,
    With holley crown'd,
But th' ancient, tuneful, laurell'd Nine,   5
    From classic ground.

I mourn'd the card that Fortune dealt,
To see where bonie Whitefords dwelt;   Ballochmyle
But other prospects made me melt;
    That village near;   Mauchline
There Nature, Friendship, Love, I felt,   11
    Fond-mingling dear!

Hail! Nature's pang, more strong than death!
Warm Friendship's glow, like kindling wrath!
Love, dearer than the parting breath   15
    Of dying friend!
Not ev'n with life's wild devious path,
    Your force shall end!

*With deep-struck, reverential awe,
The learned *Sire* and *Son* I saw,
To Nature's God and Nature's law
    They gave their lore,
This, all its source and end to draw,   125
    That, to adore.

BRYDON's brave Ward† I well could spy,
Beneath old SCOTIA's smiling eye;
Who call'd on Fame, low standing by,
    To hand him on,   130
Where many a Patriot-name on high
    And Hero shone.

* Catrine, the seat of the late Doctor, and present Professor Stewart.
† Colonel Fullarton.

The Pow'r that gave the soft alarms
In blooming Whiteford's rosy charms,   20
Still threats the tiny, feather'd arms,
    The barbed dart,
While lovely Wilhelminia warms   Miss Wilhelminia
    The coldest heart.   Alexander

126 *additional stanzas follow in* S *to* complete *Duan First.* Text *from* H-H.:

Where Lugar leaves his moorland plaid,   Cumnock
Where lately Want was idly laid,
I marked busy, bustling Trade,
    In fervid flame,
Beneath a Patroness's aid,   5
    Of noble name.

Wild, countless hills I could survey,
And countless flocks as wild as they;
But other scenes did charms display,
    That better please,   10
Where polish'd manners dwell with Gray,   Mr. Farquhar
    In rural ease.   Gray

Where Cessnock pours with gurgling sound;   Auchinskieth
And Irwine, marking out the bound,
Enamour'd of the scenes around,   15
    Slow runs his race,
A name I doubly honor'd found,   Caprington
    With knightly grace.

Brydone's brave ward, I saw him stand,   Colonel Fullarton
Fame humbly offering her hand,   20

Duan Second

With musing-deep, astonish'd stare,
I view'd the heavenly-seeming *Fair*;
A whisp'ring *throb* did witness bear   135
    Of kindred sweet,
When with an elder Sister's air
    She did me greet.

'All hail! *my own* inspired Bard!
'In me thy native Muse regard!   140
'Nor longer mourn thy fate is hard,
    'Thus poorly low!
'I come to give thee such *reward*,
    'As *we* bestow.

'Know, the great *Genius* of this Land,   145
'Has many a light, aerial band,
'Who, all beneath his high command,
    'Harmoniously,
'As *Arts* or *Arms* they understand,
    'Their labors ply.   150

And near, his kinsman's rustic band,   Dr. Fullarton
    With one accord,
Lamenting their late blessed land
    Must change its lord.

The owner of a pleasant spot,   25
Near sandy wilds, I last did note;   Orangefield
A heart too warm, a pulse too hot
    At times, o'erran;
But large in ev'ry feature wrote,
    Appear'd the Man.   30

133–8 *S has*

Duan the Second.

All these in colours, strong imprest,
I marked chief among the rest,
While favor'd by my honor'd guest,
    In converse sweet;
Who, as I said, in blushes drest,
    Thus did me greet.
'All hail &c.

The rest of this Duan is exactly the same as the printed copies; only the following stanza was forgot in the hurry of writing out for the press.
Lines 161–8 follow

'They Scotia's Race among them share;
'Some fire the *Sodger* on to dare;
'Some rouse the *Patriot* up to bare
      'Corruption's heart:
'Some teach the *Bard*, a darling care,   155
      'The tuneful Art.

' 'Mong swelling floods of reeking gore,
'They ardent, kindling spirits pour;
'Or, mid the venal Senate's roar,
      'They, sightless, stand,   160
'To mend the honest *Patriot-lore*,
      'And grace the hand.

'And when the Bard, or hoary Sage,
'Charm or instruct the future age,
'They bind the wild, Poetic rage   165
      'In energy,
'Or point the inconclusive page
      'Full on the eye.

'Hence, Fullarton, the brave and young;
'Hence, Dempster's truth-prevailing tongue;   170
'Hence, sweet harmonious Beattie sung
      'His "Minstrel lays;"
'Or tore, with noble ardour stung,
      'The *Sceptic*'s bays.

'To lower Orders are assign'd,   175
'The humbler ranks of Human-kind,
'The rustic Bard, the lab'ring Hind,
      'The Artisan;
'All chuse, as, various they're inclin'd,
      'The various man.   180

161 To] And *S*   163–8 *om. 86. Text from 87*   164 Charm or instruct]
Instruct, or charm *S*   165–8 *S has*
      'They point the inconclusive page
            'Full on the eye,
      'Or bind the wild, poetic rage
            'In energy.

'When yellow waves the heavy grain,
'The threat'ning *Storm*, some, strongly, rein;
'Some teach to meliorate the plain,
            'With *tillage-skill*;
'And some instruct the Shepherd-train,   185
            'Blythe o'er the hill.

'Some hint the Lover's harmless wile;
'Some grace the Maiden's artless smile;
'Some soothe the Lab'rer's weary toil,
            'For humble gains,   190
'And make his *cottage-scenes* beguile
            'His cares and pains.

'Some, bounded to a district-space,
'Explore at large Man's *infant race*,
'To mark the embryotic trace,   195
            'Of *rustic Bard*;
'And careful note each op'ning grace,
            'A guide and guard.

'*Of these am I*—Coila my name;
'And this district as mine I claim,   200
'Where once the *Campbells*, chiefs of fame,
            'Held ruling pow'r:
'I mark'd thy embryo-tuneful flame,
            'Thy natal hour.

'With future hope, I oft would gaze,   205
'Fond, on thy little, early ways,
'Thy rudely-caroll'd, chiming phrase,
            'In uncouth rhymes,
'Fir'd at the simple, artless lays
            'Of other times.   210

'I saw thee seek the sounding shore,
'Delighted with the dashing roar;
'Or when the *North* his fleecy store
            'Drove thro' the sky,
'I saw grim Nature's visage hoar,   215
            'Struck thy young eye.

201 *Campbells* 87–94: *Campbell's* 86

'Or when the deep-green-mantl'd Earth,
'Warm-cherish'd ev'ry floweret's birth,
'And joy and music pouring forth,
          'In ev'ry grove,   220
'I saw thee eye the gen'ral mirth
          'With boundless love.

'When ripen'd fields, and azure skies,
'Call'd forth the *Reaper*'s rustling noise,
'I saw thee leave their ev'ning joys,   225
          'And lonely stalk,
'To vent thy bosom's swelling rise,
          'In pensive walk.

'When *youthful Love*, warm-blushing, strong,
'Keen-shivering shot thy nerves along,   230
'Those accents, grateful to thy tongue,
          'Th' adored *Name*,
'I taught thee how to pour in song,
          'To soothe thy flame.

'I saw thy pulse's maddening play,   235
'Wild-send thee Pleasure's devious way,
'Misled by Fancy's *meteor-ray*,
          'By Passion driven;
'But yet the *light* that led astray,
          'Was *light* from Heaven.   240

'I taught thy manners-painting strains,
'The *loves*, the *ways* of simple swains,
'Till now, o'er all my wide domains,
          'Thy fame extends;
'And some, the pride of *Coila*'s plains,   245
          'Become thy friends.

'Thou canst not learn, nor I can show,
'To paint with *Thomson*'s landscape-glow;
'Or wake the bosom-melting throe,
          'With *Shenstone*'s art;   250
'Or pour, with *Gray*, the moving flow,
          'Warm on the heart.

'Yet all beneath th' unrivall'd Rose,
'The lowly Daisy sweetly blows;
'Tho' large the forest's Monarch throws   255
          'His army shade,
'Yet green the juicy Hawthorn grows,
          'Adown the glade.

'Then never murmur nor repine;
'Strive in thy *humble sphere* to shine;   260
'And trust me, not *Potosi's mine*,
          'Nor *King's regard*,
'Can give a bliss o'ermatching thine,
          'A *rustic Bard*.

'To give my counsels all in one,   265
'Thy *tuneful flame* still careful fan;
'Preserve *the dignity of Man*,
          'With Soul erect;
'And trust, the UNIVERSAL PLAN
          'Will all protect.   270

'*And wear thou this*'—She solemn said,
And bound the *Holly* round my head:
The polish'd leaves, and berries red,
          Did rustling play;
And, like a passing thought, she fled,   275
          In light away.

262 *King's 87–94: Kings 86*

63. Epistle to John Goldie in Kilmarnock, Author of,
The Gospel recovered—

August — 1785

O GOWDIE, terror o' the whigs,
Dread o' black coats and reverend wigs!
Sour Bigotry on his last legs
      Girns and looks back,
Wishing the ten Egyptian plagues   5
      May sieze you quick.—

Poor gapin, glowrin Superstition!
Waes me, she's in a sad condition:
Fye! bring Black Jock* her state-physician,
      To see her water: 10
Alas! there's ground for great suspicion,
      She'll ne'er get better.—

Enthusiasm's past redemption,
Gane in a gallopin consumption:
Not a' her quacks wi' a' their gumption   15
      Can ever mend her;
Her feeble pulse gies strong presumption,
      She'll soon surrender.—

Auld Orthodoxy lang did grapple
For every hole to get a stapple;   20
But now, she fetches at the thrapple
      And fights for breath;
Haste, gie her name up in the Chapel†
      Near unto death.—

* The Revᵈ J. R–ss–ll — Kilmᶜᵏ   † Chapel — Mʳ Russel's kirk—

Epistle to John Goldie. *Text from the Glenriddell MS (pp. 2–4), collated with Stewart, 1802 (p. 234), and Cromek (p. 364). Title in Stewart* Letter to John Goudie, Kilmarnock, on the Publication of his Essays. *Stewart has ll. 1–12, 19–24, 13–18, and 25–30 only; Cromek ll. 43–54 only*
  3 his] her *Stewart*   4 Girns and] Girnin' *Stewart*   6 May] Wad *Stewart*
9, 23 *notes om. Stewart*   11 for] o' *Stewart*   great] *correcting* strong *in MS*
15 her] the *Stewart*   16 Can] Will *Stewart*   18 She'll soon surrender]
Death soon will end her *Stewart*   20 For . . . stapple;] But now she's got an
unco ripple, *Stewart*   21–22, 23–24 *transposed in Stewart*   21 But now,]
See how *Stewart*   22 fights] gasps *Stewart*   24 Near] Nigh *Stewart*

It's you and Taylor* are the chief   25
To blame for a' this black mischief;
But could the L—d's ain folk get leave,
    A toom tar-barrel
And twa red peats wad bring relief
    And end the quarrel.—   30

For me, my skill's but very sma',
And skill in Prose I've nane ava;
But quietlenswise, between us twa,
    Weel may ye speed;
And tho' they sud you sair misca',   35
    Ne'er fash your head.—

E'en swinge the dogs; and thresh them sicker!
The mair they squeel ay chap the thicker;
And still 'mang hands a hearty bicker
    O' something stout;   40
It gars an Owther's pulse beat quicker,
    And helps his wit.—

There's naething like the honest nappy;
Whare'll ye e'er see men sae happy,
Or women sonsie, saft and sappy,   45
    'Tween morn and morn,
As them wha like to taste the drappie
    In glass or horn.—

I've seen me daez't upon a time,
I scarce could wink or see a styme;   50
Just ae hauf-mutchkin does me prime,
    (Ought less, is little)
Then back I rattle on the rhyme,
    As gleg's a whittle.—
      I am &c.

* Taylor — Dᴿ Taylor of Norwich—

25 It 's] 'Tis *Stewart*   26 To . . . black] Wha are to blame for this *Stewart*
27 could . . . folk get] gin . . . focks gat *Stewart*   29 bring] send *Stewart*

64. Man was Made to Mourn, A Dirge

Peggy Bawn

I

W_{HEN} chill November's surly blast
    Made fields and forests bare,
One ev'ning, as I wand'red forth,
    Along the banks of A<small>IRE</small>,
I spy'd a man, whose aged step   5
    Seem'd weary, worn with care;
His face was furrow'd o'er with years,
    And hoary was his hair.

II

Young stranger, whither wand'rest thou?
    Began the rev'rend Sage;   10
Does thirst of wealth thy step constrain,
    Or youthful Pleasure's rage?
Or haply, prest with cares and woes,
    Too soon thou hast began,
To wander forth, with me, to mourn   15
    The miseries of Man.

Man was made to Mourn. *Text from the edition of 1786, collated with the* First
Commonplace Book (*1CPB; dated August 1785*), the *Kilmarnock MS* (*Kil*), *and the
editions of 1787, 1793, 1794. Title in Kil* A Ballad; *in 1CPB* A Song—Tune Peggy
Bawn
   13 with] by *1CPB*

III

The Sun that overhangs yon moors,
  Out-spreading far and wide,
Where hundreds labour to support
  A haughty lordling's pride;   20
I've seen yon weary winter-sun
  Twice forty times return;
And ev'ry time has added proofs,
  That Man was made to mourn.

IV

O Man! while in thy early years,   25
  How prodigal of time!
Mispending all thy precious hours,
  Thy glorious, youthful prime!
Alternate Follies take the sway;
  Licentious Passions burn;   30
Which tenfold force gives Nature's law,
  That Man was made to mourn.

V

Look not alone on youthful Prime,
  Or Manhood's active might;
Man then is useful to his kind,   35
  Supported is his right:
But see him on the edge of life,
  With Cares and Sorrows worn,
Then Age and Want, Oh! ill-match'd pair!
  Show Man was made to mourn.   40

VI

A few seem favourites of Fate,
  In Pleasure's lap carest;
Yet, think not all the Rich and Great,
  Are likewise truly blest.

17 The ... moors] Yon sun that hangs o'er Carrick Moors *1CPB Kil*   18 Out-spreading] That spread so *1CPB Kil*   20 A haughty lordling's] The lordly Cassilis *1CPB Kil*   27 thy] those *1CPB*   31 gives] give *1CPB* 33–40 Look . . . mourn.] *om. here in 1CPB and given later*   37 on . . . life] 'on the edge of days' *1CPB*   38 Sorrows] labors *1CPB Kil*   42 Pleasure's] Fortune's *1CPB Kil*

But Oh! what crouds in ev'ry land,   45
  All wretched and forlorn,
Thro' weary life this lesson learn,
  That Man was made to mourn!

VII

Many and sharp the num'rous Ills
  Inwoven with our frame!   50
More pointed still we make ourselves,
  Regret, Remorse and Shame!
And Man, whose heav'n-erected face,
  The smiles of love adorn,
Man's inhumanity to Man   55
  Makes countless thousands mourn!

VIII

See, yonder poor, o'erlabour'd wight,
  So abject, mean and vile,
Who begs a brother of the earth
  To give him leave to toil;   60
And see his lordly *fellow-worm*,
  The poor petition spurn,
Unmindful, tho' a weeping wife,
  And helpless offspring mourn.

IX

If I'm design'd yon lordling's slave,   65
  By Nature's law design'd,
Why was an independent wish
  E'er planted in my mind?
If not, why am I subject to
  His cruelty, or scorn?   70
Or why has Man the will and pow'r
  To make his fellow mourn?

46 All] Are *94*   All . . . forlorn] To wants and sorrows born *1CPB*
49 Many . . . Ills] Many the ills that Nature's hand *1CPB*   50 Inwoven]
Has woven *1CPB*   64 offspring] children *1CPB*   65 I'm design'd] I am
doom'd *1CPB Kil*   66 law] hand *1CPB Kil*   70 cruelty, or] *correcting*
insolence and *in 1CPB*

X

Yet, let not this too much, my Son,
    Disturb thy youthful breast:
This partial view of human-kind   75
    Is surely not the *last*!
The poor, oppressed, honest man
    Had never, sure, been born,
Had there not been some recompence
    To comfort those that mourn!   80

XI

O Death! the poor man's dearest friend,
    The kindest and the best!
Welcome the hour, my aged limbs
    Are laid with thee at rest!
The Great, the Wealthy fear thy blow,   85
    From pomp and pleasure torn;
But Oh! a blest relief to those
    That weary-laden mourn!

65. A Song.—On Miss P—— K——

Loch Eroch Side

77 man] heart *1CPB*   78 never, sure,] surely ne'er *1CPB*   86 pomp and
pleasure] pomps, and pleasures *1CPB Kil*   87 to 87 (*st*) 93 94: for *MSS 86 87 (sk)*
A Song. *Text from SMM, 1787 (78; unsigned), collated with the Alloway MS,
Stewart and Meikle's tract, and Stewart, 1802 (pp. 210–11; S). Title from the MS;*

YOUNG Peggy blooms our boniest lass,
  Her blush is like the morning,
The rosy dawn, the springing grass,
  With early gems adorning:
Her eyes outshine the radiant beams   5
  That gild the passing shower,
And glitter o'er the chrystal streams,
  And chear each fresh'ning flower.

Her lips more than the cherries bright,
  A richer die has grac'd them,   10
They charm th' admiring gazer's sight
  And sweetly tempt to taste them:
Her smile is as the ev'ning mild,
  When feath'red pairs are courting,
And little lambkins wanton wild,   15
  In playful bands disporting.

Were Fortune lovely Peggy's foe,
  Such sweetness would relent her,
As blooming spring unbends the brow
  Of surly, savage winter.   20
Detraction's eye no aim can gain
  Her winning pow'rs to lessen;
And fretful envy grins in vain,
  The poison'd tooth to fasten.

Ye Pow'rs of Honor, Love and Truth,   25
  From ev'ry ill defend her;
Inspire the highly favor'd Youth
  The Destinies intend her;
Still fan the sweet connubial flame,
  Responsive in each bosom;   30
And bless the dear parental name
  With many a filial blossom.

no title in SMM. Tune in MS and S The last time I came o'er the moor; *in SMM*
Loch Eroch Side
    2 Her blush is] She's blushing like *S*   3 dawn, . . . grass,] dawn . . . grass *MS*
4 early] pearly *MS S*   7 o'er] on *MS S*   streams] stream *S*   9 cherries]
cherry's *S*   13 smile is as] smiles is like *S*   20 surly, savage] savage, surly
S: MS defective   21 aim . . . gain] arm . . . join *S*   23 fretful] spiteful
MS S   24 The] Her *MS*   28 Destinies] distinies *SMM*   32 blossom.]
Blossom!!! *MS*

66. The Braes o' Ballochmyle

THE Catrine woods were yellow seen,
The flowers decay'd on Catrine lee,
Nae lav'rock sang on hillock green,
But Nature sicken'd on the e'e.
Thro' faded groves Maria sang,   5
Hersel in beauty's bloom the while,
And ay the wild-wood echoes rang,
Fareweel the braes o' Ballochmyle.

Low in your wintry beds, ye flowers,
Again ye'll flourish fresh and fair;   10
Ye birdies dumb, in with'ring bowers,
Again ye'll charm the vocal air.

The Braes o' Ballochmyle. *Text from SMM, 1790 (276; unsigned), collated with Stewart, 1802 (p. 332), and SC, 1805 (151)*

But here alas! for me nae mair
    Shall birdie charm, or floweret smile;
Fareweel the bonnie banks of Ayr,   15
    Fareweel, fareweel! sweet Ballochmyle!

67. [Third Epistle] to J. Lapraik

Sept. 13th, 1785.

Guid speed an' furder to you Johny,
    Guid health, hale han's, an' weather bony;
Now when ye're nickan down fu' cany
      The staff o' bread,
May ye ne'er want a stoup o' brany   5
      To clear your head.

May Boreas never thresh your rigs,
Nor kick your rickles aff their legs,
Sendin' the stuff o'er muirs an' haggs
      Like drivin' wrack;   10
But may the tapmast grain that wags
      Come to the sack.

I'm bizzie too, an' skelpin' at it,
But bitter, daudin showers hae wat it,
Sae my auld stumpie pen I gat it   15
      Wi' muckle wark,
An' took my jocteleg an' whatt it,
      Like ony clark.

It's now twa month that I'm your debtor,
For your braw, nameless, dateless letter,   20
Abusin' me for harsh ill nature
      On holy men,
While deil a hair yoursel ye're better,
      But mair profane.

13 mair] mair; *SMM*: mair, *SC*   13–16 But . . . Ballochmyle!] *Stewart has*
    Nae joys, alas! for me are here,
    Nae pleasure find I in this soil,
    Until Maria 'gain appear,
      Fareweel the braes o' Ballochmyle.

Third Epistle to J. Lapraik. *Text from Cromek*, Reliques, *1808 (pp. 389–91)*

But let the kirk-folk ring their bells,   25
Let's sing about our noble sels;
We'll cry nae jads frae heathen hills
      To help, or roose us,
But browster wives an' whiskie stills,
      They are the muses.   30

Your friendship sir, I winna quat it,
An' if ye mak' objections at it,
Then han' in nieve some day we'll knot it,
      An' witness take,
An' when wi' Usquabae we've wat it   35
      It winna break.

But if the beast and branks be spar'd
Till kye be gaun without the herd,
An' a' the vittel in the yard,
      An' theekit right,   40
I mean your ingle-side to guard
      Ae winter night.

Then muse-inspirin' aqua-vitæ
Shall make us baith sae blythe an' witty,
Till ye forget ye're auld an' gutty,   45
      An' be as canty
As ye were nine year less than thretty,
      Sweet ane an' twenty!

But stooks are cowpet wi' the blast,
An' now the sinn keeks in the west,   50
Then I maun rin amang the rest
      An' quat my chanter;
Sae I subscribe mysel in haste,
      Yours, RAB THE RANTER.

40 theekit] theckit *Cromek*   45 gutty] gatty *Cromek*   54 Yours] Your's
Cromek

68. To the Rev. John M'Math, Inclosing a copy of *Holy Willie's Prayer*, which he had requested

Sept. 17*th*, 1785.

WHILE at the stook the shearers cow'r
    To shun the bitter blaudin' show'r,
Or in gulravage rinnin scow'r
        To pass the time,
To you I dedicate the hour   5
        In idle rhyme.

My musie, tir'd wi' mony a sonnet
On gown, an' ban', an' douse black bonnet,
Is grown right eerie now she 's done it,
        Lest they shou'd blame her,   10
An' rouse their holy thunder on it
        And anathem her.

I own 'twas rash, an' rather hardy,
That I, a simple, countra bardie,
Shou'd meddle wi' a pack sae sturdy,   15
        Wha, if they ken me,
Can easy, wi' a single wordie,
        Louse h–ll upon me.

But I gae mad at their grimaces,
Their sighan, cantan, grace-prood faces,   20
Their three-mile prayers, an' hauf-mile graces,
        Their raxan conscience,
Whase greed, revenge, an' pride disgraces
        Waur nor their nonsense.

There's *Gaun*, miska't waur than a beast,   25
Wha has mair honor in his breast
Than mony scores as guid's the priest
        Wha sae abus't him:
An' may a bard no crack his jest
        What way they've use't him?   30

To the Rev. John M'Math. *Text from Cromek*, Reliques, *1808 (pp. 392–6)*
  28 him:] him. *Cromek*   30 him ?] him. *Cromek*

See him, the poor man's friend in need,
The gentleman in word an' deed,
An' shall his fame an' honor bleed
      By worthless skellums,
An' not a muse erect her head   35
      To cowe the blellums?

O Pope, had I thy satire's darts
To gie the rascals their deserts,
I'd rip their rotten, hollow hearts,
      An' tell aloud   40
Their jugglin' hocus pocus arts
      To cheat the crowd.

God knows, I'm no the thing I shou'd be,
Nor am I even the thing I cou'd be,
But twenty times, I rather wou'd be   45
      An atheist clean,
Than under gospel colors hid be
      Just for a screen.

An honest man may like a glass,
An honest man may like a lass,   50
But mean revenge, an' malice fause
      He'll still disdain,
An' then cry zeal for gospel laws,
      Like some we ken.

They take religion in their mouth;   55
They talk o' mercy, grace an' truth,
For what?—to gie their malice skouth
      On some puir wight,
An' hunt him down, o'er right an' ruth,
      To ruin streight.   60

All hail, Religion! maid divine!
Pardon a muse sae mean as mine,
Who in her rough imperfect line
      Thus daurs to name thee;
To stigmatize false friends of thine   65
      Can ne'er defame thee.

61 Religion] religion *Cromek*

Tho' blotch't an' foul wi' mony a stain,
An' far unworthy of thy train,
With trembling voice I tune my strain
      To join with those,   70
Who boldly dare thy cause maintain
      In spite of foes:

In spite o' crowds, in spite o' mobs,
In spite of undermining jobs,
In spite o' dark banditti stabs   75
      At worth an' merit,
By scoundrels, even wi' holy robes,
      But hellish spirit.

O Ayr, my dear, my native ground,
Within thy presbytereal bound   80
A candid lib'ral band is found
      Of public teachers,
As men, as Christians too renown'd
      An' manly preachers.

Sir, in that circle you are nam'd;   85
Sir, in that circle you are fam'd;
An' some, by whom your doctrine's blam'd
      (Which gies you honor)
Even Sir, by them your heart's esteem'd,
      An' winning manner.   90

Pardon this freedom I have ta'en,
An' if impertinent I've been,
Impute it not, good Sir, in ane
      Whase heart ne'er wrang'd ye,
But to his utmost would befriend   95
      Ought that belang'd ye.

83 Christians] christians *Cromek*

69. To a Mouse, On turning her up in her Nest, with the Plough, November, 1785.

WEE, sleeket, cowran, tim'rous *beastie*,
O, what a panic's in thy breastie!
Thou need na start awa sae hasty,
      Wi' bickering brattle!
I wad be laith to rin an' chase thee,   5
      Wi' murd'ring *pattle*!

I'm truly sorry Man's dominion
Has broken Nature's social union,
An' justifies that ill opinion,
      Which makes thee startle,   10
At me, thy poor, earth-born companion,
      An' *fellow-mortal*!

I doubt na, whyles, but thou may *thieve*;
What then? poor beastie, thou maun live!
A *daimen-icker* in a *thrave*   15
      'S a sma' request:
I'll get a blessin wi' the lave,
      An' never miss't!

Thy wee-bit *housie*, too, in ruin!
It's silly wa's the win's are strewin!   20
An' naething, now, to big a new ane,
      O' foggage green!
An' bleak *December's winds* ensuin,
      Baith snell an' keen!

Thou saw the fields laid bare an' wast,   25
An' weary *Winter* comin fast,
An' cozie here, beneath the blast,
      Thou thought to dwell,
Till crash! the cruel *coulter* past
      Out thro' thy cell.   30

To a Mouse. *Text from the edition of 1786, collated with the editions of 1787, 1793, 1794. H–H. record a manuscript (not traced) with these variants:*
23 bleak] cauld *MS*   25 bare] bleak *MS*   28 Thou] Then *MS*

That wee-bit heap o' leaves an' stibble,
Has cost thee monie a weary nibble!
Now thou's turn'd out, for a' thy trouble,
    But house or hald,
To thole the Winter's *sleety dribble*,   35
    An' *cranreuch* cauld!

But Mousie, thou art no thy-lane,
In proving *foresight* may be vain:
The best laid schemes o' *Mice* an' *Men*,
    Gang aft agley,   40
An' lea'e us nought but grief an' pain,
    For promis'd joy!

Still, thou art blest, compar'd wi' *me*!
The *present* only toucheth thee:
But Och! I *backward* cast my e'e,   45
    On prospects drear!
An' *forward*, tho' I canna *see*,
    I *guess* an' *fear*!

70. The Holy Fair*

A robe of seeming truth and trust
    Hid crafty Observation;
And secret hung, with poison'd crust,
    The dirk of Defamation:
A mask that like the gorget show'd,
    Dye-varying, on the pigeon;
And for a mantle large and broad,
    He wrapt him in Religion.—

                              Hypocrisy a-la-Mode.

* *Holy Fair* is a common phrase in the West of Scotland for a sacramental occasion.

---

34 house] hame *MS*   38 may be] whyles in *MS*   40 Gang aft] Aft
gang *MS*   43 Still, thou] But thou *MS*
The Holy Fair. *Text from the Irvine MS (I), collated with the Kilmarnock MS (Kil)
and B.M. MS Egerton 1656 (ff. 21–24ʳ; Eg), and the editions of 1786, 1787, 1793
(HL; copy with holograph corrections in the Huntington Library), 1794. Kil adds*
Composed in Autumn 1785 *to the title. Footnote added in 87–94. Of the MSS, only I
has the epigraph*
Epigraph. 2 *Observation* 93 94: observation *I 86 87*

I

UPON a simmer *Sunday morn*,
    When Nature's face is fair,
I walked forth to view the corn,
    An' snuff the callor air:
The rising sun, owre GALSTON muirs,   5
    Wi' glorious light was glintan;
The hares were hirplan down the furrs,
    The lav'rocks they were chantan
            Fu' sweet that day.

II

As lightsomely I glowr'd abroad,   10
    To see a scene sae gay,
Three *hizzies*, early at the road,
    Cam skelpan up the way.
Twa had manteeles o' dolefu' black,
    But ane wi' lyart lining;   15
The *third*, that gaed a wee aback,
    Was in the fashion shining
            Fu' gay that day.

III

The *twa* appear'd like sisters twin,
    In feature, form an' claes;   20
Their visage—wither'd, lang an' thin,
    An' sour as onie slaes:
The *third* cam up, hap-step-an'-loup,
    As light as onie lambie,—
An' wi' a curchie low did stoop,   25
    As soon as e'er she saw me,
            Fu' kind that day.

IV

Wi' bonnet aff, quoth I, 'Sweet lass,
    'I think ye seem to ken me;
'I'm sure I've seen that bonie face,   30
    'But yet I canna name ye.—'

1 Upon] 'Twas on *Eg*   15 wi'] had *Eg*   18 gay] braw *Eg*
21 visage—] visage *86–94*: faces *Eg*   28 quoth I,] cothie *Eg*

Quo' she, an' laughan as she spak,
   An' taks me by the hands,
'Ye, for my sake, hae gien the feck
   'Of a' the *ten commands*   35
       A screed some day.

V

'My name is Fun—your cronie dear,
   'The nearest friend ye hae;
'An' this is Superstition here,
   'An' that's Hypocrisy: 40
'I'm gaun to ********* *holy fair*,
   'To spend an hour in daffin;
'Gin ye'll go there, yon runkl'd pair,
   'We will get famous laughin
       At them this day.'   45

VI

Quoth I, 'With a' my heart, I'll do 't;
   'I'll get my Sunday's sark on,
'An' meet you on the holy spot;
   'Faith we'se hae fine remarkin!'
Then I gaed hame, at crowdie-time,   50
   An' soon I made me ready;
For roads were clad, frae side to side,
   Wi' monie a weary body,
       In droves that day.

VII

Here, farmers gash, in ridin graith,   55
   Gaed hoddan by their cotters;
There, swankies young, in braw braid-claith,
   Are springan owre the gutters.

34 gien] broke *Eg*   35 *commands Kil HL* 94: *comman's MSS* 86: *commauns*
87–93   36 A screed some] By night or *Eg*   41 *********] M——
Eg Kil   46–49 Quoth . . . remarkin!] *Eg has*
               Quothie, I'll get my tither coat,
               An' on my Sunday's sark,
               An' meet ye in the yard without
               At op'nin' o' the wark.

58 springan] *correcting* spangin *in Eg*

The lasses, skelpan barefit, thrang,
   In silks an' scarlets glitter;   60
Wi' *sweet-milk cheese*, in mony a whang,
   An' *farls*, bak'd wi' butter,
         Fu' crump that day.

VIII

When by the *plate* we set our nose,
   Weel heaped up wi' ha'pence,   65
A greedy glowr *Black-bonnet* throws,
   An' we maun draw our tippence.
Then in we go to see the show,
   On ev'ry side they're gath'ran;
Some carryan dails, some chairs an' stools,   70
   An' some are busy bleth'ran
         Right loud that day.

IX

Here, stands a shed to fend the show'rs,
   An' screen our countra Gentry;
There, *Racer-Jess*, an' twathree wh—res,   75
   Are blinkan at the entry:
Here sits a raw o' tittlan jads,
   Wi' heaving breasts an' bare neck;
An' there, a batch o' *Wabster lads*,
   Blackguarding frae K*******ck   80
         For *fun* this day.

X

Here, some are thinkan on their sins,
   An' some upo' their claes;
Ane curses feet that fyl'd his shins,
   Anither sighs an' pray's: 85

59 The] *correcting* Here *in Eg*   66 *Black-bonnet*] the Elder *Eg*   72 Right]
Fu' *Eg*   75 There, *Racer-Jess*] Bet Barb–r there *Eg Kil*   76 Are] *correcting*
Sit *in I*: Sit *Eg Kil*   at] in *Eg*]   79 *lads*,] brawds *Eg Kil*   80 K*******ck]
Kilm–rn–ck *Eg Kil*   83 some upo'] ithers on *Eg*

On this hand sits a Chosen swatch,
  Wi' screw'd-up, grace-proud faces;
On that, a set o' chaps, at watch,
  Thrang winkan on the lasses
      To *chairs* that day.   90

XI

O happy is that man, an' blest!
  Nae wonder that it pride him!
Whase ain dear lass, that he likes best,
  Comes clinkan down beside him!
Wi' arm repos'd on the *chair back*,   95
  He sweetly does compose him;
Which, by degrees, slips round her *neck*,
  An's loof upon her *bosom*
      Unkend that day.

XII

Now a' the congregation o'er,   100
  Is silent expectation;
For ****** speels the holy door,
  Wi' tidings o' d—mn–t—n:
Should *Hornie*, as in ancient days,
  'Mang sons o' G— present him,   105
The vera sight o' ******'s face,
  To's ain *het hame* had sent him
      Wi' fright that day.

XIII

Hear how he clears the points o' Faith
  Wi' rattlin an' thumpin!   110
Now meekly calm, now wild in wrath,
  He's stampan, an' he's jumpan!

86 a Chosen 87–94: a godly *Eg*: an Elect *I Kil* 86   87 screw'd-up . . .
faces] 'mercy beggin' faces' *Eg*   88 at] on *Eg Kil*   89 on] at *Eg Kil*
93 likes] loves *Eg*   100 Now a'] But now *Eg*   101 silent] hush't wi' *Eg*
102, 106 ******] 86–94: Sawnie *Eg Kil: del. I*   102 speels] climbs *Eg*
103 d—mn–t—n 87–94: s–lv–t—n *MSS* 86   104 ancient days] *correcting* days
of yore *in I*   107 To 's ain *het hame*] Tae H–ll wi' speed *Eg*   108 Wi']
For *Eg*   111 in] wi' *Eg*

His lengthen'd chin, his turn'd up snout,
   His eldritch squeel an' gestures,
O how they fire the heart devout,   115
   Like cantharidian plaisters
      On sic a day!

XIV

But hark! the *tent* has chang'd it's voice;
   There's peace an' rest nae langer;
For a' the *real judges* rise,   120
   They canna sit for anger.
***** opens out his cauld harangues,
   On *practice* and on *morals*;
An' aff the godly pour in thrangs,
   To gie the jars an' barrels   125
      A lift that day.

XV

What signifies his barren shine,
   Of *moral pow'rs* an' *reason*;
His English style, an' gesture fine,
   Are a' clean out o' season.   130
Like SOCRATES or ANTONINE,
   Or some auld pagan heathen,
The *moral man* he does define,
   But ne'er a word o' *faith* in
      That's right that day.   135

XVI

In guid time comes an antidote
   Against sic poosion'd nostrum;
For *******, frae the water-fit,
   Ascends the *holy rostrum*:

---

122 ***** opens out] Geordie begins *Eg Kil*   123 On . . . on] O' . . . of *Eg*
127–8 What . . . *reason*] *Eg has*

      Its no nae Gospel truth divine
      Tae cant o' Sense an' Reason

130 Are] Is *Eg*   132 pagan] wicket *Eg Kil*   138 *******, frae the] sairy
Willy *Eg Kil*

See, up he's got the Word o' G——,   140
   An' meek an' mim has view'd it,
While COMMON-SENSE has taen the road,
   An' aff, an' up the *Cowgate**
      Fast, fast that day.

XVII

Wee ****** niest, the Guard relieves,   145
   An' Orthodoxy raibles,
Tho' in his heart he weel believes,
   An' thinks it auld wives' fables:
But faith! the birkie wants a *Manse*,
   So, cannilie he hums them;   150
Altho' his *carnal* Wit an' Sense
   Like hafflins-wise o'ercomes him
      At times that day.

XVIII

Now, butt an' ben, the Change-house fills,
   Wi' *yill-caup* Commentators:
Here's crying out for bakes an' gills,   155
   An' there, the pint-stowp clatters;
While thick an' thrang, an' loud an' lang,
   Wi' *Logic*, an' wi' *Scripture*,
They raise a din, that, in the end,   160
   Is like to breed a rupture
      O' wrath that day.

XIX

Leeze me on Drink! it gies us mair
   Than either School or Colledge:
It kindles Wit, it waukens Lear,   165
   It pangs us fou o' Knowledge.

---

  * A street so called, which faces the *tent* in——.

---

143 *Foot-note added in 87*   144 Fast, fast] In haste *Eg*   145 ******]
M—r *Kil*   niest] *om. Eg*   163 *Stanzas XIX, XX are in reverse order in Eg.*
Note after 162 in Kil: The next verse after the following ought to be in here
164 Colledge] *corrected to* College *in HL*   165 kindles] kain'les *Eg*

Be't *whisky-gill* or *penny-wheep,*
   Or onie stronger potion,
It never fails, on drinkin deep,
   To kittle up our *notion,*   170
          By night or day.

                    XX

The lads an' lasses, blythely bent
   To mind baith *saul* an' *body,*
Sit round the table, weel content,
   An' steer about the *Toddy.*   175
On this ane's dress, an' that ane's leuk,
   They're makin observations;
While some are cozie i' the neuk,
   An' forming *assignations*
          To meet some day.   180

                    XXI

But now the L——'s ain trumpet touts,
   Till a' the hills are rairan,
An' echos back return the shouts,
   Black ****** is na spairan:
His piercin words, like highlan swords,   185
   Divide the joints an' marrow;
His talk o' H–ll, whare devils dwell,
   Our vera* 'Sauls does harrow'
          Wi' fright that day.

                    XXII

A vast, unbottom'd, boundless *Pit,*   190
   Fill'd fou o' *lowan brunstane,*
Whase raging flame, an' scorching heat,
   Wad melt the hardest whunstane!

---

* Shakespeare's Hamlet.

   167–243 *Missing from Kil*   173 To . . . *body*] Their lowan drowth tae
quench *Eg*   175 *Toddy.*] punch; *Eg*   182 are] is *Eg*   183 echos . . .
return] echo . . . returns *Eg*: echos *corrected to* echoes in *HL*   184 ******]
Jock, he *Eg*   185 highlan] twa-edg't *Eg*   188 Our vera 'Sauls] 'Our vera
sauls *Eg*

The *half-asleep* start up wi' fear,
  An' think they hear it roaran,   195
When presently it does appear,
  'Twas but some neebor *snoran*
      Asleep that day.

XXIII

'Twad be owre lang a tale to tell,
  How monie stories past,   200
An' how they crouded to the yill,
  When they were a' dismist:
How drink gaed round, in cogs an' caups,
  Amang the furms an' benches;
An' *cheese* an' *bread*, frae women's laps,   205
  Was dealt about in lunches,
      An' dawds that day.

XXIV

In comes a gausie, gash *Guidwife*,
  An' sits down by the fire,
Syn draws her *kebbuck* an' her knife;   210
  The lasses they are shyer.
The auld *Guidmen*, about the *grace*,
  Frae side to side they bother,
Till some ane by his bonnet lays,
  An' gies them't, like a *tether*,   215
      Fu' lang that day.

XXV

Wae sucks! for him that gets nae lass,
  Or lasses that hae naething!
Sma' need has he to say a grace,
  Or melvie his braw claething!   220
O *Wives* be mindfu', ance yoursel,
  How bonie lads ye wanted,
An' dinna, for a *kebbuck-heel*,
  Let lasses be affronted
      On sic a day!   225

196 When] While *Eg*   203 drink] yill *Eg*   205 *cheese* an' *bread*] bread an' cheese *Eg*   210 Syn] Then *Eg*

XXVI

Now *Clinkumbell*, wi' rattlan tow,
    Begins to jow an' croon;
Some swagger hame, the best they dow,
    Some wait the afternoon.
At slaps the billies halt a blink,   230
    Till lasses strip their shoon:
Wi' *faith* an' *hope*, an' *love* an' *drink*,
    They're a' in famous tune
                For crack that day.

XXVII

How monie hearts this day converts,   235
    O' Sinners and o' Lasses!
Their hearts o' stane, gin night are gane
    As saft as ony flesh is.
There's some are fou o' *love divine*;
    There's some are fou o' *brandy*;   240
An' monie jobs that day begin,
    May end in *Houghmagandie*
                Some ither day.

71. The Twa Dogs. A Tale

'TWAS in that place o' *Scotland*'s isle,
    That bears the name o' auld king COIL,
Upon a bonie day in June,
When wearing thro' the afternoon,
Twa Dogs, that were na thrang at hame,   5
Forgather'd ance upon a time.

226–7 Now . . . croon;] *Eg has*
                Then Robin Gib wi' weary jow
                Begins tae clink an' croon,
231 strip] *correcting* change *in Eg*   237 gane *Eg:* gane, *I 86–94*

The Twa Dogs. *Text from the Irvine MS (I), collated with the Kilmarnock MS (Kil) and fragments, and the editions of 1786, 1787, 1793 (HL: copy with holograph corrections in the Huntington Library), 1794*

The first I'll name, they ca'd him *Ceasar*,
Was keepet for his Honor's pleasure;
His hair, his size, his mouth, his lugs,
Show'd he was nane o' Scotland's dogs;   10
But whalpet some place far abroad,
Whare sailors gang to fish for Cod.

His locked, letter'd, braw brass-collar,
Show'd him the *gentleman* an' *scholar*;
But tho' he was o' high degree,   15
The fient a pride na pride had he,
But wad hae spent an hour caressan,
Ev'n wi' a Tinkler-gipsey's *messan*:
At *Kirk* or *Market*, *Mill* or *Smiddie*,
Nae tawtied *tyke*, tho' e'er sae duddie,   20
But he wad stan't, as glad to see him,
An' stroan't on stanes an' hillocks wi' him.

The tither was a *ploughman's collie*,
A rhyming, ranting, raving billie,
Wha for his friend an' comrade had him,   25
And in his freaks had *Luath* ca'd him;
After some dog in **Highlan Sang*,
Was made lang syne, lord knows how lang.

He was a gash an' faithfu' *tyke*,
As ever lap a sheugh, or dyke!   30
His honest, sonsie, baws'nt *face*,
Ay gat him friends in ilka place;
His *breast* was white, his towzie *back*,
Weel clad wi' coat o' glossy black;
His gawsie tail, wi' upward curl,   35
Hung owre his hurdies wi' a swirl.

Nae doubt but they were fain o' ither,
An' unco pack an' thick the gither;
Wi' social *nose* whyles snuff'd an' snowcket;
Whyles mice an' modewurks they howcket;   40

* Cuchullin's dog in Ossian's Fingal.

Whyles scour'd awa in lang excursion,
An' worry'd ither in *diversion*;
Untill wi' daffin weary grown,
Upon a knowe they sat them down,
An' there began a lang digression   45
About the *lords o' the creation.*

CEASAR

I've aften wonder'd, honest *Luath*,
What sort o' life poor dogs like you have;
An' when the *gentry*'s life I saw,
What way *poor bodies* liv'd ava.   50

Our *Laird* gets in his racked rents,
His coals, his kane, an' a' his stents;
He rises when he likes himsel;
His flunkies answer at the bell;
He ca's his coach; he ca's his horse;   55
He draws a bonie, silken purse
As lang's my *tail*, whare thro' the steeks,
The yellow, letter'd *Geordie* keeks.

Frae morn to een it's nought but toiling,
At baking, roasting, frying, boiling: 60
An' tho' the gentry first are steghan,
Yet ev'n the *ha' folk* fill their peghan
Wi' sauce, ragouts, an' sic like trashtrie,
That's little short o' downright wastrie.
Our *Whipper-in*, wee, blastiet wonner,   65
Poor, worthless elf, it eats a dinner,
Better than ony *Tenant-man*
His Honor has in a' the lan':
An' what poor *Cot-folk* pit their painch in,
I own it's past my comprehension.—   70

42 in] for *Kil*   43–44 Untill . . . down, *HL 94: MSS and 86 have*
            Till tir'd at last wi' mony a farce,
            They set them down upon their arse:
87 *and* 93 *have* Till tir'd . . . their a—   58 yellow,] yellow *86–94*
65 *Whipper-in 86–94: whipperin MSS*

LUATH

Trowth, *Ceasar*, whyles they're fash'd eneugh;
A *Cotter* howckan in a sheugh,
Wi' dirty stanes biggan a dyke,
Bairan a quarry, an' sic like,
Himsel, a wife, he thus sustains,   75
A smytrie o' wee, duddie weans,
An' nought but his han'-daurk, to keep
Them right an' tight in *thack an' raep.*

An' when they meet wi' sair disasters,
Like loss o' health, or want o' masters,   80
Ye maist wad think, a wee touch langer,
An' they maun starve o' cauld an' hunger:
But how it comes, I never kent yet,
They're maistly wonderfu' contented;
An' buirdly chiels, an' clever hizzies,   85
Are bred in sic a way as this is.

CEASAR

But then, to see how ye're negleket,
How huff'd, an' cuff'd, an' disrespeket!
L—d man, our gentry care as little
For *delvers*, *ditchers*, an' sic cattle;   90
They gang as saucy by poor folk,
As I wad by a stinkan brock.

I've notic'd, on our Laird's *court-day*,
An' mony a time my heart's been wae,
Poor *tenant-bodies*, scant o' cash,   95
How they maun thole a *factor*'s snash;
He'll stamp an' threaten, curse an' swear,
He'll *apprehend* them, *poind* their gear,
While they maun stand, wi' aspect humble,
An' hear it a', an' fear an' tremble!   100

I see how folk live that hae riches,
But surely poor-folk maun be *wretches*!

71 they're] their *Kil 86 87*   eneugh] enough *86–94*

LUATH

They're no sae wretched 's ane wad think;
Tho' constantly on poortith's brink,
They're sae accustom'd wi' the sight,   105
The view o't gies them little fright.

Then chance an' fortune are sae guided,
They're ay in less or mair provided;
An' tho' fatigu'd wi' close employment,
A blink o' rest's a sweet enjoyment.   110

The dearest comfort o' their lives,
Their grushie weans, an' faithfu' wives;
The *prattling things* are just their pride,
That sweetens a' their fire-side.

An' whyles, twalpennie-worth o' *nappy*   115
Can mak the bodies unco happy;
They lay aside their private cares,
To mind the Kirk an' State affairs;
They'll talk o' *patronage* an' *priests*,
Wi' kindling fury i' their breasts,   120
Or tell what new taxation's comin,
An' ferlie at the folk in Lon'on.

As bleak-fac'd Hallowmass returns,
They get the jovial, rantan *Kirns*,
When *rural life*, of ev'ry station,   125
Unite in common recreation;
Love blinks, Wit slaps, an' social Mirth
Forgets there's *care* upo' the earth.

That *merry day* the year begins,
They bar the door on frosty win's;   130
The nappy reeks wi' mantling ream,
An' sheds a heart-inspiring steam;

119–20 They'll . . . breasts,] *om. Kil*   121 Or tell] Foretell *Kil*   122 ferlie]
wonder *Kil*   125 of] in *Kil*   126 Unite] Unites *Kil*   130 win's]
winds *HL*

The luntan pipe, an' sneeshin mill,
Are handed round wi' right guid will;
The cantie, auld folks, crackan crouse,   135
The young anes rantan thro' the house—
My heart has been sae fain to see them,
That I for joy hae *barket* wi' them.

Still it's owre true that ye hae said,
Sic game is now owre aften play'd;   140
There's monie a creditable *stock*
O' decent, honest, fawsont folk,
Are riven out baith root an' branch,
Some rascal's pridefu' greed to quench,
Wha thinks to knit himsel the faster   145
In favor wi' some *gentle Master*,
Wha, aiblins, thrang a *parliamentin*,
For *Britain's guid* his saul indentin—

CEASAR

Haith lad, ye little ken about it;
For Britain's guid! guid faith! I doubt it.   150
Say rather, gaun as PREMIERS lead him,
An' saying *aye* or *no*'s they bid him:
At Operas an' Plays parading,
Mortgaging, gambling, masquerading:
Or maybe, in a frolic daft,   155
To HAGUE or CALAIS takes a waft,
To make a *tour* an' take a whirl,
To learn *bon ton* an' see the worl'.

There, at VIENNA or VERSAILLES,
He rives his father's auld entails;   160
Or by MADRID he takes the rout,
To thrum *guittarres* an' fecht wi' *nowt*;
Or down *Italian Vista* startles,
Wh—re-hunting amang groves o' myrtles:
Then bowses drumlie *German-water*,   165
To make himsel look fair an' fatter,

145 Wha] *correcting* Or *in I*   162 thrum . . . fecht] play . . . fight *Kil*

An' clear the consequential sorrows,
Love-gifts of Carnival Signioras.
For Britain's guid! for her destruction!
Wi' dissipation, feud an' faction!   170

LUATH

Hech man! dear sirs! is that the gate,
They waste sae mony a braw estate!
Are we sae foughten an' harass'd
For gear to gang that gate at last!

O would they stay aback frae courts,   175
An' please themsels wi' countra sports,
It wad for ev'ry ane be better,
The *Laird*, the *Tenant*, an' the *Cotter*!
For thae frank, rantan, ramblan billies,
Fient haet o' them 's illhearted fellows;   180
Except for breakin o' their timmer,
Or speakin lightly o' their *Limmer*;
Or shootin of a hare or moorcock,
The ne'er-a-bit they're ill to poor folk.

But will ye tell me, master *Cesar*,   185
Sure *great folk*'s life's a life o' pleasure?
Nae cauld nor hunger e'er can steer them,
The vera thought o't need na fear them.

CESAR

L—d man, were ye but whyles where I am,
The *gentles* ye wad ne'er envy them!   190

It's true, they needna starve or sweat,
Thro' Winter's cauld, or Summer's heat;
They've nae sair-wark to craze their banes,
An' fill *auld-age* wi' grips an' granes:

167-8 An' . . . Signioras. *87-94: MSS and 86 have*
            An' purge the bitter ga's an' cankers,
            O' curst *Venetian* b—res an' ch—ncres.
[shankers *Kil*] 187 nor] or *Kil*

But *human-bodies* are sic fools,   195
For a' their Colledges an' Schools,
That when nae *real* ills perplex them,
They *mak* enow themsels to vex them;
An' ay the less they hae to sturt them,
In like proportion, less will hurt them.   200

A country fellow at the pleugh,
His *acre*'s till'd, he's right eneugh;
A country girl at her wheel,
Her *dizzen*'s done, she's unco weel;
But Gentlemen, an' Ladies warst,   205
Wi' ev'n down *want o' wark* they're curst.
They loiter, lounging, lank an' lazy;
Tho' deil-haet ails them, yet uneasy;
Their days, insipid, dull an' tasteless,
Their nights, unquiet, lang an' restless.   210

An' ev'n their sports, their balls an' races,
Their galloping thro' public places,
There's sic parade, sic pomp an' art,
The joy can scarcely reach the heart.

The *Men* cast out in *party-matches*,   215
Then sowther a' in deep debauches.
Ae night, they're mad wi' drink an' wh–ring,
Niest day their life is past enduring.

The *Ladies* arm-in-arm in clusters,
As great an' gracious a' as sisters;   220
But hear their *absent thoughts* o' ither,
They're a' run-deils an' jads the gither.
Whyles, owre the wee bit cup an' platie,
They sip the *scandal-potion* pretty;

201 country fellow at the] countra fallow at his *Kil*   202 till'd] *correcting*
done *in Kil*   203 country girl] countra lassie *Kil*   206 they're] are *86–94*
211 their balls] like balls *Kil*   212 Their] An' *Kil*

Or lee-lang nights, wi' crabbet leuks,   225
Pore owre the devil's *pictur'd beuks*;
Stake on a chance a farmer's stackyard,
An' cheat like ony *unhang'd blackguard*.

There's some exceptions, man an' woman;
But this is Gentry's life in common.   230

By this, the sun was out o' sight,
An' darker gloamin brought the night:
The *bum-clock* humm'd wi' lazy drone,
The kye stood rowtan i' the loan;
When up they gat, an' shook their lugs,   235
Rejoic'd they were na *men* but *dogs*;
An' each took off his several way,
Resolv'd to meet some ither day.

72. The Cotter's Saturday Night.
Inscribed to R. A****, Esq.

Let not Ambition mock their useful toil,
  Their homely joys, and destiny obscure;
Nor Grandeur hear, with a disdainful smile,
  The short and simple annals of the Poor.
                                            GRAY.

                    I

M y lov'd, my honor'd, much respected friend,
    No mercenary Bard his homage pays;
With honest pride, I scorn each selfish end,
    My dearest meed, a friend's esteem and praise:

225–6 Or . . . beuks;] *fragment (ll. 225–30) collated by Dewar (not traced) has*
              Or pore hale nights, wi' crabbed leuks,
              Outowre the deil's pictur'd beuks.

228 *unhang'd*] unhang *fragment (Dewar)*   229 exceptions] exception *93 94*
238 some ither] another *Kil*

The Cotter's Saturday Night. *Text from the Irvine MS (I), collated with the Kil-marnock MS (Kil) and B.M. MS Egerton 1656 (ff. 30ʳ–32ᵛ; Eg), and the editions of 1786, 1787, 1793, 1794. Variants recorded by Henley and Henderson from the copy sent to Aitken (MS not traced) are noted below (Ait). Title and epigraph, without inscription, following* The Twa Dogs *in Kil; on the next page a fresh title* The Cotter's Saturday-Teen. Inscribed to Mr. Robert Aitken, Ayr, *and epigraph. Sub-title in Eg* A Scotch Poem

To you I sing, in simple Scottish lays,   5
  The *lowly train* in life's sequester'd scene;
The native feelings strong, the guileless ways,
  What A**** in a *Cottage* would have been;
Ah! tho' his worth unknown, far happier there I ween!

II

November chill blaws loud wi' angry sugh;   10
  The short'ning winter-day is near a close;
The miry beasts retreating frae the pleugh;
  The black'ning trains o' craws to their repose:
The toil-worn COTTER frae his labor goes,
  This night his weekly moil is at an end,   15
Collects his *spades*, his *mattocks* and his *hoes*,
  Hoping the *morn* in ease and rest to spend,
And weary, o'er the muir, his course does hameward bend.

III

At length his lonely *Cot* appears in view,
  Beneath the shelter of an aged tree;   20
Th' expectant wee-things, toddlan, stacher thro'
  To meet their *Dad*, wi' flichterin noise and glee.
His wee-bit ingle, blinkan bonilie,
  His clean hearth-stane, his thrifty *Wifie*'s smile,
The *lisping infant*, prattling on his knee,   25
  Does a' his weary kiaugh and care beguile,
And makes him quite forget his labor and his toil.

IV

Belyve, the *elder bairns* come drapping in,
  At *Service* out, amang the Farmers roun';
Some ca' the pleugh, some herd, some tentie rin   30
  A cannie errand to a neebor toun:
Their eldest hope, their *Jenny*, woman-grown,
  In youthfu' bloom, Love sparkling in her e'e,
Comes hame, perhaps to show a braw new gown,
  Or deposite her sair-won penny-fee,   35
To help her *Parents* dear, if they in hardship be.

8 A****] Aitken *Kil Eg*   13 trains] flocks *Kil Eg (Ait)*   21 toddlan]
tottlin *Kil Eg*   26 kiaugh and care] carking cares *93 94*

V

With joy unfeign'd, *brothers* and *sisters* meet,
    And each for other's weelfare kindly spiers:
The social hours, swift-wing'd, unnotic'd, fleet;
    Each tells the uncos that he sees or hears.   40
The *Parents partial* eye their hopeful years;
    Anticipation forward points the view;
The *Mother* wi' her needle and her sheers
    Gars auld claes look amaist as weel's the new;
The *Father* mixes a', wi' admonition due.   45

VI

Their Master's and their Mistress's command,
    The *youngkers* a' are warned to obey;
And mind their labors wi' an eydent hand,
    And ne'er, tho' out o' sight, to jauk or play:
'And O! be sure to fear the LORD alway!   50
'And mind your *duty*, duely, morn and night!
'Lest in temptation's path ye gang astray,
    'Implore His counsel and assisting might:
'They never sought in vain, that sought the LORD aright.'

VII

But hark! a rap comes gently to the door;   55
    Jenny, wha kens the meaning o' the same,
Tells how a neebor lad came o'er the muir,
    To do some errands, and convoy her hame.
The wily Mother sees the *conscious flame*
    Sparkle in *Jenny*'s e'e, and flush her cheek,   60
With heart-struck, anxious care enquires his name,
    While *Jenny* hafflins is afraid to speak;
Weel-pleas'd the Mother hears, it's nae wild, worthless
    Rake.

VIII

With kindly welcome, *Jenny* brings him ben;
    A *strappan youth*, he takes the Mother's eye;   65
Blythe *Jenny* sees the *visit*'s no ill-taen;
    The Father cracks of horses, pleughs and kye.

39 social] tender *Eg* (*Ait*)   40 or] an' *Kil*   44 Gars] Maks *Kil*: Makes *Eg*
49 or] an' *Kil*   50 fear] *correcting* mind *in Eg*   51 mind] *correcting* tent
in Eg   54 that] wha *Kil Eg* (*Ait*)   59 sees] spys (*Ait*)

The *youngster*'s artless heart o'erflows wi' joy,
  But blate and laithfu', scarce can weel behave;
The Mother, wi' a woman's wiles, can spy   70
  What makes the *youth* sae bashfu' and sae grave;
Weel-pleas'd to think her *bairn*'s respected like the lave.

IX

O happy love! where love like this is found!
  O heart-felt raptures! bliss beyond compare!
I've paced much this weary, *mortal round*,   75
  And sage EXPERIENCE bids me this declare—
'If Heaven a draught of heavenly pleasure spare,
  'One *cordial* in this melancholly *Vale*,
' 'Tis when a youthful, loving, *modest* Pair,
  'In other's arms, breathe out the tender tale,   80
'Beneath the milk-white thorn that scents the ev'ning
    gale.'

X

Is there, in human-form, that bears a heart—
  A wretch! a villain! lost to love and truth!
That can, with studied, sly, ensnaring art,
  Betray sweet *Jenny*'s unsuspecting youth?   85
Curse on his perjur'd arts! dissembling smoothe!
  Are *Honor*, *Virtue*, *Conscience*, all exil'd?
Is there no Pity, no relenting Ruth,
  Points to the Parents fondling o'er their Child?
Then paints the *ruin'd Maid*, and *their* distraction wild! 90

XI

But now the Supper crowns their simple board,
  The healsome *Porritch*, chief of SCOTIA's food:
The soupe their *only Hawkie* does afford,
  That 'yont the hallan snugly chows her cood:

68 artless] witless *Kil Eg* (*Ait*)   71 bashfu'] aukward *Eg* (*Ait*)   73 love like this] suchen love *Kil Eg* (*Ait*)   75 I've paced much] I've traced long *Eg*: I've paced long *Kil*: I, who have traced long (*Ait*)   76 And . . . this] From deep-felt sage Experience can (*Ait*)   77 draught] drop *Eg*   81 ev'ning] *correcting* balmy *in I*   86 perjur'd] *correcting* coward *in I*   87 *Honor*, *Virtue*, *Conscience*] Virtue, Honour, Conscience *Eg*: Virtue, Conscience, Honor *Kil*   91 Supper . . . simple] chearful Supper crowns the (*Ait*)

The *Dame* brings forth, in complimental mood,   95
  To grace the lad, her weel-hain'd kebbuck, fell;
And aft he's prest, and aft he ca's it guid;
  The frugal *Wifie*, garrulous, will tell,
How 'twas a towmond auld, sin' Lint was i' the bell.

XII

The chearfu' Supper done, wi' serious face,   100
  They, round the ingle, form a circle wide;
The Sire turns o'er, with patriarchal grace,
  The big *ha'-Bible*, ance his *Father*'s pride:
His bonnet rev'rently is laid aside,
  His *lyart haffets* wearing thin and bare;   105
Those strains that once did sweet in ZION glide,
  He wales a portion with judicious care;
'*And let us worship* GOD!' he says with solemn air.

XIII

They chant their artless notes in simple guise;
  They tune their hearts, by far the noblest aim: 110
Perhaps *Dundee*'s wild-warbling measures rise,
  Or plaintive *Martyrs*, worthy of the name;
Or noble *Elgin* beets the heaven-ward flame,
  The sweetest far of SCOTIA's holy lays:
Compar'd with these, *Italian trills* are tame;   115
  The tickl'd ears no heart-felt raptures raise;
Nae unison hae they, with our CREATOR's praise.

XIV

The priest-like Father reads the sacred page,
  How *Abram* was the Friend of GOD on high;
Or, *Moses* bade eternal warfare wage,   120
  With *Amalek*'s ungracious progeny;
Or how the *royal Bard* did groaning lye,
  Beneath the stroke of Heaven's avenging ire;
Or *Job*'s pathetic plaint, and wailing cry;
  Or rapt *Isiah*'s wild, seraphic fire;   125
Or other *Holy Seers* that tune the *sacred lyre*.

96 To] T *Eg*   98 The frugal] The thrifty *Eg*: Meanwhile the (*Ait*)   garrulous, will] garrulous 'll *Kil Eg*   100 chearfu'] social (*Ait*)   114 sweetest]
chiefest *Eg*

XV

Perhaps the *Christian Volume* is the theme;
  How *guiltless blood* for *guilty man* was shed;
How HE, who bore in Heaven the second name,
  Had not on Earth whereon to lay His head: 130
How His first *followers* and *servants* sped;
  The *Precepts sage* they wrote to many a land:
How *he*, who lone in *Patmos*, banished,
  Saw in the sun a mighty angel stand;
And heard great *Bab'lon*'s doom pronounc'd by Heaven's
    command.   135

XVI

Then kneeling down to HEAVEN'S ETERNAL KING,
  The *Saint*, the *Father*, and the *Husband* prays:
Hope 'springs exulting on triumphant wing,'*
  That *thus* they all shall meet in future days:
There, ever bask in *uncreated rays*,   140
  No more to sigh, or shed the bitter tear,
Together hymning their CREATOR'S praise
  In *such society*, yet still more dear;
While circling Time moves round in an eternal sphere.

XVII

Compar'd with this, how poor Religion's pride,   145
  In all the pomp of *method*, and of *art*,
When men display to congregations wide,
  Devotion's ev'ry grace, except the *heart*!
The POWER, incens'd, the Pageant will desert,
  The pompous strain, the sacredotal stole;   150
But haply, in some *Cottage* far apart,
  May hear, well pleas'd, the language of the *Soul*;
And in His *Book of Life* the Inmates poor enroll.

* Popes Windsor Forest.

---

132 The] What (*Ait*)   138 *Foot-note om. in Kil Eg*   141 or] nor *Kil Eg*

XVIII

Then homeward all take off their sev'ral way;
 The youngling *Cottagers* retire to rest: 155
The Parent-pair their *secret homage* pay,
 And proffer up to Heaven the warm request,
 That 'HE who stills the *raven*'s clam'rous nest,
 'And decks the *lily* fair in flow'ry pride,
 'Would, in the way His *Wisdom* sees the best, 160
 'For *them* and for their *little ones* provide;
'But chiefly, in their hearts with *Grace divine* preside.'

XIX

From Scenes like these, old SCOTIA's grandeur springs,
 That makes her lov'd at home, rever'd abroad:
Princes and lords are but the breath of kings, 165
 'An honest man's the noble work of GOD:'
And *certes*, in fair Virtue's heavenly road,
 The *Cottage* leaves the *Palace* far behind:
What is a lordling's pomp? a cumbrous load,
 Disguising oft the *wretch* of human kind, 170
Studied in arts of Hell, in wickedness refin'd!

XX

O SCOTIA! my dear, my native soil!
 For whom my warmest wish to Heaven is sent!
Long may thy hardy sons of *rustic toil*
 Be blest with health and peace and sweet content! 175
And O may Heaven their simple lives prevent
 From *Luxury*'s contagion, weak and vile!
Then howe'er *crowns* and *coronets* be rent,
 A *virtuous Populace* may rise the while,
And stand a wall of fire, around their much-lov'd ISLE. 180

XXI

O THOU! who pour'd the *patriotic tide*,
 That stream'd thro' great, unhappy WALLACE' heart;
Who dar'd to, nobly, stem tyrannic pride,
 Or *nobly die*, the second glorious part:

154 all take off their] each takes off his *Eg (Ait)* 166 noble] *later corrected*
to noblest *in Eg* 182 thro'] in *Kil*

(The Patriot's GOD, peculiarly thou art,   185
   His *friend, inspirer, guardian* and *reward!*)
O never, never SCOTIA's realm desert,
   But still the *Patriot*, and the *Patriot-bard*,
In bright succession raise, her *Ornament* and *Guard*!

THE following POEM will, by many Readers, be well enough
understood; but, for the sake of those who are unacquainted
with the manners and traditions of the country where the scene
is cast, Notes are added, to give some account of the principal
Charms and Spells of that Night, so big with Prophecy to the   [5]
Peasantry in the West of Scotland. The passion of prying into
Futurity makes a striking part of the history of Human-nature,
in it's rude state, in all ages and nations; and it may be some
entertainment to a philosophic mind, if any such should honor
the Author with a perusal, to see the remains of it, among the   [10]
more unenlightened in our own.

73. Halloween*

Yes! let the Rich deride, the Proud disdain,
The simple pleasures of the lowly train;
To me more dear, congenial to my heart,
One native charm, than all the gloss of art.
                               GOLDSMITH.

I

UPON that *night*, when Fairies light,
   On *Cassilis Downans*† dance,
Or owre the lays, in splendid blaze,
   On sprightly coursers prance;

---

* Is thought to be a night when Witches, Devils, and other mischief-making
beings, are all abroad on their baneful, midnight errands: particularly, those aerial
people, the Fairies, are said, on that night, to hold a grand Anniversary.

† Certain little, romantic, rocky, green hills, in the neighbourhood of the ancient
seat of the Earls of Cassilis.

Halloween. *Text from the edition of 1786, collated with the Alloway MS (Al; ll. 1–135),
the Kilmarnock MS (Kil; lines 147–252, with appended Notes on the preceding Poem),
and the editions of 1787, 1793, 1794. Al has the epigraph from Gray used in 72; and
lacks notes. Title in Al* Halloween.—A Scotch Poem.—*Kil has no note on* Halloween.

  2 *foot-note* ancient] *not in* Kil.   Kil *adds* famous in country-story for being the
haunt of Fairies.   3 in] with *Al*   4 sprightly] knightly *Al*

Or for *Colean*, the rout is taen,   5
    Beneath the moon's pale beams;
There, up the *Cove*,* to stray an' rove,
    Amang the rocks an' streams
            To sport that night.

II

Amang the bonie, winding banks,   10
    Where *Doon* rins, wimplin, clear,
Where BRUCE† ance rul'd the martial ranks,
    An' shook his *Carrick* spear,
Some merry, friendly, countra folks,
    Together did convene,   15
To *burn* their nits, an' *pou* their stocks,
    An' haud their *Halloween*
            Fu' blythe that night.

III

The lasses feat, an' cleanly neat,
    Mair braw than when they're fine;   20
Their faces blythe, fu' sweetly kythe,
    Hearts leal, an' warm, an' kin':
The lads sae trig, wi' wooer-babs,
    Weel knotted on their garten,
Some unco blate, an' some wi' gabs,   25
    Gar lasses hearts gang startin
            Whyles fast at night.

IV

Then, first an' foremost, thro' the kail,
    Their *stocks*‡ maun a' be sought ance;

---

* A noted cavern near Colean-house, called the Cove of Colean; which, as well as Cassilis Downans, is famed, in country story, for being a favourite haunt of Fairies.

† The famous family of that name, the ancestors of ROBERT the great Deliverer of his country, were Earls of Carrick.

‡ The first ceremony of Halloween, is, pulling each a *Stock*, or plant of kail. They must go out, hand in hand, with eyes shut, and pull the first they meet with: its being

---

7 *foot-note* which . . . Fairies.] said to be a kind of head-quarters of the Fairies, particularly on Halloween, which is allowed on all hands, to be the anniversary meeting of these aerial people. *Kil*   11 wimplin] wimplean *Al*   12 rul'd] rul't *Al*   20 braw than] sweet nor *Al*   23 sae trig] right sprush *Al* 29 *note in Kil:* STOCKS the first ceremony of Halloween is pulling, each, a plant, or

They steek their een, an' grape an' wale,   30
   For muckle anes, an' straught anes.
Poor hav'rel *Will* fell aff the drift,
   An' wander'd thro' the *Bow-kail*,
An' pow't, for want o' better shift,
   A *runt* was like a sow-tail   35
      Sae bow't that night.

V

Then, straught or crooked, yird or nane,
   They roar an' cry a' throw'ther;
The vera *wee-things*, toddlan, rin,
   Wi' stocks out owre their shouther: 40
An' gif the *custock*'s sweet or sour,
   Wi' joctelegs they taste them;
Syne coziely, aboon the door,
   Wi' cannie care, they've plac'd them
      To lye that night.   45

VI

The lasses staw frae 'mang them a',
   To pou their *stalks o' corn*;*
But *Rab* slips out, an' jinks about,
   Behint the muckle thorn:

big or little, straight or crooked, is prophetic of the size and shape of the grand object of all their Spells—the husband or wife. If any *yird*, or earth, stick to the root, that is *tocher*, or fortune; and the taste of the *custoc*, that is, the heart of the stem, is indicative of the natural temper and disposition. Lastly, the stems, or to give them their ordinary appellation, the *runts*, are placed somewhere above the head of the door; and the christian names of the people whom chance brings into the house, are, according to the priority of placing the *runts*, the names in question.

* They go to the barn-yard, and pull each, at three several times, a stalk of Oats. If the third stalk wants the *top-pickle*, that is, the grain at the top of the stalk, the party in question will come to the marriage-bed any thing but a Maid.

---

stock of kail—they go out with eyes shut, hand in hand, pull the first they meet with, according as it big or little, straight or crooked, so is the size or shape of the grand object in question—the HUSBAND or WIFE, the taste of the heart of the stem, or as it is called, the CUSTOCK, indicates the disposition, and lastly, the stems or runts are placed over the head of the door, and the names of the people whom chance brings into the house, according to the priority of placing the runts, are the NAMES in question.   33 wander'd] waunert *Al*   37 yird] lan' *Al*   39 toddlan] tottlean *Al*   43 Syne] Then *Al*   47 *foot-note* at three . . . Oats.] three corn stalks; *Kil*   If . . . the stalk,] if they want the top-grain or pickle, *Kil*   will come . . . but a Maid 87–94: wants the maidenhead *Ki* : will want the Maidenhead *86*

He grippet *Nelly* hard an' fast;   50
  Loud skirl'd a' the lasses;
But her *tap-pickle* maist was lost,
  When kiutlan in the *Fause-house**
    Wi' him that night.

VII

The auld Guidwife's weel-hoordet *nits*†   55
  Are round an' round divided,
An' monie lads an' lasses fates
  Are there that night decided:
Some kindle, couthie, side by side,
  An' *burn* thegither trimly;   60
Some start awa, wi' saucy pride,
  An' jump out owre the chimlie
    Fu' high that night.

VIII

Jean slips in twa, wi' tentie e'e;
  Wha 'twas, she wadna tell;   65
But this is *Jock*, an' this is *me*,
  She says in to hersel:
He bleez'd owre her, an' she owre him,
  As they wad never mair part,
Till fuff! he started up the lum,   70
  An' *Jean* had e'en a sair heart
    To see't that night.

---

* When the corn is in a doubtful state, by being too green, or wet, the Stack-builder, by means of old timber, &c. makes a large apartment in his stack, with an opening in the side which is fairest exposed to the wind: this he calls a *Fause-house*.
  † Burning the nuts is a favourite charm. They name the lad and lass to each particular nut, as they lay them in the fire; and according as they burn quietly together, or start from beside one another, the course and issue of the Courtship will be.

---

51 skirl'd] skirl't *Al*   53 kiutlan] kiuetlean *Al*   53 *note in Kil:* FAUSE HOUSE a large hole the stack-builder makes in the side which is fairest exposed to the wind, if the corn is in a doubtful state for greeness or wetness.   55 *foot-note* is a favourite . . . fire;] this is a favorite charm: they name the lad and lass to each particular nut, *Kil*   56–58 divided . . . decided] dividet . . . decidet *Al* 59 kindle] kain'le *Al*   67 to] till *Al*   70 fuff!] fizz—*Al*   started] startet *Al* 72 To] Tae *Al*

IX

Poor *Willie*, wi' his *bow-kail runt*,
  Was *brunt* wi' primsie *Mallie*;
An' *Mary*, nae doubt, took the drunt,   75
  To be compar'd to *Willie*:
Mall's nit lap out, wi' pridefu' fling,
  An' her ain fit, it brunt it;
While *Willie* lap, an' swoor by *jing*,
  'Twas just the way he wanted   80
            To be that night.

X

Nell had the *Fause-house* in her min',
  She pits hersel an' *Rob* in;
In loving bleeze they sweetly join,
  Till white in ase they're sobbin: 85
Nell's heart was dancin at the view;
  She whisper'd *Rob* to leuk for't;
Rob, stownlins, prie'd her bonie mou,
  Fu' cozie in the neuk for't,
            Unseen that night.   90

XI

But *Merran* sat behint their backs,
  Her thoughts on *Andrew Bell*;
She lea'es them gashan at their cracks,
  An' slips out by hersel:
She thro' the yard the nearest taks,   95
  An' for the *kiln* she goes then,
An' darklins grapet for the *bauks*,
  And in the *blue-clue** throws then,
            Right fear't that night.

* Whoever would, with success, try this spell, must strictly observe these directions. Steal out, all alone, to the *kiln*, and, darkling, throw into the *pot*, a clew of blue
yarn: wind it in a new clew off the old one; and towards the latter end, something
will hold the thread: demand, *wha hauds?* i.e. who holds? and answer will be returned
from the kiln-pot, by naming the christian and sirname of your future Spouse.

73 Poor] Puire *Al*   76 compar'd to] compar't wi' *Al*   85 ase] auss *Al*
86 dancin] dancean *Al*   88 prie'd ... mou] prie't ... mow *Al*   98 *note
in Kil:* BLEW CLEW they go, all alone and throw in to the pot, or bottom of

XII

An' ay she *win't*, an' ay she swat,   100
 I wat she made nae jaukin;
Till something *held* within the *pat*,
 Guid L——d! but she was quaukin!
But whether 'twas the *Deil* himsel,
 Or whether 'twas a *bauk-en*',   105
Or whether it was *Andrew Bell*,
 She did na wait on talkin
   To spier that night.

XIII

Wee Jenny to her Graunie says,
 'Will ye go wi' me Graunie?   110
'I'll *eat the apple** at the *glass*,
 'I gat frae uncle Johnie:'
She fuff't her pipe wi' sic a lunt,
 In wrath she was sae vap'rin,
She notic't na, an aizle brunt   115
 Her braw, new, worset apron
   Out thro' that night.

XIV

'Ye little Skelpie-limmer's-face!
 'I daur you try sic sportin,
'As seek the *foul Thief* onie place,   120
 'For him to spae your fortune:

---

* Take a candle, and go, alone, to a looking glass: eat an apple before it, and some traditions say you should comb your hair all the time: the face of your conjugal companion, *to be*, will be seen in the glass, as if peeping over your shoulder.

---

the kiln, a clue of blue yarn, they keep the end of the thread in their hand and wind the yarn in a new clue, off the old one which is in the pot—something will hold the thread towards the latter end—ask WHA HAUDS? answer is returned by naming the PERSON in question. 109 to] till *Al* 111 *note in Kil:* EAT THE APPLE they take a candle, and go to a looking-glass, and eat an apple, looking in the glass, the face of the husband or wife to be, is seen in the glass as if peeping over your shoulder. 114 vap'rin] vap'ran *Al*

'Nae doubt but ye may get a *sight*!
  'Great cause ye hae to fear it;
'For monie a ane has gotten a fright,
  'An' liv'd an' di'd deleeret,
          'On sic a night.   125

XV

'Ae Hairst afore the *Sherra-moor*,
  'I mind't as weel's yestreen,
'I was a gilpey then, I'm sure,
  'I was na past fyfteen: 130
'The Simmer had been cauld an' wat,
  'An' *Stuff* was unco green;
'An' ay a rantan *Kirn* we gat,
  'An' just on *Halloween*
          'It fell that night.   135

XVI

'Our *Stibble-rig* was *Rab M'Graen*,
  'A clever, sturdy fallow;
'His Sin gat *Eppie Sim* wi' wean,
  'That liv'd in Achmacalla:
'He gat *hemp-seed*,* I mind it weel,   140
  'An' he made unco light o't;
'But monie a day was *by himsel*,
  'He was sae sairly frighted
          'That vera night.'

---

* Steal out, unperceived, and sow a handful of hemp seed; harrowing it with any
thing you can conveniently draw after you. Repeat, now and then, 'Hemp seed I
saw thee, Hemp seed I saw thee; and him (or her) that is to be my true-love, come
after me and pou thee.' Look over your left shoulder, and you will see the appearance
of the person invoked, in the attitude of pulling hemp. Some traditions say, 'come
after me and shaw thee,' that is, show thyself; in which case it simply appears.
Others omit the harrowing, and say, 'come after me and harrow thee.'

---

125 liv'd an' di'd deleeret] liv't an' die't deliret *Al*   140 *foot-note* Steal
out . . . now and then,] HEMP-SEED take hemp-seed, steal out perceiv'd, sow it,
harrow it, and repeat the words *Kil*   Look] then look *Kil*   appearance]
exact figure *Kil*   invoked] desired *Kil*   Some traditions . . . thee.'] *Not
in Kil*

XVII

Then up gat fechtan *Jamie Fleck*,   145
    An' he swoor by his conscience,
That he could *saw hemp-seed* a peck;
    For it was a' but nonsense:
The auld guidman raught down the pock,
    An' out a handfu' gied him;   150
Syne bad him slip frae 'mang the folk,
    Sometime when nae ane see'd him,
            An' try't that night.

XVIII

He marches thro' amang the stacks,
    Tho' he was something sturtan;   155
The *graip* he for a *harrow* taks,
    An' haurls at his curpan:
And ev'ry now an' then, he says,
    'Hemp-seed I saw thee,
'An' her that is to be my lass,   160
    'Come after me an' draw thee
            'As fast this night.'

XIX

He whistl'd up *lord Lenox' march*,
    To keep his courage cheary;
Altho' his hair began to arch,   165
    He was sae fley'd an' eerie:
Till presently he hears a squeak,
    An' then a grane an' gruntle;
He by his showther gae a keek,
    An' tumbl'd wi' a wintle   170
            Out owre that night.

XX

He roar'd a horrid murder-shout,
    In dreadfu' desperation!
An' young an' auld come rinnan out,
    An' hear the sad narration: 175

151 slip] steal *Kil*

He swoor 'twas hilchan *Jean M'Craw*,
   Or crouchie *Merran Humphie*,
Till stop! she trotted thro' them a';
   An' wha was it but *Grumphie*
          Asteer that night?   180

XXI

Meg fain wad to the *Barn* gaen,
   To *winn three wechts o' naething*;*
But for to meet the Deil her lane,
   She pat but little faith in:
She gies the Herd a pickle nits,   185
   An' twa red cheeket apples,
To watch, while for the *Barn* she sets,
   In hopes to see *Tam Kipples*
          That vera night.

XXII

She turns the key, wi' cannie thraw,   190
   An' owre the threshold ventures;
But first on *Sawnie* gies a ca',
   Syne bauldly in she enters:
A *ratton* rattl'd up the wa',
   An' she cry'd, L—d preserve her!   195
An' ran thro' midden-hole an' a',
   An' pray'd wi' zeal and fervour,
          Fu' fast that night.

---

* This charm must likewise be performed, unperceived and alone. You go to the *barn*, and open both doors; taking them off the hinges, if possible; for there is danger, that the Being, about to appear, may shut the doors, and do you some mischief. Then take that instrument used in winnowing the corn, which, in our country-dialect, we call a *wecht*; and go thro' all the attitudes of letting down corn against the wind. Repeat it three times; and the third time, an apparition will pass thro' the barn, in at the windy door, and out at the other, having both the figure in question and the appearance or retinue, marking the employment or station in life.

---

182 *note in Kil:* THREE WECHT O' NAETHING go out, all alone, to the barn, open both the doors, take them off the hinges, otherwide the aerial being about to appear may shut the doors and do some mischief to you,—take a wecht and go thro all attitudes of letting down corn against the wind,—do this three times, the third time, a being will pass thro the barn, in at the windy door and out at the other, it will have the figure in question, with the dress and retinue marking the station of life.   188 *Kipples*] HIPPLES *Kil*   194 rattl'd] rappl't *Kil*

XXIII

They hoy't out Will, wi' sair advice;
    They hecht him some fine braw ane;   200
It chanc'd the *Stack* he *faddom't thrice,**
    Was timmer-propt for thrawin:
He taks a swirlie, auld *moss-oak,*
    For some black, grousome *Carlin*;
An' loot a winze, an' drew a stroke,   205
    Till skin in blypes cam haurlin
                Aff 's nieves that night.

XXIV

A wanton widow *Leezie* was,
    As cantie as a kittlen;
But Och! that night, amang the shaws,   210
    She gat a fearfu' settlin!
She thro' the whins, an' by the cairn,
    An' owre the hill gaed scrievin,
Whare *three Lairds' lan's met at a burn,*†
    To dip her *left sark-sleeve* in,   215
                Was bent that night.

XXV

Whyles owre a linn the burnie plays,
    As thro' the glen it wimpl't;
Whyles round a rocky scar it strays;
    Whyles in a wiel it dimpl't;   220

* Take an opportunity of going, unnoticed, to a *Bear-stack*, and fathom it three times round. The last fathom of the last time, you will catch in your arms, the appearance of your future conjugal yoke-fellow.

† You go out, one or more, for this is a social spell, to a south-running spring or rivulet, where 'three Lairds' lands meet,' and dip your left shirt-sleeve. Go to bed in sight of a fire, and hang your wet sleeve before it to dry. Ly awake; and sometime near midnight, an apparition, having the exact figure of the grand object in question, will come and turn the sleeve, as if to dry the other side of it.

---

201 *note in Kil:* FATHOM THE STACK go out and fathom three times round a bear stack, your last fathom, the third time, the desired object will be in your arms. 214 *note in Kil:* DIPPING THE SHIRT SLIEVE go out, one or more, to a south-running spring or burn, where three Laird's lands meet, dip your left shirt slieve, go to bed that night in view of a fire, hang your wet slieve over a stool before the fire to dry, lye awake and sometime in the night the object in question will come and turn the shirt before the fire as if to dry the other side of the slieve.

Whyles glitter'd to the nightly rays,
  Wi' bickerin, dancin dazzle;
Whyles cooket underneath the braes,
  Below the spreading hazle
          Unseen that night.   225

XXVI

Amang the brachens, on the brae,
  Between her an' the moon,
The Deil, or else an outler Quey,
  Gat up an' gae a croon:
Poor *Leezie*'s heart maist lap the hool;   230
  Near lav'rock-height she jumpet,
But mist a fit, an' in the *pool*,
  Out owre the lugs she plumpet,
          Wi' a plunge that night.

XXVII

In order, on the clean hearth-stane,   235
  The *Luggies** three are ranged;
And ev'ry time great care is taen,
  To see them duely changed:
Auld, uncle *John*, wha *wedlock's joys*,
  Sin' *Mar's-year* did desire,   240
Because he gat the toom dish thrice,
  He heav'd them on the fire,
          In wrath that night.

* Take three dishes; put clean water in one, foul water in another, and leave the third empty: blindfold a person, and lead him to the hearth where the dishes are ranged; he (or she) dips the left hand: if by chance in the clean water, the future husband or wife will come to the bar of Matrimony, a Maid; if in the foul, a widow; if in the empty dish, it foretells, with equal certainty, no marriage at all. It is repeated three times; and every time the arrangement of the dishes is altered.

---

228 outler] outlier *Kil*   236 *note in Kil:* LUGGIES THREE take three dishes, put foul water in one, clean water in another, and the third empty, blindfold a person and lead him to the hearth where the dishes must be placed, he (or she) dips a hand, if in the clean water, the husband or wife to be is a maid, if the foul, a widow, if the empty dishes, it fortells no marriage at all,—it is repeated three times.

XXVIII

Wi' merry sangs, an' friendly cracks,
    I wat they did na weary;   245
And unco tales, an' funnie jokes,
    Their sports were cheap an' cheary:
Till *butter'd So'ns,** wi' fragrant lunt,
    Set a' their gabs a steerin;
Syne, wi' a social glass o' strunt,   250
    They parted aff careerin
           Fu' blythe that night.

74. [The Mauchline Wedding]

I

WHEN Eighty-five was seven month auld,
    And wearing thro' the aught,
When rotting rains and Boreas bauld
    Gied farmer-folks a faught;
Ae morning quondam Mason Will,   5
    Now Merchant Master Miller,
Gaed down to meet wi' Nansie Bell
    And her Jamaica siller,
          To wed, that day.—

2

The rising sun o'er Blacksideen†   10
    Was just appearing fairly,
When Nell and Bess‡ get up to dress
    Seven lang half-hours o'er early!

---

* Sowens, with butter instead of milk to them, is always the *Halloween Supper*.
† a hill—   ‡ Miller's two sisters—

---

246 unco tales, an' funnie] mony funny tales an' *Kil*   248 *note in Kil as in*
86–94

The Mauchline Wedding. *Text from the Lochryan MS (letter to Mrs. Dunlop, 21 August 1788)*

Now presses clink and drawers jink,
   For linnens and for laces;   15
But modest Muses only *think*
   What ladies' under dress is,
      On sic a day.—

3

But we'll suppose the stays are lac'd,
   And bony bosom steekit;   20
Tho', thro' the lawn—but guess the rest—
   An Angel scarce durst keekit:
Then stockins fine, o' silken twine,
   Wi' cannie care are drawn up;
And gartened tight, whare mortal wight—   25

   .   .   .   .   .

      .   .   .   .

But now the gown wi' rustling sound,
   Its silken* pomp displays;
Sure there's no sin in being vain
   O' siccan bony claes!
Sae jimp the waist, the tail sae vast—   30
   Trouth, they were bony Birdies!
O Mither Eve, ye wad been grave
   To see their ample hurdies
      Sae large that day!!!

Then Sandy† wi's red jacket bra'   35
   Comes, whip-jee-whoa! about,
And in he gets the bony twa—
   Lord send them safely out!
And auld John‡ Trot wi' sober phiz
   As braid and bra's a Bailie,   40
His shouthers and his Sunday's giz
   Wi' powther and wi' ulzie
      Weel smear'd that day—

---

* The ladies' first silk gowns, got for the occasion
† Driver of the post chaise   ‡ M—'s father—

---

25 *Comment in MS*—As I never wrote it down, my recollection does not entirely serve me.—   43 *Comment in MS* Against my Muse had come thus far, Miss Bess and I were once more in Unison, so I thought no more of the Piece.—

75. The Auld Farmer's New-year-morning Salutation to his Auld Mare, Maggie, on giving her the accustomed ripp of corn to hansel in the New-year

A *Guid New-year* I wish thee, Maggie!
  Hae, there's a ripp to thy auld baggie:
Tho' thou's howe-backet, now, an' knaggie,
     I've seen the day,
Thou could hae gaen like ony staggie   5
     Out-owre the lay.

Tho' now thou's dowie, stiff an' crazy,
An' thy auld hide as white's a daisie,
I've seen thee dappl't, sleek an' glaizie,
     A bonie gray: 10
He should been tight that daur't to *raize* thee,
     Ance in a day.

Thou ance was i' the foremost rank,
A *filly* buirdly, steeve an' swank,
An' set weel down a shapely shank,   15
     As e'er tread yird;
An' could hae flown out-owre a stank,
     Like onie bird.

It's now some nine-an'-twenty year,
Sin' thou was my *Guidfather's Meere*;   20
He gied me thee, o' tocher clear,
     An' fifty mark;
Tho' it was sma', 'twas *weel-won* gear,
     An' thou was stark.

The Auld Farmer's . . . Salutation. *Text from the edition of 1786, collated with the Kilmarnock MS (Kil) and the editions of 1787, 1793, 1794*
  1 thee, *87–94*: you *Kil 86*   7–12 *om. here in Kil; given at the end*
6, 17 Out-owre *87–94*: Out owre *86*   17 flown] *correcting* gane *in Kil*
19 nine-an'-twenty year *87–94*: nine-an'-twenty-year *86*   20 *Guidfather's*]
Guidfather *Kil*   23 Tho' . . . 'twas] It was but sma', but *Kil*

When first I gaed to woo my *Jenny*,   25
Ye then was trottan wi' your Minnie:
Tho' ye was trickie, slee an' funnie,
    Ye ne'er was donsie;
But hamely, tawie, quiet an' cannie,
    An' unco sonsie.   30

That *day*, ye pranc'd wi' muckle pride,
When ye bure hame my bonie *Bride*:
An' sweet an' gracefu' she did ride
    Wi' maiden air!
Kyle-Stewart I could bragged wide,   35
    For sic a *pair*.

Tho' now ye dow but hoyte and hoble,
An' wintle like a saumont-coble,
That day, ye was a jinker noble,
    For heels an' win'!   40
An' ran them till they a' did wauble,
    Far, far behin'!

When thou an' I were young an' skiegh,
An' *Stable-meals* at Fairs were driegh,
How thou wad prance, an' snore, an' scriegh,   45
    An' tak the road!
Towns-bodies ran, an' stood abiegh,
    An' ca't thee mad.

When thou was corn't, an' I was mellow,
We took the road ay like a Swallow: 50
At *Brooses* thou had ne'er a fellow,
    For pith an' speed;
But ev'ry tail thou pay't them hollow,
    Whare'er thou gaed.

The sma', droop-rumpl't, hunter cattle,   55
Might aiblins waur't thee for a brattle;
But *sax Scotch mile*, thou try't their mettle,
    An' gart them whaizle:
Nae whip nor spur, but just a wattle
    O' saugh or hazle.   60

55 droop-rumpl't *87–94*: droot-rumpl't *Kil 86*   57 *mile*] miles *87–94*
56 aiblins waur't] may be wart *Kil*

Thou was a noble *Fittie-lan'*,
As e'er in tug or tow was drawn!
Aft thee an' I, in aught hours gaun,
      On guid March-weather,
Hae turn'd *sax rood* beside our han',   65
      For days thegither.

Thou never braing't, an' fetch't, an' flisket,
But thy *auld tail* thou wad hae whisket,
An' spread abreed thy weel-fill'd *brisket*,
      Wi' pith an' pow'r,   70
Till sprittie knowes wad rair't an' risket,
      An' slypet owre.

When frosts lay lang, an' snaws were deep,
An' threaten'd *labor* back to keep,
I gied thy *cog* a wee-bit heap   75
      Aboon the timmer;
I ken'd my *Maggie* wad na sleep
      For that, or Simmer.

In *cart* or *car* thou never reestet;
The steyest brae thou wad hae fac't it;   80
Thou never lap, an' sten't, an' breastet,
      Then stood to blaw;
But just thy step a wee thing hastet,
      Thou snoov't awa.

My Pleugh is now thy *bairn-time* a';   85
Four gallant brutes, as e'er did draw;
Forby sax mae, I've sell't awa,
      That thou hast nurst:
They drew me thretteen pund an' twa,
      The vera warst.   90

Monie a sair daurk we twa hae wrought,
An' wi' the weary warl' fought!
An' monie an *anxious day*, I thought
      We wad be beat!
Yet here to *crazy Age* we're brought,   95
      Wi' something yet.

65 *sax*] five *Kil*   93 an] an' 86   95 Yet] *corrected to* But *in Kil*

An' think na, my auld, trusty *Servan'*,
That now perhaps thou's less deservin,
An' thy *auld days* may end in starvin',
      For my last fow,   100
A heapet *Stimpart*, I'll reserve ane
      Laid by for you.

We've worn to crazy years thegither;
We'll toyte about wi' ane anither;
Wi' tentie care I'll flit thy tether,   105
      To some hain'd rig,
Whare ye may nobly rax your leather,
      Wi' sma' fatigue.

76. Address to the Deil

O Prince, O chief of many throned pow'rs,
That led th' embattl'd Seraphim to war—
                  MILTON.

O THOU, whatever title suit thee!
  Auld Hornie, Satan, Nick, or Clootie,
Wha in yon cavern grim an' sooty
      Clos'd under hatches,
Spairges about the brunstane cootie,   5
      To scaud poor wretches!

Hear me, *auld Hangie*, for a wee,
An' let poor, *damned bodies* bee;
I'm sure sma' pleasure it can gie,
      Ev'n to a *deil*,   10
To skelp an' scaud poor dogs like me,
      An' hear us squeel!

103 thegither] wi' ither *Kil*   106–8 To some . . . fatigue.] *Kil has*
                        An' clap thy back,
            An' mind the days we've haen the gither,
                    An' ca' the crack.

Address to the Deil. *Text from the Irvine MS (I), collated with the Kilmarnock MS*
(Kil) and the editions of 1786, 1787, 1793, 1794
  9 pleasure] comfort *Kil*

Great is thy pow'r, an' great thy fame;
Far ken'd, an' noted is thy name;
An' tho' yon *lowan heugh*'s thy hame,   15
    Thou travels far;
An' faith! thou's neither lag nor lame,
      Nor blate nor scaur.

Whyles, ranging like a roaring lion,
For prey, a' holes an' corners tryin;   20
Whyles, on the strong-wing'd Tempest flyin,
    Tirlan the *kirks*;
Whyles, in the human bosom pryin,
      Unseen thou lurks.

I've heard my rev'rend *Graunie* say,   25
In lanely glens ye like to stray;
Or where auld, ruin'd castles, gray,
    Nod to the moon,
Ye fright the nightly wand'rer's way,
      Wi' eldritch croon.   30

When twilight did my *Graunie* summon,
To say her pray'rs, douse, honest woman,
Aft 'yont the dyke she's heard you bumman,
    Wi' eerie drone;
Or, rustling, thro' the boortries coman,   35
      Wi' heavy groan.

Ae dreary, windy, winter night,
The stars shot down wi' sklentan light,
Wi' you, *mysel*, I gat a fright
    Ayont the lough;   40
Ye, like a *rash-buss*, stood in sight,
      Wi' waving sugh:

The cudgel in my nieve did shake,
Each bristl'd hair stood like a stake,

---

15 *lowan heugh*'s] howe, het hole's *Kil*   27 auld, ruin'd] auld-ruin'd *94*
37 windy] dowie *Kil*   44 Each] Ilk *Kil*

When wi' an eldritch, stoor *quaick, quaick,*   45
    Amang the springs,
Awa ye squatter'd like a *drake,*
    On whistling wings.

Let *Warlocks* grim, an' wither'd *Hags,*
Tell, how wi' you, on ragweed nags,   50
They skim the muirs an' dizzy crags,
    Wi' wicked speed;
And in kirk-yards renew their leagues,
    Owre howcket dead.

Thence, countra wives, wi' toil an' pain,   55
May plunge an' plunge the *kirn* in vain;
For Och! the yellow treasure's taen,
    By witching skill;
An' dawtit, twal-pint *Hawkie*'s gane
    As yell's the Bill.   60

Thence, mystic knots mak great abuse,
On *Young-Guidmen,* fond, keen an' croose;
When the best *warklum* i' the house,
    By cantraip wit,
Is instant made no worth a louse,   65
    Just at the bit.

When thowes dissolve the snawy hoord,
An' float the jinglan icy boord,
Then, *Water-kelpies* haunt the foord,
    By your direction,   70
An' nighted Trav'llers are allur'd
    To their destruction.

---

57 Och *MSS*: Oh *86–94*   58 witching] wicket *correcting* cantraip *in Kil*
61–66 Thence . . . bit.] *Given at the end in Kil to replace a cancelled stanza:*

    Thence, knots are coosten, spells contriv'd,
    An' the brisk bridegroom, newly wiv'd
    Just at the kittle point arriv'd,
        Fond, keen, an' croose,
    Is by some spitefu' jad depriv'd
        O 's warklum's use.

61 mak] *correcting* breed *in I:* breed *Kil*   65 instant . . . worth] made as
useless as *Kil*   68 icy boord] icy-boord *87–94*   69 haunt] *correcting* ply *in
Kil*   71 nighted] nightly *Kil*

An' aft your moss-traversing *Spunkies*
Decoy the wight that late an' drunk is:
The bleezan, curst, mischievous monkies   75
      Delude his eyes,
Till in some miry slough he sunk is,
      Ne'er mair to rise.

When MASONS' mystic *word* an' *grip*,
In storms an' tempests raise you up,   80
Some cock, or cat, your rage maun stop,
      Or, strange to tell!
The *youngest Brother* ye wad whip
      Aff straught to *H–ll*.

Lang syne in *Eden*'s bonie yard,   85
When youthfu' lovers first were pair'd,
An' all the Soul of Love they shar'd,
      The raptur'd hour,
Sweet on the fragrant, flow'ry swaird,
      In shady bow'r: 90

Then you, ye auld, snick-drawing dog!
Ye cam to Paradise incog,
An' play'd on man a cursed brogue,
      (Black be your fa'!)
An' gied the infant warld a shog,   95
      'Maist ruin'd a'.

D'ye mind that day, when in a bizz,
Wi' reeket duds, an' reestet gizz,
Ye did present your smoutie phiz
      'Mang better folk,   100
An' sklented on the *man of Uz*
      Your spitefu' joke?

75 bleezan] dancin *Kil*   79 MASONS' 86: MASON'S *MSS*: Masons 87–94
85–90 Lang . . . bow'r:] *Given at the end in Kil to replace a cancelled stanza:*
          Langsyne, in Eden's happy scene,
          When strappin Edie's days were green,
          An' Eve was like my bonie Jean,
              My dearest part,
       A dancin, sweet, young, handsome quean
            Wi' guileless heart:

99 smoutie] ugly *Kil*   101 *Uz*] *correcting Uzz in I: Uzz Kil 86–94*

An' how ye gat him i' your thrall,
An' brak him out o' house an' hal',
While scabs an' botches did him gall,   105
     Wi' bitter claw,
An' lows'd his ill-tongu'd, wicked *Scawl*
     Was warst ava?

But a' your doings to rehearse,
Your wily snares an' fechtin fierce,   110
Sin' that day *MICHAEL did you pierce,
     Down to this time,
Wad ding a' *Lallan* tongue, or *Erse*,
     In Prose or Rhyme.

An' now, auld *Cloots*, I ken ye're thinkan,   115
A certain *Bardie*'s rantin, drinkin,
Some luckless hour will send him linkan,
     To your black pit;
But faith! he'll turn a corner jinkan,
     An' cheat you yet.   120

But fare you weel, auld *Nickie-ben*!
O wad ye tak a thought an' men'!
Ye aiblins might—I dinna ken—
     Still hae a *stake*—
I'm wae to think upo' yon den,   125
     Ev'n for your sake.

* Vide Milton, Book 6th

---

116 A certain *Bardie*'s rantin,] That Robin's rantin, swearin, *Kil*   117 hour
will] hour'll *Kil*

77. Scotch Drink

Gie him strong Drink *until he wink,*
That's sinking in despair;
An' liquor *guid, to fire his bluid,*
    That's prest wi' grief an' care:
There let him bowse an' deep carouse,   5
    Wi' bumpers flowing o'er,
Till he forgets his loves *or* debts,
    An' minds his griefs no more.

                    Solomon's Proverbs, Ch. 31st V. 6, 7.

LET other Poets raise a fracas
    'Bout vines, an' wines, an' druken *Bacchus,*
An' crabbed names an' stories wrack us,
            An' grate our lug,
I sing the juice *Scotch bear* can mak us,   5
            In glass or jug.

O thou, my MUSE! guid, auld SCOTCH DRINK!
Whether thro' wimplin worms thou jink,
Or, richly brown, ream owre the brink,
            In glorious faem,   10
Inspire me, till I *lisp* an' *wink,*
            To sing thy name!

Let husky Wheat the haughs adorn,
And Aits set up their awnie horn,
An' Pease an' Beans, at een or morn,   15
            Perfume the plain,
Leeze me on thee *John Barleycorn,*
            Thou king o' grain!

On thee aft Scotland chows her cood,
In souple scones, the wale o' food!   20
Or tumbling in the boiling flood
            Wi' kail an' beef;
But when thou pours thy strong *heart's blood,*
            There thou shines chief.

Scotch Drink. *Text from the Irvine MS (I), collated with the Kilmarnock MS (Kil)*
and the editions of 1786, 1787, 1793, 1794
    Epigraph. 2, 4 *That's*] Wha's *Kil*   4 *an'*] correcting or *in Kil*   5 *him . . .*
an'] correcting them . . . wi' *in Kil*   7 or *Kil* 86-94: an' *I*

Food fills the wame, an' keeps us livin: 25
Tho' life's a gift no worth receivin,
When heavy-dragg'd wi' pine an' grievin;
   But oil'd by thee,
The wheels o' life gae down-hill, scrievin,
   Wi' rattlin glee.   30

Thou clears the head o' doited Lear;
Thou chears the heart o' drooping Care;
Thou strings the nerves o' Labor-sair,
   At's weary toil;
Thou ev'n brightens dark Despair,   35
   Wi' gloomy smile.

Aft, clad in massy, siller weed,
Wi' Gentles thou erects thy head;
Yet, humbly kind, in time o' need,
   The *poorman*'s wine,   40
His wee drap pirratch, or his bread,
   Thou kitchens fine.

Thou art the life o' public haunts;
But thee, what were our fairs an' rants?
Ev'n godly meetings o' the saunts,   45
   By thee inspir'd,
When gaping they besiege the *tents*,
   Are doubly fir'd.

That *merry night* we get the corn in,
O sweetly, then, thou reams the horn in!   50
Or reekan on a *New-year-mornin*
   In cog or bicker,
An' just a wee drap *sp'ritual burn* in,
   An' *gusty sucker*!

When Vulcan gies his bellys breath,   55
An' Ploughmen gather wi' their graith,
O rare! to see thee fizz an' fraeth
   I' the lugget caup!
Then *Burnewin* comes on like Death,
   At ev'ry chap.   60

26 Tho'] *correcting* But *in I*: But *Kil* 41 pirratch] parritch *87–94*

Nae mercy, then, for airn *or* steel;
The brawnie, banie, Ploughman-chiel
Brings hard owrehip, wi' sturdy wheel,
   The strong forehammer,
Till block an' studdie ring an' reel   65
   Wi' dinsome clamour.

When skirlin weanies see the light,
Thou maks the gossips clatter bright,
How fumbling coofs their dearies slight,
   Wae worth the name!   70
Nae Howdie gets a social night,
   Or plack frae them.

When neebors anger at a plea,
An' just as wud as wud can be,
How easy can the *barley-bree*   75
   Cement the quarrel!
It's ay the cheapest Lawyer's fee
   To taste the barrel.

Alake! that e'er my *Muse* has reason
To wyte her countrymen wi' treason!   80
But mony daily weet their weason
   Wi' liquors nice,
An' hardly, in a winter season,
   E'er spier her price.

Wae worth that *Brandy*, burnan trash!   85
Fell source o' monie a pain an' brash!
Twins mony a poor, doylt, druken hash
   O' half his days;
An' sends, beside, auld *Scotland*'s cash
   To her warst faes.   90

70–72 Wae . . . them. 87–94: *MSS and 86 have*
   Wae worth them for 't,
 While healths gae round to him wha, *tight*,
   Gies famous sport.
83 winter] winter's *94*

Ye Scots wha wish auld Scotland well,
Ye chief, to you my tale I tell,
Poor, plackless devils like *mysel*,
            It sets you ill,
Wi' bitter, dearthfu' *wines* to mell,   95
            Or *foreign gill*.

May *Gravels* round his blather wrench,
An' *Gouts* torment him, inch by inch,
Wha twists his gruntle wi' a glunch
            O' sour disdain,   100
Out owre a glass o' *Whisky-punch*
            Wi' honest men!

O *Whisky*! soul o' plays an' pranks!
Accept a *Bardie*'s gratefu' thanks!
When wanting thee, what tuneless cranks   105
            Are my poor Verses!
Thou comes—they rattle i' their ranks
            At ither's arses!

Thee, *Ferintosh*! O sadly lost!
Scotland lament frae coast to coast!   110
Now colic-grips, an' barkin hoast,
            May kill us a';
For loyal *Forbes' Charter'd boast*
            Is taen awa!

Thae curst horse-leeches o' th' Excise,   115
Wha mak the *Whisky stills* their prize!
Haud up thy han' *Deil*! ance, twice, thrice!
            There, sieze the blinkers!
An' bake them up in brunstane pies
            For poor damn'd *Drinkers*.   120

Fortune, if thou'll but gie me still
Hale breeks, a scone, an' *Whisky gill*,
An' rowth o' *rhyme* to rave at will,
            Tak a' the rest,
An' deal 't about as thy blind skill   125
            Directs thee best.

104 gratefu'] humble 94   115–20 Thae . . . *Drinkers*.] *om. Kil; marked* A
verse wanting, *and supplied later in the MS*

78. Brose and Butter

JENNY sits up i' the laft,
    Jockie wad fain a been at her;
But there cam a wind out o' the west
    Made a' the winnocks to clatter.

O gie my love brose, lasses;   5
    O gie my love brose and butter;
For nane in Carrick wi' him
    Can gie a c——t its supper.

The laverock lo'es the grass,
    The paetrick lo'es the stibble: 10
And hey, for the gardiner lad,
    To gully awa wi' his dibble!
    O gie, &c.

My daddie sent me to the hill
    To pu' my minnie some heather;
An' drive it in your fill,   15
    Ye're welcome to the leather.
    O gie, &c.

The Mouse is a merry wee beast,
    The Moudiewart wants the een;
And O' for a touch o' the thing
    I had in my nieve yestreen.   20
    O gie, &c.

Brose and Butter. *Text from MMC (pp. 38–39), collated with the Adam MS (verso o
a draft letter to Margaret Kennedy, autumn 1785). Sequence in MS: ll. 5–8, 1–4, a
stanza not in MMC, 13–20, 9–12. MS lacks ll. 21–24. After l. 4 it has*

> A dow 's a dainty dish;
>   A goose is hollow within;
> A sight wad mak you blush,
>   But a' the fun 's to fin'.

3 But] *om. MS*   4 winnocks] windows *MS*   5 O gie . . . lasses] Gie . . .
brose *MS*   7–8 For . . . supper.] *MS has*

> An' gie my Love brose, brose,
>   Yestreen he wanted his supper.

9 laverock lo'es] lark she loves *MS*   10 paetrick lo'es] hen she loves *MS*
17, 18 The] A *MS*   wee *MS*: wi' *MMC*   19 a] the *MS*

We a' were fou yestreen,
 The night shall be its brither;
And hey, for a roaring pin
 To nail twa wames thegither!
  O gie, &c.

79. To J. S****

Friendship, mysterious cement of the soul!
Sweet'ner of Life, and solder of Society!
I owe thee much—

         BLAIR.

D EAR S****, the sleest, pawkie thief,
 That e'er attempted stealth or rief,
Ye surely hae some warlock-breef
  Owre human hearts;
For ne'er a bosom yet was prief   5
  Against your arts.

For me, I swear by sun an' moon,
And ev'ry star that blinks aboon,
Ye've cost me twenty pair o' shoon
  Just gaun to see you;   10
And ev'ry ither pair that's done,
  Mair taen I'm wi' you.

That auld, capricious carlin, *Nature*,
To mak amends for scrimpet stature,
She's turn'd you off, a human-creature   15
  On her *first* plan,
And in her freaks, on ev'ry feature,
  She's wrote, *the Man*.

*To J. S****. Text from the edition of 1786, collated with the Kilmarnock MS (Kil)
and the editions of 1787, 1793, 1794. Title in Kil* Address to J. Smith; *epigraph*
Friendship! mysterious cement of &c. *added later*
 1 S****] Smith *Kil*   7–12 For . . . you.] *om. here in Kil and added at the
end of the MS* 13–18 That . . . Man.] *not in Kil*

Just now I've taen the fit o' rhyme,
My barmie noddle's working prime,
My fancy yerket up sublime
   Wi' hasty summon:
Hae ye a leisure-moment's time
   To hear what 's comin?

Some rhyme a neebor's name to lash;
Some rhyme, (vain thought!) for needfu' cash;
Some rhyme to court the countra clash,
   An' raise a din;
For me, an *aim* I never fash;
   I rhyme for *fun*.

The star that rules my luckless lot,
Has fated me the russet coat,
An' damn'd my fortune to the groat;
   But, in requit,
Has blest me with a *random-shot*
   O' countra wit.

This while my notion's taen a sklent,
To try my fate in guid, black *prent*;
But still the mair I'm that way bent,
   Something cries, 'Hoolie!
'I red you, honest man, tak tent!
   Ye'll shaw your folly.

'There's ither Poets, much your betters,
'Far seen in *Greek*, deep men o' *letters*,
'Hae thought they had ensur'd their debtors,
   'A' future ages;
'Now moths deform in shapeless tatters,
   'Their unknown pages.'

20

25

30

35

40

45

23 Hae ye a leisure-moment's *correcting* Will ye lay-bye a wee whyles *in Kil*
24 To] An' *Kil* 25-30 Some . . . *fun*.] *Given in Kil at the end of the MS to replace a cancelled stanza:*
     Some rhyme because they like to clash,
     An' gie a neebor's name a lash;
     An' some (vain thought) for needfu' cash;
       An' some for fame;
     For me, I string my dogg'rel trash
       For fun at hame.

47 tatters] *om. Kil*

Then farewel hopes of Laurel-boughs,
To garland my poetic brows!   50
Henceforth, I'll rove where busy ploughs
⠀⠀⠀⠀Are whistling thrang,
An' teach the lanely heights an' howes
⠀⠀⠀⠀My rustic sang.

I'll wander on with tentless heed,   55
How never-halting moments speed,
Till fate shall snap the brittle thread;
⠀⠀⠀⠀Then, all unknown,
I'll lay me with th' *inglorious dead*,
⠀⠀⠀⠀Forgot and gone!   60

But why, o' Death, begin a tale?
Just now we're living sound an' hale;
Then top and maintop croud the sail,
⠀⠀⠀⠀Heave *Care* o'er-side!
And large, before Enjoyment's gale,   65
⠀⠀⠀⠀Let's tak the tide.

This life, sae far's I understand,
Is a' enchanted fairy-land,
Where Pleasure is the Magic-wand,
⠀⠀⠀⠀That, wielded right,   70
Maks Hours like Minutes, hand in hand,
⠀⠀⠀⠀Dance by fu' light.

The *magic-wand* then let us wield;
For, ance that five an' forty's speel'd,
See, crazy, weary, joyless Eild,   75
⠀⠀⠀⠀Wi' wrinkl'd face,
Comes hostan, hirplan owre the field,
⠀⠀⠀⠀Wi' creeping pace.

---

53 teach] tell *Kil*⠀⠀⠀⠀62 we're] I'm *Kil*⠀⠀⠀⠀63 croud] *correcting* hoist *in Kil*
64 Heave *Care* o'er-side] *correcting* All hands aloft *in Kil*⠀⠀⠀⠀66 tak the tide]
correcting send adrift *in Kil*

When ance *life's day* draws near the gloamin,
Then fareweel vacant, careless roamin;   80
An' fareweel chearfu' tankards foamin,
      An' social noise;
An' fareweel dear, deluding woman,
      The joy of joys!

O *Life*! how pleasant in thy morning,   85
Young Fancy's rays the hills adorning!
Cold-pausing Caution's lesson scorning,
      We frisk away,
Like school-boys, at th' expected warning,
      To joy and play.   90

We wander there, we wander here,
We eye the *rose* upon the brier,
Unmindful that the *thorn* is near,
      Among the leaves;
And tho' the puny wound appear,   95
      Short while it grieves.

Some, lucky, find a flow'ry spot,
For which they never toil'd nor swat;
They drink the *sweet* and eat the *fat*,
      But care or pain;   100
And haply, eye the barren hut,
      With high disdain.

With steady aim, some Fortune chase;
Keen hope does ev'ry sinew brace;
Thro' fair, thro' foul, they urge the race,   105
      And sieze the prey:
Then canie, in some cozie place,
      They close the *day*.

83 deluding] bewitching *Kil*   97 spot] spat *Kil*   101 And . . . barren]
And eye the barren, hungry *Kil*   107 canie, in some cozie] cozie, in some
canie *Kil*

And others, like your humble servan',
Poor wights! nae rules nor roads observin;   110
To right or left, eternal swervin,
    They zig-zag on;
Till curst with Age, obscure an' starvin,
    They aften groan.

Alas! what bitter toil an' straining—   115
But truce with peevish, poor complaining!
Is Fortune's fickle *Luna* waning?
    E'en let her gang!
Beneath what light she has remaining,
    Let's sing our Sang.   120

My pen I here fling to the door,
And kneel, ye *Pow'rs*, and warm implore,
'Tho' I should wander *Terra* o'er,
    'In all her climes,
'Grant me but this, I ask no more,   125
    'Ay rowth o' rhymes.

'Gie dreeping roasts to *countra Lairds*,
'Till icicles hing frae their beards;
'Gie fine braw claes to fine *Life-guards*,
    'And *Maids of Honor*;   130
'And yill an' whisky gie to *Cairds*,
    'Until they sconner.

'A *Title*, DEMPSTER merits it;
'A *Garter* gie to WILLIE PIT;
'Gie Wealth to some be-ledger'd Cit,   135
    'In cent per cent;
'But give me real, sterling Wit,
    'And I'm content.

'While ye are pleas'd to keep me hale,
'I'll sit down o'er my scanty meal,   140

122 ye *Pow'rs, Kil*: 'Ye *Pow'rs*, 86: 'Ye Pow'rs! 87–94 134 A *Garter* gie]
correcting Honor, gie that *in Kil* 135 Gie Wealth ... Cit] *correcting* If he goes
on to merit it *in Kil* 139 ye] you *Kil*

'Be't *water-brose*, or *muslin-kail*,
          'Wi' chearfu' face,
'As lang's the Muses dinna fail
          'To say the grace.'

An anxious e'e I never throws   145
Behint my lug, or by my nose;
I jouk beneath Misfortune's blows
          As weel's I may;
Sworn foe to *sorrow*, *care*, and *prose*,
          I rhyme away.   150

O ye, douse folk, that live by rule,
Grave, tideless-blooded, calm and cool,
Compar'd wi' you—O fool! fool! fool!
          How much unlike!
Your hearts are just a standing pool,   155
          Your lives, a dyke!

Nae hare-brain'd, sentimental traces,
In your unletter'd, nameless faces!
In *arioso* trills and graces
          Ye never stray,   160
But *gravissimo*, solemn basses
          Ye hum away.

Ye are sae *grave*, nae doubt ye're *wise*;
Nae ferly tho' ye do despise
The hairum-scairum, ram-stam boys,   165
          The rattling squad:
I see ye upward cast your eyes—
          —Ye ken the road—

Whilst I—but I shall haud me there—
Wi' you I'll scarce gang *ony where*—   170
Then *Jamie*, I shall say nae mair,
          But quat my sang,
Content *with* You to mak a *pair*,
          Whare'er I gang.

151 douse folk, that] guid folk wha *Kil*   155 hearts] *correcting* lives *in Kil*
157 hare-brain'd] hair-brain'd *87–94*   166 rattling *87–94*: rantin *Kil*: rambling *86*

80. The rantin dog the Daddie o't

Whar'll bonny Annie lie

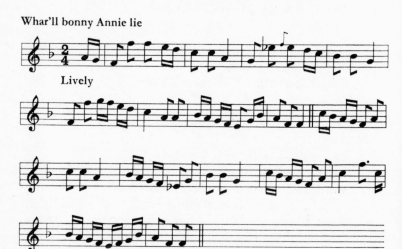

Lively

O Wha my babie-clouts will buy,
O Wha will tent me when I cry;
Wha will kiss me where I lie,
The rantin dog the daddie o't.

O Wha will own he did the faut,   5
O Wha will buy the groanin maut,
O Wha will tell me how to ca't,
The rantin dog the daddie o't.

When I mount the Creepie-chair,
Wha will sit beside me there,   10
Gie me Rob, I'll seek nae mair,
The rantin dog the Daddie o't.

Wha will crack to me my lane;
Wha will mak me fidgin fain;
Wha will kiss me o'er again,   15
The rantin dog the Daddie o't.

The rantin dog the Daddie o't. *Text from SMM, 1790 (277; signed Z)*

81. The Author's Earnest Cry and Prayer*, to the Right Honorable and Honorable, the Scotch Representatives in the House of Commons

> *Dearest of Distillation! last and best!—*
> *—How art thou lost!—*
> Parody on Milton.

Ye Irish Lords, ye *knights* an' *squires*,
  Wha represent our Brughs an' Shires,
An' dousely manage our affairs
      In *Parliament*,
To you a simple Bardie's pray'rs   5
      Are humbly sent.

Alas! my roupet *Muse* is haerse!
Your Honors' hearts wi' grief 'twad pierce,
To see her sittan on her arse
      Low i' the dust,   10
An' scriechan out prosaic verse,
      An' like to brust!

Tell them wha hae the chief direction,
Scotland and *me*'s in great affliction,
E'er sin' they laid that curst restriction   15
      On Aquavitæ;
An' rouse them up to strong conviction,
      An' move their pity.

* This was wrote before the Act anent the Scotch Distilleries, of session 1786; for which Scotland and the Author return their most grateful thanks.

The Author's Earnest Cry and Prayer. *Text from the Irvine MS, collated with the Kilmarnock MS (Kil) and the editions of 1786, 1787, 1793 (HL; copy with holograph corrections in the Huntington Library), 1794. Foot-note to title added in 87–94. Title to the Right . . . Honorable, deleted in HL*
  5 Bardie's] Poet's HL 94   8 Honors' hearts] Honor's hearts MSS 86 87: Honors heart 93 94

Stand forth and tell yon PREMIER YOUTH
The honest, open, naked truth;   20
Tell him o' mine an' Scotland's drouth,
          His servants humble:
The muckle devil blaw you south,
          If ye dissemble!

Does ony *great man* glunch an' gloom?   25
Speak out an' never fash your thumb!
Let *posts* an' *pensions* sink or swoom
          Wi' them wha grant them:
If honestly they canna come,
          Far better want them.   30

In gath'rin votes ye were na slack,
Now stand as tightly by your tack:
Ne'er claw your lug, an' fidge your back,
          An' hum an' haw,
But raise your arm, an' tell your crack   35
          Before them a'.

Paint Scotland greetan owre her thrissle;
Her *mutchkin stowp* as toom's a whissle;
An' damn'd Excise-men in a bussle,
          Seizan a *Stell*,   40
Triumphant crushan't like a muscle
          Or laimpet shell.

Then on the tither hand present her,
A blackguard *Smuggler*, right behint her,
An', cheek-for-chow, a chuffie *Vintner*,   45
          Colleaguing join,—
Picking her pouch as bare as Winter,
          Of a' kind coin.

Is there, that bears the name o' SCOT,
But feels his heart's bluid rising hot,   50
To see his poor, auld Mither's *pot*,
          Thus dung in staves;
An' plunder'd o' her hindmost groat,
          By gallows knaves?

31 In . . . were] At . . . was *Kil*

Alas! I'm but a nameless wight,   55
Trode i' the mire out o' sight!
But could I like MONTGOMERIES fight,
            Or gab like BOSWEL,
There's some *sark-necks* I wad *draw* tight,
            An' *tye* some *hose* well.   60

God bless your Honors, can ye see't,
The kind, auld, cantie Carlin greet,
An' no get warmly to your feet,
            An' gar them hear it,
An' tell them, wi' a patriot-heat,   65
            Ye winna bear it?

Some o' you nicely ken the laws,
To round the period an' pause,
An' with rhetoric clause on clause
            To mak harangues;   70
Then echo thro' Saint Stephen's wa's
            Auld Scotland's wrangs.

Dempster, a true-blue Scot I'se warran;
Thee, aith-detesting, chaste *Kilkerran*;
An' that glib-gabbet Highlan Baron,   75
            The Laird o' *Graham*;
And ane, a chap that's damn'd auldfarran,
            Dundass his name.

Erskine, a spunkie norland billie;
True Campbels, *Frederic* an' *Ilay*;   80
An' Livistone, the bauld *Sir Willie*;
            An' mony ithers,
Whom auld Demosthenes or Tully
            Might own for brithers.

84 *Cancelled stanza follows in Kil:*
            Thee Sodger Hugh—my watchman stented,
            If Bardies e'er are represented;
            I ken if that your sword were wanted
                        Ye'd lend your hand,
            But when there's ought to say anent it,
                        Ye're at a stand.

Arouse my boys! exert your mettle,   85
To get auld Scotland back her *kettle*!
Or faith! I'll wad my new pleugh-pettle,
          Ye'll see't or lang,
She'll teach you, wi' a reekan whittle,
          Anither sang.   90

This while she's been in crankous mood,
Her *lost Militia* fir'd her bluid;
(Deil na they never mair do guid,
          Play'd her that pliskie!)
An' now she's like to rin red-wud   95
          About her *Whisky*.

An' L—d! if ance they pit her till 't,
Her tartan petticoat she'll kilt
An' durk an' pistol at her belt,
          She'll tak the streets,   100
An' rin her whittle to the hilt,
          I' th' first she meets!

For G—d-sake, Sirs! then speak her fair,
An' straik her cannie wi' the hair,
An' to the *muckle house* repair,   105
          Wi' instant speed,
An' strive, wi' a' your Wit an' Lear,
          To get remead.

Yon ill-tongu'd tinkler, *Charlie Fox*,
May taunt you wi' his jeers an' mocks;   110
But gie him 't het, my hearty cocks!
          E'en cowe the cadie!
An' send him to his dicing box,
          An' sportin lady.

Tell yon guid bluid of auld *Boconnock*'s,   115
I'll be his debt twa mashlum bonnocks,

85 Arouse] Rouse up *Kil*   86 auld Scotland] *correcting* your Mither *in Kil*
93 na] nor *Kil*

An' drink his health in auld *Nanse Tinnock's
   Nine times a week,
If he some scheme, like tea an' winnocks,
   Wad kindly seek.   120

Could he some *commutation* broach,
I'll pledge my aith in guid braid Scotch,
He need na fear their foul reproach
   Nor erudition,
Yon mixtie-maxtie, queer hotch-potch, 125
   The *Coalition*.

Auld Scotland has a raucle tongue;
She's just a devil wi' a rung;
An' if she promise auld or young
   To tak their part,   130
Tho' by the neck she should be strung,
   She'll no desert.

And now, ye chosen FIVE AND FORTY,
May still your Mither's heart support ye;
Then tho' a *Minister* grow dorty,   135
   An' kick your place,
Ye'll snap your fingers, poor an' hearty,
   Before his face.

God bless your Honors, a' your days,
Wi' sowps o' kail an' brats o' claise,   140
In spite of a' the thievish kaes
   That haunt St. *Jamie's*!
Your humble Bardie sings an' prays
   While *Rab* his name is.

* A worthy old Hostess of the Author's in *Mauchline*, where he sometimes
studies Politics over a glass of guid auld *Scotch Drink*.

---

143 Bardie] Poet *HL 94*

Postscript

Let half-starv'd slaves in warmer skies,   145
See future wines, rich-clust'ring, rise;
Their lot auld Scotland ne'er envies,
   But blyth an' frisky,
She eyes her freeborn, martial boys,
   Tak aff their Whisky.   150

What tho' their Phebus kinder warms,
While Fragrance blooms and Beauty charms!
When wretches range, in famish'd swarms,
   The scented groves,
Or hounded forth, *dishonor* arms,   155
   In hungry droves.

Their *gun*'s a burden on their shouther;
They downa bide the stink o' *powther*;
Their bauldest thought's a hank'ring swither,
   To stan' or rin,   160
Till skelp—a shot—they're aff, a' throu'ther,
   To save their skin.

But bring a SCOTCHMAN frae his hill,
Clap in his cheek a *highlan gill*,
Say, such is royal GEORGE's will,   165
   An' there's the foe,
He has nae thought but how to kill
   Twa at a blow.

Nae cauld, faint-hearted doubtings tease him;
Death comes, with fearless eye he sees him;   170
Wi' bluidy hand a welcome gies him;
   An' when he fa's,
His latest draught o' breathin lea'es him
   In faint huzzas.

Sages their solemn een may steek,   175
An' raise a philosophic reek,

146 future wines, rich-clust'ring] Vines, an' wines, an' olives *Kil*

An' physically causes seek,
    In *clime* an' *season*,
But tell me *Whisky*'s name in Greek,
    I'll tell the reason.   180

SCOTLAND, my auld, respected Mither!
Tho' whyles ye moistify your leather,
Till when ye speak, ye aiblins blether;
    Yet deil-mak-matter!
FREEDOM and WHISKY gang thegither,   185
    Tak aff your whitter.

82. Sketch

HAIL, Poesie! thou nymph reserv'd!
  In chase o' thee, what crowds hae swerv'd
Frae Common Sense, or sunk ennerv'd
    'Mang heaps o' clavers;
And Och! o'er aft thy joes hae starv'd   5
    'Mid a' thy favors!

Say, Lassie, why thy train amang,
While loud the trumps heroic clang,
And Sock and buskin skelp alang
    To death or marriage;   10
Scarce ane has tried the Shepherd-sang
    But wi' miscarriage?

In Homer's craft Jock Milton thrives;
Eschylus' pen Will Shakespeare drives;
Wee Pope, the knurlin, 'till him rives   15
    Horatian fame;
In thy sweet sang, Barbauld, survives
    E'en Sappho's flame.

183–6 Till . . . whitter. *HL 94: MSS and 86–93 have*
    Till whare ye sit, on craps o' heather,
      Ye tine your dam;
    FREEDOM and WHISKY gang thegither,
      Tak aff your dram!

Sketch. *Text from Davidson Cook's transcript of the Law MS* (Burns Chronicle, *1927, pp. 14–15), collated with Currie (iv. 357–9)*
  8 trumps] trump's *Currie*   9 and] or *Currie*

But thee, Theocritus, wha matches?
They're no' Herd's ballats, Maro's catches;   20
Squire Pope but busks his skinklin patches
          O' Heathen tatters:
I pass by hunders, nameless wretches,
          That ape their betters.

In this braw age o' wit and lear,   25
Will nane the Shepherd's whistle mair
Blaw sweetly in his native air
          And rural grace;
And wi' the far-fam'd Grecian share
          A rival place?   30

Yes! there is ane; a Scotish callan!
There's ane: come forrit, honest Allan!
Thou need na jouk behint the hallan,
          A chiel sae clever;
The teeth o' Time may gnaw Tamtallan,   35
          But thou's for ever.

Thou paints auld Nature to the nines,
In thy sweet Caledonian lines;
Nae gowden stream thro' myrtles twines
          Where Philomel,   40
While nightly breezes sweep the vines,
          Her griefs will tell!

Thy rural loves are Nature's sel';
Nae bombast spates o' nonsense swell;
Nae snap conceits, but that sweet spell   45
          O' witchin' loove,
That charm that can the strongest quell,
          The sternest move.

In gowany glens thy burnie strays,
Where bonie lasses bleach their claes;   50

20 Herd's] herd's *Currie*   27 his] its *Currie*   41 While . . . vines,] *alternative to* While midnight gales rustle clustering vines, *in MS*   43–48, 49–54 *Transposed in Currie*

Or trots by hazelly shaws and braes
    Wi' hawthorns gray,
Where blackbirds join the shepherd's lays
    At close o' day.

83. To a Louse, On Seeing one on a Lady's Bonnet at Church

Ha! whare ye gaun, ye crowlan ferlie!
    Your impudence protects you sairly:
I canna say but ye strunt rarely,
        Owre *gawze* and *lace*;
Tho' faith, I fear ye dine but sparely,   5
        On sic a place.

Ye ugly, creepan, blastet wonner,
Detested, shunn'd, by saunt an' sinner,
How daur ye set your fit upon her,
        Sae fine a *Lady*!   10
Gae somewhere else and seek your dinner,
        On some poor body.

Swith, in some beggar's haffet squattle;
There ye may creep, and sprawl, and sprattle,
Wi' ither kindred, jumping cattle,   15
        In shoals and nations;
Whare *horn* nor *bane* ne'er daur unsettle,
        Your thick plantations.

Now haud you there, ye're out o' sight,
Below the fatt'rels, snug and tight,   20
Na faith ye yet! ye'll no be right,
        Till ye've got on it,
The vera tapmost, towrin height
        O' *Miss's bonnet*.

To A Louse. *Text from the edition of 1786, collated with Bodl. MS. Add. A. 111 and the editions of 1787, 1793, 1794*
Title in MS: On seeing a Louse on a young lady's bonnet at Church.

 1 crowlan] blastet *MS*   5 dine] feed *MS*   9 your] a *MS*   11 Gae]
Swith! *MS*   13 Swith,] Gae, *MS*   14–15 *transposed in MS*   21 faith]
haith *MS*   23 tapmost, towrin] upmost, tapmast *MS*

My sooth! right bauld ye set your nose out,   25
As plump an' gray as onie grozet:
O for some rank, mercurial rozet,
      Or fell, red smeddum,
I'd gie you sic a hearty dose o't,
      Wad dress your droddum!   30

I wad na been surpriz'd to spy
You on an auld wife's *flainen toy*;
Or aiblins some bit duddie boy,
      On 's *wylecoat*;
But Miss's fine *Lunardi*, fye!   35
      How daur ye do't?

O *Jenny* dinna toss your head,
An' set your beauties a' abroad!
Ye little ken what cursed speed
      The blastie's makin!   40
Thae *winks* and *finger-ends*, I dread,
      Are notice takin!

O wad some Pow'r the giftie gie us
To see oursels as others see us!
It wad frae monie a blunder free us   45
      An' foolish notion:
What airs in dress an' gait wad lea'e us,
      And ev'n Devotion!

31 wad na] shouldna *MS*   33 aiblins] may be *MS*   35 *Lunardi*] Lunardo
MS   37 *Jenny*] *Jeany*, *MS*   44 *oursels*] oursel *MS*   *others*] ithers *MS*

84. Love and Liberty—A Cantata

Recitativo—

WHEN lyart leaves bestrow the yird,
 Or wavering like the Bauckie-bird[1],
Bedim cauld Boreas' blast;
When hailstanes drive wi' bitter skyte,
And infant Frosts begin to bite,   5
 In hoary cranreuch drest;
Ae night at e'en a merry core
 O' randie, gangrel bodies,
In Poosie-Nansie's[2] held the splore,
 To drink their orra dudies: 10
  Wi' quaffing, and laughing,
   They ranted an' they sang;
  Wi' jumping, an' thumping,
   The vera girdle rang.

First, niest the fire, in auld, red rags,   15
Ane sat; weel brac'd wi' mealy bags,
 And knapsack a' in order;
His doxy lay within his arm;
Wi' USQUEBAE an' blankets warm,
 She blinket on her Sodger: 20
An' ay he gies the tozie drab
 The tither skelpan kiss,
While she held up her greedy gab,
 Just like an aumous dish:
  Ilk smack still, did crack still,   25
   Just like a cadger's whip;
  Then staggering, an' swaggering,
   He roar'd this ditty up—

---

1 The old Scotch name for the Bat.
2 The Hostess of a noted Caravansary in M——, well known to and much frequented by the lowest orders of Travellers and Pilgrims.

Love and Liberty—A Cantata. *Text from the Alloway MS (Al; given to David Woodburn, ?1786, and used for Stewart and Meikle's printing, 1799), collated with the Don MS, the transcript in Edinburgh University Library MS Laing iii. 586 (ff. 46ʳ–51ʳ), The Merry Muses of Caledonia, c. 1800 (MMC; songs only at ll. 57–80,*

---

1 bestrow] bestrew *Don*   3 Bedim] Thick load *Don*   9 Poosie] Pussie *Don*
Note om. Stewart   24 *Note in Don* Aumous-dish) alms-dish   26 Just like]
Like onie *Don*   27 staggering, an' swaggering] swaggering and staggering *Don*

Air. *Tune, Soldier's joy*

I am a Son of Mars who have been in many wars,
    And show my cuts and scars wherever I come;   30
This here was for a wench, and that other in a trench,
    When welcoming the French at the sound of the drum.
                        Lal de daudle &c.

My Prenticeship I past where my LEADER breath'd his last,
    When the bloody die was cast on the heights of ABRAM;
And I served out my TRADE when the gallant *game* was play'd,
    And the MORO low was laid at the sound of the drum. 36

I lastly was with Curtis among the *floating batt'ries*,
    And there I left for witness, an arm and a limb;
Yet let my Country need me, with ELLIOT to head me,
    I'd clatter on my stumps at the sound of a drum.   40

129–48, and 208–35), Stewart (1801, pp. 1–19; 1802, pp. 289–301), and Cromek,
Select Scotish Songs, 1810. See Commentary. The Laing transcript follows the text in
the Don MS. Title from Don. Title in Stewart: The Jolly Beggars: A Cantata (1801),
The Jolly Beggars; or, Tatterdemallions: A Cantata (1802)

32 *Chorus in Don* Fal lal de dal &c.   34 When] And *Don*

And now tho' I must beg, with a wooden arm and leg,
  And many a tatter'd rag hanging over my bum,
I'm as happy with my wallet, my bottle and my Callet,
  As when I us'd in scarlet to follow a drum.

What tho', with hoary locks, I must stand the winter shocks,
  Beneath the woods and rocks oftentimes for a home,   46
When the tother bag I sell and the tother bottle tell,
  I could meet a troop of HELL at the sound of a drum.

Recitativo—

He ended; and the kebars sheuk,
  Aboon the chorus roar;   50
While frighted rattons backward leuk,
  An' seek the benmost bore:
A fairy FIDDLER frae the neuk,
  He skirl'd out, ENCORE.
But up arose the martial CHUCK,   55
  An' laid the loud uproar—

Air. *Tune, Sodger laddie*

41–44 And now . . . a drum.] *om. Don*   43 wallet,] wallet *Al*   45 What]
Now *Don*   53 fairy Fiddler frae] Merry Andrew i' *Cromek*

I Once was a Maid, tho' I cannot tell when,
And still my delight is in proper young men:
Some one of a troop of Dragoons was my dadie,
No wonder I'm fond of a Sodger laddie.   60
   Sing lal de dal &c.

The first of my Loves was a swaggering blade,
To rattle the thundering drum was his trade;
His leg was so tight and his cheek was so ruddy,
Transported I was with my Sodger laddie.

But the godly old Chaplain left him in the lurch,   65
The sword I forsook for the sake of the church;
He ventur'd the Soul, and I risked the Body,
'Twas then I prov'd false to my Sodger laddie.

Full soon I grew sick of my sanctified *Sot*,
The Regiment at large for a husband I got;   70
From the gilded Spontoon to the Fife I was ready;
I asked no more but a Sodger laddie.

But the Peace it reduc'd me to beg in despair,
Till I met my old boy in a Cunningham fair;
His rags regimental they flutter'd so gaudy,
My heart it rejoic'd at a Sodger laddie.   75

And now I have lived—I know not how long,
And still I can join in a cup and a song;
But whilst with both hands I can hold the glass steady,
Here's to thee, My Hero, My Sodger laddie.   80

61 Loves] Lovers *MMC* 67 ventur'd . . . risked] risked . . . ventur'd *Don*
74 boy] body *MMC* in] at *Don MMC Stewart Cromek* 76 a] my *MMC*
Stewart 78 join] joy *MMC* 79 But] And *Don*
80 *An additional recitative and air, in Burns's holograph but written at a different
time, follow in Al and were printed in Stewart (1802):*

Recitative

Poor Merry-andrew, in $^{the}_{a}$ neuk,
   Sat guzzling wi' a Tinkler-hizzie;
They mind't na wha the chorus teuk,
   Between themsels they were sae busy:
At length wi' drink an' courting dizzy,
   He stoiter'd up an' made a face;
Then turn'd, an' laid a smack on Grizzie,
   Syne tun'd his pipes wi' grave grimace.

   Air. Tune, Auld Sir Symon.

Sir Wisdom's a fool when he's fou;
   Sir Knave is a fool in a Session,
He's there but a prentice, I trow,
   But I am a fool by profession.

My Grannie she bought me a beuk,
   An' I held awa to the school;
I fear I my talent misteuk,
   But what will ye hae of a fool.

For drink I would venture my neck;
   A hizzie's the half of my Craft:
But what could ye other expect
   Of ane that's avowedly daft.

I, ance, was ty'd up like a stirk,
   For civilly swearing and quaffing;
I, ance, was abus'd i' the kirk,
   For towsing a lass i' my daffin.

Poor Andrew that tumbles for sport,
   Let nae body name wi' a jeer;
There's even, I'm tauld, i' the Court
   A Tumbler ca'd the Premier.

Observ'd ye yon reverend lad
   Mak faces to tickle the Mob;
He rails at our mountebank squad,
   Its rivalship just i' the job.

And now my conclusion I'll tell,
   For faith I'm confoundedly dry:
The chiel that's a fool for himsel,
   Guid L—d, he's far dafter than I.

See Commentary

Recitativo—

Then niest outspak a raucle Carlin,
Wha ken't fu' weel to cleek the Sterlin;
For mony a pursie she had hooked,
An' had in mony a well been douked:
Her LOVE had been a HIGHLAND LADDIE,   85
But weary fa' the waefu' woodie!
Wi' sighs an' sobs she thus began
To wail her braw JOHN HIGHLANDMAN—

Air. *Tune, O an' ye were dead Gudeman*

Brisk

A HIGHLAND lad my Love was born,
The lalland laws he held in scorn;   90
But he still was faithfu' to his clan,
My gallant, braw JOHN HIGHLANDMAN.

84 douked] doukit *Don:* ducked *Stewart*   85 Love] Dove *Stewart*
90, 103 lalland] Lawland *Don*   91 he] om. *Don*

Chorus—

Sing hey my braw John Highlandman!
Sing ho my braw John Highlandman!
There's not a lad in a' the lan'   95
Was match for my John Highlandman.

With his Philibeg, an' tartan Plaid,
An' guid Claymore down by his side,
The ladies' hearts he did trepan,
My gallant, braw John Highlandman.   100
        Sing hey &c.

We ranged a' from Tweed to Spey,
An' liv'd like lords an' ladies gay:
For a lalland face he feared none,
My gallant, braw John Highlandman.
        Sing hey &c.

They banish'd him beyond the sea,   105
But ere the bud was on the tree,
Adown my cheeks the pearls ran,
Embracing my John Highlandman.
        Sing hey &c.

But Och! they catch'd him at the last,
And bound him in a dungeon fast,   110
My curse upon them every one,
They've hang'd my braw John Highlandman.
        Sing hey &c.

And now a Widow I must mourn
The Pleasures that will ne'er return;
No comfort but a hearty can,   115
When I think on John Highlandman.
        Sing hey &c.

103 none] nane *Stewart (1802)*   109 But Och!] But, oh! *Stewart*
113–16 And now . . . Highlandman.] *om. Don*   114 The Pleasures that will]
Departed joys that *Cromek*

Recitativo—

A pigmy Scraper wi' his Fiddle,
Wha us'd to trystes an' fairs to driddle,
Her strappan limb an' gausy middle,
      (He reach'd nae higher)   120
Had hol'd his HEARTIE like a riddle,
      An' blawn 't on fire.

Wi' hand on hainch, and upward e'e,
He croon'd his gamut, ONE, TWO, THREE,
Then in an ARIOSO key,   125
      The wee Apollo
Set off wi' ALLEGRETTO glee
      His GIGA SOLO—

Air. *Tune, Whistle owre the lave o't*

Lively

LET me ryke up to dight that tear,
An' go wi' me an' be my DEAR;   130
An' then your every CARE an' FEAR
May whistle owre the lave o't.

Chorus—

I am a Fiddler to my trade,
An' a' the tunes that e'er I play'd,
The sweetest still to WIFE or MAID,   135
Was whistle owre the lave o't.

117 wi' his] on a *Don*   118 to trystes] at trysts *Stewart (1802)*   129 ryke]
reach *Don*   130 an'] to *MMC Stewart (1801)*

At KIRNS an' WEDDINS we'se be there,
An' O sae nicely's we will fare!
We'll bowse about till Dadie CARE
 Sing whistle owre the lave o't.   140
   I am &c.

Sae merrily's the banes we'll pyke,
An' sun oursells about the dyke;
An' at our leisure when ye like
 We'll whistle owre the lave o't.
   I am &c.

But bless me wi' your heav'n o' charms, 145
An' while I kittle hair on thairms
HUNGER, CAULD, an' a' sic harms
 May whistle owre the lave o't.
   I am &c.

Recitativo—

Her charms had struck a sturdy CAIRD,
 As weel as poor GUTSCRAPER;   150
He taks the Fiddler by the beard,
 An' draws a roosty rapier—
He swoor by a' was swearing worth
 To speet him like a Pliver,
Unless he would from that time forth 155
 Relinquish her for ever:

Wi' ghastly e'e poor TWEEDLEDEE
 Upon his hunkers bended,
An' pray'd for grace wi' ruefu' face,
 An' so the quarrel ended;   160
But tho' his little heart did grieve,
 When round the TINKLER prest her,
He feign'd to snirtle in his sleeve
 When thus the CAIRD address'd her—

---

146 *Note in Don* thairms) small guts = fiddle strings   152 roosty] rusty *Don Stewart* (*1802*)   155 would from] wad frae *Stewart* (*1802*)   that] *correcting this in Al*   158 *Note in Don* hunkers) the position of one going to sit down on the floor   160 so] sae *Don Stewart* (*1802*)   162 TINKLER] tinker *Stewart*

Air. *Tune, Clout the Caudron*

My bonie lass I work in brass,   165
    A Tinkler is my station;
I've travell'd round all Christian ground
    In this my occupation;
I've ta'en the gold an' been enroll'd
    In many a noble squadron;   170
But vain they search'd when off I march'd
    To go an' clout the Caudron.
            I've ta'en the gold &c.

Despise that Shrimp, that withered Imp,
    With a' his noise an' cap'rin;
An' take a share, with those that bear   175
    The *budget* and the *apron*!
And *by* that Stowp! my faith an' houpe,
    And *by* that dear Kilbaigie*,
If e'er ye want, or meet with scant,
    May I ne'er weet my craigie!   180
            And by that Stowp, &c.

* A peculiar sort of Whiskie so called: a great favorite with Poosie Nansie's Clubs.

---

169 gold an'] gold, I've *Stewart Cromek*   170 noble] gallant *Don*
173–4 Despise ... cap'rin] *Cromek gives a variant:*

    That monkey face, despise that race,
    Wi' a' their noise and cap'ring

173 Shrimp, that withered Imp] imp so gent and gimp *Don*   178 *Note in
Don* a well-known kind of Whisky, much used as a beverage, morning, noon and
night, in Pussie Nansies.

Recitativo—

The Caird prevail'd—th' unblushing fair
    In his embraces sunk;
Partly wi' LOVE o'ercome sae sair,
    An' partly she was drunk:
SIR VIOLINO with an air,   185
    That show'd a man o' spunk,
Wish'd UNISON between the PAIR,
    An' made the bottle clunk
            To their health that night.

But hurchin Cupid shot a shaft,   190
    That play'd a DAME a shavie—
The Fiddler RAK'D her, FORE AND AFT,
    Behint the Chicken cavie:
Her lord, a wight of HOMER's craft*,
    Tho' limpan wi' the Spavie,   195
He hirpl'd up an' lap like daft,
    An' shor'd them DAINTY DAVIE
            O' *boot* that night.

He was a care-defying blade,
    As ever BACCHUS listed!   200
Tho' Fortune sair upon him laid,
    His heart she ever miss'd it.
He had no WISH but—to be glad,
    Nor WANT but—when he thristed;
He hated nought but—to be sad,   205
    An' thus the Muse suggested
            His sang that night.

---

* Homer is allowed to be the eldest Ballad singer on record.

---

192 The Fiddler] A Sailor *Don Cromek*   203 no] nae *Don Stewart* (*1802*)
204 thristed] thirsted *Stewart*

Air. *Tune, For a' that an' a' that*

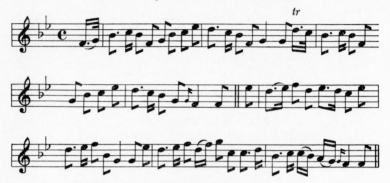

I am a Bard of no regard,
   Wi' gentle folks an' a' that;
But Homer like the glowran byke,   210
   Frae town to town I draw that.

Chorus—

   For a' that an' a' that,
      An' twice as muckle's a' that,
   I've lost but Ane, I've Twa behin',
   I've Wife eneugh for a' that.   215

I never drank the Muses' Stank,
   Castalia's burn an' a' that,
But there it streams an' richly reams,
   My Helicon I ca' that.
        For a' that &c.

Great love I bear to all the Fair,   220
   Their humble slave an' a' that;
But lordly Will, I hold it still
   A mortal sin to thraw that.
        For a' that &c.

In raptures sweet this hour we meet,
   Wi' mutual love an' a' that;   225
But for how lang the flie may stang,
   Let Inclination law that.
        For a' that &c.

224 raptures] rapture *Don MMC*

Their tricks an' craft hae put me daft,
   They've ta'en me in, an' a' that,
But clear your decks an' here 's the SEX!   230
   I like the jads for a' that.
      For a' that an' a' that
        An' twice as muckle's a' that,
   My DEAREST BLUID to do them guid,
      They're welcome till 't for a' that.   235

        Recitativo—

So sung the BARD—and Nansie's waws
Shook with a thunder of applause
   Re-echo'd from each mouth!
They toom'd their pocks, they pawn'd their duds,
They scarcely left to coor their fuds   240
   To quench their lowan drouth:
Then owre again the jovial thrang
   The Poet did request
To lowse his PACK an' wale a sang,
   A BALLAD o' the best.   245
      He, rising, rejoicing,
        Between his TWA DEBORAHS,
     Looks round him an' found them
      Impatient for the Chorus.

   Air. *Tune, Jolly Mortals, fill your glasses*

    SEE the smoking bowl before us,   250
     Mark our jovial, ragged ring!
    Round and round take up the Chorus,
     And in raptures let us sing—

228 hae] have *Stewart* (*1801*)   230 here's] here's, *Don*   234 bluid] bluid, *Don
MMC Stewart*   239 pocks, they . . . duds] pouches, pawned their pocks *Don*
240 They] And *Don*   fuds] backs *Don*   241 To quench] Quenching
Don   243 did] does *Don: corrected to* did *in Laing transcript*   248 Looks
round him] Look'd round him *Don. Cromek gives a variant* Look'd round them

Chorus—

A fig for those by law protected!
    LIBERTY's a glorious feast!   255
Courts for Cowards were erected,
    Churches built to please the PRIEST.

What is TITLE, what is TREASURE,
    What is REPUTATION's care?
If we lead a life of pleasure,   260
    'Tis no matter HOW or WHERE.
        A fig, &c.

With the ready trick and fable
    Round we wander all the day;
And at night, in barn or stable,
    Hug our doxies on the hay.   265
        A fig for &c.

Does the train-attended CARRIAGE
    Thro' the country lighter rove?
Does the sober bed of MARRIAGE
    Witness brighter scenes of love?
        A fig for &c.

Life is all a VARIORUM,   270
    We regard not how it goes;
Let them cant about DECORUM,
    Who have character to lose.
        A fig for &c.

272 cant] prate *Don*   273 character] characters *Stewart*

Here's to Budgets, Bags and Wallets!
   Here's to all the wandering train!   275
Here's our ragged Brats and Callets!
   One and all cry out, Amen!
      A fig for those by Law protected,
        Liberty's a glorious feast!
      Courts for Cowards were erected,   280
        Churches built to please the Priest.

274, 275 Here's to] Here is, *Don*   275 the] our *Don: correcting* our *in Al*
276 Here's] Here's, *Don*

III

POEMS
1 7 8 6

MOSSGIEL AND
EDINBURGH

85. The Ordination

For sense they little owe to frugal Heav'n—
To please the Mob they hide the little giv'n.

I

K********* Wabsters, fidge an' claw,
  An' pour your creeshie nations;
An' ye wha leather rax an' draw,
  Of a' denominations;
Swith to the *Laigh Kirk*, ane an' a',   5
  An' there tak up your stations;
Then aff to *B–gb*—'s in a raw,
  An' pour divine libations
              For joy this day.

II

Curst Common-sense, that imp o' h–ll,   10
  Cam in wi' Maggie Lauder*;
But O******* aft made her yell,
  An' R***** sair misca'd her:

---

* Alluding to a scoffing ballad which was made on the admission of the late Reverend and worthy Mr L—— to the *Laigh Kirk*.

The Ordination. *Text from the Edinburgh edition, 1787, collated with those of 1793, 1794*
  H–H. record variants in two MSS (not traced). In the first: Title in MS: A Scotch Poem, by Rab Rhymer   7 *B–gb*—'s] Crookes's *MS*   28 let . . . read] wale a text a proper verse *MS*   30 graceless . . . Dad] Ham leugh at his father's arse *MS*   32 drove . . . blade] did four buttocks pierce *MS*   34 the scauldin jad] wi' scaulding hearse *MS*   38–41 And bind . . . feed] *MS has:*
              Wi' form'la an' confession;
              An' lay your hands upon his head
              An' seal his high commission,
              The Holy flock to tent an' feed
50 *kail*] fowls *MS*   54 ilka] every *MS*   90 Fast, fast] In haste *MS*   111–12 Morality's . . . quarter] *MS has*
              Get up—wha ever's fit to rise
              An' thro' the room let's thorter
The second MS has the same variants in lines 28–34, 38–41, and these: 90 Fast,] Fu *MS*   111 demure decoys] delusive joys *MS*

This day M'******* taks the flail,
  An' he's the boy will blaud her!   15
He'll clap a *shangan* on her tail,
  An' set the bairns to daud her
        Wi' dirt this day.

III

Mak haste an' turn king David owre,
  An' lilt wi' holy clangor;   20
O' double verse come gie us four,
  An' skirl up the Bangor:
This day the Kirk kicks up a stoure,
  Nae mair the knaves shall wrang her,
For Heresy is in her pow'r,   25
  And gloriously she'll whang her
        Wi' pith this day.

IV

Come, let a proper text be read,
  An' touch it aff wi' vigour,
How graceless *Ham** leugh at his Dad,   30
  Which made *Canaan* a niger;
Or *Phineas*† drove the murdering blade,
  Wi' wh—re-abhorring rigour;
Or *Zipporah*‡, the scauldin jad,
  Was like a bluidy tiger   35
        I' th' inn that day.

V

There, try his mettle on the creed,
  And bind him down wi' caution,
That *Stipend* is a carnal weed
  He takes but for the fashion;   40
And gie him o'er the flock, to feed,
  And punish each transgression;
Especial, *rams* that cross the breed,
  Gie them sufficient threshin,
        Spare them nae day.   45

* Genesis, ch. ix. vers. 22.   † Numbers, ch. xxv. vers. 8.
‡ Exodus, ch. iv. vers. 25.

VI

Now auld K*********, cock thy tail,
　　An' toss thy horns fu' canty;
Nae mair thou'lt rowte out-owre the dale,
　　Because thy pasture's scanty;
For lapfu's large o' *gospel kail*　　　　　　　50
　　Shall fill thy crib in plenty,
An' *runts* o' *grace* the pick an' wale,
　　No gi'en by way o' dainty
　　　　　　　But ilka day.

VII

Nae mair by *Babel's streams* we'll weep,　　55
　　To think upon our *Zion*;
And hing our fiddles up to sleep,
　　Like baby-clouts a-dryin:
Come, screw the pegs wi' tunefu' cheep,
　　And o'er the thairms be tryin;　　　　60
Oh, rare! to see our elbucks wheep,
　　And a' like lamb-tails flyin
　　　　　　　Fu' fast this day!

VIII

Lang, *Patronage*, wi' rod o' airn,
　　Has shor'd the Kirk's undoin,　　　　65
As lately *F—nw—ck*, sair forfairn,
　　Has proven to its ruin:
Our Patron, honest man! *Gl*******,
　　He saw mischief was brewin;
And like a godly, elect bairn,　　　　　　70
　　He's wal'd us out a true ane,
　　　　　　　And sound this day.

IX

Now R******** harangue nae mair,
　　But steek your gab for ever;
Or try the wicked town of A**,　　　　　75
　　For there they'll think you clever;

Or, nae reflection on your lear,
   Ye may commence a Shaver;
Or to the *N–th–rt–n* repair,
   And turn a Carpet-weaver   80
      Aff-hand this day.

X

M***** and you were just a match,
   We never had sic twa drones;
Auld *Hornie* did the *Laigh Kirk* watch,
   Just like a winkin baudrons: 85
And ay he catch'd the tither wretch,
   To fry them in his caudrons;
But now his Honor maun detach,
   Wi' a' his brimstone squadrons,
      Fast, fast this day.   90

XI

See, see auld Orthodoxy's faes
   She's swingein thro' the city!
Hark, how the nine-tail'd cat she plays!
   I vow it's unco pretty:
There, Learning, with his Greekish face,   95
   Grunts out some Latin ditty;
And Common Sense is gaun, she says,
   To mak to *Jamie Beattie*
      Her plaint this day.

XII

But there's Morality himsel,   100
   Embracing all opinions;
Hear, how he gies the tither yell,
   Between his twa companions!
See, how she peels the skin an' fell,
   As ane were peelin onions!   105
Now there, they're packed aff to h–ll,
   And banish'd our dominions,
      Henceforth this day.

XIII

O happy day! rejoice, rejoice!
    Come bouse about the porter!   110
Morality's demure decoys
    Shall here nae mair find quarter:
M'*******, R*****, are the boys
    That Heresy can torture;
They'll gie her on a rape a hoyse,   115
    And cowe her measure shorter
        By th' head some day.

XIV

Come, bring the tither mutchkin in,
    And here's, for a conclusion,
To ev'ry *New-light** mother's son,   120
    From this time forth, Confusion:
If mair they deave us wi' their din,
    Or Patronage intrusion,
We'll light a spunk, and, ev'ry skin,
    We'll rin them aff in fusion   125
        Like oil, some day.

86. The Inventory

To Mr Robt Aiken in Ayr, in answer to his mandate requiring an
account of servants, carriages, carriage-horses, riding horses, wives,
children, &c.

SIR, as your mandate did request,
I send you here a faithfu' list,
O' gudes an' gear, an' a' my graith,
To which I'm clear to gi'e my aith.

---

* *New-light* is a cant phrase, in the West of Scotland, for those religious opinions
which Dr Taylor of Norwich has defended so strenuously.

The Inventory. *Text from Stewart, 1801 (pp. 46–49), collated with the MS in the
possession of Mr. Paul Fenimore Cooper, New York (C), the Don MS, and Currie (iv.
372–5). Except at ll. 8, 10, and 11, Currie follows C. Title from Stewart; sub-title
from Don. Title in C and Currie:* Answer to a Mandate sent by the surveyor of the

3 O' . . . my] My horses, servants, carts and *C*: My servants, horses, pleughs and
Don   4 clear to gi'e] free to tak *C Don*

Imprimis then, for carriage cattle,⎫   5
I have four brutes o' gallant mettle,⎬
As ever drew afore a pettle.   ⎭
My **Lan' afore*'s a gude auld *has been*,
An' wight an' wilfu' a' his days been.
My †*Lan' ahin*'s a weel gaun fillie,   10
That aft has borne me hame frae Killie‡,
An' your auld burrough mony a time,
In days when riding was nae crime—
But ance whan in my wooing pride
I like a blockhead boost to ride,   15
The wilfu' creature sae I pat to,
(L—d pardon a' my sins an' that too!)
I play'd my fillie sic a shavie,
She's a' bedevil'd wi' the spavie.
My §*Furr ahin*'s a wordy beast,   20
As e'er in tug or tow was trac'd.—
The fourth's a Highland Donald hastie,
A d—n'd red wud Kilburnie blastie;
Foreby a *Cowt*, o' *Cowt's* the wale,
As ever ran afore a tail.   25
If he be spar'd to be a beast,
He'll draw me fifteen pun' at least.—
Wheel carriages I ha'e but few,
Three carts, an' twa are feckly new;
Ae auld wheelbarrow, mair for token,   30
Ae leg an' baith the trams are broken;

---

* The fore horse on the left-hand in the plough.
† The hindmost on the left-hand in the plough.   ‡ Kilmarnock.
§ The same on the right-hand in the plough.

---

windows, carriages, &c. to each farmer, ordering them to send a signed list of their
horses, servants, wheel carriages, &c. and whether they were married men or
bachelors, and what children they had.—*Footnote in C:* the Surveyor was M^r R.
Aiken. *See Commentary*
6 have] hae *C Don*   7 afore] before *C Don*   8, 10 *Lan'*] *hand- Currie*
8 *afore's*] -afore, *C Don*   10 *ahin's*] -ahin, *C Don*   11 That] Wha *C. Note
not in C*   hame] safe *Currie*   14–19 But . . . spavie.] *not in C*   15 block-
head] haverel *Don*   17 too *Don*: to *Stewart*   20 *ahin's*] -ahin, *C Don*   wordy]
guid, gray *C*: stark, gray *Don*   22 fourth 's] fourth, *C Don*   25 afore]
before *C Don*   26 If] An' *C*: Gif *Don (correcting* And)   30 Ae] An *C Don*
31 leg . . . trams] tram . . . feet *Don*

I made a poker o' the spin'le,
An' my auld mither brunt the trin'le.—
For men, I've three mischievous boys,
Run de'ils for rantin' an' for noise;   35
A gaudsman ane, a thrasher t'other,
Wee Davock hauds the nowt in fother.
I rule them as I ought, discreetly,
An' aften labour them compleatly.
An' ay on Sundays duly nightly,   40
I on the questions *targe* them tightly;
Till faith, wee Davock's turn'd sae gleg,
Tho' scarcely langer than your leg,
He'll screed you aff Effectual Calling,
As fast as ony in the dwalling.—   45
I've nane in female servan' station,
(L—d keep me ay frae a' temptation!)
I ha'e nae wife; and that my bliss is,
An' ye have laid nae tax on misses;
An' then if kirk folks dinna clutch me,   50
I ken the devils dare na touch me.
Wi' weans I'm mair than weel contented,
Heav'n sent me ane mae than I wanted.
My sonsie smirking dear-bought Bess, ⎫
She stares the daddy in her face,   ⎬   55
Enough of ought ye like but grace;   ⎭
But her, my bonny sweet wee lady,
I've paid enough for her already,
An' gin ye tax her or her mither,
B' the L—d! ye'se get them a' thegither.   60

And now, remember Mr. A–k–n,
Nae kind of licence out I'm takin';
Frae this time forth, I do declare,
I'se ne'er ride horse nor hizzie mair;

33 mither *C Don*: mother *Stewart*   35 rantin'] *corrected to* fechtin *in Don*
41 *targe*] tairge *C Don*   42 turn'd] grown *C Don*   43 your] my *C
Don*   49 have] hae *C Don*   50–51 An' . . . me.] *not in C Don*
52 Wi'] For *C Don*   54 sonsie] blinking *Don*   55 stares the daddy]
stares, the daddie, *Don*   59 An' gin] And if *C Don*   63–64 Frae . . . mair;]
not in C Don

Thro' dirt and dub for life I'll paidle,   65
Ere I sae dear pay for a saddle;
My travel a' on foot I'll shank it,
I've sturdy bearers, Gude be thankit.—
The Kirk an' you may tak' you that,
It puts but little in your pat;   70
Sae dinna put me in your buke,
Nor for my ten white shillings luke.

This list wi' my ain han' I wrote it,
Day an' date as under notit,
Then know all ye whom it concerns,   75
Subscripsi huic,

ROBERT BURNS.

Mossgeil, February 22d, 1786.

87. To Mr. John Kennedy

Mossgiel, 3rd March, 1786.

Now Kennedy if foot or horse
    E'er bring you in by Mauchline Corss,
L—d man there's lasses there wad force
        A hermit's fancy,
And down the gate in faith they're worse   5
        And mair unchancy.

But as I'm sayin, please step to Dow's
And taste sic gear as Johnnie brews,
Till some bit callan bring me news
        That you are there,   10
And if we dinna hae a bouze
        Ise ne'er drink mair.

65–66, 67–68 *Transposed in Don*   67–68 My . . . thankit.] *C and Don have*
            I've sturdy stumps the Lord be thanked,
            And a' my gates on foot I'll shank it.
69–72 The . . . luke.] *not in C Don*   73 I] I've *C Don*   74 Day] The day
C Don   76 *Don is dated* Mossgiel May— 1786: *no date in C*

To Mr. John Kennedy. *Text from Cunningham, 1834 (vii. 334–5; Cun)*
11 hae] had *Cun*

It 's no I like to sit an' swallow
Then like a swine to puke an' wallow,
But gie me just a true good fallow   15
            Wi' right ingine,
And spunkie ance to make us mellow,
            And then we'll shine.

Now if ye're ane o' warl's folk,
Wha rate the wearer by the cloak   20
An' sklent on poverty their joke
            Wi' bitter sneer,
Wi' you no friendship I will troke
            Nor cheap nor dear.

But if as I'm informed weel   25
Ye hate as ill 's the vera de'il
The flinty heart that canna feel—
            Come Sir, here's tae you:
Hae there's my haun', I wiss you weel
            And Gude be wi' you.   30

88. Adam A——'s Prayer

Gude pity me, because I'm little,
    For though I am an elf o' mettle,
And can, like ony wabster's shuttle,
            Jink there or here;
Yet, scarce as lang 's a gude kail whittle,   5
            I'm unco queer.

And now thou kens our waefu' case,
For *Geordie's Jurr* we're in disgrace,
Because we've stang'd her through the place,
            And hurt her spleuchan,   10
For which we darena show our face
            Within the clachan.

30 Gude *H–H.*, *from a MS* (*not traced*): gude *Cun*

Adam A[rmour']s Prayer. *Text from the* Scots Magazine, January *1808* (*SM*)

And now we're dern'd in dens and hollows,
And hunted as was William Wallace,
Wi' Constables, those blackguard fallows,   15
          And Sodgers baith;
But gude preserve us frae the gallows,
          That shamefu' death!

Auld, grim, black-bearded Geordie's sell;
Oh, shake him o'er the mouth o' hell,   20
There let him hing, and roar, and yell,
          Wi' hideous din,
And if he offers to rebel,
          Then heave him in.

When Death comes in wi' glimmering blink,   25
And tips auld druken Nanz the wink,
May Satan gie her a— a clink
          Within his yet,
And fill her up wi' brimstone drink
          Red, reeking, het.   30

There's Jockie and the hav'rel Jenny,
Some Devil seize them in a hurry,
And waff them in th' infernal wherry
          Straught through the lake,
And gie their hides a noble curry,   35
          Wi' oil of aik.

As for the *Jurr*, poor worthless body,
She's got mischief enough already,
Wi' stanged hips, and buttocks bloody,
          She's suffer'd sair;   40
But may she wintle in a woodie,
          If she w——e mair.

13 dern'd] darn'd *SM*   18 death!] death. *SM*   20 Oh,] O' *SM*   30 Red,
reeking,] Red reeking *SM*

89. Song. On Miss W. A.

Tune, Ettrick banks

'TWAS ev'n, the dewy fields were green,
　　On ev'ry blade the pearls hang,
The Zephyr wanton'd round the bean,
　　And bore its fragrant sweets alang;
In ev'ry glen the Mavis sang,   5
　　All nature list'ning seem'd the while;
Except where greenwood Echos rang
　　Amang the braes o' Ballochmyle.

Song. *Text from the Alloway MS (Al), collated with MSS Stair and Mossgiel*
(*Dewar's transcript*), The Polyhymnia, *18 (P; 1799)*, Currie, *1800 (i. 125; with the*
letter to Miss Alexander), and SC, 1801 (108; air, Johny's Gray Breeks). Title in
Stair *A Song . . . . On accidentally seeing Miss W—— A—— in an evening walk.*
Holograph note in Al *The above Song cannot be published without the consent of*
the Lady, which I have desired a common friend to ask.—
　　Dewar collated a MS with Currie's reading in ll. 15–16, And there *in l. 23, and*
the readings of the text at ll. 15–16, 23–24 given as alternatives at the end of the third
stanza
　　2–4 hang . . . alang] hung . . . along *SC*　　　7 Except] Unless *P*

With careless step I onward stray'd,
    My heart rejoic'd in Nature's joy,   10
When, musing in a lonely glade,
    A Maiden fair I chanc'd to spy:
Her look was like the Morning's eye,
    Her air like Nature's vernal smile,
The lilies' hue and roses' die   15
    Bespoke the Lass o' Ballochmyle.

Fair is a morn in flow'ry May,
    And sweet an ev'n in Autumn mild;
When roving through the garden gay,
    Or wand'ring in the lonely wild;   20
But Woman, Nature's darling child,
    There all her charms she does compile,
And all her other works are foil'd
    By th' bony Lass o' Ballochmyle.

O if she were a country Maid,   25
    And I the happy country Swain!
Though shelt'red in the lowest shed
    That ever rose on Scotia's plain:
Through weary Winter's wind and rain,
    With joy, with rapture I would toil,   30
And nightly to my bosom strain
    The bony Lass o' Ballochmyle.

Then Pride might climb the slipp'ry steep
    Where fame and honors lofty shine:
And Thirst of gold might tempt the deep   35
    Or downward seek the Indian mine:

15–16 The . . . Ballochmyle.] *footnote variant in Currie, whose text has*

        Perfection whispered passing by,
        Behold the lass o' Ballochmyle!

SC gives Currie's version as a variant

15 lilies'] lily *Stair*   17 a] the *Currie SC*   18 an ev'n] a night *Stair*
Mossgiel P: is night *Currie SC*   23 And all] Even there *Currie SC*   25 if]
gin *P*: had *Currie SC*   were] been *Currie SC*   28 Scotia's] Scotland's *Currie*
SC   33 might] may *P*   36 seek] dig *P*   Indian *Stair*: indian *Al*

Give me the Cot below the pine,
   To tend the flocks or till the soil,
And ev'ry day has joys divine
   With th' bony Lass o' Ballochmyle.   40

90. Letter to J——s T——t, Gl—nc——r

Auld com'rade dear and brither sinner,
   How's a' the folk about Gl—nc——r;
How do ye this blae eastlin win',
That's like to blaw a body blin':
For me my faculties are frozen,   5
My dearest member nearly dozen'd:
I've sent you here by Johnie Simson,
Twa sage Philosophers to glimpse on!
Smith, wi' his sympathetic feeling,
An' Reid, to common sense appealing.   10
Philosophers have fought an' wrangled,
An' meikle Greek an' Latin mangled,
Till with their Logic-jargon tir'd,
An' in the depth of science mir'd,
To common sense they now appeal,   15
What wives an' wabsters see an' feel;
But, hark ye, friend, I charge you strictly,
Peruse them an' return them quickly;
For now I'm grown sae cursed douse,
I pray an' ponder *butt* the house,   20
My shins, my lane, I there sit roastin,
Perusing Bunyan, Brown and Boston;
Till by an' by, if I haud on,
I'll grunt a real Gospel groan:
Already I begin to try it,   25
To cast my een up like a Pyet,
When by the gun she tumbles o'er,

---

39 has] brings *P*: have *Currie*

Letter to J——s T——t. *Text from Stewart, 1802 (pp. 321–3), collated with Oliver's
and Duncan's editions, 1801*
   9–10 Smith . . . Reid] Reid . . . Smith *Stewart*

Flutt'ring an' gasping in her gore:
Sae shortly you shall see me bright,
A burning an' a shining light. 30

My heart-warm love to guid auld Glen,
The ace an' wale of honest men;
When bending down with auld gray hairs,
Beneath the load of years and cares,
May he who made him still support him, 35
An' views beyond the grave comfort him.

His worthy fam'ly far and near,
God bless them a' wi' grace and gear.

My auld school-fellow, Preacher Willie,
The manly tar, my mason billie, 40
An' Auchenbay, I wish him joy;
If he's a parent, lass or boy,
May he be dad, and Meg the mither,
Just five and forty years thegither!
An' no forgetting wabster Charlie, 45
I'm tauld he offers very fairly,
An' L—d, remember singing Sannock,
Wi' hale-breeks, saxpence an' a bannock;
An' next, my auld acquaintance, Nancy,
Since she is fitted to her fancy; 50
An' her kind stars hae airted till her,
A guid chiel wi' a pickle siller:
My kindest, best respects I sen' it,
To cousin Kate an' sister Janet,
Tell them frae me, wi' chiels be cautious; 55
For, faith, they'll ablins fin' them fashious:
To grant a heart is fairly civil,
But to grant a maidenhead's the devil!
An' lastly, Jamie, for yoursel,
May guardian angels tak a spell, ⎫ 60
An' steer you seven miles south o' hell;⎭

40 billie] Billie *Stewart*

But first, before you see heav'ns glory,
May ye get mony a merry story,
Mony a laugh and mony a drink,
An' ay aneugh o' needfu' clink.   65

Now fare ye well, an' joy be wi' you,
For my sake this I beg it o' you,
Assist poor Simson a' ye can,
Ye'll fin' him just an honest man:
Sae I conclude and quat my chanter,   70
Yours, saint or sinner,
                    RAB THE RANTER.

91. [To Mrs. C——]

T H O U flattering mark of friendship kind
        Still may thy pages call to mind
    The dear, the beauteous donor:
Though sweetly female every part
Yet such a head, and more the heart,   5
    Does both the sexes honor.
She showed her taste refined and just
    When she selected thee,
Yet deviating own I must,
    For so approving me.   10
        But kind still, I mind still,
            The giver in the gift;
        I'll bless her and wiss her
            A Friend aboon the Lift.

65 aneugh] a neugh *Stewart*   71 Yours] Your's *Stewart*   RAB] ROB
Stewart

To Mrs. C——. *Text from the Cowie MS, collated with Cunningham, 1834 (vii. 336;
letter to Aiken, 3 April 1786)*
    11 I] I'll *Cun*   14 aboon] above *Cun*

92. To a Mountain-Daisy, On turning one down, with the Plough, in April — 1786

WEE, modest, crimson-tipped flow'r,
  Thou's met me in an evil hour;
For I maun crush amang the stoure
      Thy slender stem:
To spare thee now is past my pow'r,   5
      Thou bonie gem.

Alas! it's no thy neebor sweet,
The bonie *Lark*, companion meet!
Bending thee 'mang the dewy weet!
      Wi's spreckl'd breast,   10
When upward-springing, blythe, to greet
      The purpling East.

Cauld blew the bitter-biting *North*
Upon thy early, humble birth;
Yet chearfully thou glinted forth   15
      Amid the storm,
Scarce rear'd above the *Parent-earth*
      Thy tender form.

The flaunting *flow'rs* our Gardens yield,
High-shelt'ring woods and wa's maun shield,   20
But thou, beneath the random bield
      O' clod or stane,
Adorns the histie *stibble-field*,
      Unseen, alane.

To a Mountain-Daisy. *Text from the edition of 1786, collated with a MS of lines 1–24
(see Commentary) and the editions of 1787, 1793, 1794. Title in MS* The Gowan.—
A Scotch Poem.—On turning down a mountain-daisie with the plough, April—
1786
    3–6 For . . . gem.] *MS has*

              Alas, to spare thee's past my pow'r,
                    Thou bonie gem;
              For I maun crush amang the stowre
                    Thy slender stem.
    8 bonie] harmless *MS*   10 Wi 's] Wi' *87–94*

There, in thy scanty mantle clad,   25
Thy snawie bosom sun-ward spread,
Thou lifts thy unassuming head
   In humble guise;
But now the *share* uptears thy bed,
   And low thou lies!   30

Such is the fate of artless Maid,
Sweet *flow'ret* of the rural shade!
By Love's simplicity betray'd,
   And guileless trust,
Till she, like thee, all soil'd, is laid   35
   Low i' the dust.

Such is the fate of simple Bard,
On Life's rough ocean luckless starr'd!
Unskilful he to note the card
   Of *prudent Lore*,   40
Till billows rage, and gales blow hard,
   And whelm him o'er!

Such fate to *suffering worth* is giv'n,
Who long with wants and woes has striv'n,
By human pride or cunning driv'n   45
   To Mis'ry's brink,
Till wrench'd of ev'ry stay but Heav'n,
   He, ruin'd, sink!

Ev'n thou who mourn'st the *Daisy*'s fate,
That fate is thine—no distant date;   50
Stern Ruin's *plough-share* drives, elate,
   Full on thy bloom,
Till crush'd beneath the *furrow*'s weight,
   Shall be thy doom!

93. The Lament. Occasioned by the Unfortunate Issue of a Friend's Amour

Alas! how oft does goodness wound itself!
And sweet Affection *prove the spring of Woe!*
Home.

I

O Thou pale Orb, that silent shines,
  While care-untroubled mortals sleep!
Thou seest a *wretch*, who inly pines,
  And wanders here to wail and weep!
With Woe I nightly vigils keep,   5
  Beneath thy wan, unwarming beam;
And mourn, in lamentation deep,
  How *life* and *love* are all a dream!

II

I joyless view thy rays adorn,
  The faintly-marked, distant hill: 10
I joyless view thy trembling horn,
  Reflected in the gurgling rill.
My fondly-fluttering heart, be still!
  Thou busy pow'r, Remembrance, cease!
Ah! must the agonizing thrill,   15
  For ever bar returning Peace!

III

No idly-feign'd, poetic pains,
  My sad, lovelorn lamentings claim:
No shepherd's pipe—Arcadian strains;
  No fabled tortures, quaint and tame.   20
The *plighted faith;* the *mutual flame;*
  The *oft-attested Powers above;*
The *promis'd Father's tender name;*
  These were the pledges of my love!

The Lament. *Text from the edition of 1786, collated with the editions of 1787, 1793,*
1794
  3 who] that 93 94

IV

Encircled in her clasping arms,   25
  How have the raptur'd moments flown!
How have I wish'd for Fortune's charms,
  For her dear sake, and her's alone!
And, must I think it! is she gone,
  My secret-heart's exulting boast?   30
And does she heedless hear my groan?
  And is she ever, ever lost?

V

Oh! can she bear so base a heart,
  So lost to Honor, lost to Truth,
As from the *fondest lover* part,   35
  The *plighted husband* of her youth?
Alas! Life's path may be unsmooth!
  Her way may lie thro' rough distress!
Then, who her pangs and pains will soothe,
  Her sorrows share and make them less?   40

VI

Ye winged Hours that o'er us past,
  Enraptur'd more, the more enjoy'd,
Your dear remembrance in my breast,
  My fondly-treasur'd thoughts employ'd.
That breast, how dreary now, and void,   45
  For her too scanty once of room!
Ev'n ev'ry *ray* of *Hope* destroy'd,
  And not a *Wish* to gild the gloom!

VII

The morn that warns th' approaching day,
  Awakes me up to toil and woe: 50
I see the hours, in long array,
  That I must suffer, lingering, slow.
Full many a pang, and many a throe,
  Keen Recollection's direful train,
Must wring my soul, ere Phoebus, low,   55
  Shall kiss the distant, western main.

VIII

And when my nightly couch I try,
   Sore-harass'd out, with care and grief,
My toil-beat nerves, and tear-worn eye,
   Keep watchings with the nightly thief: 60
Or if I slumber, Fancy, chief,
   Reigns, hagard-wild, in sore afright:
Ev'n day, all-bitter, brings relief,
   From such a horror-breathing night.

IX

O! thou bright Queen, who, o'er th' expanse, 65
   Now highest reign'st, with boundless sway!
Oft has thy silent-marking glance
   Observ'd us, fondly-wand'ring, stray!
The time, unheeded, sped away,
   While Love's *luxurious pulse* beat high,   70
Beneath thy silver-gleaming ray,
   To mark the mutual-kindling eye.

X

Oh! scenes in strong remembrance set!
   Scenes, never, never to return!
Scenes, if in stupor I forget,   75
   Again I feel, again I burn!
From ev'ry joy and pleasure torn,
   Life's weary vale I'll wander thro';
And hopeless, comfortless, I'll mourn
   A faithless woman's broken vow.   80

94. Despondency, an Ode

I

OPPRESS'D with grief, oppress'd with care,
  A burden more than I can bear,
   I set me down and sigh:
O Life! Thou art a galling load,
Along a rough, a weary road,   5
   To wretches such as I!

Despondency, an Ode. *Text from the edition of 1786, collated with the editions of 1787, 1793, 1794*

Dim-backward as I cast my view,
  What sick'ning Scenes appear!
What Sorrows *yet* may pierce me thro',
  Too justly I may fear!   10
    Still caring, despairing,
      Must be my bitter doom;
    My woes here, shall close ne'er,
      But with the *closing tomb*!

II

Happy! ye sons of Busy-life,   15
Who, equal to the bustling strife,
  No other view regard!
Ev'n when the wished *end*'s deny'd,
Yet while the busy *means* are ply'd,
  They bring their own reward: 20
Whilst I, a hope-abandon'd wight,
  Unfitted with an *aim*,
Meet ev'ry sad-returning night,
  And joyless morn the same.
    You, bustling and justling,   25
      Forget each grief and pain;
    I, listless, yet restless,
      Find ev'ry prospect vain.

III

How blest the Solitary's lot,
Who, all-forgetting, all-forgot,   30
  Within his humble cell,
The cavern wild with tangling roots,
Sits o'er his newly-gather'd fruits,
  Beside his crystal well!
Or haply, to his ev'ning thought,   35
  By unfrequented stream,
The *ways of men* are distant brought,
  A faint-collected dream:
    While praising, and raising
      His thoughts to Heaven on high,   40
    As wand'ring, meand'ring,
      He views the solemn sky.

IV

Than I, no *lonely Hermit* plac'd
Where never human footstep trac'd,
   Less fit to play the part,   45
The *lucky moment* to improve,
And *just* to stop, and *just* to move,
   With *self-respecting* art:
But ah! those pleasures, Loves and Joys
   Which I too keenly taste,   50
The *Solitary* can despise,
   Can want, and yet be blest!
     He needs not, he heeds not,
       Or human love or hate;
     Whilst I here, must cry here,   55
       At perfidy ingrate!

V

Oh, enviable, early days,
When dancing thoughtless Pleasure's maze,
   To Care, to Guilt unknown!
How ill exchang'd for riper times,   60
To feel the follies, or the crimes,
   Of others, or my own!
Ye tiny elves that guiltless sport,
   Like linnets in the bush,
Ye little know the ills ye court,   65
   When Manhood is your wish!
     The losses, the crosses,
       That *active man* engage;
     The fears all, the tears all,
       Of dim declining *Age*!   70

95. Jeremiah 15ᵗʰ Ch. 10 V.

A<small>H</small>, woe is me, my Mother dear!
  A man of strife ye've born me:
For sair contention I maun bear,
   They hate, revile and scorn me.—

Jeremiah 15ᵗʰ Ch. 10 V. *Text from the Glenriddell MS (p. 124), collated with the Adam MS*

I ne'er could lend on bill or band,   5
    That five per cent might blest me;
And borrowing, on the tither hand,
    The de'il a ane wad trust me.—

Yet I, a coin-denied wight,
    By Fortune quite discarded,   10
Ye see how I am, day and night,
    By lad and lass blackguarded.—

96. Epitaph on a Henpecked Country Squire

As father Adam first was fool'd,
    A case that's still too common,
Here lyes a man a woman rul'd,
    The devil rul'd the woman.

97. Epigram on said Occasion

O DEATH, hadst thou but spar'd his life,
    Whom we, this day, lament!
We freely wad exchang'd the *wife*,
    An' a' been weel content.

Ev'n as he is, cauld in his graff,   5
    The *swap* we yet will do 't;
Tak thou the Carlin's carcase aff,
    Thou'se get the *saul* o' *boot*.

98. Another

One Queen Artemisa, as old stories tell,
    When depriv'd of her husband she loved so well,
In respect for the love and affection he'd show'd her,
She reduc'd him to dust, and she drank up the
        Powder.

Epitaph and Epigrams. *Text from the edition of 1786. Not reprinted*

But Queen N**********, of a diff'rent complexion, 5
When call'd on to order the fun'ral direction,
Would have *eat* her dead lord, on a slender pretence,
Not to show her respect, but—*to save the expence.*

99. Extempore— to Mr Gavin Hamilton

To you, Sir, this summons I've sent,
  Pray whip till the pownie is fraething;
But if you demand what I want,
  I honestly answer you, naething.—

Ne'er scorn a poor Poet like me,   5
  For idly just living and breathing,
While people of every degree
  Are busy employed about—naething.—

Poor Centum per centum may fast,
  And grumble his hurdies their claithing;   10
He'll find, when the balance is cast,
  He's gane to the devil for—naething.—

The Courtier cringes and bows,
  Ambition has likewise its plaything;
A Coronet beams in his brows,   15
  And what is a Coronet? naething.—

Some quarrel the presbyter gown,
  Some quarrel Episcopal graithing,
But every good fellow will own
  Their quarrel is all about—naething.—   20

The lover may sparkle and glow,
  Approaching his bonie bit gay thing;
But marriage will soon let him know,
  He's gotten a buskit up naething.—

Extempore. *Text from the* Second Commonplace Book, *pp. 29–31, collated with the*
transcript in the Glenriddell MS (pp. 111–13)

The Poet may jingle and rhyme,   25
   In hopes of a laureate wreathing,
And when he has wasted his time,
   He's kindly rewarded with naething.—

The thundering bully may rage,
   And swagger and swear like a heathen;   30
But collar him fast, I'll engage
   You'll find that his courage is naething.—

Last night with a feminine whig,
   A Poet she could na put faith in,
But soon we grew lovingly big,   35
   I taught her, her terrors were naething.—

Her whigship was wonderful pleased,
   But charmingly tickled wi' ae thing;
Her fingers I lovingly squeezed,
   And kissed her and promised her—naething.— 40

The Priest anathemas may threat,
   Predicament, Sir, that we're baith in;
But when honor's reveillé is beat,
   The holy artillery's naething.—

And now I must mount on the wave,   45
   My voyage perhaps there is death in;
But what of a watery grave!
   The drowning a Poet is naething.—

And now as grim death's in my thought,
   To you, Sir, I make this bequeathing: 50
My service as lang as ye've ought,
   And my friendship, by G—, when ye've
     naething.—

100. On a Scotch Bard Gone to the West Indies

A' YE wha live by sowps o' drink,
  A' ye wha live by crambo-clink,
A' ye wha live and never think,
     Come, mourn wi' me!
Our *billie*'s gien us a' a jink,   5
     An' owre the Sea.

Lament him a' ye rantan core,
Wha dearly like a random-splore;
Nae mair he'll join the *merry roar*,
     In social key;   10
For now he's taen anither shore,
     An' owre the Sea!

The bonie lasses weel may wiss him,
And in their dear *petitions* place him:
The widows, wives, an' a' may bless him,   15
     Wi' tearfu' e'e;
For weel I wat they'll sairly miss him
     That's owre the Sea!

O Fortune, they hae room to grumble!
Hadst thou taen aff some drowsy bummle,   20
Wha can do nought but fyke an' fumble,
     'Twad been nae plea;
But he was gleg as onie wumble,
     That's owre the Sea!

Auld, cantie KYLE may weepers wear,   25
An' stain them wi' the saut, saut tear:
'Twill mak her poor, auld heart, I fear,
     In flinders flee:
He was her *Laureat* monie a year,
     That's owre the Sea!   30

On a Scotch Bard. *Text from the edition of 1786, collated with the Adam and Hunting-*
ton Library (HL) *MSS and the editions of 1787, 1793, 1794*
    1 A'] A' O *Adam*   5 Our . . . a'] Our billie Tam has taen *Adam*: Our
billie, Rob, has ta'en *HL*   11 For . . . taen] He's canter't to *HL*   14 in . . .
place] pray kind Fortune to redress *HL*   19 they] *corrected to* we *in Adam*
21 Wha] That *Adam HL*   27 mak] gar *HL*

He saw Misfortune's cauld *Nor-west*
Lang-mustering up a bitter blast;
A Jillet brak his heart at last,
   Ill may she be!
So, took a birth afore the mast,   35
   An' owre the Sea.

To tremble under Fortune's cummock,
On scarce a bellyfu' o' *drummock*,
Wi' his proud, independant stomach,
   Could ill agree;   40
So, row't his hurdies in a *hammock*,
   An' owre the Sea.

He ne'er was gien to great misguidin,
Yet coin his pouches wad na bide in;
Wi' him it ne'er was *under hidin*;   45
   He dealt it free:
The *Muse* was a' that he took pride in,
   That's owre the Sea.

Jamaica bodies, use him weel,
An' hap him in a cozie biel: 50
Ye'll find him ay a dainty chiel,
   An' fou o' glee:
He wad na wrang'd the vera *Diel*,
   That's owre the Sea.

Fareweel, my *rhyme-composing billie*!   55
Your native soil was right ill-willie;
But may ye flourish like a lily,
   Now bonilie!
I'll toast ye in my hindmost *gillie*,
   Tho' owre the Sea!   60

34 may] may't *Adam HL* 38 On] An' *HL* 55 Fareweel, my *rhyme-composing*] Then fare-you-weel, my rhymin *HL* 58 Now] So *93* 59 ye 87–94: you *Adam HL 86*

101. [Second Epistle to Davie]

AULD NIBOR,

I'M three times, doubly, o'er your debtor,
For your auld-farrent, frien'ly letter;
Tho' I maun say 't, I doubt ye flatter,
      Ye speak sae fair;
For my puir, silly, rhymin' clatter   5
      Some less maun sair.

Hale be your heart, hale be your fiddle;
Lang may your elbuck jink an' diddle,
Tae cheer you thro' the weary widdle
      O' war'ly cares,   10
Till bairns' bairns kindly cuddle
      Your auld, gray hairs.

But DAVIE, lad, I'm red ye're glaikit;
I'm tauld the Muse ye hae negleckit;
An' gif it's sae, ye sud be licket   15
      Until ye fyke;
Sic hauns as you sud ne'er be faikit,
      Be hain't wha like.

For me, I'm on Parnassus brink,
Rivan the words tae gar them clink;   20
Whyles daez't wi' love, whyles daez't wi' drink,
      Wi' jads or masons;
An' whyles, but ay owre late, I think
      Braw sober lessons.

Of a' the thoughtless sons o' man,   25
Commen' me to the Bardie clan;
Except it be some idle plan
      O' rhymin clink,
The devil-haet, that I sud ban,
      They never think.   30

Second Epistle to Davie. *Text from David Sillar*, Poems, *1789; title* To the Author
30 never] ever *Sillar*

Nae thought, nae view, nae scheme o' livin',
Nae cares tae gie us joy or grievin':
But just the pouchie put the nieve in,
            An' while ought's there,
Then, hiltie, skiltie, we gae scrivin',   35
            An' fash nae mair.

Leeze me on rhyme! it's ay a treasure,
My chief, amaist my only pleasure,
At hame, a-fiel, at wark or leisure,
            The Muse, poor hizzie!   40
Tho' rough an' raploch be her measure,
            She's seldom lazy.

Haud tae the Muse, my dainty Davie:
The warl' may play you [monie] a shavie;
But for the Muse, she'll never leave ye,   45
            Tho' e'er sae puir,
Na, even tho' limpan wi' the spavie
            Frae door tae door.

102. [To] Mr Gavin Hamilton, Mauchline

I HOLD it, Sir, my bounden duty
To warn you how that Master TOOTIE,
    Alias, Laird M^cgawn,
Was here to hire yon lad away
'Bout which ye spak the ither day,   5
    An' wad hae done't aff han':
But lest he learn the callan tricks,
    As faith I muckle doubt him,
Like scrapin out auld Crummies' nicks,
    An' tellin lies about them;   10

44 monie Ed.: om. Sillar

To Mr Gavin Hamilton. Text from the Alloway MS (dated, and superscribed for posting), collated with Cromek, Reliques, 1808 (p. 397). Sub-title in Cromek (Recommending a Boy.)
5 which] whom Cromek

As lieve then I'd have then,
    Your CLERKSHIP he should sair;
If sae be ye may be
    Not fitted otherwhere.—

Altho' I say't, he's gleg enough,   15
An' 'bout a HOUSE that's rude an' rough,
    The boy might learn to SWEAR;
But then wi' you, he'll be sae taught,
An' get sic fair EXAMPLE straught,
    I hae na ony fear.   20
Ye'll catechize him, ev'ry quirk,
    An' shore him weel wi' HELL;
An' gar him follow to the kirk—
    —Ay, when ye gang YOURSEL.
      If ye then maun be then   25
        Frae hame, this comin Friday,
      Then please Sir, to lea'e Sir,
        The orders wi' your LADY.—

My word of HONOR I hae gien,
In PAISLEY JOHN's, that night at een,   30
    To meet the WARLD's WORM;
To try to get the twa to gree,
An' name the airles, an' the fee,
    In legal mode an' form:
I ken, he weel a SNICK can draw,   35
    When simple bodies let him;
An' if a DEVIL be at a',
    In faith, he's sure to get him.—
      To phrase you, an' praise you,
        Ye ken your LAUREAT scorns: 40
      The PRAY'R still, you share still,
        Of grateful MINSTREL BURNS.

Mossgaville
Wednesday 3d May
1786.

103. A Dedication To G**** H******* Esq;

Expect na, Sir, in this narration,
  A fleechan, fleth'ran *Dedication*,
To roose you up, an' ca' you guid,
An' sprung o' great an' noble bluid;
Because ye're sirnam'd like *His Grace*,   5
Perhaps related to the race:
Then when I'm tir'd—and sae are *ye*,
Wi' monie a fulsome, sinfu' lie,
Set up a face, how I stop short,
For fear your modesty be hurt.   10

   This may do—maun do, Sir, wi' them wha
Maun please the Great-folk for a wamefou;
For me! sae laigh I need na bow,
For, LORD be thanket, *I can plough*;
And when I downa yoke a naig,   15
Then, LORD be thanket, *I can beg*;
Sae I shall say, an' that's nae flatt'rin,
It's just *sic Poet* an' *sic Patron*.

   The Poet, some guid Angel help him,
Or else, I fear, some *ill ane* skelp him!   20
He may do weel for a' he's done yet,
But only—he's no just begun yet.

   The Patron, (Sir, ye maun forgie me,
I winna lie, come what will o' me)
On ev'ry hand it will allow'd be,   25
He's just—nae better than he should be.

   I readily and freely grant,
He downa see a poor man want;
What's no his ain, he winna tak it;
What ance he says, he winna break it;   30
Ought he can lend he'll no refus't,
Till aft his guidness is abus'd;

A Dedication. *Text from the edition of 1786, collated with those of 1787, 1793, 1794*

And rascals whyles that do him wrang,
Ev'n *that*, he does na mind it lang:
As Master, Landlord, Husband, Father,   35
He does na fail his part in either.

    But then, nae thanks to him for a' that;
Nae *godly symptom* ye can ca' that;
It's naething but a milder feature,
Of our poor, sinfu', corrupt Nature: 40
Ye'll get the best o' moral works,
'Mang black *Gentoos*, and Pagan *Turks*,
Or Hunters wild on *Ponotaxi*,
Wha never heard of Orth–d–xy.
That he's the poor man's friend in need,   45
The GENTLEMAN in word and deed,
It's no through terror of D–mn–t–n;
It's just a carnal inclination.

    Morality, thou deadly bane,
Thy tens o' thousands thou hast slain!   50
Vain is his hope, whase stay an' trust is,
In *moral* Mercy, Truth and Justice!

    No—stretch a point to catch a plack;
Abuse a Brother to his back;
Steal thro' the *winnock* frae a wh–re,   55
But point the Rake that taks the *door*;
Be to the Poor like onie whunstane,
And haud their noses to the grunstane;
Ply ev'ry art o' *legal* thieving;
No matter—stick to *sound believing*.   60

    Learn three-mile pray'rs, an' half-mile graces,
Wi' weel spread looves, an' lang, wry faces;
Grunt up a solemn, lengthen'd groan,
And damn a' Parties but your own;
I'll warrant then, ye're nae Deceiver,   65
A steady, sturdy, staunch *Believer*.

48 *additional line in 86 to complete a triplet:* And Och! that's nae r–g–n–r–t—n!

O ye wha leave the springs o' C–lv–n,
For *gumlie dubs* of your ain delvin!
Ye sons of Heresy and Error,
Ye'll *some day* squeel in quaking terror!   70
When Vengeance draws the sword in wrath,
And in the fire throws the *sheath*;
When Ruin, with his sweeping *besom*,
Just frets till Heav'n commission gies him;
While o'er the *Harp* pale Misery moans,⎫   75
And strikes the ever-deep'ning tones, ⎬
Still louder shrieks, and heavier groans! ⎭

   Your pardon, Sir, for this digression,
I maist forgat my *Dedication*;
But when Divinity comes cross me,   80
My readers still are sure to lose me.

   So Sir, you see 'twas nae daft vapour,
But I maturely thought it proper,
When a' my works I did review,
To *dedicate* them, Sir, to You: 85
Because (ye need na tak it ill)
I thought them something like *yoursel*.

   Then patronize them wi' your favor,
And your Petitioner shall ever—
I had amaist said, *ever pray*,   90
But that's a word I need na say:
For prayin I hae little skill o't;
I'm baith dead-sweer, an' wretched ill o't;
But I'se repeat each poor man's *pray'r*,
That kens or hears about you, Sir—   95

   'May ne'er Misfortune's gowling bark,
'Howl thro' the dwelling o' the CLERK!
'May ne'er his gen'rous, honest heart,
'For that same gen'rous spirit smart!
'May K******'s far-honor'd name   100
'Lang beet his hymeneal flame,

81 still 87–94: then 86

'Till H*******'s, at least a diz'n,
'Are frae their nuptial labors risen:
'Five bonie Lasses round their table,
'And sev'n braw fellows, stout an' able,   105
'To serve their King an' Country weel,
'By word, or pen, or pointed steel!
'May Health and Peace, with mutual rays,
'Shine on the ev'ning o' his days;
'Till his wee, curlie *John*'s ier-oe,   ⎫   110
'When ebbing life nae mair shall flow,   ⎬
'The last, sad, mournful rites bestow!'   ⎭

   I will not wind a lang conclusion,
With complimentary effusion:
But whilst your wishes and endeavours,   115
Are blest with Fortune's smiles and favours,
I am, Dear Sir, with zeal most fervent,
Your much indebted, humble servant.

   But if, which Pow'rs above prevent,
That iron-hearted Carl, *Want*,   120
Attended, in his grim advances,
By *sad mistakes*, and *black mischances*,
While hopes, and joys, and pleasures fly him,
Make you as poor a dog as I am,
Your *humble servant* then no more;   125
For who would humbly serve the Poor?
But by a poor man's hopes in Heav'n!
While recollection's pow'r is giv'n,
If, in the vale of humble life,
The victim sad of Fortune's strife,   130
I, through the tender-gushing tear,
Should recognise my *Master dear*,
If friendless, low, we meet together,
Then, Sir, your hand—my FRIEND and BROTHER.

104. A Bard's Epitaph

Is there a whim-inspir'd fool,
Owre fast for thought, owre hot for rule,
Owre blate to seek, owre proud to snool,
      Let him draw near;
And o'er this grassy heap sing dool,   5
      And drap a tear.

Is there a Bard of rustic song,
Who, noteless, steals the crouds among,
That weekly this area throng,
      O, pass not by!   10
But with a frater-feeling strong,
      Here, heave a sigh.

Is there a man whose judgment clear,
Can others teach the course to steer,
Yet runs, himself, life's mad career,   15
      Wild as the wave,
Here pause—and thro' the starting tear,
      Survey this grave.

The poor Inhabitant below
Was quick to learn and wise to know,   20
And keenly felt the friendly glow,
      And *softer flame*;
But thoughtless follies laid him low,
      And stain'd his name!

Reader attend—whether thy soul   25
Soars fancy's flights beyond the pole,
Or darkling grubs this earthly hole,
      In low pursuit,
Know, prudent, cautious, *self-controul*
      Is Wisdom's root.   30

A Bard's Epitaph. *Text from the edition of 1786, collated with those of 1787, 1793, 1794*

105. Epistle to a Young Friend

May — 1786.

I

I LANG hae thought, my youthfu' friend,
    A Something to have sent you,
Tho' it should serve nae other end
    Than just a kind memento;
But how the subject theme may gang,   5
    Let time and chance determine;
Perhaps it may turn out a Sang;
    Perhaps, turn out a Sermon.

II

Ye'll try the world soon my lad,
    And ANDREW dear believe me,   10
Ye'll find mankind an unco squad,
    And muckle they may grieve ye:
For care and trouble set your thought,
    Ev'n when your end's attained;
And a' your views may come to nought,   15
    Where ev'ry nerve is strained.

III

I'll no say, men are villains a';
    The real, harden'd wicked,
Wha hae nae check but *human law*,
    Are to a few restricked: 20
But Och, mankind are unco weak,
    An' little to be trusted;
If *Self* the wavering balance shake,
    It's rarely right adjusted!

Epistle to a Young Friend. *Text from the edition of 1786, collated with the Kilmarnock MS (Kil), Edinburgh University MS Laing II. 210–12, and the editions of 1787, 1793, 1794. The MSS have no title, and are dated* Mossgiel 15ᵗʰ May 1786
    5 how] *correcting* what *in Kil*   gang] *correcting* be *in MSS*   14 end 's]
view's *MSS*   15 views] schemes *MSS*   17–32 *Stanzas III and IV transposed in MSS*   21 Och, mankind are unco] gen'rally mankind are *MSS*

IV

Yet they wha fa' in Fortune's strife,   25
    Their fate we should na censure,
For still th' *important end* of life,
    They equally may answer:
A man may hae an *honest heart*,
    Tho' Poortith hourly stare him;   30
A man may tak a neebor's part,
    Yet hae nae *cash* to spare him.

V

Ay free, aff han', your story tell,
    When wi' a bosom crony;
But still keep something to yoursel   35
    Ye scarcely tell to ony.
Conceal yoursel as weel's ye can
    Frae critical dissection;
But keek thro' ev'ry other man,
    Wi' sharpen'd, sly inspection.   40

VI

The *sacred lowe* o' weel plac'd love,
    Luxuriantly indulge it;
But never tempt th' *illicit rove*,
    Tho' naething should divulge it:
I wave the quantum o' the sin;   45
    The hazard of concealing;
But Och! it hardens *a' within*,
    And petrifies the feeling!

26 should] would 94   48 *Additional stanza in MSS:*

    If ye hae made a step aside,
        Some hap-mistake, o'ertaen you;
    Yet, still keep up a decent pride,
        An' ne'er owre far demean you.
    Time comes wi' kind, oblivious shade,
        An' daily darker sets it;
    An', if nae mae mistakes are made,
        The world soon forgets it.

VII

To catch Dame Fortune's golden smile,
　　Assiduous wait upon her;　　　　　　　　　　50
And gather gear by ev'ry wile,
　　That's justify'd by Honor:
Not for to *hide* it in a *hedge*,
　　Nor for a *train-attendant*;
But for the glorious priviledge　　　　　　　　55
　　Of being *independant*.

VIII

The *fear o' Hell*'s a hangman's whip,
　　To haud the wretch in order;
But where ye feel your *Honor* grip,
　　Let that ay be your border:　　　　　　　　60
It's slightest touches, instant pause—
　　Debar a' side-pretences;
And resolutely keep it's laws,
　　Uncaring consequences.

IX

The great CREATOR to revere,　　　　　　　　65
　　Must sure become the *Creature*;
But still the preaching cant forbear,
　　And ev'n the rigid feature:
Yet ne'er with Wits prophane to range,
　　Be complaisance extended;　　　　　　　　70
An *atheist-laugh*'s a poor exchange
　　For *Deity offended*!

X

When ranting round in Pleasure's ring,
　　Religion may be blinded;
Or if she gie a *random-fling*,　　　　　　　　75
　　It may be little minded;
But when on Life we're tempest-driven,
　　A Conscience but a canker—
A correspondence fix'd wi' Heav'n,
　　Is sure a noble *anchor*!　　　　　　　　　80

61 It's] The *MSS*

XI

Adieu, dear, amiable Youth!
    Your *heart* can ne'er be wanting!
May Prudence, Fortitude and Truth
    Erect your brow undaunting!
In *ploughman phrase* 'GOD send you speed,'   85
    Still daily to grow wiser;
And may ye better reck the *rede*,
    Than ever did th' *Adviser*!

106. [Lines written on a Bank-note]

WAE worth thy pow'r, thou cursed leaf!
    Fell source of all my woe and grief!
For lake o' thee I've lost my lass;
For lake o' thee I scrimp my glass;
I see the children of Affliction   5
Unaided, thro' thy curst restriction;
I've seen th' Oppressor's cruel smile
Amid his hapless victim's spoil;
And for thy potence vainly wish'd
To crush the Villain in the dust: 10
For lake o' thee I leave this much-lov'd shore,
Never perhaps to greet old Scotland more!

                              R. B.—Kyle.

81 Adieu] Fareweel *MSS*   88 *MSS signed* Robt Burns.

Lines written on a Bank-note. *Text from the original MS at Alloway*

107. Highland Lassie O —

To its own tune —

McLauchlin's Scots Measure

Slowish

Chorus

N<small>AE</small> gentle dames tho' ne'er sae fair
Shall ever be my Muse's care;
Their titles a' are empty show,
Gie me my Highland Lassie, O.—

Chorus —

Within the glen sae bushy, O,   5
Aboon the plain sae rashy, O,
I set me down wi' right gude will
To sing my Highland Lassie, O.—

Highland Lassie O. *Text from the Hastie MS, f. 25*, collated with *SMM, 1788 (117;*
signed X), and SC, 1798 (37). To its own tune *corrects* Tune, M<small>c</small>Lachlin's Scots
measure *in MS. In SC the song is set to the air* The Deuk's dang o'er my Daddy,
arranged in eight-line stanzas, with the note This was an early production, and seems
to have been written on the Poet's Highland Mary
    1 ne'er] e'er *SC*   2 ever . . . Muse's] *correcting* be my simple Muse's *in MS*

O were yon hills and vallies mine,
Yon palace and yon gardens fine;   10
The world then the love should know
I bear my Highland Lassie, O.—
    Within the glen &c.

But fickle Fortune frowns on me,
And I maun cross the raging sea;
But while my crimson currents flow,   15
I love my Highland Lassie, O.—
    Within the glen &c.

Altho' thro' foreign climes I range,
I know her heart will never change;
For her bosom burns with honor's glow,
My faithful Highland Lassie, O.—   20
    Within the glen &c.

For her I'll dare the billow's roar;
For her I'll trace a distant shore;
That Indian wealth may lustre throw
Around my Highland Lassie, O.—
    Within the glen &c.

She has my heart, she has my hand,   25
By secret Truth and Honor's band:
Till the mortal stroke shall lay me low,
I'm thine, my Highland Lassie, O.—
    Farewel, the glen sae bushy! O
    Farewel, the plain sae rashy! O   30
    To other lands I now must go
    To sing my Highland Lassie, O.—

16 I] I'll *SC*   21 billow's] billows' *SC*   26 secret] sacred *SC*

108. [Address of Beelzebub]

To the R^t Honble JOHN, EARL OF BREADALBANE, President of the R^t Honble the HIGHLAND SOCIETY, which met, on the 23^d of May last, at the Shakespeare, Covent garden, to concert ways and means to frustrate the designs of FIVE HUNDRED HIGHLANDERS who, as the Society were informed by M^r McKenzie of Applecross, were so audacious as to attempt an escape from theire lawful lords and masters whose property they are emigrating from the lands of M^r McDonald of Glengary to the wilds of CANADA, in search of that fantastic thing —LIBERTY—

LONG LIFE, My lord, an' health be yours,
  Unskaith'd by hunger'd HIGHLAN BOORS!
Lord grant, nae duddie, desp'rate beggar,
Wi' durk, claymore, or rusty trigger
May twin auld SCOTLAND o' a LIFE,   5
She likes—as BUTCHERS like a KNIFE!

Faith, you and Applecross were right
To keep the highlan hounds in sight!
I doubt na! they wad bid nae better
Than let them ance out owre the water;   10
Then up amang thae lakes an' seas
They'll mak what rules an' laws they please.

Some daring Hancocke, or a Frankline,
May set their HIGHLAN bluid a ranklin;
Some Washington again may head them,   15
Or some MONTGOMERY, fearless, lead them;
Till, God knows what may be effected,
When by such HEADS an' HEARTS directed:
Poor, dunghill sons of dirt an' mire,
May to PATRICIAN RIGHTS ASPIRE;   20
Nae sage North, now, nor sager Sackville,
· To watch an' premier owre the pack vile!
An' whare will ye get Howes an' Clintons
To bring them to a right repentance,
To cowe the rebel generation,   25
An' save the honor o' the NATION?

Address of Beelzebub. *Text from the Watson MSS (1127)*

THEY! an' be d—mn'd! what right hae they
To Meat, or Sleep, or light o' day,
Far less to riches, pow'r, or freedom,
But what your lordships PLEASE TO GIE THEM?   30

BUT, hear me, my lord! Glengary, hear!
Your HAND'S OWRE LIGHT ON THEM, I fear:
Your FACTORS, GREIVES, TRUSTEES an' BAILIES,
I canna say but they do gailies;
They lay aside a' tender mercies   35
An' tirl the HALLIONS to the BIRSIES;
Yet, while they're only poin'd, and herriet,
They'll keep their stubborn Highlan spirit.
But smash them! crush them a' to spails!
An' rot the DYVORS i' the JAILS!   40
The young dogs, swinge them to the labour,
Let WARK an' HUNGER mak them sober!
The HIZZIES, if they're oughtlins fausont,
Let them in DRURY LANE be lesson'd!
An' if the wives, an' dirty brats,   45
Come thiggan at your doors an' yets,
Flaffan wi' duds, an' grey wi' beese,
Frightan awa your deucks an' geese;
Get out a HORSE-WHIP, or a JOWLER,
The langest thong, the fiercest growler,   50
An' gar the tatter'd gipseys pack
Wi' a' their bastarts on their back!

Go on, my lord! I lang to meet you
An' in my HOUSE AT HAME to greet you;
Wi' COMMON LORDS ye shanna mingle,   55
The benmost newk, beside the ingle
At my right hand, assign'd your seat
'Tween HEROD's hip, an' POLYCRATE;
Or, if ye on your station tarrow,
Between ALMAGRO and PIZARRO;   60
A seat, I'm sure ye're weel deservin't;
An' till ye come—your humble servant
                                    BEELZEBUB.
HELL 1st June Anno Mundi 5790

54–58 *MS defective; lines completed in another hand*

109. Libel Summons —

I N Truth and Honour's name—AMEN—
Know all men by these Presents plain:—

This fourth o' June, at Mauchline given,
The year 'tween eighty five and seven,
WE, Fornicators by profession,   5
As per extractum from each Session,
In way and manner here narrated,
Pro bono Amor congregated;
And by our brethren constituted,
A COURT OF EQUITY deputed.—   10
WITH special authoris'd direction
To take beneath our strict protection,
The stays-out-bursting, quondam maiden,
With GROWING LIFE and anguish laden;
Who by the rascal is deny'd,   15
That led her thoughtless steps aside.—
He who disowns the ruin'd Fair-one,
And for her wants and woes does care none;
The wretch that can refuse subsistence
To those whom he has given existence;   20

Libel Summons. *Text from (a) the Hastie MS (Ha), ff. 176ʳ–177ᵛ (ll. 1–98, 159–70)
and (b) B.M. MS Egerton 1656, ff. 8ʳ–10ʳ (Eg 1; ll. 99–158), collated with MS Eg 2
(f. 11; ending at l. 60) and Scott Douglas's transcript set into the back of his copy of
MMC (SD). Title from Ha; title in SD* The Court of Equity. A poem, by Robert
Burns; *no title in other MSS. See Commentary*
    3 fourth o' June] twalt o' May *Eg 1–2 SD*   5 Fornicators] old prac-
titioners *SD*   6 extractum . . . each] extracts frae Books o' *SD*   7–8 In . . .
congregated;] *not in Eg 1–2*   8 Pro bono Amor] All *con amore SD*   9 And]
Are, *SD*   12 beneath] within *SD*   strict protection] *correcting* keen inspection
in SD   13 stays-out-bursting] stays-unlacing *Eg 1–2*: open stay-laced *SD*
15 Who] *corrected to* That *in Eg 2*   rascal] Scoundrel *Eg 1–2*: miscreant *SD*
16 That] Who *Eg 1–2*   17–24 He . . . favors:] *Eg 1 has only*
                    The knave who takes a private stroke
                    Beneath his sanctimonious cloke:
In SD this couplet follows l. 22. Eg 2 has ll. 19–20, The knave . . . cloke, *and ll. 23–24
only*   19 that] who *Eg 2 SD*   refuse] deny *SD*   subsistence] assistance *Eg 2*
20 those . . . given] life he raked into *SD*

He who when at a lass's by-job,
Defrauds her wi' a fr–g or dry-b–b;
The coof that stands on clishmaclavers
When women haflins offer favors:—
All who in any way or manner   25
Distain the Fornicator's honor,
We take cognisance thereanent,
The proper Judges competent.—

First, Poet B—s he takes the chair;
Allow'd by a', his title's fair;   30
And pass'd nem. con. without dissension,
He has a duplicate pretension.—
Next, Merchant Smith, our worthy Fiscal,
To cow each pertinaceous rascal;
In this, as every other state,   35
His merit is conspicuous great:
Richmond the third, our trusty Clerk,
The minutes regular to mark,
And sit dispenser of the law,
In absence of the former twa;   40
The fourth our Messenger at Arms,
When failing all the milder terms,
Hunter, a hearty, willing brother,
Weel skill'd in *dead and living leather.—
Without Preamble less or more said,   45
We, body politic aforesaid,

* A Tanner.

21–22, 23–24 *Transposed in SD*   21 He . . . by-job,] *correcting* The selfish,
d–mn'd, dry-bobbing *in Ha*: The sneak wha, at . . . by-job *SD*   23–24 clishmaclavers . . . favors] *clishmaclaver* . . . favour *SD*   23 that stands] wha stan's
Eg 2 SD   24 women] lasses *overwritten in Ha*: lasses *Eg 2 SD*   25 All . .
or] In short, all who in any *SD*   who] *correcting* those *in Eg 1*   26 Distain
the Fornicator's] Shall stain the Fornicator's *correcting* Shall shirk to act like Man
of *in SD*   27 We] To *SD*   28 The proper] We are the *SD*   30 fair]
clear *SD*   31–32 *Transposed in SD*   31 And pass'd] To pass *SD*   32 has
shews *SD*   33 Next, Merchant] The second, *Eg 1–2*   worthy] *corrected to*
trusty *in SD*   35 as . . . state] his very foes admit *SD*   37 trusty] worthy
SD   38 The] Our *Eg 1–2 SD*   regular to] he will duly *SD*   39 And sit]
A fit *SD*   40 former] *corrects* tither *in Eg 1*: ither *SD*   41 The] And *SD*
42 all] a' *SD*   43 hearty, willing] willing, hearty *Eg 2 SD*   brother] brither
SD   44, 55 *Notes in Ha only*

With legal, due WHEREAS, and WHEREFORE,
We are appointed here to care for
The interests of our constituents,
And punish contraveening truants,   50
Keeping a proper regulation
Within the lists of FORNICATION.—

WHEREAS, our FISCAL, by petition,
Informs us there is strong suspicion,
You, Coachman *Dow, and Clockie †BROWN,   55
Baith residenters in this town;
In other words, you, JOCK, and, SANDY,
Hae been at wark at HOUGHMAGANDIE;
And now when facts are come to light,
The matter ye deny outright.—   60

FIRST, YOU, JOHN BROWN, there's witness borne,
And affidavit made and sworn,
That ye hae bred a hurly-burly
'Bout JEANY MITCHEL's tirlie-whirlie,
And blooster'd at her regulator,   65
Till a' her wheels gang clitter-clatter.—
And farther still, ye cruel Vandal,
A tale might even in hell be scandal!

    * A coachman.   † A Clockmaker.

---

47 With legal] Shall now wi' *SD*   48 We . . . care] Dispatch the business we
cam here *SD*   49–50 *Transposed in SD as*

> And punish contravening truants,
> At instance of our constituants;

51 Keeping a] And thus by *SD*: And keep *Eg 2*   52 Within] We'll purge *SD*
53 WHEREAS . . . by] Our fiscal here, by his *SD*   55 You] That *SD*
58 wark at] warks o' *SD*   59 when facts are] when it is *Eg 1*: the matter 's
Eg 2   come] brought *SD*   60 The matter ye] Your part in 't, ye *Eg 2*:
Those facts ye baith *SD*   60 *Eg 2 ends*   61 FIRST, YOU, JOHN] YOU
CLOCKIE *Eg 1*: First, CLOCKY *SD*   62 *Lines 79–82 follow in SD*   63 That
ye . . . bred] That YE . . . rais'd *Eg 1*: And that ye wroucht *SD*   64 'Bout]
In *Eg 1 SD*   64, 76 JEANY] *correction (? not autograph) of* MAGGY *in Eg 1*
65–66 And . . . clitter-clatter.] *not in Eg 1. SD has*

> That ye her pend'lum tried to alter
> And graizled at her regulator:

That ye hae made repeated trials
Wi' drugs and draps in doctor's phials,   70
Mixt, as ye thought, wi' fell infusion,
Your ain begotten wean to poosion.—
And yet ye are sae scant o' grace,
Ye daur to lift your brazen face,
And offer for to take your aith,   75
Ye never lifted JEANY's claith.—
But tho' ye should yoursel manswear,
Laird Wilson's sclates can witness bear,
Ae e'ening of a MAUCHLINE fair,
That JEANY's masts they saw them bare;   80
For ye had furl'd up her sails,
And was at play—at heads and tails.—

NEXT, SANDY DOW, you're here indicted
To have, as publickly you're wyted,
Been clandestinely upward whirlin   85
The petticoats o' MAGGY BORELAN,
And giein her canister a rattle,
That months to come it winna settle.—
And yet, ye offer your protest,
Ye never herried Maggy's nest;   90
Tho', it's weel ken'd that at her gyvel
Ye hae gien mony a kytch and kyvel.—

THEN BROWN AND DOW, before design'd,
For clags and clauses there subjoin'd,
WE, Court aforesaid, cite and summon,   95
That on the fifth o' July comin,

69 That . . . repeated] Ye've made repeated wicked *Eg 1*   70 draps] droggs *SD*
71 wi'] in *SD*   74 Ye . . . to lift] Ye . . . set up *Eg 1*: As . . . to lift *SD*
75 for to take] there to gie *SD*   77–78 But . . . bear,] *om. SD*   77 ye . . .
manswear] by Heaven an' Hell ye swear *Eg 1*   should] *follows* wickedly (*del.*) *in Ha*
79 Ae . . . MAUCHLINE] Last Mauchline February *SD*   80 JEANY's] Maggie's *Eg 1*
they saw] ye laid *SD*   82 at] o' *SD*   83 NEXT, SANDY . . . you're here]
YOU COACHMAN . . . are here *Eg 1*: Next, Sandy . . . ye are *SD*   84 To . . .
you're] As publicly ye hae been *SD*   85 Been clandestinely upward] For aft
clandestinely up- *SD*   87 giein] gied *Eg 1*   88 to come it] hereafter *SD*
89 offer your] loon, ye still *SD*   92 Ye . . . kyvel.] Ye've done what Time
will soon unravel. *SD*   93 before] above *Eg 1 SD*   94 clauses there] claims
hereto *SD*   95 WE,] The *SD*   96 fifth o' July] fourth o' June in *Eg 1*:
fourth o' June just *SD*

The hour o' cause, in our Court-ha',
At Whitefoord's arms, ye answer LAW!

[BUT, as reluctantly we PUNISH,
An' rather, mildly would admonish: 100
Since Better PUNISHMENT prevented,
Than OBSTINACY sair repented.—

THEN, for that ANCIENT SECRET'S SAKE,
You have the honor to partake;
An' for that NOBLE BADGE you wear,   105
YOU, SANDIE DOW, our BROTHER dear,
We give you as a MAN an' MASON,
This private, sober, friendly lesson.—

YOUR CRIME, a manly deed we view it,
As MAN ALONE, can only do it;   110
But, in denial persevering,
Is to a SCOUNDREL'S NAME adhering.
The BEST o' MEN, hae been surpris'd;
The BEST o' WOMEN been advis'd:
NAY, CLEVEREST LADS hae haen a TRICK O'T,   115
AN', BONNIEST LASSES taen a LICK O'T.—

98 At .. LAW!] At Whitefoord Arms, ye'll answer a'. *SD. SD adds*
              Exculpate proof ye needna bring,
              For we're resolved about the thing—
99–158 *Text from Eg 1*   99 BUT] Yet *SD*   100 mildly would] would with
zeal *SD*   101–2 Since ... repented.] *om. SD*   101 Since] *correcting* Far *in*
Eg 1   103 THEN ... SECRET'S] We ... Secret *SD*   108 private] serious *SD*
109 view] trow *SD*   110 only] *corrected to* rightly *in SD*   111–12 *SD has*
              And he's nae man that won't avow it;
              Therefore, confess, and join our core,
              And keep reproach outside the door.
114 BEST O'] doucest *SD*   115 NAY, ... haen] The ... had *SD*   116 AN',]
The *SD*   116 *SD adds*
              Kings hae been proud our name to own—
              The brightest jewel in their crown;
              The rhyming sons o' bleak Parnassus,
              Were ay red-wud about the lasses,
              And saul and body, all would venture,
              Rejoicing in our list to enter,
              E'en (wha wad trow't?)—the cleric order
              Aft slyly break the hallow'd border,
              And show—in ᵏⁱᵗᵗˡᵉ time and place—
                         certain
              They are as scant o' boasted grace,
              As ony o' the human race.

Then Brother Dow, if you're asham'd⎫
In such a QUORUM to be nam'd,   ⎬
Your conduct much is to be blam'd. ⎭
See, ev'n HIMSEL—there's GODLY BRYAN,   120
The auld WHATRECK he has been tryin;
When such as he put to their han',
What man on CHARACTER need stan'?
Then Brother dear, lift up your brow,
And, like yoursel, the TRUTH avow;   125
Erect a dauntless face upon it,
An' say, 'I am the man has done it;
'I SANDIE DOW GAT MEG WI' WEAN,
'An's fit to do as much again.'
Ne'er mind their solemn rev'rend faces,   130
Had they—in proper times an' places,
But SEEN AN' FUN'—I mukle dread it,
They just would done as you an' WE did.—
To TELL THE TRUTH's a manly lesson,
An' doubly proper in A MASON.—   135

You MONSIEUR BROWN, as it is proven,
JEAN MITCHEL's wame by you was hoven;
Without you by a quick repentance   ⎫
Acknowledge Jean's an' your acquaintance, ⎬
Depend on't, this shall be your sentence.— ⎭   140
Our beadles to the Cross shall take you,
And there shall mither naked make you;
Some canie grip near by your middle,
They shall it bind as tight's a fiddle;
The raep they round the PUMP shall tak   145
An' tye your han's behint your back;

117 Then . . . you're] So, . . . be not *SD*   118 such] sic *SD*   119–25 Your
. . . avow;] *om. SD*   126 Erect . . . face] But lift . . . brow *SD*
128 WEAN] bairn *SD*   129 's] *om. SD*   130–5 Ne'er . . . MASON.] *om. SD*
136–7 YOU . . . hoven;] *SD has*

        For you, John Brown, sae black your faut is,
        Sae double-dyed, we gie you notice,

137 JEAN] MEG *Eg 1*   138 you] ye, *SD*   139 Jean's *SD*: MEG's *Eg 1*
140 Depend on't,] Remember *SD*   141 beadles] beagles *SD*   141–2 take
you . . . make you] tak ye . . . mak ye *SD*   143–4 Some . . . fiddle;] *om. SD*
145 The raep . . . shall] Around the rump a rape they'll *SD*   146 behint]
ahint *SD*

Wi' just an ell o' string allow'd
To jink an' hide you frae the croud:
There ye shall stan', a legal seizure,
In during Jeanie Mitchel's pleasure;   150
So be, her pleasure dinna pass
Seven turnings of a half-hour glass:
Nor shall it in her pleasure be
To louse you out in less than THREE.—

THIS, our futurum esse DECREET,   155
We mean it not to keep a secret;
But in OUR SUMMONS here insert it,
And whoso dares, may controvert it.—]

THIS, mark'd before the date and place is,
SIGILLUM EST, PER,

                    B—S THE PRESES.   160

This Summons and the signet mark,
EXTRACTUM EST, PER,

                    RICHMOND, CLERK.

AT MAUCHLINE, idem date of June,
'Tween six and seven, the afternoon,
You twa, in propria personæ,   165
Within design'd, SANDY and JOHNY,
This SUMMONS legally have got,
As vide witness underwrote:
Within the house of JOHN DOW, vinter,
NUNC FACIO HOC,

                    GULLELMUS HUNTER.   170

148 you] ye SD   149 legal] lawful SD   150 Jeanie SD: Maggie Eg 1
151 dinna pass] don't surpass SD   152 Seven] Five SD   154 louse you
out] turn you loose SD   156 it not to keep] not to be kept SD   158 dares,
may controvert] dare—let him subvert SD   159-70 Text from Ha
159 THIS . . . before] Thus . . above, SD   160 SIGILLUM] SUBSIGNUM Eg 1
161 and] wi' SD   163 idem . . . June] idem . . . May SD: twenty fifth of
May Eg 1   164 'Tween . . . afternoon] About the twalt hour o' the day Eg 1:
'Tween four and five, decline of day SD   165 twa] two Eg 1   166 Within]
Before Eg 1 SD   167 have got] you've got it SD   168 underwrote] under-
noted SD

110. Epitaph on John Dove, Innkeeper, Mauchline

H ERE lies Johnny Pidgeon,
   What was his religion,
Whae'er desires to ken,
To some other warl
Maun follow the carl,   5
For here Johnny Pidgeon had nane.

Strong ale was ablution,
Small beer persecution,
A dram was *memento mori*;
But a full flowing bowl,   10
Was the saving his soul,
And Port was celestial glory.

111. Epitaph on a Wag in Mauchline

L AMENT 'im Mauchline husbands a',
   He aften did assist ye;
For had ye staid whole weeks awa'
   Your wives they ne'er had miss'd ye.

Ye Mauchline bairns as on ye pass,   5
   To school in bands thegither,
O tread ye lightly on his grass,
   Perhaps he was your father.

Epitaph on John Dove. *Text from Stewart, 1801 (p. 32)*

Epitaph on a Wag. *Text from Stewart, 1801 (p. 54). Another version was published in* The Court of Equity, *1910, with the title* Johannes Fuscus hic jacet quondam horologiorum Faber in M——. *It has* Tho ye had bidden years awa' *in l. 3 and a few trivial variants*

112. [On Willie Chalmers]

Madam,

W^I' braw new branks in mickle pride,
        And eke a braw new brechan,
My Pegasus I'm got astride,
        And up Parnassus pechin;
Whiles owre a bush wi' downward crush,   5
        The doited beastie stammers;
Then up he gets, and off he sets,
        For sake o' *Willie Chalmers.*

I doubt na, lass, that weel kenned name
        May cost a pair o' blushes;   10
I am nae stranger to your fame,
        Nor his warm-urged wishes.
Your bonnie face sae mild and sweet,
        His honest heart enamours,
And faith ye'll no be lost a whit,   15
        Tho' waired on *Willie Chalmers.*

Auld Truth hersel' might swear ye're fair,
        And Honour safely back her,
And Modesty assume your air,
        And ne'er a ane mistak' her: 20
And sic twa love-inspiring e'en,
        Might fire even holy Palmers;
Nae wonder then they've fatal been
        To honest *Willie Chalmers.*

I doubt na Fortune may you shore   25
        Some mim-mou'd pouthered priestie,
Fu' lifted up wi' Hebrew lore,
        And band upon his breastie;
But oh! what signifies to you
        His lexicons and grammars;   30
The feeling heart's the royal blue,
        And that's wi' *Willie Chalmers.*

On Willie Chalmers. *Text from Lockhart, 1830 (pp. 159–60). See Commentary*
25 shore] shore, *Lockhart*

Some gapin' glowrin' countra laird,
   May warsle for your favour;
May claw his lug, and straik his beard,   35
   And host up some palaver.
My bonie maid, before ye wed
   Sic clumsy-witted hammers,
Seek Heaven for help, and barefit skelp
   Awa' wi' *Willie Chalmers*.   40

Forgive the Bard! my fond regard
   For ane that shares my bosom,
Inspires my muse to gie 'm his dues,
   For de'il a hair I roose him.
May powers aboon unite you soon,   45
   And fructify your amours,—
And every year come in mair dear
   To you and *Willie Chalmers*.

113. A Dream

Thoughts, words and deeds, the Statute blames with reason;
But surely Dreams were ne'er indicted Treason.

On reading, in the public papers, the Laureate's Ode, with the other
parade of June 4th, 1786, the Author was no sooner dropt asleep,
than he imagined himself transported to the Birth-day Levee; and,
in his dreaming fancy, made the following Address.

I

G UID-MORNIN to your MAJESTY!
   May heaven augment your blisses,
On ev'ry new *Birth-day* ye see,
   A humble Poet wishes!
My Bardship here, at your Levee,   5
   On sic a day as this is,
Is sure an uncouth sight to see,
   Amang thae Birth-day dresses
         Sae fine this day.

A Dream. *Text from the edition of 1786, collated with those of 1787, 1793, 1794*
  4 Poet *93 94*: Bardie *86 87*

II

I see ye're complimented thrang,   10
 By many a *lord* an' *lady*;
'God save the King''s a cukoo sang
 That's unco easy said ay:
The *Poets* too, a venal gang,
 Wi' rhymes weel-turn'd an' ready,   15
Wad gar you trow ye ne'er do wrang,
 But ay unerring steady,
     On sic a day.

III

For me! before a Monarch's face,
 Ev'n *there* I winna flatter;   20
For neither Pension, Post, nor Place,
 Am I your humble debtor:
So, nae reflection on YOUR GRACE,
 Your Kingship to bespatter;
There's monie *waur* been o' the Race,   25
 And aiblins *ane* been better
    Than You this day.

IV

'Tis very true, my sovereign King,
 My skill may weel be doubted;
But *Facts* are cheels that winna ding,   30
 An' downa be disputed:
Your *royal nest*, beneath *Your* wing,
 Is e'en right reft an' clouted,
And now the third part o' the string,
 An' less, will gang about it   35
    Than did ae day.

V

Far be't frae me that I aspire
 To blame your Legislation,
Or say, ye wisdom want, or fire,
 To rule this mighty nation;   40

But faith! I muckle doubt, my SIRE,
  Ye've trusted 'Ministration,
To chaps, wha, in a *barn* or *byre*,
  Wad better fill'd their station
           Than *courts* yon day.   45

VI

And now Ye've gien auld *Britain* peace,
  Her broken shins to plaister;
Your sair taxation does her fleece,
  Till she has scarce a tester:
For me, thank God, my life's a *lease*,   50
  Nae *bargain* wearing faster,
Or faith! I fear, that, wi' the geese,
  I shortly boost to pasture
           I' the craft some day.

VII

I'm no mistrusting *Willie Pit*,   55
  When taxes he enlarges,
(An' *Will*'s a true guid fallow's get,
  A Name not Envy spairges)
That he intends to pay your *debt*,
  An' lessen a' your *charges*;   60
But, G–d-sake! let nae *saving-fit*
  Abridge your bonie *Barges*
           An' *Boats* this day.

VIII

Adieu, my LIEGE! may Freedom geck
  Beneath your high protection;   65
An' may Ye rax Corruption's neck,
  And gie her for dissection!
But since I'm here, I'll no neglect,
  In loyal, true affection,
To pay your QUEEN, with due respect,   70
  My fealty an' subjection
           This great Birth-day.

57 *Will*'s] *Will*'s 86 87

IX

Hail, *Majesty most Excellent!*
  While Nobles strive to please Ye,
Will Ye accept a Compliment,   75
  A simple Poet gies Ye?
Thae bonie Bairntime, Heav'n has lent,
  Still higher may they heeze Ye
In bliss, till Fate some day is sent,
  For ever to release Ye   80
        Frae Care that day.

X

For you, young Potentate o' W——,
  I tell your *Highness* fairly,
Down Pleasure's stream, wi' swelling sails,
  I'm tauld ye're driving rarely;   85
But some day ye may gnaw your nails,
  An' curse your folly sairly,
That e'er ye brak *Diana*'s *pales*,
  Or rattl'd dice wi' *Charlie*
        By night or day.   90

XI

Yet aft a ragged *Cowte*'s been known,
  To mak a noble *Aiver*;
So, ye may dousely fill a Throne,
  For a' their clish-ma-claver:
There, Him at *Agincourt* wha shone,   95
  Few better were or braver;
And yet, wi' funny, queer *Sir* John*,
  He was an unco shaver
        For monie a day.

XII

For you, right rev'rend O——,   100
  Nane sets the *lawn-sleeve* sweeter,
Altho' a ribban at your lug
  Wad been a dress compleater:

---

* Sir John Falstaff, Vide Shakespeare.

---

76 Poet *93 94*: Bardie *86 87*   88 *Diana*'s *87–94*: Diana's *86*

As ye disown yon paughty dog,
   That *bears* the Keys of Peter,   105
Then swith! an' get a *wife* to hug,
   Or trouth! ye'll stain the *Mitre*
          Some luckless day.

XIII

Young, royal TARRY-BREEKS, I learn,
   Ye've lately come athwart her;   110
A glorious* *Galley*, stem and stern,
   Weel rigg'd for *Venus barter*;
But first hang out that she'll discern
   Your *hymeneal Charter*,
Then heave aboard your *grapple airn*,   115
   An', large upon her *quarter*,
          Come full that day.

XIV

Ye lastly, bonie blossoms a',
   Ye *royal Lasses* dainty,
Heav'n mak you guid as weel as braw,   120
   An' gie you *lads* a plenty:
But sneer na *British-boys* awa;
   For Kings are unco scant ay,
An' German-Gentles are but *sma'*,
   They're better just than *want ay*   125
          On onie day.

XV

God bless you a'! consider now,
   Ye're unco muckle dautet;
But ere the *course* o' life be through,
   It may be bitter sautet: 130
An' I hae seen their *coggie* fou,
   That yet hae tarrow't at it,
But or the *day* was done, I trow,
   The laggen they hae clautet
          Fu' clean that day.   135

* Alluding to the Newspaper account of a certain royal Sailor's Amour.

123 Kings *87–94*: King's *86*

114. [To Dr. John Mackenzie]

FRIDAY first's the day appointed
By our Right Worshipful Anointed,
　　To hold our grand Procession,
To get a blade o' Johnie's Morals,
And taste a swatch o' Manson's barrels, 　　　5
　　I' the way of our Profession:
Our Master and the Brotherhood
　　Wad a' be glad to see you;
For me, I wad be mair than proud
　　To share the MERCIES wi' you. 　　　10
　　If Death then wi' skaith then
　　　　Some mortal heart is hechtin,
　　Inform him, an' storm him,
　　　　That SATURDAY ye'll fecht him.

115. The Farewell. To the Brethren of St. James's Lodge, Tarbolton

Tune, Goodnight and joy be wi' you a'

Brisk

To Dr. John Mackenzie. *Text from the Adam MS, signed* Robt Burns *and dated* Mossgiel, 14th June, A.M. 5790.

The Farewell. *Text from the edition of 1786, collated with SMM, 1803 (600), and the editions of 1787, 1793, 1794. SMM lacks a title*

I

Adieu! a heart-warm, fond adieu!
 Dear brothers of the *mystic tye*!
Ye favour'd, ye enlighten'd Few,
 Companions of my social joy!
Tho' I to foreign lands must hie,   5
 Pursuing Fortune's slidd'ry ba',
With melting heart, and brimful eye,
 I'll mind you still, tho' far awa'.

II

Oft have I met your social Band,
 And spent the chearful, festive night;   10
Oft, honor'd with supreme command,
 Presided o'er the *Sons of light*:
And by that *Hieroglyphic* bright,
 Which none but *Craftsmen* ever saw!
Strong Mem'ry on my heart shall write   15
 Those happy scenes when far awa'!

III

May Freedom, Harmony and Love
 Unite you in the *grand Design*,
Beneath th' Omniscient Eye above,
 The glorious ARCHITECT Divine!   20
That you may keep th' *unerring line*,
 Still rising by the *plummet's law*,
Till *Order* bright, completely shine,
 Shall be my Pray'r when far awa'.

IV

And *You*, farewell! whose merits claim,   25
 Justly that *highest badge* to wear!
Heav'n bless your honor'd, noble Name,
 To MASONRY and SCOTIA dear!
A last request, permit me here,
 When yearly ye assemble a',   30
One *round*, I ask it with a *tear*,
 To him, *the Bard, that 's far awa'*.

3 favour'd, ye enlighten'd *SMM 93 94*: favored, *enlighten'd 86 87*   8, 16,
24, 32 awa' *SMM 93 94*: awa *86 87*

116. The Farewell

The valiant, in himself, what can he suffer?
Or what does he regard his single woes?
But when, alas! he multiplies himself,
To dearer selves, to the lov'd tender fair,
To those whose bliss, whose beings hang upon him,
To helpless children,—then, Oh then he feels
The point of misery festering in his heart,
And weakly weeps his fortunes like a coward:
Such, such am I!—undone!
　　　　　　　　　Thomson's *Edward and Eleanora.*

FAREWELL, old Scotia's bleak domains,
　Far dearer than the torrid plains,
　　Where rich ananas blow!
Farewell, a mother's blessing dear!
A brother's sigh! a sister's tear!　　　　　　5
　My Jean's heart-rending throe!
Farewell, my Bess! tho' thou'rt bereft
　　Of my paternal care,
A faithful brother I have left,
　　My part in him thou'lt share!　　　　　10
　　　Adieu too, to you too,
　　　　My Smith, my bosom frien';
　　When kindly you mind me,
　　　O then befriend my Jean!

What bursting anguish tears my heart;　　　15
From thee, my Jeany, must I part!
　　Thou, weeping, answ'rest—'No!'
Alas! misfortune stares my face,
And points to ruin and disgrace,
　　I for thy sake must go!　　　　　　　20
Thee, Hamilton, and Aiken dear,
　　A grateful, warm adieu:
I, with a much-indebted tear,
　　Shall still remember you!
　　　All-hail then, the gale then,　　　25
　　　　Wafts me from thee, dear shore!
　　It rustles, and whistles
　　　I'll never see thee more!

The Farewell. *Text from Hamilton Paul's edition, 1819 (p. 197)*

117. Tam Samson's* Elegy

An honest man's the noblest work of God—
POPE.

H AS auld K********* seen the Deil?
     Or great M'*******† thrawn his heel?
Or R********‡ again grown weel,
          To preach an' read?
'Na, waur than a'!' cries ilka chiel,   5
     'Tam Samson's dead!'

K********* lang may grunt an' grane,
An' sigh an' sab, an' greet her lane,
An' cleed her bairns, man, wife, an' wean,
          In mourning weed;   10
To Death she's dearly pay'd the kane,
     Tam Samson's dead!

The Brethren o' the mystic *level*
May hing their head in wofu' bevel,
While by their nose the tears will revel,   15
          Like ony bead;
Death's gien the Lodge an unco devel,
     Tam Samson's dead!

When Winter muffles up his cloak,
And binds the mire like a rock;   20
When to the loughs the Curlers flock,
          Wi' gleesome speed,
Wha will they station at the *cock*,
     Tam Samson's dead?

* When this worthy old Sportsman went out last muir-fowl season, he supposed it
was to be, in Ossian's phrase, 'the last of his fields;' and expressed an ardent wish to
die and be buried in the muirs. On this hint the Author composed his Elegy and
Epitaph.

† A certain Preacher, a great favourite with the Million. *Vide* the ORDINATION,
p. [214].

‡ Another Preacher, an equal favourite with the Few, who was at that time ailing.
For him see also the ORDINATION, stanza IX.

Tam Samson's Elegy. *Text from the Edinburgh edition, 1787, collated with those of
1793, 1794*
   8 sab] sob *87 (sk) 93*   22 speed] spied *87*

He was the king of a' the Core,   25
To guard, or draw, or wick a bore,
Or up the rink like *Jehu* roar
      In time o' need;
But now he lags on Death's *hog-score*,
      Tam Samson's dead!   30

Now safe the stately Sawmont sail,
And Trouts bedropp'd wi' crimson hail,
And Eels weel kend for souple tail,
      And Geds for greed,
Since dark in Death's *fish-creel* we wail   35
      Tam Samson dead!

Rejoice, ye birring Paitricks a';
Ye cootie Moorcocks, crousely craw;
Ye Maukins, cock your fud fu' braw,
      Withoutten dread;   40
Your mortal Fae is now awa',
      Tam Samson's dead!

That woefu' morn be ever mourn'd
Saw him in shootin graith adorn'd,
While pointers round impatient burn'd,   45
      Frae couples freed;
But, Och! he gaed and ne'er return'd!
      Tam Samson's dead!

In vain Auld-age his body batters;
In vain the Gout his ancles fetters;   50
In vain the burns cam down like waters,
      An acre-braid!
Now ev'ry auld wife, greetin, clatters,
      'Tam Samson's dead!'

Owre mony a weary hag he limpit,   55
An' ay the tither shot he thumpit,
Till coward Death behind him jumpit,
      Wi' deadly feide;
Now he proclaims, wi' tout o' trumpet,
      Tam Samson's dead!   60

When at his heart he felt the dagger,
He reel'd his wonted bottle-swagger,
But yet he drew the mortal trigger
   Wi' weel-aim'd heed;
'L—d, five!' he cry'd, an' owre did stagger; 65
   Tam Samson's dead!

Ilk hoary Hunter mourn'd a brither;
Ilk Sportsman-youth bemoan'd a father;
Yon auld gray stane, amang the heather,
   Marks out his head, 70
Whare *Burns* has wrote, in rhyming blether,
   Tam Samson's dead!

There, low he lies, in lasting rest;
Perhaps upon his mould'ring breast
Some spitefu' muirfowl bigs her nest, 75
   To hatch an' breed:
Alas! nae mair he'll them molest!
   Tam Samson's dead!

When August winds the heather wave,
And Sportsmen wander by yon grave, 80
Three vollies let his mem'ry crave
   O' pouther an' lead,
Till Echo answer frae her cave,
   Tam Samson's dead!

Heav'n rest his saul, whare'er he be! 85
Is th' wish o' mony mae than me:
He had twa fauts, or maybe three,
   Yet what remead?
Ae social, honest man want we:
   Tam Samson's dead! 90

THE EPITAPH

Tam Samson's weel-worn clay here lies,
 Ye canting Zealots, spare him!
If Honest Worth in heaven rise,
 Ye'll mend or ye win near him.

73–78 There . . . dead!] *added in 93 94; holograph insertion in Geddes' copy of 87*
(*Huntington Library*) *beginning* Here, low he lies . . .

PER CONTRA

Go, Fame, an' canter like a filly   95
Thro' a' the streets an' neuks o' *Killie*,*
Tell ev'ry social, honest billie
    To cease his grievin,
For yet, unskaith'd by Death's gleg gullie,
    Tam Samson's livin!   100

118. [To John Kennedy]

FAREWEL D . .ʳ Friend! may Guid-luck hit you,
  And 'mang her favorites admit you!
If e'er Detraction shore to smit you,
    May nane believe him!
And ony deil that thinks to get you,
    Good Lord deceive him!!!

119A. [Epistle from a Taylor to *Robert Burns*]

[WHAT waefu' news is this I hear,
  Frae greeting I can scarce forbear,
Folk tells me, ye're gawn aff this year,
    Out o'er the sea,
And lasses wham ye lo'e sae dear   5
    Will greet for thee.

Weel wad I like war ye to stay,
But Robin since ye will away,
I ha'e a word yet mair to say,
    And maybe twa;   10
May he protect us night an' day,
    That made us a'.

---

  * *Killie* is a phrase the country-folks sometimes use for the name of a certain town in the West.

To John Kennedy. *Text from the Massachusetts Historical Society MS (letter to Kennedy, August 1786; Ferguson's facsimile)*

Epistle from a Taylor. *Text from Stewart, 1801 (pp. 25–27)*

Whar thou art gaun, keep mind frae me,
Seek him to bear thee companie,
And, Robin, whan ye come to die,   15
   Ye'll won aboon,
An' live at peace an' unity
   Ayont the moon.

Some tell me, Rab, ye dinna fear
To get a wean, an' curse an' swear,   20
I'm unco wae, my lad, to hear
   O' sic a trade,
Cou'd I persuade ye to forbear,
   I wad be glad.

Fu' weel ye ken ye'll gang to *hell*,   25
Gin ye persist in doin' ill—
Waes me! ye 're hurlin' down the hill
   Withouten dread,
An' ye'll get leave to swear your fill
   After ye 're dead.   30

There,* walth o' women ye'll get near,
But gettin' weans ye will forbear,
Ye'll never say, my bonnie dear
   Come, gie's a kiss—
Nae kissing there—ye'll girn an' sneer,   35
   An' ither hiss.

O Rab! lay by thy foolish tricks,
An' steer nae mair the female sex,
Or some day ye'll come through the pricks,
   An' that ye'll see;   40
Ye'll fin' hard living wi' Auld Nicks;
   I'm wae for thee.

But what's this comes wi' sic a knell,
Amaist as loud as ony bell,
While it does mak' my conscience tell   45
   Me what is true,
I'm but a ragget cowt mysel',
   Owre sib to you!

* In hell.

We're owre like those wha think it fit,
To stuff their noddles fu' o' wit,   50
An' yet content in darkness sit,
         Wha shun the light,
To let them see down to the pit,
         That lang dark night.

But fareweel, Rab, I maun awa',   55
May he that made us keep us a',
For that wad be a dreadfu' fa'
         And hurt us sair,
Lad, ye wad never mend ava,
         Sae, Rab, tak' care.]   60

119B. Robert Burns' Answer

WHAT ails ye now, ye lousie b——h,
     To thresh my back at sic a pitch?
Losh man! hae mercy wi' your natch,
         Your bodkin's bauld,
I did na suffer ha'f sae much   5
         Frae Daddie Auld.

What tho' at times when I grow crouse,
I gi'e their wames a random pouse,
Is that enough for you to souse
         Your servant sae?   10
Gae mind your seam, ye prick the louse,
         An' jag the flae.

King David o' poetic brief,
Wrought 'mang the lasses sic mischief
As fill'd his after life wi' grief   15
         An' bloody rants,
An' yet he's rank'd amang the chief
         O' lang syne saunts.

Robert Burns' Answer. *Text from Stewart, 1801 (pp. 28–31)*

And maybe, Tam, for a' my cants,
My wicked rhymes, an' drucken rants,   20
I'll gie auld cloven Clooty's haunts
        An unco slip yet,
An' snugly sit amang the saunts
        At Davie's hip yet.

But fegs, the Session says I maun   25
Gae fa' upo' anither plan,
Than garren lasses cowp the cran
        Clean heels owre body,
And sairly thole their mither's ban,
        Afore the howdy.   30

This leads me on, to tell for sport,
How I did wi' the Session sort—
Auld Clinkum at the inner port
        Cry'd three times, 'Robin!'
'Come hither lad, an' answer for't,   35
        'Ye're blam'd for jobbin'.'

Wi' pinch I put a Sunday's face on,
An' snoov'd awa' before the Session—
I made an open fair confession,
        I scorn'd to lie;   40
An' syne Mess John, beyond expression,
        Fell foul o' me.

A furnicator lown he call'd me,
An' said my fau't frae bliss expell'd me;
I own'd the tale was true he tell'd me,   45
        'But what the matter,'
Quo' I, 'I fear unless ye geld me,
        'I'll ne'er be better.'

'Geld you!' quo' he, 'and whatfore no,
'If that your right hand, leg or toe,   50
'Should ever prove your sp'ritual foe,
        'You shou'd remember
'To cut it aff, an' whatfore no,
        'Your dearest member.'

'Na, na,' quo' I, 'I'm no for that,   55
'Gelding's nae better than 'tis ca't,
'I'd rather suffer for my faut,
                  'A hearty flewit,
'As sair owre hip as ye can draw 't!
                  'Tho' I should rue it.   60

'Or gin ye like to end the bother,
'To please us a', I've just ae ither,
'When next wi' yon lass I forgather,
                  'Whate'er betide it,
'I'll frankly gi'e her 't a' thegither,   65
                  'An' let her guide it.'

But, Sir, this pleas'd them warst ava,
An' therefore, Tam, when that I saw,
I said 'Gude night', and cam' awa',
                  And left the Session;   70
I saw they were resolved a'
                  On my oppression.

120. The Brigs of Ayr, a Poem. Inscribed to J. B*********, *Esq;* Ayr

THE simple Bard, rough at the rustic plough,
    Learning his tuneful trade from ev'ry bough;
The chanting linnet, or the mellow thrush,
Hailing the setting sun, sweet, in the green thorn bush,

67 ava] of ava *Stewart*

The Brigs of Ayr. *Text from the Edinburgh edition, 1787, collated with the Alloway MSS (Aa, Ab) and the editions of 1793, 1794. Aa contains a draft of lines 25–96, 127–8, and a draft of the letter sent to Ballantine with the poem; Ab is a complete version, with the title* The Brigs of Ayr.—An Eclogue.—*and Ballantine's name in full. See Commentary*

H–H. *record two other MSS (not traced). The first has most of the variants given below from Ab and the following:*
    69 airy] fairy *MS*   142 taste] trade *MS*   190 Common-sense] sense's Port *MS*

The second has the variants given below in ll. 55–56, 184–5 (the second couplet

The soaring lark, the perching red-breast shrill,   5
Or deep-ton'd plovers, grey, wild-whistling o'er the hill;
Shall he, nurst in the Peasant's lowly shed,
To hardy Independence bravely bred,
By early Poverty to hardship steel'd,
And train'd to arms in stern Misfortune's field,   10
Shall he be guilty of their hireling crimes,
The servile, mercenary Swiss of rhymes?
Or labour hard the panegyric close,
With all the venal soul of dedicating Prose?
No! though his artless strains he rudely sings,   15
And throws his hand uncouthly o'er the strings,

reading Nae difference but whase mainmast is tallest, / All comfortably charg'd
alike in leaden ballast), *and the following:*
  51 left . . . took] leaves . . . takes *MS*   52 wheel'd] wheels *MS*   79 seem'd]
look'd *MS*   101 ruin'd] tasteless *MS*   175 than . . . to] I doubt than
ye can *MS*   186 Men] Wights *MS*   187 in Bonds] in musty bonds *MS*
191 stept] veer'd *MS*

In the Burns Chronicle, *1926, pp. 61–62, is a transcript of a MS (not traced) con-
taining what were probably experiments in a dedication to Ballantine:*

	Sir,
[recto]	think not with a mercenary view

Some servile Sycophant approaches you.
To you my Muse would sing these simple lays,
To you my heart its grateful homage pays,
I feel the weight of all your kindness past,   5
But thank you not as wishing it to last:
Scorn'd be the wretch whose earth-born grov'lling soul
Would in his ledger-hopes his Friends enroll.
Tho I, a lowly nameless, rustic Bard,
Who ne'er must hope your goodness to reward,   10
Yet man to man, Sir, let us fairly meet,
And like masonic Level, equal greet.
How poor the balance! ev'n what Monarch's plan,
Between two noble creatures such as Man.
That to your Friendship I am strongly tied   15
I still shall own it, Sir, with grateful pride,
When haply roaring seas between us tumble wide.

[verso]   Or if among so many cent'ries waste,
Thro the long vista of dark ages past,
Some much-lov'd honor'd name a radiance cast,
Perhaps some Patriot of distinguish'd worth,
I'll match him if My Lord will please step forth.   5
Or Gentleman and Citizen combine,
And I shall shew his peer in Ballantine:
Tho' honest men were parcell'd out for sale,
He might be shown a sample for the hale.

He glows with all the spirit of the Bard,
Fame, honest fame, his great, his dear reward.
Still, if some Patron's gen'rous care he trace,
Skill'd in the secret, to bestow with grace;   20
When B********* befriends his humble name,
And hands the rustic Stranger up to fame,
With heartfelt throes his grateful bosom swells,
The godlike bliss, to give, alone excels.

'Twas when the stacks get on their winter-hap,   25
And thack and rape secure the toil-won crap;
Potatoe-bings are snugged up frae skaith
Of coming Winter's biting, frosty breath;
The bees, rejoicing o'er their summer-toils,   ⎫
Unnumber'd buds, an' flow'rs' delicious spoils,   ⎬ 30
Seal'd up with frugal care in massive, waxen piles,   ⎭
Are doom'd by Man, that tyrant o'er the weak,
The death o' devils, smoor'd wi' brimstone reek:
The thund'ring guns are heard on ev'ry side,
The wounded coveys, reeling, scatter wide;   35
The feather'd field-mates, bound by Nature's tie,
Sires, mothers, children, in one carnage lie:
(What warm, poetic heart but inly bleeds,
And execrates man's savage, ruthless deeds!)
Nae mair the flow'r in field or meadow springs;   40
Nae mair the grove with airy concert rings,
Except perhaps the Robin's whistling glee,
Proud o' the height o' some bit half-lang tree:

---

17 the Bard] *correcting* a Bard *in Ab*   18 great,] great *87*   25 *Aa begins*
26 toil-won] *correcting* dear-won *in Aa*   21 his] the *Ab*   27 are snugged
up frae] screen'd snugly frae the *corrected to* are screen'd frae coming *in Aa*
28 coming] nipping *Aa*   29–33 The bees . . . reek:] *Aa has*

Th' industrious bees, rejoicing owre their stores,
The lazy drones a' banish'd out o' doors,
Are sent by cruel man new hames to seek,
Or die like devils, smoor'd wi' brunstane reek;

followed by line 40 deleted   30 flow'rs' delicious] flowerets' nect'rine *Ab*
33 brimstone] brunstane *Ab*   36 by] in *Aa*   37 mothers, children,] sons
and daughters *Aa*

The hoary morns precede the sunny days,
Mild, calm, serene, wide-spreads the noon-tide blaze, } 45
While thick the gossamour waves wanton in the rays.

'Twas in that season; when a simple Bard,
Unknown and poor, simplicity's reward,
Ae night, within the ancient brugh of *Ayr*,
By whim inspir'd, or haply prest wi' care,   50
He left his bed and took his wayward rout,
And down by *Simpson*'s* wheel'd the left about:
(Whether impell'd by all-directing Fate,
To witness what I after shall narrate;
Or whether, rapt in meditation high,   55
He wander'd out he knew not where nor why)
The drowsy *Dungeon-clock*† had number'd two,
And *Wallace Tow'r*† had sworn the fact was true:
The tide-swoln Firth, with sullen-sounding roar,
Through the still night dash'd hoarse along the shore: 60
All else was hush'd as Nature's closed e'e;
The silent moon shone high o'er tow'r and tree:
The chilly Frost, beneath the silver beam,
Crept, gently-crusting, o'er the glittering stream.—

When, lo! on either hand the list'ning Bard,   65
The clanging sugh of whistling wings is heard;

* A noted tavern at the *Auld Brig* end.   † The two steeples.

44 precede] precedes *Ab*   45 wide-spreads] wide-pours *Aa*   47 season;]
season, *MSS* 94   51 He . . . and] Alang the Brig he *Aa*   53–54 *not in Aa*
55–56 Or whether . . . why] *Aa has (with transposition marks)*

(Whither, rapt up in meditation high,
He wander'd forth he knew not where nor why;
Or, penitential pangs for former sins
Led him to rove by quondam Merran Din's).

Ab transposes the couplets, with alterations Or penitential . . . Or whether rapt . . .
57 *Dungeon-clock*] Steeple-clock *Aa Ab (without note)*   59 sullen-sounding]
hoarsely-sounding *Aa*   60 hoarse] white *Aa*   61 All else was hush'd]
corrected from All else beside was quiet to h *in Aa*   62 silent] *corrected from*
silver *in Aa*   65–68 When . . . hare;] *Aa, Ab have*

When lo! before our Bardie's wond'ring een,
The Brigs of Ayr's twa guardian Sprites are seen!

Ab deletes the couplet, and proceeds with lines 65–68   66 is] are *Ab*

Two dusky forms dart thro' the midnight air,
Swift as the *Gos** drives on the wheeling hare;
Ane on th' *Auld Brig* his airy shape uprears,
The ither flutters o'er the *rising piers*:   70
Our warlock Rhymer instantly descry'd
The Sprites that owre the *Brigs of Ayr* preside.
(That Bards are second-sighted is nae joke,
And ken the lingo of the sp'ritual folk;
Fays, Spunkies, Kelpies, a', they can explain them,   75
And ev'n the vera deils they brawly ken them.)
Auld Brig appear'd of ancient Pictish race,
The vera wrinkles Gothic in his face:
He seem'd as he wi' Time had warstl'd lang,
Yet, teughly doure, he bade an unco bang.   80
New Brig was buskit in a braw, new coat,
That he, at *Lon'on*, frae ane *Adams* got;
In's hand five taper staves as smooth 's a bead,
Wi' virls an' whirlygigums at the head.
The Goth was stalking round with anxious search,   85
Spying the time-worn flaws in ev'ry arch;
It chanc'd his new-come neebor took his e'e,
And e'en a vex'd and angry heart had he!
Wi' thieveless sneer to see his modish mien,
He, down the water, gies him this guid-een—   90

AULD BRIG

I doubt na, frien', ye'll think ye're nae sheep-shank,
Ance ye were streekit owre frae bank to bank!
But gin ye be a Brig as auld as me,
Tho' faith, that day, I doubt, ye'll never see;
There'll be, if that date come, I'll wad a boddle,   95
Some fewer whigmeleeries in your noddle.

---

* The gos-hawk, or falcon.

---

68 *Footnote lacking in MSS*   69 *Brig* his airy shape] bows, his dusky form *Aa*
71–72 *not in Aa*   86 Spying] Viewing *Aa*   89 thieveless] thyveless *MSS*   94 day 94:
date *MSS* 87 93   day, I doubt, ye'll] I doubt that date ye *Aa*   95 There 'll . . .
come] *correcting* But if ye do, they'll be *in Aa*   if] gin *Aa*: gif *Ab*   date 94:
day *MSS* 87 93   96 *Aa adds and concludes:*

    Och, waes my heart! for them that's dead an' rotten,
    To think how their auld, royal Art's forgotten!

NEW BRIG

Auld Vandal, ye but show your little mense,
Just much about it wi' your scanty sense;
Will your poor, narrow foot-path of a street,
Where twa wheel-barrows tremble when they meet,   100
Your ruin'd, formless bulk o' stane and lime,
Compare wi' bonie *Brigs* o' modern time?
There's men of taste wou'd tak the *Ducat-stream*,*
Tho' they should cast the vera sark and swim,
Ere they would grate their feelings wi' the view   105
Of sic an ugly, Gothic hulk as you.

AULD BRIG

Conceited gowk! puff'd up wi' windy pride!
This mony a year I've stood the flood an' tide;
And tho' wi' crazy eild I'm sair forfairn,
I'll be a *Brig* when ye're a shapeless cairn!   110
As yet ye little ken about the matter,
But twa-three winters will inform ye better.
When heavy, dark, continued, a'-day rains
Wi' deepening deluges o'erflow the plains;
When from the hills where springs the brawling *Coil*,   115
Or stately *Lugar*'s mossy fountains boil,
Or where the *Greenock* winds his moorland course,
Or haunted *Garpal*† draws his feeble source,

* A noted ford, just above the Auld Brig.
† The banks of *Garpal Water* is one of the few places in the West of Scotland
where those fancy-scaring beings, known by the name of *Ghaists*, still continue
pertinaciously to inhabit.

        The chiels that bigget me were Masons prime, ⎫
        Fu' brawly could they bake the stane an' lime, ⎬
        That ages it would stan't the teeth o' time: ⎭
        They wrought sic warks that your fine Architects,
        They couldna do the like o't for their necks!
                New-Brig.

The rest of the page is blank

   99–102 Will . . . time?] *Ab has*

        Will your auld, formless bulk o' stane an' lime
        Compare wi' bony Brigs o' modern time?

103 *Footnote not in Ab*   105 Ere *Ab*: E'er *87–94*   108 stood] stan't *Ab*
117 his] its *Ab*   118, 123 *Footnotes not in Ab*   118 his] its *Ab*

Arous'd by blustering winds an' spotting thowes,
In mony a torrent down the snaw-broo rowes;   120
While crashing ice, borne on the roaring speat,
Sweeps dams, an' mills, an' brigs, a' to the gate;
And from *Glenbuck*,* down to the *Ratton-key*,†
Auld *Ayr* is just one lengthen'd, tumbling sea;
Then down ye'll hurl, deil nor ye never rise!   125
And dash the gumlie jaups up to the pouring skies.
A lesson sadly teaching, to your cost,
That Architecture's noble art is lost!

NEW BRIG

Fine *architecture*, trowth, I needs must say 't o't!
The L——d be thankit that we've tint the gate o't!   130
Gaunt, ghastly, ghaist-alluring edifices,
Hanging with threat'ning jut like precipices;
O'er-arching, mouldy, gloom-inspiring coves,
Supporting roofs fantastic, stony groves:
Windows and doors in nameless sculptures drest,   135
With order, symmetry, or taste unblest;
Forms like some bedlam Statuary's dream,
The craz'd creations of misguided whim;
Forms might be worshipp'd on the bended knee, ⎫
And still the *second dread command* be free,   ⎬   140
Their likeness is not found on earth, in air, or sea. ⎭
Mansions that would disgrace the building-taste
Of any mason reptile, bird, or beast;
Fit only for a doited Monkish race,
Or frosty maids forsworn the dear embrace,   145
Or Cuifs of latter times, wha held the notion,
That sullen gloom was sterling, true devotion:
Fancies that our guid Brugh denies protection,
And soon may they expire, unblest with resurrection!

* The source of the river of Ayr.
† A small landing-place above the large key.

119 spotting] spotted *Ab*   121 While] *correcting* And *in Ab*   122 mills]
milns *Ab*   134 roofs 94: roofs— *Ab*: roofs, 87 93   142 building-taste]
bigging taste *Ab*   146 latter 94: later *Ab* 87 93   148 guid] *om. Ab*

AULD BRIG

O ye, my dear-remember'd, ancient yealings,   150
Were ye but here to share my wounded feelings!
Ye worthy *Proveses*, an' mony a *Bailie*,
Wha in the paths o' righteousness did toil ay;
Ye dainty *Deacons*, an' ye douce *Conveeners*,
To whom our moderns are but causey-cleaners;   155
Ye godly *Councils* wha hae blest this town;
Ye godly *Brethren* o' the sacred gown,
Wha meekly gae your *hurdies* to the *smiters*;
And (what would now be strange) ye *godly Writers*:
A' ye douce folk I've borne aboon the broo,   160
Were ye but here, what would ye say or do!
How would your spirits groan in deep vexation,
To see each melancholy alteration;
And, agonising, curse the time and place
When ye begat the base, degen'rate race!   165
Nae langer Rev'rend Men, their country's glory,
In plain, braid Scots hold forth a plain, braid story:
Nae langer thrifty Citizens, an' douce,
Meet owre a pint, or in the Council-house;
But staumrel, corky-headed, graceless Gentry,   170
The herryment and ruin of the country;
Men, three-parts made by Taylors and by Barbers,
Wha waste your weel-hain'd gear on d——d *new Brigs*
    and *Harbours*!

NEW BRIG

Now haud you there! for faith ye've said enough,
And muckle mair than ye can mak to through.   175
As for your Priesthood, I shall say but little,
Corbies and *Clergy* are a shot right kittle:
But, under favor o' your langer beard,
Abuse o' Magistrates might weel be spar'd;

164–5 And . . . race!] *not in Ab*   167 Scots] Scotch *Ab*   171 the] their *Ab*
175 *Additional lines in Ab:*

> That's ay a string auld, doyted Graybeards harp on,
> A topic for their peevishness to carp on.

To liken them to your auld-warld squad,   180
I must needs say, comparisons are odd.
In *Ayr*, Wag-wits nae mair can have a handle
To mouth 'A Citizen', a term o' scandal:
Nae mair the Council waddles down the street,
In all the pomp of ignorant conceit;   185
Men wha grew wise priggin owre hops an' raisins,
Or gather'd lib'ral views in Bonds and Seisins.
If haply Knowledge, on a random tramp,
Had shor'd them with a glimmer of his lamp,
And would to Common-sense for once betray'd them,   190
Plain, dull Stupidity stept kindly in to aid them.

What farther clishmaclaver might been said,
What bloody wars, if Sprites had blood to shed,
No man can tell; but, all before their sight,
A fairy train appear'd in order bright: 195
Adown the glittering stream they featly danc'd;
Bright to the moon their various dresses glanc'd:
They footed o'er the wat'ry glass so neat,
The infant ice scarce bent beneath their feet:
While arts of Minstrelsy among them rung,   200
And soul-ennobling Bards heroic ditties sung.

O had *M'Lauchlan**, thairm-inspiring Sage,   ⎫
Been there to hear this heavenly band engage,   ⎬
When thro' his dear *Strathspeys* they bore with ⎪
    Highland rage;   ⎭

* A well known performer of Scottish music on the violin.

---

180 squad] bodies *Ab*   181 odd] odious *Ab*   182 a] *om. Ab*
184–5 Nae . . . conceit;] *Ab has*

> Nae mair down street the Council *Quorum* waddles
> With wigs like main sails on their logger noddles:
> No difference but bulkiest or tallest,
> With comfortable Dulness in for ballast:
> Nor shoals nor currents need a Pilot's caution,
> For regularly slow, they only witness motion.

191 dull Stupidity stept kindly] kind Stupidity stept *Ab*   202 *Footnote not in Ab*

Or when they struck old Scotia's melting airs,   205
The lover's raptur'd joys or bleeding cares;
How would his Highland lug been nobler fir'd,
And ev'n his matchless hand with finer touch inspir'd!
No guess could tell what instrument appear'd,
But all the soul of Music's self was heard;   210
Harmonious concert rung in every part,
While simple melody pour'd moving on the heart.

The Genius of the Stream in front appears,
A venerable Chief advanc'd in years;
His hoary head with water-lilies crown'd,   215
His manly leg with garter tangle bound.
Next came the loveliest pair in all the ring,
Sweet Female Beauty hand in hand with Spring;
Then, crown'd with flow'ry hay, came Rural Joy,
And Summer, with his fervid-beaming eye: 220
All-chearing Plenty, with her flowing horn,
Led yellow Autumn wreath'd with nodding corn;
Then Winter's time-bleach'd locks did hoary show,
By Hospitality with cloudless brow.
Next follow'd Courage with his martial stride,   225
From where the *Feal* wild-woody coverts hide:
Benevolence, with mild, benignant air,
A female form, came from the tow'rs of *Stair*:
Learning and Worth in equal measures trode,
From simple *Catrine*, their long-lov'd abode: 230
Last, white-rob'd Peace, crown'd with a hazle wreath,
To rustic Agriculture did bequeath
The broken, iron instruments of Death,
At sight of whom our Sprites forgat their kindling wrath.

205 struck] touch'd *Ab*   221 her] his *Ab*   234 Le Fin— *follows in Ab*

121. Wrote on the blank leaf of a copy of my first Edition, which I sent to an old Sweetheart, then married—

ONCE fondly lov'd, and still rememb'red dear,
   Sweet early Object of my youthful vows,
Accept this mark of friendship, warm, sincere,
   Friendship—'tis all cold duty now allows.

And while you read the simple, artless rhymes,   5
   One friendly sigh for him—he asks no more,
Who, distant, burns in flaming torrid climes,
   Or haply lies beneath th' Atlantic roar.

'TWAS the girl I mention in my letter to Dr Moore, where I speak of taking the sun's altitude.—Poor Peggy! Her husband is my old acquaintance and a most worthy fellow.—When I was taking leave of my Carrick relations intending to go to the West Indies, when I took farewel of her, neither she nor I could speak a syllable. —Her husband escorted me three miles on my road, and we both parted with tears.—

Wrote . . . to an old Sweetheart. *Text from the Alloway MS (Al A), collated with MSS Adam, Al B, the Huntington Library MS (Geddes's copy of 87), and the transcript in the Glenriddell MS (p. 63; Glen). The MSS have only trivial variations in their titles. The footnote is an autograph interpolation in Glen. Footnote in Al A* I was then going to the West Indies.—
   3 mark] gift *Adam*   5 while] *correcting* when *in Al A*: when *Adam Al B Geddes Glen*   the] these *Adam*

122. Song

Tune, Roslin Castle

Slow

tr

I

T HE gloomy night is gath'ring fast,
Loud roars the wild, inconstant blast,
Yon murky cloud is foul with rain,
I see it driving o'er the plain;
The Hunter now has left the moor,   5
The scatt'red coveys meet secure,
While here I wander, prest with care,
Along the lonely banks of *Ayr*.

Song, *Text from the Edinburgh edition, 1787, collated with the Stair MS, SMM, 1790
(284; unsigned), and the editions of 1793, 1794. H–H. record variants from a holograph in a copy of 86 (not traced) agreeing with the Stair MS in ll. 13–14, 23, 30.
Title in SMM* The Bonie Banks of Ayr
  5–6 *repeated in SMM*   6 meet] left *93*

II

The Autumn mourns her rip'ning corn
By early Winter's ravage torn;   10
Across her placid, azure sky,
She sees the scowling tempest fly:
Chill runs my blood to hear it rave,
I think upon the stormy wave,
Where many a danger I must dare,   15
Far from the bonie banks of *Ayr*.

III

'Tis not the surging billow's roar,
'Tis not that fatal, deadly shore;
Tho' Death in ev'ry shape appear,
The Wretched have no more to fear: 20
But round my heart the ties are bound,
That heart transpierc'd with many a wound;
These bleed afresh, those ties I tear,
To leave the bonie banks of *Ayr*.

IV

Farewell, old *Coila*'s hills and dales,   25
Her heathy moors and winding vales;
The scenes where wretched Fancy roves,
Pursuing past, unhappy loves!
Farewell, my friends! farewell, my foes!
My peace with these, my love with those—   30
The bursting tears my heart declare,
Farewell, the bonie banks of *Ayr*!

13–14 Chill . . . wave,] *MS has*

>   The whistling Storm affrightens me;
>   I think upon the raging sea;

23 These . . . those] Those . . . these *MS*   30 My . . . those] My love with
these, my peace with those *MS*   31 The] These *MS*

123. The Northern Lass

She raise and loot me in

TH OUGH cruel Fate should bid us part,
    Far as the Pole and Line,
Her dear idea round my heart
    Should tenderly entwine:

Though mountains rise, and desarts howl,   5
    And oceans roar between;
Yet dearer than my deathless soul
    I still would love my Jean.—

The Northern Lass. *Text from the Hastie MS, f. 26ʳ, collated with the Stair MS and
SMM, 1788 (118; signed R). Title from SMM. Cancelled title in Hastie MS* Lines to
MᶜPherson's Farewell. *Title in Stair MS* Song.—Tune, She rose and loot me in
    2 Far as] As far 's *Stair*   5 rise] frown *Stair*

124. A Fragment—

Chorus

GREEN grow the rashes O,
Green grow the rashes O,
The lasses they hae wimble bores,
The widows they hae gashes O.

1

In sober hours I am a priest;   5
  A hero when I'm tipsey, O;
But I'm a king and ev'ry thing,
  When wi' a wanton Gipsey, O.
    Green grow &c.

2

'Twas late yestreen I met wi' ane,
  An' wow, but she was gentle, O!   10
Ae han' she pat roun' my cravat,
  The tither to my p—— O.
    Green grow &c.

3

I dought na speak—yet was na fley'd—
  My heart play'd duntie, duntie, O;
An' ceremony laid aside,   15
  I fairly fun' her c—ntie, O.—
    Green grow &c.
                              Multa desunt—

A Fragment. *Text from the MS (letter to Richmond, 3 September 1786)*

125. The Calf

To the Rev. Mr——, on his text, MALACHI, *ch. iv. vers. 2* 'And
they shall go forth, and grow up, like CALVES of the stall.'

RIGHT, Sir! your text I'll prove it true,
  Tho' Heretics may laugh;
For instance, there's yoursel just now,
  God knows, an unco *Calf*!

And should some Patron be so kind,   5
  As bless you wi' a kirk,
I doubt na, Sir, but then we'll find,
  Ye're still as great a *Stirk*.

But, if the Lover's raptur'd hour
  Shall ever be your lot,   10
Forbid it, ev'ry heavenly Power,
  You e'er should be a *Stot*!

Tho', when some kind, connubial Dear
  Your But-and-ben adorns,
The like has been that you may wear   15
  A noble head of *horns*.

And, in your lug, most reverend J——,
  To hear you roar and rowte,
Few men o' sense will doubt your claims
  To rank amang the *Nowte*.   20

And when ye're number'd wi' the dead,
  Below a grassy hillock,
Wi' justice they may mark your head—
  'Here lies a famous *Bullock*!'

The Calf. *Text from the Edinburgh edition, 1787, collated with those of 1793, 1794.*
Scott Douglas records a MS (not traced) with these variants:

 5 should . . . be so] when . . . shall be *MS* 6 As] To *MS* 9 raptur'd]
mystic *MS* 10 Shall] Should *MS* 13 Tho' . . . some] And . . . a *MS*
17 in your lug] to conclude *MS* 22 Below] Beneath *MS*
24 Here] He're *87 (sk) 93*

126. Nature's Law

Humbly inscribed to Gavin Hamilton, Esq.

'Great Nature spoke; observant man obey'd'—POPE.

LET other heroes boast their scars,
    The marks of sturt and strife;
And other poets sing of wars,
    The plagues of human life;
Shame fa' the fun; wi' sword and gun   5
    To slap mankind like lumber!
I sing his name, and nobler fame,
    Wha multiplies our number.

Great Nature spoke, with air benign,
    'Go on, ye human race;   10
This lower world I you resign;
    Be fruitful and increase.
The liquid fire of strong desire
    I've pour'd it in each bosom;
Here, on this hand, does Mankind stand,   15
    And there, is Beauty's blossom.'

The Hero of these artless strains,
    A lowly bard was he,
Who sung his rhymes in Coila's plains,
    With meikle mirth an' glee;   20
Kind Nature's care had given his share
    Large, of the flaming current;
And, all devout, he never sought
    To stem the sacred torrent.

He felt the powerful high behest   25
    Thrill, vital, thro' and thro';
And sought a correspondent breast,
    To give obedience due:
Propitious Powers screen'd the young flow'rs,
    From mildews of abortion;   30
And lo! the Bard—a great reward—
    Has got a double portion!

Nature's Law. *Text from the Aldine edition, 1839 (ii. 150)*

Auld cantie Coil may count the day,
    As annual it returns,
The third of Libra's equal sway,   35
    That gave another Burns,
With future rhymes, an' other times,
    To emulate his sire,
To sing auld Coil in nobler style,
    With more poetic fire.   40

Ye Powers of peace, and peaceful song,
    Look down with gracious eyes;
And bless auld Coila, large and long,
    With multiplying joys;
Lang may she stand to prop the land,   45
    The flow'r of ancient nations;
And Burnses spring, her fame to sing,
    To endless generations!

127. **Extempore Verses on Dining with Lord
Daer**

Mossgiel, October 25th.

THIS wot all ye whom it concerns,
  I, rhymer Rab, alias BURNS,
        October twenty-third,
A ne'er to be forgotten day!
Sae far I sprachl'd up the brae,   5
        I dinner'd wi' a LORD.

I've been at drucken Writers' feasts;
Nay, been bitch fou 'mang godly Priests;
        (Wi' rev'rence be it spoken!)
I've even join'd the honour'd jorum,   10
When mighty Squireships o' the Quorum,
        Their hydra drouth did sloken.

Extempore Verses. *Text from Stewart, 1802 (pp. 267–8), collated with Currie, 1801*
(i. 134). Title and date from Stewart
  2 Rab] Robin *Currie*

But wi' a LORD!—stand out my shin!
A LORD—a PEER—an EARL's SON—
       Up higher yet, my bonnet!   15
An' such a LORD—lang Scotch ell twa;
Our PEERAGE he looks o'er them a',
       As I look o'er my sonnet.

But, O! for Hogarth's magic pow'r,
To shew Sir Bardie's willyart glowr,   20
       An' how he star'd an' stammer'd!
When goavan's he'd been led wi' branks,
An' stumpan on his ploughman shanks,
       He in the parlour hammer'd.

To meet good Stuart little pain is,   25
Or Scotia's sacred Demosthenes,
       Thinks I, they are but men!
But Burns, my Lord—Guid G—d! I doited!
My knees on ane anither knoited,
       As faultering I gaed ben!   30

I sidling shelter'd in a neuk,
An' at his Lordship staw a leuk,
       Like some portentous omen;
Except GOOD SENSE, an' SOCIAL GLEE,
An' (what surpris'd me) MODESTY,   35
       I marked nought uncommon.

I watch'd the symptoms o' the GREAT,
The GENTLE PRIDE, the LORDLY STATE,
       The arrogant assuming;
The fient a pride, nae pride had he,   40
Nor sauce, nor state, that I could see,
       Mair than an honest Ploughman.

---

16 ell] ells *Currie*   17 looks o'er] o'erlooks *Currie*   22 's he'd been] as
if *Currie*   25-30 To meet . . . ben!] *om. Currie. See Commentary*   32 staw
a leuk] steal't a look *Currie*

Then from his Lordship I shall learn,
Henceforth to meet with unconcern,
      One rank as well's another;   45
Nae honest, worthy man need care,
To meet wi' NOBLE, youthfu' DAER,
      For he but meets a BROTHER.

128. The Sons of old Killie

Tune—Shawnboy

Lively

Y E sons of old Killie, assembled by Willie,
   To follow the noble vocation;
Your thrifty old mother has scarce such another
   To sit in that honoured station.
I've little to say, but only to pray,   5
   As praying's the ton of your fashion;
A prayer from the muse you well may excuse,
   'Tis seldom her favourite passion.

The Sons of old Killie. *Text from Cunningham, 1834 (iv. 32). Cunningham prints a
note from Burns's MS:* This song, wrote by Mr. Burns, was sung by him in the
Kilmarnock Kilwinning Lodge, in 1786, and given by him to Mr. Parker, who was
Master of the Lodge.

Ye powers who preside o'er the wind and the tide,
   Who marked each element's border;   10
Who formed this frame with beneficent aim,
   Whose sovereign statute is order;
Within this dear mansion may wayward contention
   Or withered envy ne'er enter;
May secresy round be the mystical bound,   15
   And brotherly love be the centre.

129. Epistle to Capt.ⁿ Will.ᵐ Logan at Park—

Oct: 30ᵗʰ, 1786.

HAIL, thairm-inspirin, rattlin Willie!
  Though Fortune's road be rough an' hilly
To ev'ry fiddling, rhyming billie,
     We never heed;
But tak it like th' unbacked Fillie,   5
     Proud o' her speed.

When idly goavin whyles we saunter,
Yirr, Fancy barks,—awa we canter,
Up-hill, down-brae, till some mishanter,
     Some black Bog-hole,   10
Arreest us; then the scathe an' banter
     We're forc'd to thole.

Hale be your HEART! Hale be your FIDDLE!
Lang may your elbuck jink an' didle,
To chear you through the weary widdle   15
     O' this vile Warl:
Until ye on a cummock dridle,
     A gray-hair'd Carl!

Epistle to Capt.ⁿ Will.ᵐ Logan. *Text from Edinburgh University MS Dc.6.111*
(Stewart), collated with the Auld transcript in the same library and Cunningham, 1834
(iii. 9–12; Cun). Title in Cun Epistle to Major Logan; *in Auld (in a different hand)*
To the late Major Logan of Ayr
   5 unbacked] unbracked *Auld*   11 Arreest] Arrests *Cun*   scathe] *correcting*
skaith *in Stewart*   16 vile] wild *Cun*   17 cummock] crummock *Cun*

Come WEALTH, come POORTITH, late or soon,
Heav'n send your HEART-STRINGS ay IN TUNE! 20
An' screw your TEMPER-PINS aboon,
      A FIFTH or mair,
The melancholious, sairie croon
      O' cankrie CARE!

May still your Life, from day to day, 25
Nae LENTE LARGO, in the play,
But ALLEGRETTO FORTE, gay,
      Harmonious flow:
A sweeping, kindling, bauld STRATHSPEY,
      Encore! Bravo! 30

A' blessins on the cheary *gang*
Wha dearly like a Jig or sang;
An' never balance RIGHT and WRANG
      By square and rule,
But as the CLEGS o' FEELING stang, 35
      Are wise or fool!

My hand-wal'd CURSE keep hard in chase
The harpy, hoodock, purse-proud RACE,
Wha count on POORTITH as disgrace!
      Their tuneless hearts, 40
May FIRE-SIDE DISCORDS jar a BASS
      To a' their PARTS!

But come—your hand—my careless brither—
I' th' tither WARLD, if there's anither,
An' that there is, I've little swither 45
      About the matter;
We cheek-for-chow shall jog the gither,
      I 'se ne'er bid better.

We've fauts an' failins,—granted clearly:
We're frail, backsliding Mortals meerly: 50

---

23 sairie] fairie *Auld*: lazie *Cun*   31 A' blessins] A blessing *Cun*
33 balance] think o' *Auld Cun*   37 hand-wal'd] hand wald *Auld*   41 BASS]
base *Cun*

Eve's bonie Squad, Priests wyte them sheerly,
    For our grand fa':
But still—but still—I like them dearly;
    God bless them a'!

Ochon! for poor Castalian Drinkers,   55
When they fa' foul o' earthly Jinkers!
The witching, curst, delicious blinkers
    Hae put me hyte;
An' gart me weet my waukrife winkers,
    Wi' girnan spite.   60

But by yon Moon! an' that's high swearin;
An' every Star within my hearin!
An' by her een! wha was a dear ane,
    I'll ne'er forget;
I hope to gie the Jads a clearin   65
    In fair play yet!

My loss I mourn, but not repent it:
I'll seek my pursie whare I tint it:
Ance to the Indies I were wonted,
    Some cantraip hour,   70
By some sweet Elf I may be dinted,
    Then, Vive l'Amour!

Faites mes Baisemains respectueuse,
To sentimental Sister Susie,
An' honest Lucky; no to roose ye,   75
    Ye may be proud,
That sic a couple Fate allows ye
    To grace your blood.

Nae mair, at present, can I measure;
An' trowth my rhymin ware's nae treasure;   80
But when in Ayr, some half hour's leisure,
    Be 't light, be 't dark,
Sir Bard will do himsel the pleasure
    To call at Park.

58 Hae put me] *correcting* Aft pit us *in Stewart*   59 me weet my] *correcting*
us weet our *in Stewart*   71 I may] I'll yet *Auld Cun*   73 respectueuse]
correcting or I'll abuse ye *in Stewart:* respectuaise *Auld*   84 *Signed* Robt Burns
and dated Mosgiel, 30 Octr 1786 *in Auld and Cun*

130. A Winter Night

Poor naked wretches, wheresoe'er you are,
That bide the pelting of this pityless storm!
How shall your houseless heads, and unfed sides,
Your loop'd and window'd raggedness, defend you
From seasons such as these—
                                            SHAKESPEARE.

WHEN biting *Boreas*, fell and doure,
   Sharp shivers thro' the leafless bow'r;
When *Phœbus* gies a short-liv'd glow'r,
         Far south the lift,
Dim-dark'ning thro' the flaky show'r,   5
         Or whirling drift.

Ae night the Storm the steeples rocked,
Poor Labour sweet in sleep was locked,
While burns, wi' snawy wreeths up-choked,
         Wild-eddying swirl,   10
Or thro' the mining outlet bocked,
         Down headlong hurl.

List'ning, the doors an' winnocks rattle,
I thought me on the ourie cattle,
Or silly sheep, wha bide this brattle   15
         O' winter war,
And thro' the drift, deep-lairing, sprattle,
         Beneath a scar.

Ilk happing bird, wee, helpless thing!
That, in the merry months o' spring,   20
Delighted me to hear thee sing,
         What comes o' thee?
Whare wilt thou cow'r thy chittering wing,
         An' close thy e'e?

A Winter Night. *Text from the Edinburgh edition, 1787, collated with the Alloway*
MS and the editions of 1793, 1794. The MS lacks the epigraph
  3 When] An' MS   8 Labour . . . was] *correcting* Cot-folk . . . were *in MS*
13 List'ning,] Listening *MS*   15 Or] *correcting* An' *in MS*   17 drift, deep-
lairing, sprattle,] drift deep-lairing sprattle *MS*

Ev'n you on murd'ring errands toil'd,   25
Lone from your savage homes exil'd,
The blood-stain'd roost, and sheep-cote spoil'd,
    My heart forgets,
While pityless the tempest wild
      Sore on you beats.   30

Now *Phœbe*, in her midnight reign,
Dark-muffl'd, view'd the dreary plain;
Still crouding thoughts, a pensive train,
    Rose in my soul,
When on my ear this plaintive strain,   35
      Slow-solemn, stole—

'Blow, blow, ye Winds, with heavier gust!
'And freeze, thou bitter-biting Frost!
'Descend, ye chilly, smothering Snows!
'Not all your rage, as now, united shows   40
    'More hard unkindness, unrelenting,
    'Vengeful malice, unrepenting,
'Than heaven-illumin'd Man on brother Man bestows!

'See stern Oppression's iron grip,
    'Or mad Ambition's gory hand,   45
'Sending, like blood-hounds from the slip,
    'Woe, Want, and Murder o'er a land!
'Ev'n in the peaceful rural vale,
    'Truth, weeping, tells the mournful tale,
'How pamper'd Luxury, Flatt'ry by her side,   50
    'The parasite empoisoning her ear,
    'With all the servile wretches in the rear,
'Looks o'er proud Property, extended wide;
    'And eyes the simple, rustic Hind,
    'Whose toil upholds the glitt'ring show,   55
    'A creature of another kind,
    'Some coarser substance, unrefin'd,
'Plac'd for her lordly use thus far, thus vile, below!

27 blood-stain'd] *alternative to* feathery *in MS*   35 When] *correcting* Till
in MS   36 Slow-solemn,] Slow, solemn, *MS*   45 mad] *correcting* proud
in MS

'Where, where is Love's fond, tender throe,
'With lordly Honor's lofty brow,   60
   'The pow'rs you proudly own?
'Is there, beneath Love's noble name,
'Can harbour, dark, the selfish aim,
   'To bless himself alone!
'Mark Maiden-innocence a prey   65
   'To love-pretending snares,
'This boasted Honor turns away,
'Shunning soft Pity's rising sway,
'Regardless of the tears, and unavailing pray'rs!
'Perhaps, this hour, in Mis'ry's squalid nest,   70
'She strains your infant to her joyless breast,
'And with a Mother's fears shrinks at the rocking blast!

'Oh ye! who, sunk in beds of down,
'Feel not a want but what yourselves create,
'Think, for a moment, on his wretched fate,   75
'Whom friends and fortune quite disown!
'Ill-satisfy'd, keen Nature's clam'rous call,
   'Stretch'd on his straw he lays himself to sleep,
'While thro' the ragged roof and chinky wall,
   'Chill, o'er his slumbers, piles the drifty heap!   80
'Think on the dungeon's grim confine,
   'Where Guilt and poor Misfortune pine!
'Guilt, erring Man, relenting view!
'But shall thy legal rage pursue
   'The Wretch, already crushed low   85
'By cruel Fortune's undeserved blow?
'Affliction's sons are brothers in distress;
'A Brother to relieve, how exquisite the bliss!'

   I heard nae mair, for *Chanticleer*
      Shook off the pouthery snaw,   90
   And hail'd the morning with a cheer,
      A cottage-rousing craw.

   But deep this truth impress'd my mind—
      Thro' all his works abroad,
   The heart benevolent and kind   95
      The most resembles GOD.

60 lordly] daring *MS*   75 wretched] hapless *MS*

131. [Extempore Reply to an Invitation]

S^{IR}, Yours this moment I unseal,
 And faith I'm gay and hearty!
To tell the truth and shame the deil,
 I am as fou as Bartie:
But Foorsday, sir, my promise leal,   5
 Expect me o' your partie,
If on a beastie I can speel
 Or hurl in a cartie.
     Yours,
       ROBERT BURNS.
MACHLIN,
Monday Night, 10 o'clock

132. Lying at a Reverend Friend's house one night, the Author left the following *Verses* in the room where he slept:—

I

O THOU dread Pow'r, who reign'st above!
 I know Thou wilt me hear;
When for this scene of peace and love,
 I make my pray'r sincere.

II

The hoary Sire—the mortal stroke,   5
 Long, long be pleas'd to spare;
To bless his little filial flock,
 And show what good men are.

Extempore Reply. *Text from Chambers–Wallace, 1896 (iv. 319). H–H. record a MS (not traced) in agreement with this text*

O Thou dread Pow'r. *Text from the Edinburgh edition, 1787, collated with NLS MS 661 and the editions of 1793, 1794. Title in MS A Prayer.*
 1 dread . . . reign'st above!] in whom we live and move! *MS*   6 be pleas'd to] in goodness *MS*

III

She, who her lovely Offspring eyes
  With tender hopes and fears,   10
O bless her with a Mother's joys,
  But spare a Mother's tears!

IV

Their hope, their stay, their darling youth,
  In manhood's dawning blush;
Bless him, Thou God of love and truth,   15
  Up to a Parent's wish.

V

The beauteous, seraph Sister-band,
  With earnest tears I pray,
Thou know'st the snares on ev'ry hand,
  Guide Thou their steps alway.   20

VI

When soon or late they reach that coast,
  O'er life's rough ocean driven,
May they rejoice, no wand'rer lost,
  A Family in Heaven!

133. [The Night was still]

THE night was still, and o'er the hill
  The moon shone on the castle wa';
The mavis sang, while dew-drops hang
  Around her on the castle wa'.

Sae merrily they danc'd the ring,   5
  Frae e'enin till the cocks did craw,
And aye the owerword o' the spring
  Was Irvine's bairns are bonnie a'.

11 O] Long *MS*   13 hope, their stay] stay and prop *MS*   16 Parent's]
parents' *94*

The Night was still. *Text from Blackie,* The Land of Burns, *1840 (p. 58)*

134. [Rusticity's ungainly Form]

RUSTICITY's ungainly form
   May cloud the highest mind;
But when the heart is nobly warm,
   The good excuse will find.

Propriety's cold cautious rules   5
   Warm Fervour may o'erlook;
But spare poor Sensibility
   The ungentle harsh rebuke.

135. Address to Edinburgh

I

EDINA! *Scotia*'s darling seat!
   All hail thy palaces and tow'rs,
Where once beneath a Monarch's feet
   Sat Legislation's sov'reign pow'rs!
From marking wildly-scatt'red flow'rs,   5
   As on the banks of *Ayr* I stray'd,
And singing, lone, the ling'ring hours,
   I shelter in thy honor'd shade.

II

Here Wealth still swells the golden tide,
   As busy Trade his labours plies;   10
There Architecture's noble pride
   Bids elegance and splendor rise;
Here Justice, from her native skies,
   High wields her balance and her rod;
There Learning, with his eagle eyes,   15
   Seeks Science in her coy abode.

Rusticity's ungainly Form. *Text from Blackie,* The Land of Burns, *1840 (p. 58)*

Address to Edinburgh. *Text from the Edinburgh edition,* 1787, *collated with MSS Adam and Don, and the editions of* 1793, 1794
    5 marking] gathering *Don*   8 thy] *correcting* your *in Adam*: your *Don*
9 still swells] slow-swells *Adam Don*   14 High wields] High-wields *Adam Don*

III

Thy Sons, *Edina*, social, kind,
  With open arms the Stranger hail;
Their views enlarg'd, their lib'ral mind,
  Above the narrow, rural vale: 20
Attentive still to Sorrow's wail,
  Or modest Merit's silent claim;
And never may their sources fail!
  And never envy blot their name!

IV

Thy Daughters bright thy walks adorn,   25
  Gay as the gilded summer sky,
Sweet as the dewy, milk-white thorn,
  Dear as the raptur'd thrill of joy!
Fair B—— strikes th' adoring eye,
  Heav'n's beauties on my fancy shine;   30
I see the *Sire of Love* on high,
  And own his work indeed divine!

V

There, watching high the least alarms,
  Thy rough, rude Fortress gleams afar;
Like some bold Vet'ran, gray in arms,   35
  And mark'd with many a seamy scar:
The pond'rous wall and massy bar,
  Grim-rising o'er the rugged rock,
Have oft withstood assailing War,
  And oft repell'd th' Invader's shock.   40

VI

With awe-struck thought, and pitying tears,
  I view that noble, stately Dome,
Where *Scotia*'s kings of other years,
  Fam'd heroes! had their royal home:

---

20 rural] rustic *Adam*   21 Sorrow's] *correcting* Pity's *in Adam*: Pity's *Don*
22 Or] *corrected to* And *in Adam*   29 B——] Burnet *Adam*   33 watching
high] watching-high *Adam*   39 Have oft withstood] *corrected to* Oft has it
stood *in Adam*: Oft has it stood *Don*

Alas, how chang'd the times to come!　　　　45
　　Their royal Name low in the dust!
Their hapless Race wild-wand'ring roam!
　　Tho' rigid Law cries out, 'twas just!

VII

Wild-beats my heart, to trace your steps,
　　Whose ancestors, in days of yore,　　　　50
Thro' hostile ranks and ruin'd gaps
　　Old *Scotia*'s bloody lion bore:
Ev'n *I* who sing in rustic lore,
　　Haply *my Sires* have left their shed,
And fac'd grim Danger's loudest roar,　　　　55
　　Bold-following where your Fathers led!

VIII

Edina! Scotia's darling seat!
　　All hail thy palaces and tow'rs,
Where once, beneath a Monarch's feet,
　　Sat Legislation's sov'reign pow'rs!　　　　60
From marking wildly-scatt'red flow'rs,
　　As on the banks of *Ayr* I stray'd,
And singing, lone, the ling'ring hours,
　　I shelter in thy honor'd shade.

136. To a Haggis

Fair fa' your honest, sonsie face,
　　Great Chieftan o' the Puddin-race!
Aboon them a' ye tak your place,
　　　　Painch, tripe, or thairm:
Weel are ye wordy of a *grace*　　　　5
　　　　As lang's my arm.

---

48 Law] *corrected to* truth *in Adam*: Truth *Don*　　49 Wild-beats my heart]
My heart beats wild *MSS*　　trace] *correcting* meet *in Adam*　　53 in] with *MSS*
61 marking] gath'ring *Don*　　64 thy] your *MSS*

To a Haggis. *Text from the Edinburgh edition, 1787, collated with the* Caledonian
Mercury (*19 December 1786*) *and the* Scots Magazine (*January 1787*) *and the
editions of 1793, 1794*

The groaning trencher there ye fill,
Your hurdies like a distant hill,
Your *pin* wad help to mend a mill
   In time o' need,   10
While thro' your pores the dews distil
   Like amber bead.

His knife see Rustic-labour dight,
An' cut you up wi' ready slight,
Trenching your gushing entrails bright 15
   Like onie ditch;
And then, O what a glorious sight,
   Warm-reekin, rich!

Then, horn for horn they stretch an' strive,
Deil tak the hindmost, on they drive, 20
Till a' their weel-swall'd kytes belyve
   Are bent like drums;
Then auld Guidman, maist like to rive,
   Bethankit hums.

Is there that owre his French *ragout*, 25
Or *olio* that wad staw a sow,
Or *fricassee* wad mak her spew
   Wi' perfect sconner,
Looks down wi' sneering, scornfu' view
   On sic a dinner? 30

Poor devil! see him owre his trash,
As feckless as a wither'd rash,
His spindle shank a guid whip-lash,
   His nieve a nit;
Thro' bluidy flood or field to dash, 35
   O how unfit!

But mark the Rustic, *haggis-fed*,
The trembling earth resounds his tread,
Clap in his walie nieve a blade,
   He'll mak it whissle; 40
An' legs, an' arms, an' heads will sned,
   Like taps o' thrissle.

Ye Pow'rs wha mak mankind your care,
And dish them out their bill o' fare,
Auld Scotland wants nae skinking ware   45
       That jaups in luggies;
But, if ye wish her gratefu' pray'r,
       Gie her a *Haggis*!

137. Verses intended to be written below a noble Earl's picture

WHOSE is that noble, dauntless brow?
    And whose that eye of fire?
And whose that generous, Princely mien,
    Ev'n rooted Foes admire?

Stranger, to justly show that brow,   5
    And mark that eye of fire,
Would take HIS hand, whose vernal tints,
    His other Works admire.

Bright as a cloudless Summer-sun,
    With stately port he moves;   10
His guardian Seraph eyes with awe
    The noble Ward he loves.

Among th' illustrious Scottish Sons
    That Chief thou may'st discern,
Mark Scotia's fond-returning eye,   15
    It dwells upon GLENCAIRN.

43–48 Ye . . . *Haggis*!] *the periodicals have*
    Ye Powers wha gie us a' that 's gude,
    Still bless auld Caledonia's brood
    Wi' great John Barleycorn's heart's blude
        In stowps or luggies;
    And on our board that king o' food,
        A glorious Haggice.
45 skinking *87* (*sk*) *93 94*: stinking *87* (*st, London*)

Verses. *Text from the MS at Lady Stair's House, Edinburgh, collated with the Don MS.*
Title in Don Verses intended to have been written below the picture of a noble Earl.
   9 cloudless Summer-sun] cloudless, summer Sun *Don*   13 illustrious]
illustrious, *Don*

138. Song

Tune, Jockey's Gray Breeks

Brisk

I

AGAIN rejoicing Nature sees
    Her robe assume its vernal hues,
Her leafy locks wave in the breeze
    All freshly steep'd in morning dews.

CHORUS*

And maun I still on Menie† doat,   5
    And bear the scorn that's in her e'e!
For it's jet, jet black, an' it's like a hawk,
    An' it winna let a body be!

---

* This Chorus is part of a song composed by a gentleman in Edinburgh,
a particular friend of the Author's.
    † *Menie* is the common abbreviation of *Marianne.*

Song. *Text from the Edinburgh edition, 1787, collated with those of 1793, 1794*

II

In vain to me the cowslips blaw,
In vain to me the vi'lets spring;   10
In vain to me, in glen or shaw,
The mavis and the lintwhite sing.
And maun I still, &c.

III

The merry Ploughboy cheers his team,
Wi' joy the tentie Seedsman stalks,
But life to me's a weary dream,   15
A dream of ane that never wauks.
And maun I still, &c.

IV

The wanton coot the water skims,
Amang the reeds the ducklings cry,
The stately swan majestic swims,
And ev'ry thing is blest but I.   20
And maun I still, &c.

V

The Sheep-herd steeks his faulding slap,
And owre the moorlands whistles shill,
Wi' wild, unequal, wand'ring step
I meet him on the dewy hill.
And maun I still, &c.

VI

And when the lark, 'tween light and dark,   25
Blythe waukens by the daisy's side,
And mounts and sings on flittering wings,
A woe-worn ghaist I hameward glide.
And maun I still, &c.

VII

Come Winter, with thine angry howl,
  And raging bend the naked tree;   30
Thy gloom will soothe my chearless soul,
  When Nature all is sad like me!

And maun I still on Menie *doat,*
  And bear the scorn that's in her e'e!
For it's jet, jet black, an' it's like a hawk,
  An' it winna let a body be.

IV

POEMS
1787

EDINBURGH; BORDER TOUR;
HIGHLAND TOURS

139. To Miss L——,

With BEATTIE'S POEMS *for a New-Year's Gift*. Jan. 1. 1787.

AGAIN the silent wheels of time
    Their annual round have driv'n,
And you, tho' scarce in maiden prime,
    Are so much nearer Heav'n.

No gifts have I from Indian coasts   5
    The infant year to hail;
I send you more than India boasts
    In *Edwin*'s simple tale.

Our Sex with guile and faithless love
    Is charg'd, perhaps too true;   10
But may, dear Maid, each Lover prove
    An *Edwin* still to you.

To Miss L——. *Text from the Edinburgh edition, 1787, collated with the Huntington Library MS and the editions of 1793, 1794*

140. [There was a lad]

Tune, Daintie Davie

Brisk

THERE was a lad was born in Kyle,
  But what na day o' what na style,
I doubt it's hardly worth the while
  To be sae nice wi' Robin.
        Robin was a rovin' Boy,   5
          Rantin' rovin', rantin' rovin';
        Robin was a rovin' Boy,
          Rantin' rovin' Robin.

There was a lad. *Text from Cromek,* Reliques, *1808 (p. 341), collated with the*
Second Commonplace Book, *pp. 3–4 (2CPB). Title in 2CPB* A Fragment—Tune,
Daintie Davie

  1 lad was] birkie *2CPB*   4 *et passim* Robin] Davie *2CPB*   5–8 *Chorus in*
2CPB:

        Leeze me on thy curly pow,
          Bonie Davie, daintie Davie;
        Leeze me on thy curly pow,
          Thou 'se ay my daintie Davie.

Our monarch's hindmost year but ane
Was five-and-twenty days begun,   10
'Twas then a blast o' Janwar' Win'*
    Blew hansel in on Robin.

The Gossip keekit in his loof,
Quo' scho wha lives will see the proof,
This waly boy will be nae coof,   15
    I think we'll ca' him Robin.

He'll hae misfortunes great and sma',
But ay a heart aboon them a';
He'll be a credit till us a',
    We'll a' be proud o' Robin.   20

But sure as three times three mak nine,
I see by ilka score and line,
This chap will dearly like our kin',
    So leeze me on thee, Robin.

Guid faith quo' scho I doubt you Stir,   25
Ye'll gar the lasses lie aspar;
But twenty fauts ye may hae waur—
    So blessins on thee, Robin.

141. Elegy on the Death of Robert Ruisseaux

Now Robin lies in his last lair,
  He'll gabble rhyme, nor sing nae mair,
Cauld poverty, wi' hungry stare,
    Nae mair shall fear him;
Nor anxious fear, nor cankert care   5
    E'er mair come near him.

* Jan. 25ᵗʰ 1759. the date of my Bardship's vital existence.—

11 *Footnote from 2CPB*   14 scho . . . will] she, . . . 'll *2CPB*   19 be . . .
a'] gie his Daddie's name a blaw *2CPB*   21 mak] maks *2CPB*   25 Stir
2 CPB: Sir *Cromek*   26 Ye'll *2CPB*: Ye *Cromek*   lie aspar *2CPB*: om. *Cromek*

Elegy on the Death of Robert Ruisseaux. *Text from Cromek*, Reliques, *1808*
(*p. 343*)

To tell the truth, they seldom fash't him,
Except the moment that they crush't him;
For sune as chance or fate had hush't 'em
          Tho' e'er sae short,   10
Then wi' a rhyme or song he lash't 'em,
          And thought it sport.

Tho' he was bred to kintra wark,
And counted was baith wight and stark,
Yet that was never Robin's mark   15
          To mak a man;
But tell him, he was learn'd and clark,
          Ye roos'd him then!

142. Epitaph. Here lies Robert Fergusson, Poet

Born, September 5th, 1751—Died 16th October, 1774

No sculptur'd marble here, nor pompous lay,
          'No story'd urn nor animated bust;'
This simple stone directs pale SCOTIA's way
          To pour her sorrows o'er her POET's dust.

[She mourns, sweet, tuneful youth, thy hapless fate, 5
          Tho' all the pow'rs of song thy fancy fir'd;
Yet Luxury and Wealth lay by in state,
          And thankless starv'd what they so much admir'd.

This humble tribute with a tear he gives,
          A brother Bard, he can no more bestow;   10
But dear to fame thy Song immortal lives,
          A nobler monument than Art can show.]

Epitaph. *Text from the Alloway MS (Al; on the verso of a draft of Burns's letter to the Bailies of the Canongate, 6 February 1787), collated with the inscription sent to Peter Stuart ? February ? 1787 (Currie, ii. 59). The inscription has ll. 1–4 only. Title from Al. Heading from Currie: Al has* Here lies Robert Ferguson, Poet. He was born . . . and died . . . 1774.
     1 sculptur'd marble *Currie:* pageant bearings *Al*   3 pale *Currie:* old *Al*

[On Fergusson]

143.

Curse on ungrateful man, that can be pleas'd,
    And yet can starve the author of the pleasure!

O thou, my elder brother in Misfortune,
By far my elder Brother in the muse,
With tears I pity thy unhappy fate!   5
Why is the Bard unfitted for the world,
Yet has so keen a relish of its Pleasures?

144.

Ill-fated Genius! Heaven-taught Fergusson,
    What heart that feels and will not yield a tear,
To think Life's sun did set e'er well begun
    To shed its influence on thy bright career.

O why should truest Worth and Genius pine   5
    Beneath the iron grasp of Want and Woe,
While titled knaves and idiot-greatness shine
    In all the splendour Fortune can bestow?

145. To a Painter

Dear —, I'll gie ye some advice,
    You'll tak it no uncivil:
You shouldna paint at angels, man,
    But try and paint the Devil.

On Fergusson. *Text of 143 from holograph inscription in a copy of Fergusson's poems presented to Rebeccah Carmichael at Edinburgh, 19 March 1787 (facsimile in H-H., ii. 416), collated with Cromek,* Reliques, *1808 (p. 424). Lines 1–2 are written over Fergusson's portrait, the remainder beneath it. Text of 144 from Chambers, 1851 (iii. 221; from holograph inscription on a blank leaf of the* World). *See Commentary*

143. 4 muse] muses *Cromek*   6 unfitted for] unpitied by *Cromek*

To a Painter. *Text from Chambers-Wallace (iv. 309)*

To paint an angel's kittle wark,   5
Wi' Nick there's little danger;
You'll easy draw a lang-kent face,
But no sae weel a stranger.

R. B.

146. To Mᴿ E—— on his translation of and com-
mentaries on Martial

O THOU, whom Poesy abhors,
    Whom Prose has turned out of doors;
Heard'st thou yon groan?—proceed no further!
'Twas laurell'd Martial calling, Murther!

147A. [The Guidwife of Wauchope-House, to
Robert Burns, the Airshire Bard. Feb. 1787]

MY canty, witty, rhyming ploughman,
    I hafflins doubt, it is na' true, man,
That ye between the stilts was bred,
Wi' ploughman school'd, wi' ploughman fed.
I doubt it sair, ye've drawn your knowledge   5
Either frae grammar school, or colledge.
Guid troth, your saul and body baith
War' better fed, I'd gie my aith,
Than theirs, who sup sour milk and parritch,
An' bummil thro' the single caritch.   10
Whaever heard the ploughman speak,
Could tell gif Homer was a Greek?
He'd flee as soon upon a cudgel,
As get a single line of Virgil.

To Mᴿ E——. *Text from the Alloway MS (Al a), collated with MS Al b, the Esty MS (letter to Clarinda, 14 January 1788), the Lochryan–Adam MS (letter to Mrs Dunlop, 12 February 1788), the facsimile of the original inscription* (Burns Chronicle, *1894, p. 137) and Stewart, 1801 (p. 54). A transcript (not holograph) is in the Watson MSS (1119). Original heading* To Mᴿ Elphinstone—. *Title in Al b* Wrote on a blank leaf of E——'s pompous translation of Martial; *in Loch* To Mr E——
    1 Poesy] *correcting* Poetry *in facsimile*: Poetry *Stewart*   3 yon] that *Stewart*
4 calling] roaring *Stewart*

The Guidwife of Wauchope-House. *Text from Stewart, 1802 (pp. 323–4)*

An' then sae slee ye crack your jokes   15
O' Willie P—t and Charlie F—x.
Our great men a' sae weel descrive,
An' how to gar the nation thrive,
Ane maist wad swear ye dwalt amang them,
An' as ye saw them, sae ye sang them.   20
But be ye ploughman, be ye peer,
Ye are a funny blade, I swear.
An' tho' the cauld I ill can bide,
Yet twenty miles, an' mair, I'd ride,
O'er moss, an' muir, an' never grumble,   25
Tho' my auld yad shou'd gae a stumble,
To crack a winter-night wi' thee,
An' hear thy sangs, an' sonnets slee.
A guid saut herring, an' a cake
Wi' sic a chiel a feast wad make.   30
I'd rather scour your rumming yill,
Or eat o' cheese and bread my fill,
Than wi' dull lairds on turtle dine,
An' ferlie at their wit and wine.
O, gif I kend but whare ye baide,   35
I'd send to you a marled plaid;
'Twad haud your shoulders warm and braw,
An' douse at kirk, or market shaw.
Far south, as weel as north, my lad,
A' honest Scotsmen lo'e the *maud*.   40
Right wae that we're sae far frae ither;
Yet proud I am to ca' ye brither.

> Your most obed. E. S.]

147B. The Answer

GUIDWIFE,

I MIND it weel in early date,
 When I was beardless, young and blate,
   An' first cou'd thresh the barn,
Or haud a yokin at the pleugh,
An' tho' fu' foughten sair eneugh,   5
   Yet unco proud to learn.

The Answer. *Text from Stewart, 1802 (pp. 325–7), collated with Currie, 1800 (iii. 377; lines 1–42 only)*
   4 at] of *Currie*   5 fu' foughten] forfoughten *Currie*

When first amang the yellow corn
　　A man I reckon'd was;
An' with the lave ilk merry morn
　　Could rank my rig and lass;   10
　　　　Still shearing and clearing
　　　　The tither stooked raw;
　　　　With clavers and haivers
　　　　Wearing the time awa':

Ev'n then a wish (I mind its power)   15
A wish, that to my latest hour
　　Shall strongly heave my breast;
That I for poor auld Scotland's sake
Some useful plan, or book could make,
　　Or sing a sang at least.   20

The rough bur-thistle spreading wide
　　Amang the bearded bear,
I turn'd my weeding heuk aside,
　　An' spar'd the symbol dear.
　　　　No nation, no station   25
　　　　My envy e'er could raise:
　　　　A Scot still, but blot still,
　　　　I knew no higher praise.

But still the elements o' sang
In formless jumble, right an' wrang,   30
　　Wild floated in my brain;
Till on that hairst I said before,
My partner in the merry core,
　　She rous'd the forming strain.

I see her yet, the sonsy quean,   35
　　That lighted up my jingle;
Her pauky smile, her kittle een,
　　That gar't my heart-strings tingle.

14 time] day *Currie*   23 my weeding heuk] the weeder-clips *Currie*
37 pauky . . . kittle] witching . . . pauky *Currie*

So tiched, bewitched,
I rav'd ay to mysel;   40
But bashing and dashing,
I kend na how to tell.

Hale to the sex, ilk guid chiel says,
Wi' merry dance in winter-days,
    An' we to share in common: 45
The gust o' joy, the balm of woe,
The saul o' life, the heav'n below,
    Is rapture-giving woman.

Ye surly sumphs, who hate the name,
    Be mindfu' o' your mither: 50
She, honest woman, may think shame
    That ye're connected with her.
        Ye're wae men, ye're nae men,
        That slight the lovely dears:
        To shame ye, disclaim ye,   55
        Ilk honest birkie swears.

For you, na bred to barn and byre,
Wha sweetly tune the Scottish lyre,
    Thanks to you for your line.
The marled plaid ye kindly spare,   60
By me should gratefully be ware;
    'Twad please me to the Nine.

I'd be mair vauntie o' my hap,
    Douse hingin o'er my curple,
Than ony ermine ever lap,   65
    Or proud imperial purple.
        Farewell then, lang hale then,
        An' plenty be your fa':
        May losses and crosses
        Ne'er at your hallan ca'.   70

March, 1787.   R. BURNS.

39–40 So . . . mysel;] *Currie has*
                I fired, inspired,
                At ev'ry kindling keek,
42 I . . . tell] I feared ay to speak *Currie*   43 sex] set *Stewart*

148. [To Miss Isabella Macleod]

TH E crimson blossom charms the bee,
  The summer sun the swallow;
So dear this tuneful gift to me
  From lovely Isabella.

Her portrait fair upon my mind   5
  Revolving Time shall mellow;
And Mem'ry's latest effort find
  The lovely Isabella.

No Bard nor Lover's rapture this,
  In fancies vain and shallow;   10
She is, so come my soul to bliss!
  The lovely Isabella.

149. Extempore, in the Court of S——

Tune, Gillicrankie

Lord A——te

HE clench'd his pamphlets in his fist,
  He quoted and he hinted,
Till in a declamation-mist,
  His argument he tint it:
He gaped for 't, he graped for 't,   5
  He fand it was awa, man;
And what his common sense came short,
  He eked out wi' law, man.

To Miss Isabella Macleod. *Text from the Alloway MS (dated* Edin! March 16th
1787 *and signed* Rob! Burns)
    5 fair] *correcting* strong *in MS*

Extempore. *Text from B.M. MS Egerton 1656, f. 18, collated with* Cromek, Reliques,
1808 (p. 418)
    7 And] But *Cromek*

M^r Er——ne—

Collected, Harry stood awee,
    Then open'd out his arm, man;   10
His lordship sat wi' ruefu' e'e,
    And ey'd the gathering storm, man:
Like wind-driv'n hail it did assail,
    Or torrents owre a lin, man;
The BENCH sae wise lift up their eyes,   15
    Half-wauken'd wi' the din, man.

150. Extempore Epistle to M^r McAdam of
Craigengillan, (wrote in Nanse Tinnock's,
Mauchline) in answer to an obliging letter
he sent in the commencement of my poetic
career—

SIR, o'er a gill I gat your card,
    I trow it made me proud;
See wha taks notice o' the Bard!
    I lap and cry'd fu' loud.—

Now deil-ma-care about their jaw,   5
    The senseless, gawky million;
I'll cock my nose aboon them a',
    I'm roos'd by Craigengillan.—

'Twas noble, Sir; 'twas like yoursel,
    To grant your high protection: 10
A great man's smile ye ken fu' well,
    Is ay a blest infection.—

Tho', by his* banes wha in a tub
    Match'd Macedonian Sandy!
On my ain legs thro' dirt and dub,   15
    I independant stand ay.—

* Diogenes

Extempore Epistle. *Text from the Alloway MS (Al), collated with the Huntington
Library MS (HL; Geddes's copy of 87), the Glenriddell MS (Glen; pp. 72–73; transcript), and Cromek, Reliques, 1808 (p. 399). Title from Glen. Title in Al* Epistle to
. . . Craigengillan in answer . . . career; *in HL* Epistle, wrote in the commencement
. . . poetical career, to M^r M^cadam . . . in answer to an obliding letter he sent me.—
13 *footnote in Glen and Cromek only*

And when those legs to gude, warm kail
    Wi' welcome canna bear me;
A lee dyke-side, a sybow-tail,
    And barley-scone shall chear me.—   20

Heaven spare you lang to kiss the breath
    O' mony flowery simmers!
And bless your bonie lasses baith,
    I'm tald they're loosome kimmers!   25

And God bless young Dunaskin's laird,
    The blossom of our gentry!
And may he wear an auld man's beard,
    A credit to his country!

151. Prologue

Spoken by Mr. WOODS on his Benefit night, Monday, 16th April, 1787.

WHEN by a generous Public's kind acclaim,
    That dearest meed is granted—honest fame;
When *here* your favour is the *actor*'s lot,
Nor even the *man* in *private life* forgot;
What breast so dead to heav'nly Virtue's glow,   5
But heaves impassion'd with the grateful throe.

Poor is the task to please a barb'rous throng,
It needs no Siddons' powers in Southern's song;

Prologue. *Text from Stewart, 1801 (pp. 57–59), collated with the* Edinburgh Evening Courant *and the* Caledonian Mercury, *19 April 1787.*
H–H. (*ii. 382–3*) *record a draft (not traced) with these variants:*
    7 Poor . . . barb'rous] Small . . . gaping *MS*   8 It . . . song;] Unmeaning rant, extravagance of song. *MS*   8 *Followed in MS by two couplets in two versions:*

    (*i*)   Heavy stupidity all rueful views
            The Tyburn humours of the tragic Muse;
            Or roars at times the rude rough laugh between,
            As horse-play nonsense shows her comic scene.

    (*ii*)   The vacant staring crowd all rueful views
            The Tyburn humours of the tragic Muse;
            Or comic scenes the merry roar engage,
            As horseplay nonsense thunders on the stage.

But here an ancient nation fam'd afar,
For genius, learning high, as great in war—   10
Hail, CALEDONIA, name for ever dear!
Before whose sons I'm honour'd to appear!
Where every science—every nobler art—
That can inform the mind, or mend the heart,
Is known; as grateful nations oft have found   15
Far as the rude barbarian marks the bound.
Philosophy, no idle pedant dream,
Here holds her search by heaven-taught Reason's
   beam;
Here History paints, with elegance and force,
The tide of Empire's fluctuating course;   20
Here Douglas forms wild Shakespeare into plan,
And Harley* rouses all the god in man.
When well-form'd taste, and sparkling wit unite,
With manly lore, or female beauty bright,
(Beauty, where faultless symmetry and grace,   25
Can only charm us in the second place,)
Witness my heart, how oft with panting fear,
As on this night, I've met these judges here!
But still the hope Experience taught to live,
Equal to judge—you're candid to forgive.   30
No hundred-headed Riot here we meet,
With decency and law beneath his feet;
Nor Insolence assumes fair Freedom's name;
Like CALEDONIANS, you applaud or blame.

O thou, dread Power! whose empire-giving hand 35
Has oft been stretch'd to shield the honour'd land!
Strong may she glow with all her ancient fire;
May every son be worthy of his sire;
Firm may she rise with generous disdain
At Tyranny's, or direr Pleasure's chain;   40

* The Man of Feeling, wrote by Mr. M'Kenzie.

10 genius] *correcting* taste and *in MS*   11 Hail] *correcting alternatives* Fair
and Great *in MS*   13 Where] *correcting* Here *in MS*   nobler] noblest *MS*
16 Far . . . bound.] To wide civilization's utmost bound; *MS*   17 idle
pedant] more a pedant's *MS*   18 holds her] makes his *MS*   34 applaud]
praise *MS*   39 Firm] Still *MS*

Still self-dependent in her native shore,
Bold may she brave grim Danger's loudest roar,
Till Fate the curtain drop on worlds to be no more.⟩

152. Epistle to Mr Tytler of Woodhouselee, Author of a Defence of Mary Queen of Scots—

May — 1787

R EVERED Defender of beauteous Stuart,
  Of Stuart!—a Name once respected,
A Name which to love was the mark of a true heart,
But now 'tis despis'd and neglected.

Tho' something like moisture conglobes in my eye, 5
Let no man misdeem me disloyal;
A poor, friendless wand'rer may well claim a sigh,
Still more if that Wand'rer were royal.

My Fathers that *name* have rever'd on a throne,
My Fathers have died to right it; 10
Those Fathers would spurn their degenerate Son
That NAME should he scoffingly slight it.

41–43 Still . . . more.] *MS has*

> May never sallow Want her bounty stint,
> Nor selfish maxim dare the sordid hint;
> But may her virtues ever be her prop:
> These her best stay, and Thou her surest hope,
> Till Fate on worlds the eternal curtain drop.

Epistle to Mr Tytler. *Text from Dewar's transcript of the Esty MS (letter to Lady Winifred Constable, 16 December 1789), completed from Currie, 1800 (iv. 351; letter to Tytler, 4 May 1787), and collated with the transcript in Edinburgh University MS Laing III. 586 (Laing; endorsed* Sir Walter Scott, Bart Melrose). *Title in Esty and Laing* Part of an Epistle . . . Queen of Scots*: in Currie* Copy of a poetical address to Mr. William Tytler, with the present of the bard's picture. *Lines 5–12 are quoted by Burns in a letter of 26 December 1787 (? to James Steuart). H–H. record a copy (not traced) of the letter to Tytler with the readings of Currie at ll. 6, 10 (alternative to* died), *13, 15, 16, 21, 23, the as alternative to* once *at l. 3, and* Electoral *as alternative to* Hanover *at l. 18. See Commentary*

3 the] once *Laing*   6 man] one *Currie*   10 died] fallen *Currie*

Still in pray'rs for King G—— I most cordially join,
   The Queen and the rest of the gentry:
Be they wise, be they foolish, 'tis nothing of mine,   15
   Their title's allow'd in the Country.

But why of that Epocha make such a fuss,
   That brought us th' Electoral Stem?
If bringing them over was lucky for *us*,
   I'm sure 'twas as lucky for *them*!   20

But Politics, truce! we're on dangerous ground;
   Who knows how the fashions may alter:
The doctrines today that are loyalty sound,
   Tomorrow may bring us a halter.

I send you a trifle, a head of a bard,   25
   A trifle scarce worthy your care;
But accept it, good sir, as a mark of regard,
   Sincere as a saint's dying prayer.

Now life's chilly evening dim shades on your eye,
   And ushers the long dreary night;   30
But you like the star that athwart gilds the sky,
   Your course to the latest is bright.

153. [To Miss Ainslie, in Church]

FAIR maid, you need not take the hint,
   Nor idle texts pursue;
'Twas only sinners that he meant,
   Not angels such as you.

13 cordially] heartily *Currie*   15 'tis] is *Currie*   16 allow'd in the]
avow'd by my *Currie*   18–20 That . . . *them*!] *replaced by asterisks in Currie*
21 Politics] loyalty *Currie*   23 doctrines . . . are] doctrine . . . is *Currie*
25–32 I send . . . bright.] *om. Esty Laing: text from Currie*

To Miss Ainslie. *Text from the Grierson Papers* (Robert Burns: His Associates and
Contemporaries, *ed. R. T. Fitzhugh, 1943, p. 44*). *Editor's punctuation*

154. [To William Creech]

Selkirk 13th May 1787

AULD chuckie REEKIE's sair distrest,
  Down droops her ance weel-burnish'd crest,
Nae joy her bonie buskit nest
      Can yield ava;
Her darling bird that she loes best,   5
      Willie's awa.—

O Willie was a witty wight,
And had o' things an unco slight;
Auld Reekie ay he keepit tight,
      And trig and braw: 10
But now they'll busk her like a fright,
      Willie's awa.—

The stiffest o' them a' he bow'd,
The bauldest o' them a' he cow'd,
They durst nae mair than he allow'd,   15
      That was a law:
We've lost a birkie weel worth gowd,
      Willie's awa.—

Now gawkies, tawpies, gowks and fools,
Frae colleges and boarding-schools,   20
May sprout like simmer puddock-stools
      In glen or shaw;
He wha could brush them down to mools
      Willie's awa.—

The brethren o' the commerce-chaumer   25
May mourn their loss wi' doolfu' clamour;

To William Creech. *Text from the Alloway MS (letter to Creech, 13 May 1787),
collated with Cromek,* Reliques, *1808 (p. 24)*
    7 a witty] *correcting* an unco *in MS*   11 But now] *correcting* I fear *in MS*

He was a dictionar and grammar
       Amang them a':
I fear they'll now mak mony a stammer,
       Willie's awa.—   30

Nae mair we see his levee door
Philosophers and Poets pour,
And toothy Critics by the score
       In bloody raw;
The Adjutant of a' the core   35
       Willie's awa.—

Now worthy Greg'ry's latin face,
Tytler's and Greenfield's modest grace,
M^ckenzie, Stuart, such a brace
       As Rome ne'er saw;   40
They a' maun meet some ither place,
       Willie's awa.—

Poor Burns—even Scotch Drink canna quicken,
He cheeps like some bewilder'd chicken,
Scar'd frae its minnie and the cleckin   45
       By hoodie-craw:
Grief's gien his heart an unco kickin,
       Willie's awa.—

Now ev'ry sour-mou'd, girnin blellum,
And Calvin's folk are fit to fell him;   50
Ilk self-conceited, critic skellum
       His quill may draw;
He wha could brawlie ward their bellum
       Willie's awa.—

Up wimpling, stately Tweed I've sped,   55
And Eden scenes on chrystal Jed,
And Ettrick banks now roaring red
       While tempests blaw;
But ev'ry joy and pleasure's fled,
       Willie's awa.—   60

50 folk] fock, *Cromek*   51 Ilk] And *Cromek*

May I be Slander's common speech;
A text for Infamy to preach;
And lastly, streekit out to bleach
          In winter snaw
When I forget thee, WILLIE CREECH,   65
          Tho' far awa!—

May never wicked Fortune touzle him,
May never wicked men bamboozle him,
Until a pow as auld's Methusalem
          He canty claw: 70
Then to the blessed, new Jerusalem
          Fleet-wing awa.—

155. [To Symon Gray]

I

SYMON Gray,
You're dull to-day.

II

DULNESS, with redoubted sway,
Has seized the wits of Symon Gray.

III

DEAR Cimon Gray,
                    The other day,
          When you sent me some rhyme,
I could not then just ascertain
          Its worth, for want of time.

But now today, good Mr. Gray,   5
          I've read it o'er and o'er,
Tried all my skill, but find I'm still
          Just where I was before.

To Symon Gray. *Text of* I *and* II *from Chambers–Wallace (ii. 113). Text of* III
from a manuscript copy of Burns's holograph, dated Dunse, 15.th May, 1787 (*photostat
supplied by Mr John McVie), collated with H–H. (ii. 110–111; from 'a complete
copy'). H–H. make a triplet of* I *and* II, *and print as the first stanza of* III

We auld wives' minions gie our opinions,
    Solicited or no;   10
Then of its fau'ts my honest thoughts
    I'll give—and here they go.

Such d——'d bombast no time that's past
    Will show, or time to come,
So, Cimon dear, your song I'll tear,   15
    And with it wipe my [bum].

156. [To Renton of Lamerton]

Your billet, Sir, I grant receipt;
    Wi' you I'll canter ony gate;
Tho' 'twere a trip to yon blue warl
Whare Birkies march on burning marl.
Then, Sir, God willing, I'll attend ye;   5
An' to His goodness I commend ye—
                     R. Burns.

III. 13 time] age *H–H.*   14 Will . . . or] Can . . . nor *H–H.*   16 bum
H–H.: om. in MS

To Renton of Lamerton. *Text from a facsimile of Burns's note in Dobell,* The In-
gatherer, *12 (November 1930), item 34*
  2 Wi'] *correcting* I'll *in MS*

157. Bonie Dundee

Slow

'O WHAR did ye get that hauver-meal bannock?'
   O silly blind body, O dinna ye see;
I gat it frae a young brisk Sodger Laddie,
   Between Saint Johnston and bonie Dundee.

Bonie Dundee. *Text from SMM, 1787 (99; unsigned), collated with the Cowie MS
(note to Cleghorn, ? March 1787). Holograph note in Watson MSS 1790 (1143):*
Stanza of an old Song, tune bonie Dundee

> Ye're like to the timmer o' yon rotten wood,
>   Ye're like to the bark o' yon rotten tree;
> Ye slip frae me like a knotless thread,
>   An' ye'll crack your credit wi' mae than me.

Erratum in the set of Bonie Dundee that I wrote before—For happer-meal, read,
hauver-meal, i.e. meal composed of two different kinds of grain

1 did ye get] gat ye *MS*   3 young brisk] *not in MS*   4 Johnston]
Johnston's *MS*

O gin I saw the laddie that gae me 't!   5
   Aft has he doudl'd me upon his knee;
May Heaven protect my bonie Scots laddie,
   And send him safe hame to his babie and me.

My blessins upon thy sweet, wee lippie!
   My blessins upon thy bonie e'e brie!   10
Thy smiles are sae like my blyth Sodger laddie,
   Thou's ay the dearer, and dearer to me!
But I'll big a bow'r on yon bonie banks,
   Whare Tay rins wimplin by sae clear;
And I'll cleed thee in the tartan sae fine,   15
   And mak thee a man like thy dadie dear.

158. [At Roslin Inn]

MY blessings on ye, honest wife,
   I ne'er was here before;
Ye've wealth o' gear for spoon and knife—
   Heart could not wish for more.

Heav'n keep you clear o' sturt and strife,   5
   Till far ayont fourscore,
And by the Lord o' death and life,
   I'll ne'er gae by your door!

6, 9, 10 upon] on *MS*   7 protect] preserve *MS*   9 lippie] lips *MS*
11 are] *not in MS*   blyth] *not in MS*   12 ay the dearer, and dearer] dearer,
dearer ay *MS*   15 sae] *not in MS*

At Roslin Inn. *Text from Chambers, 1851 (ii. 43), collated with Hogg and Mother-well, 1834 (ii. 67; HM). See Commentary*

  1 honest] sonsie *HM*   3 Ye've . . . spoon] You've gi'en us walth for horn
HM   4 Heart could not] Nae heart could *HM*   5 clear o' sturt] free frae
care *HM*   7 by . . . and] while I toddle on thro' *HM*   8 gae] gang *HM*

159. Epigram

W HOE'ER he be that sojourns here,
       I pity much his case,
Unless he come to wait upon
    The Lord their God, his Grace.

There's naething here but Highland pride,   5
    And Highland scab and hunger;
If Providence has sent me here,
    'Twas surely in an anger.

160. On the death of Sir J. Hunter Blair—

T HE lamp of day, with ill-presaging glare,
       Dim, cloudy, sunk beyond the western wave:
Th' inconstant blast howl'd thro' the darkening air,
    And hollow whistled in the rocky cave.

Epigram. *Text from Stewart, 1801 (p. 53). Note in Stewart:* BURNS, *accompanied by a friend, having gone to Inverary at a time when some company were there on a visit to his Grace the Duke of Argyll, finding himself and his companion entirely neglected by the Inn-keeper, whose whole attention seemed to be occupied with the visitors of his Grace, expressed his disapprobation of the incivility with which they were treated in the following lines: A Stewart and Meikle tract (1799) has*

> Highland pride, Highland scab, Highland hunger,
> If God Almighty sent me here, 'twas surely in his anger.

On the death of Sir J. Hunter Blair. *Text from the Huntington Library MS (HL; Geddes's copy of 87), collated with the draft in Burns's journal of his Border tour (*JBT*), MSS Alloway (Al A, B), Esty, and Glenriddell (Glen; pp. 60–62, transcript with holograph note; see Commentary), and Currie, 1800 (iii. 381).* JBT *has ll. 1–3, 5–8 in ink (p. 47), a page of illegible writing in pencil, and ll. 37–40 in ink (p. 49). A MS has been recorded in a copy of 86 (see H–H., ii. 413–14) with these variants:*
   7 limpid . . . hallow'd,] *erst the saint's revered MS*   10 clouds, swift-wing'd,] *winged clouds MS*   14 disclos'd] *display'd MS*   17 glow] *flow MS*
20 embu'd] *embrued MS*   33 ancient] *wonted MS*   35 how] *now MS*
37 lie unsung] *fall in vain MS*   39 tongue] *strain MS*

Dewar collated a MS (not traced) with the readings of Al A and Esty at ll. 7 and 10, and the title Elegy on Sir J. H. Blair. *Title in Al A* Elegy on Sir J. H. Blair: *in Esty* Elegy on the late Sir James Hunter Blair
   2 beyond] behind *JBT:* beneath *Glen*   3 darkening] *correcting* darken'd *in* HL

Lone as I wander'd by each cliff and dell,   5
   *Once the lov'd haunts of Scotia's royal train;
Or mus'd where limpid streams, once hallow'd, well;
   Or mouldering ruins mark the sacred Fane.†

Th' increasing blast roar'd round the beetling rocks;
   The clouds, swift-wing'd, flew o'er the starry sky;   10
The groaning trees, untimely, shed their locks,
   And shooting meteors caught the startled eye.—

The paly moon rose in the livid east,
   And 'mong the cliffs disclos'd a stately Form,
In weeds of woe, that frantic beat her breast,   15
   And mix'd her wailings with the raving storm.—

Wild to my heart the filial pulses glow;
   'Twas CALEDONIA's trophy'd shield I view'd;
Her form majestic droop'd in pensive woe,
   The lightening of her eye in tears embu'd.—   20

Revers'd that spear, redoubtable in war,
   Reclin'd that banner, erst in fields unfurl'd,
That like a deathful meteor gleam'd afar,
   And brav'd the mighty monarchs of the world.—

'My patriot-Son fills an untimely grave!'   25
   With accent wild and lifted arms she cry'd;
'Low lies the hand that oft was stretch'd to save,
   'Low lies the heart that swell'd with honor's pride.—

* The king's park at Holyroodhouse.—
† S� Anthony's well and chapel.—

---

7 limpid . . . hallow'd,] erst revered waters *JBT Esty Al A: corrected in Al B*
10 clouds, swift-wing'd,] winged clouds *Esty Al A: corrected in Al B*   14 'mong
Al A Al B Esty Glen: 'mongst *HL*   15 frantic] *correcting* pensive *in Al B*
26 accent] accents *Currie*   arms] *correcting* hands *in Al B HL*   28 honor's]
honest *Currie*

'A weeping Country joins a Widow's tear,
   'The helpless Poor mix with the Orphans' cry;   30
'The drooping arts surround their Patron's bier,
   'And grateful Science heaves the heart-felt sigh.——

'I saw my Sons resume their ancient fire;
   'I saw fair Freedom's blossoms richly blow:
'But ah, how hope is born but to expire!   35
   'Relentless Fate has laid their Guardian low.——

'My Patriot falls—but shall he lie unsung,
   'While empty Greatness saves a worthless name?
'No: every Muse shall join her tuneful tongue,
   'And future ages hear his growing fame.——   40

'And I will join a Mother's tender cares,
   'Thro' future times to make his virtues last,
'That distant years may boast of other BLAIRS—'
   She said, and vanish'd with the sweeping blast.

161. [To Miss Ferrier]

MADAM

NAE Heathen Name shall I prefix,
   Frae Pindus or Parnassus;
AULD REEKIE dings them a' to sticks
   For rhyme-inspiring Lasses.——

Jove's tunefu' Dochters three times three   5
   Made Homer deep their debtor;
But gien the body half an e'e,
   Nine FERRIERS wad done better.——

---

38 empty . . . worthless] *correcting* worthless . . . empty *in JBT*

To Miss Ferrier. *Text from the Alloway MS (enclosing a copy of* **160**), *collated with Ewing's transcript from the* College Album, *1828, and Chambers, 1851 (ii. 109–10). The jottings at the end of Burns's journal of his Border tour include (before a draft of* **160**) *a draft of ll. 1–4 headed* To Miss F—— *and reading* O' gentry frae Parnassus *in l. 2. See Commentary*

Last day my mind was in a bog,
    Down George's street I stoited;   10
A creeping, cauld PROSAIC fog
    My vera senses doited.—

Do what I dought to set her free,
    My Muse lay in the mire;
Ye turn'd a neuk—I saw your e'e—   15
    She took the wing like fire.—

The mournfu' Sang I here inclose,
    In GRATITUDE I send you;
And pray in rhyme, sincere as prose,
    A' GUDE THINGS MAY ATTEND YOU.   20
                          ROB⁺. BURNS

St James' Square ⎫
Saturday even: ⎭

162. On reading, in a Newspaper, the Death of
—— M'L——, Esq. Brother to a Young Lady,
a particular Friend of the Author's

SAD thy tale, thou idle page,
    And rueful thy alarms:
Death tears the brother of her love
    From Isabella's arms.

Sweetly deckt with pearly dew   5
    The morning rose may blow;
But cold successive noontide blasts
    May lay its beauties low.

9 mind] muse *Album*   11 creeping] gloomy *Album*   14 Muse] saul
Chambers   15 Ye . . . I saw] I . . . she catch'd *Album*   16 She] And
Album   17 inclose] indite *Album*   19 And . . . prose] And [wish and]
pray in rhyme sincere *Chambers*

On reading, &c. *Text from the Edinburgh edition, 1793, collated with the Lochryan
MS (Loch), the Alloway MSS (Al A, B, C), the Huntington Library MS (HL; Geddes's
copy of 87), MSS Adam, Esty, and Glenriddell (Glen; pp. 64–65; transcript with
autograph revisions), and the edition of 1794. Title in Adam and Esty* On reading . . .
an account of the death, *&c. Most MSS have* Miss I[sabella] M'[Leod] *for* a Young
Lady, *and Esty adds* and whose Family had for some time suffered a train of misfortunes.

7 successive] *correcting* succeeding *in Loch*

Fair on Isabella's morn
  The sun propitious smil'd;   10
But, long ere noon, succeeding clouds
  Succeeding hopes beguil'd.

Fate oft tears the bosom chords
  That Nature finest strung:
So Isabella's heart was form'd,   15
  And so that heart was wrung.

Dread Omnipotence, alone,
  Can heal the wound He gave;
Can point the brimful grief-worn eyes
  To scenes beyond the grave.   20

Virtue's blossoms there shall blow,
  And fear no withering blast;
There Isabella's spotless worth
  Shall happy be at last.

---

13 Fate] *correcting* Heaven *in Al A–B*: Heaven *Loch Adam*   16 that] her *Loch
Al (A, B) HL Esty Adam Glen*   16 *Additional stanza in Al (B) HL Esty:*

      Were it in the Poet's power,
        Strong as he shares the grief
      That pierces Isabella's heart,
        To give that heart relief!

  19 brimful grief-worn] grief-worn, brimful *Loch Al (A; correcting* tearful grief-
worn) *Al B HL Esty Adam Glen*   22 withering] *correcting* threatning *in Loch*
24 *Holograph note added in Glen:* This poetic compliment, what few poetic compliments are, was from the heart.—

163. Yon wild mossy mountains—

Phebe

Slow

Y<small>ON</small> wild, mossy mountains sae lofty and wide,
That nurse in their bosom the youth o' the Clyde;
Where the grous lead their coveys thro' the heather to feed,
And the sheepherd tents his flock as he pipes on his reed.

Not Gowrie's rich valley, nor Forth's sunny shores,   5
To me hae the charms o' yon wild, mossy moors:
For there, by a lanely, sequestered stream,
Resides a sweet Lassie, my thought and my dream.—

Yon wild mossy mountains. *Text from the Hastie MS, f. 70, collated with SMM,*
1792 (331; signed X). Dewar collated a MS omitting ll. 9–12, with these variants:
1 wild] high *MS*   4 tents] eyes *MS*   5 valley] vallies *MS*
    7 sequestered] sequestred *SMM*

Amang thae wild mountains shall still be my path,
Ilk stream foaming down its ain green, narrow strath;   10
For there, wi' my Lassie, the day-lang I rove,
While o'er us, unheeded, flee the swift hours o' Love.—

She is not the fairest, altho' she is fair;
O' nice education but sma' is her skair;
Her parentage humble as humble can be;   15
But I loe the dear Lassie because she loes me.—

To Beauty what man but maun yield him a prize,
In her armour of glances, and blushes, and sighs;
And when Wit and Refinement hae polish'd her darts,
They dazzle our een, as they flie to our hearts.—   20

But Kindness, sweet Kindness, in the fond-sparkling e'e,
Has lustre outshining the diamond to me;
And the heart beating love as I'm clasp'd in her arms,
O, these are my Lassie's all-conquering charms.—

164. My Harry was a Gallant gay

Tune, Highlander's Lament

10 Ilk . . . down *SMM:* Where ilk stream faems alang *MS*   green, narrow]
correcting narrow green *in MS*   14 skair] share *SMM*   18 In her armour
of] *correcting* Her armour is *in MS*

My Harry was a Gallant gay. *Text from SMM, 1790 (209; unsigned), collated with
the Hastie MS, f. 166 (not holograph)*

MY Harry was a gallant gay,
   Fu' stately strade he on the plain;
But now he's banish'd far awa,
   I'll never see him back again.

Chorus

  O for him back again,   5
    O for him back again,
  I wad gie a' Knockhaspie's land
    For Highland Harry back again.

When a' the lave gae to their bed,
   I wander dowie up the glen;   10
I set me down and greet my fill,
   And ay I wish him back again.
    O for him &c.

O were some villains hangit high,
   And ilka body had their ain!
Then I might see the joyfu' sight,   15
  My Highlan Harry back again.
    O for him &c.

2 on] o'er *MS*   5 O] And oh! *MS*   6 O] Ah! *MS*   7 Knockhaspie's]
my father's *MS*   10 up] down *MS*   11 I . . . fill] An' sair I greet an' aft
I wish *MS*   12 And . . . him] For Highland Harry *MS*   12 *Additional
stanzas in MS:*

    'Sad was the day an' sad the hour
    'He left me and his native plain
    'And rush'd his sair wrang'd prince to join
    'But ah! he ne'er cam back again.

    'Strong was my Harry's arm in war
    'Unmatch'd in a' Culoden plain
    'Now vengeance marks him as her prey
    'I'll never see him back again.'

15–16 Then . . . again.] *MS has*

    Then I wi' joy might welcome hame
    My Prince an' Harry back again.

17 O for him &c.] *MS has*

    And oh! for him back again,
    The Auld Stewarts back again
    I wad gie a' my fathers lan'
    To see them safely back again.

165. Verses written on a window of the Inn at Carron

Wᴇ cam' na here to view your warks,
   In hopes to be mair wise,
But only, lest we gang to hell,
   It may be nae surprise:
But whan we tirl'd at your door,   5
   Your porter dought na bear us;
Sae may, shou'd we to hell's yetts come,
   Your billy Satan sair us!

166. [Lines on Stirling]

[A] Written by Somebody in the window of an inn at Stirling on seeing the Royal Palace in ruins.

Hᴇʀᴇ Stewarts once in triumph reign'd,
   And laws for Scotland's weal ordain'd;
But now unroof'd their Palace stands,
Their sceptre's fall'n to other hands;
Fallen indeed, and to the earth,   5
Whence grovelling reptiles take their birth.—
The injur'd Sᴛᴇᴡᴀʀᴛ-line are gone,
A Race outlandish fill their throne;
An idiot race, to honor lost;
Who know them best despise them most.—   10

[B] These imprudent lines were answered, very petulantly, by somebody, I believe a Revᵈ Mʳ Hamilton.—In a M.S.S. where I met with the answer, I wrote below—

Verses. *Text from Stewart, 1801 (p. 60), collated with the* Edinburgh Evening Courant, *5 October 1789 (dated 26 August 1787 and signed* R.B., Ayrshire)
  6 bear *Courant:* hear *Stewart*   7 Sae] So *Courant*

Lines on Stirling. *Text of [A] and [B] from the Glenriddell MS (p. 80; transcript with Burns's holograph note), collated with Cunningham, 1834 (iii. 294–5; Cun). Text of [C] from Cunningham*
  [A] 1 triumph] glory *Cun*   4 fall'n to] swayed by *Cun*   5–6 Fallen . . . birth.] *om. Cun*   7 are] is *Cun*   8 fill] fills *Cun*   9–10 An . . . most.] *om. Cun*

WITH Esop's lion, Burns says, sore I feel
Each other blow, but d–mn that ass's heel!

[C]   The Reproof
RASH mortal, and slanderous Poet, thy name
Shall no longer appear in the records of fame;
Dost not know that old Mansfield, who writes like the
    Bible,
Says the more 'tis a truth, Sir, the more 'tis a libel?

167. On a Schoolmaster in Cleish Parish, Fifeshire

HERE lie Willie M—hie's banes,
  O Satan, when ye tak him,
Gie him the schulin' o' your weans;
  For clever Deils he'll mak 'em!

168. Strathallan's Lament

Plaintive

[B] 1 With] Like *Cun*   2 Each other blow] All others scorn *Cun*

On a Schoolmaster. *Text from Cromek*, Reliques, *1808 (p. 420)*

Strathallan's Lament. *Text from SMM, 1788 (132; signed B), collated with SC, 1805
(178),* Currie *(iv. 273–4), and MSS Alloway, Adam, and Hastie. The Alloway MS is*

Thickest night, surround my dwelling!
   Howling tempests, o'er me rave!
Turbid torrents, wintry swelling,
   Roaring by my lonely cave.
Chrystal streamlets gently flowing,   5
   Busy haunts of base mankind,
Western breezes softly blowing,
   Suit not my distracted mind.

In the cause of Right engaged,
   Wrongs injurious to redress,   10
Honor's war we strongly waged,
   But the heavens deny'd success:
Ruin's wheel has driven o'er us,
   Not a hope that dare attend,
The wide world is all before us—   15
   But a world without a friend!

complete, but has no title. The Adam MS has ll. 9–16 only. The Hastie MS contains two
fragments: on f. 28, ll, 9–16 as in SMM, with the heading Thickest Night surround
Allan's Lament; *on f. 41, a draft headed* Song—Tune, Masterton's Lament:

   Thickest Night surround my dwelling!
      Howling tempests o'er me rave!
   Wintry torrents turbid, swell

   Streams [that glide in *del.*] the pride of orient plains,
   Never bound in Winter's chains,

H–H. record a draft with variants as below. See Commentary
   1 night, surround] darkness shrouds *H–H.:* night o'erhang *SC Currie*
3 Turbid . . . wintry] Sweeping . . . turbid *MS collated in Aldine edn., 1839*
4 Roaring by] Still surround *SC Currie*   9–12 In . . . success:] *H–H. has*

   Farewell fleeting, fickle treasure,
   Between mishap and folly shar'd;
   Farewell peace and farewell pleasure,
   Farewell flattering man's regard.

13, 15 us] me *H–H.*   14 Not . . . dare] Nor dare a hope my fate *H–H.*
15 is] *correcting* was *in Adam*

169. Written with a Pencil over the Chimney-piece, in the Parlour of the Inn at Kenmore, Taymouth

ADMIRING Nature in her wildest grace,
These northern scenes with weary feet I trace;
O'er many a winding dale and painful steep,
Th' abodes of coveyed grouse and timid sheep,
My savage journey, curious, I pursue,   5
Till fam'd Breadalbaine opens to my view.—
The meeting cliffs each deep-sunk glen divides,
The woods, wild-scattered, clothe their ample sides;
Th' outstretching lake, imbosomed 'mong the hills,
The eye with wonder and amazement fills;   10
The Tay meandering sweet in infant pride,
The palace rising on his verdant side;
The lawns wood-fringed in Nature's native taste;
The hillocks dropt in Nature's careless haste;
The arches striding o'er the new-born stream;   15
The village glittering in the noontide beam—

*   *   *   *   *   *

Poetic ardours in my bosom swell,
Lone wandring by the hermit's mossy cell:
The sweeping theatre of hanging woods;
Th' incessant roar of headlong tumbling floods—   20

*   *   *   *   *   *

Written with a Pencil. *Text from the Edinburgh edition, 1793, collated with the Alloway MS (Al), the Glenriddell MS (Glen; pp. 77–78; transcript with autograph correction), the Huntington Library MS (HL; Geddes's copy of 87), the* Edinburgh Evening Courant, *6 September 1787 (EEC), the* Edinburgh Magazine, *September 1788 (EM), the* Bee, *28 March 1792, and the edition of 1794. Dated 29 August 1787 in EEC. Title in Al Glen HL* Written in the Hermitage at Taymouth; *in the Bee* Written on a Window in Breadalbane by Mr. Robert Burns, May 9th, 1790

3 dale] *correcting* dell *in Glen:* dell *Al HL*   6 opens to *94*: opens on *93 Al Glen EEC Bee*: opens on *corrects* rises to *in HL*   7 The meeting cliffs] The meeting hills *EM*: A rifted hill *Bee*   8 ample] towering *Al Glen HL*
10 wonder] pleasure *EEC EM Bee*   12 his] its *EEC*   14 in] like *Al Glen HL*   13–16 The lawns . . . beam] *EEC EM and Bee have*

> The arches striding o'er the new-born stream,
> The village glittering in the noontide beam,
> The lawns wood-fring'd in Nature's native taste,
> Nor with one single Goth-conceit disgrac'd.

20 Th' *94*: The *Glen 93*

Here Poesy might wake her heaven taught lyre,
And look through Nature with creative fire;
Here, to the wrongs of Fate half reconcil'd,
Misfortune's lightened steps might wander wild;
And Disappointment, in these lonely bounds,   25
Find balm to soothe her bitter rankling wounds:
Here heart-struck Grief might heavenward stretch her scan,
And injured Worth forget and pardon Man.

*   *   *   *   *   *

170. The birks of Aberfeldey.—Composed on the spot

Tune, Birks of Abergeldie

Chorus

B<small>ONY</small> lassie will ye go, will ye go, will ye go;
Bony lassie will ye go to the birks of Aberfeldey.—

I

Now Simmer blinks on flowery braes,
And o'er the chrystal streamlets plays;
Come let us spend the lightsome days   5
In the birks of Aberfeldey.—

28 *Holograph note added in Glen:* I wrote this with my pencil over the chimney-
piece in the parlour of the Inn at Kenmore, at the outlet of Loch Tay.—

The birks of Aberfeldey. *Text from the Alloway MS (October 1787), collated with
SMM, 1788 (113; signed B). In SMM the chorus introduces and follows the first
stanza*

2

The little birdies blythely sing
While o'er their heads the hazels hing,
Or lightly flit on wanton wing
    In the birks of Aberfeldey.—   10

3

The braes ascend like lofty wa's,
The foamy stream deep-roaring fa's
O'erhung wi' fragrant-spreading shaws,
    The birks of Aberfeldey.—

4

The hoary cliffs are crown'd wi' flowers,   15
White o'er the linns the burnie pours
And rising weets wi' misty showers
    The birks of Aberfeldey.—

5

Let Fortune's gifts at random flee,
They ne'er shall draw a wish frae me;   20
Supremely blest wi' love and thee
    In the birks of Aberfeldey.—

7 The *SMM*: Now *MS*

171. [Amang the trees]

Tune—The King of France, he rade a race

Brisk

AMANG the trees, where humming bees
    At buds and flowers were hinging, O!
Auld Caledon drew out her drone,
    And to her pipe was singing, O!
'Twas Pibroch, Sang, Strathspey, or Reels,   5
    She dirl'd them aff, fu' clearly, O!
When there cam a yell o' foreign squeels,
    That dang her tapsalteerie, O!

Their capon craws, and queer ha ha's,
    They made our lugs grow eerie, O!   10
The hungry bike did scrape and pike
    Till we were wae and weary; O!
But a royal ghaist, wha ance was cas'd
    A prisoner aughteen year awa,
He fir'd a fiddler in the North   15
    That dang them tapsalteerie, O!

Amang the trees. *Text from Cromek*, Reliques, *1808 (p. 453), collated with Scott
Douglas (SD; iii. 167–8). SD records a MS (not traced) with these variants:*
  5 Reels] Reel *MS*   7 yell . . . squeels] curst Italian squeel *MS*
  5 or] and *SD*   11 pike] fyke *SD*

172. The Humble Petition of Bruar Water* to the Noble Duke of Athole

M^Y Lord, I know, your noble ear
    Woe ne'er assails in vain;
Embolden'd thus, I beg you'll hear
    Your humble slave complain,
How saucy Phebus' scorching beams,   5
    In flaming summer-pride,
Dry-withering, waste my foamy streams,
    And drink my crystal tide.

The lightly-jumping, glowrin trouts,
    That thro' my waters play,   10
If, in their random, wanton spouts,
    They near the margin stray;
If, hapless chance! they linger lang,
    I'm scorching up so shallow,
They're left, the whitening stanes amang,   15
    In gasping death to wallow.

Last day I grat wi' spite and teen,
    As Poet B**** came by,
That, to a Bard, I should be seen
    Wi' half my channel dry: 20
A panegyric rhyme, I ween,
    Even as I was he shor'd me;
But, had I in my glory been,
    He, kneeling, wad ador'd me.

* Bruar Falls, in Athole, are exceedingly picturesque and beautiful; but their effect is much impaired by the want of trees and shrubs.

The Humble Petition of Bruar Water. *Text from the Edinburgh edition, 1793, collated with the Huntington Library MSS (HL A, letter to Josiah Walker, 5 September 1787; HL B, Geddes's copy of 87), the Alloway MSS (Al A, B, C), the Glenriddell MS (Glen; pp. 67–71; transcript), the Edinburgh Magazine, November 1789 (EM), and the edition of 1794. Al C is defective (ll. 1–12 only). Note on the title in Al B, Glen* Bruar falls are the finest in the country, but not a bush about them which spoils much their beauty; *in Al C* Bruar falls . . . picturesque and beautiful; but not a bush to be seen about them, mars much their effect.—

11 If] When *MSS (except Al C)*   random, wanton] wanton, random *HL (A)*
EM   18 As] When *HL (A, B) Al (A, B) Glen*   B****] Burns *HL (B) Al (B) Glen*

Here, foaming down the skelvy rocks,   25
  In twisting strength I rin;
There, high my boiling torrent smokes,
  Wild-roaring o'er a linn:
Enjoying large each spring and well
  As Nature gave them me,   30
I am, altho' I say 't mysel,
  Worth gaun a mile to see.

Would then my noble master please
  To grant my highest wishes,
He'll shade my banks wi' towering trees,   35
  And bonie spreading bushes.
Delighted doubly then, my Lord,
  You'll wander on my banks,
And listen mony a grateful bird
  Return you tuneful thanks.   40

The sober laverock, warbling wild,
  Shall to the skies aspire;
The gowdspink, Music's gayest child,
  Shall sweetly join the choir:
The blackbird strong, the lintwhite clear,   45
  The mavis mild and mellow;
The robin pensive Autumn chear,
  In all her locks of yellow.

This too, a covert shall ensure,
  To shield them from the storm;   50
And coward maukin sleep secure,
  Low in her grassy form:
Here shall the shepherd make his seat,
  To weave his crown of flowers;
Or find a sheltering, safe retreat,   55
  From prone-descending showers.

25 skelvy] shelvy *HL* (*A, B*) *Al* (*B*) *Glen*: shelving *Al* (*A*)   29–32 Enjoying
. . . see.] *Cancelled in HL* (*A*)   30 gave] gives *MSS*   35 banks] streams
Al (*A*): stream *HL* (*A*)   43 gowdspink . . . gayest] Bairdie . . . youngest *HL*
(*A, B*) *Al* (*A, B*) *Glen EM*   Music's] *correcting* Nature's *in Al* (*A*)   48 In]
With *MSS*   50 storm] storms *MSS*   51 maukin] maukins *MSS EM*
52 her . . . form] their . . . forms *MSS EM*   53 make his] *correcting* find a *in*
Al (*A*)

And here, by sweet endearing stealth,
    Shall meet the loving pair,
Despising worlds with all their wealth
    As empty idle care: 60
The flowers shall vie in all their charms
    The hour of heaven to grace,
And birks extend their fragrant arms
    To screen the dear embrace.

Here haply too, at vernal dawn,   65
    Some musing bard may stray,
And eye the smoking, dewy lawn,
    And misty mountain, gray;
Or, by the reaper's nightly beam,
    Mild-chequering thro' the trees,   70
Rave to my darkly dashing stream,
    Hoarse-swelling on the breeze.

Let lofty firs, and ashes cool,
    My lowly banks o'erspread,
And view, deep-bending in the pool,   75
    Their shadows' wat'ry bed:
Let fragrant birks, in woodbines drest,
    My craggy cliffs adorn;
And, for the little songster's nest,
    The close embowering thorn.   80

So may, Old Scotia's darling hope,
    Your little angel band
Spring, like their fathers, up to prop
    Their honour'd native land!
So may, thro' Albion's farthest ken,   85
    To social-flowing glasses
The grace be—'Athole's honest men,
    'And Athole's bonnie lasses!'

57–64 And here . . . embrace.] *Cancelled in HL (A)*   65 Here haply too]
And haply here *EM*   71 my] *correcting* the *in HL (A)*   72 *Al A ends*
76 shadows'] shadow's *Glen*   77 fragrant] spreading *HL (A)*   85 ken] kin 93
88 lasses] lassies 93   *Holograph note added in Glen:* God who knows all things,
knows how my heart achs with the throes of gratitude whenever I recollect my
reception at the noble house of Athole.—

173. *A Verse composed and repeated by* Burns,
to the Master of the house, on taking leave at a
place in the Highlands, where he had been
hospitably entertained

W HEN death's dark stream I ferry o'er,
A time that surely shall come;
In Heaven itself, I'll ask no more,
Than just a Highland welcome.

174. Written with a Pencil, standing by the
Fall of Fyers, near Loch-Ness

A MONG the heathy hills and ragged woods
The roaring Fyers pours his mossy floods;
Till full he dashes on the rocky mounds,
Where, thro' a shapeless breach, his stream resounds.
As high in air the bursting torrents flow,   5
As deep recoiling surges foam below,
Prone down the rock the whitening sheet descends,
And viewless Echo's ear, astonish'd, rends.
Dim-seen, through rising mists and ceaseless showers,
The hoary cavern, wide-surrounding, lowers.   10
Still thro' the gap the struggling river toils,
And still, below, the horrid caldron boils—

*   *   *   *   *   *

A Verse. *Text from Currie, iv. 405, collated with the* Edinburgh Evening Courant,
2 July 1792 (headed Written at Dalnacardoch in the Highlands, *and signed* R.B.)

Written with a Pencil. *Text from the Edinburgh edition, 1793, collated with the*
Alloway MS (Al), the Huntington Library MS (HL; Geddes's copy of 87), the Glen-
riddell MS (Glen; pp. 79–80; transcript), and the edition of 1794. Title in MSS
Written at the Fall of Fyers
    8 astonish'd] affrighted *Al HL*   10 lowers] towers *Al HL Glen*   11–12 Still
. . . boils—] *Al and HL have*

> Still urging through the gap the river toils,
> And still the horrid deep, dark-raging boils.—

12 *Holograph note added in Glen:* I composed these lines standing on the brink of the
hideous caldron below the water-fall.—

175. Castle Gordon—*intended to be sung to Morag—*

[1]

STREAMS that glide in orient plains,
Never bound by Winter's chains;
Glowing here on golden sands,
There immixed with foulest stains
From Tyranny's empurpled hands: 5
These, their richly gleaming waves,
I leave the tyrants and their slaves,
Give me the stream that sweetly laves
    The banks by CASTLE GORDON.—

2

Torrid forests, ever gay,   10
Shading from the burning ray
Hapless wretches sold to toil;
Or the ruthless Native's way,
Bent on slaughter, blood and spoil:
Woods that ever verdant wave,   15
I leave the tyrant and the slave,
Give me the groves that lofty brave
    The storms, by CASTLE GORDON.—

3

Wildly here without control,
Nature reigns and rules the whole;   20
In that sober, pensive mood,
Dearest to the feeling soul,
She plants the forest, pours the flood:
Life's poor day I'll musing rave,
And find at night a sheltering cave,   25
Where waters flow and wild woods wave
    By bonny CASTLE GORDON.—

Castle Gordon. *Text from the* Second Commonplace Book, *pp. 27–28 (2CPB),
collated with Currie, 1800 (i.185). Lines 1–2 are jotted on the Hastie MS, f. 41ᵛ, with*
that glide in *corrected to* the pride of *and in* for by (*l. 2*)
    4 immixed] commix'd *Currie*   5 hands] bands *Currie*   7 the] to *Currie*
10 Torrid] Spicy *Currie*   19 control] *correcting* controul *in 2CPB*

176. The young Highland Rover

Tune—Morag—

L O U D blaw the frosty breezes,
     The snaws the mountains cover;
Like winter on me seizes
     Since my young Highland rover
Far wanders nations over.   5

Chorus

Where'er he go, where'er he stray,
     May Heaven be his warden;
Return him safe to fair Strathspey
     And bonie Castle-Gordon.—

The trees now naked groaning   10
     Shall soon wi' leaves be hinging,
The birdies dowie moaning
     Shall a' be blythely singing,
And every flower be springing.

Chorus

Sae I'll rejoice the lee-lang day,   15
     When by his mighty Warden
My Youth's return'd to fair Strathspey
     And bonie Castle-Gordon.

The young Highland Rover. *Text from the Hastie MS, f. 30, collated with SMM, 1788 (143; signed R), and SC, 1799 (67). Title from SMM*

177. Theniel Menzies' bony Mary—

Tune, Ruffian's rant—

Lively

IN comin by the brig o' Dye,
At Darlet we a blink did tarry;
As day was dawin in the sky
  We drank a health to bonie Mary.—

Chorus
Theniel Menzies' bonie Mary,   5
Theniel Menzies' bonie Mary,
Charlie Grigor tint his plaidie
Kissin Theniel's bonie Mary.—

Her een sae bright, her brow sae white,
  Her haffet locks as brown's a berry;   10
And ay they dimpl't wi' a smile,
  The rosy cheeks o' bonie Mary.—
    Theniel Menzies' &c.

We lap and danc'd the lee-lang day,
  Till Piper lads were wae and weary;
But Charlie gat the spring to pay   15
  For kissin Theniel's bonie Mary.—
    Theniel Menzies' &c.

Theniel Menzies' bony Mary. *Text from the Hastie MS, f. 36, collated with SMM,*
1788 (156; signed Z)

178. Lady Onlie—

Tune, Ruffian's rant

A' THE lads o' Thornie-bank
    When they gae to the shore o' Bucky,
They'll step in and tak a pint
    Wi' Lady Onlie, honest lucky.—

Chorus—

Lady Onlie, honest lucky,   5
    Brews gude ale at shore o' Bucky;
I wish her sale for her gude ale,
    The best on a' the shore o' Bucky.—

Her house sae bien, her curch sae clean,
    I wat she is a dainty Chuckie!   10
And cheary blinks the ingle gleede
    O' Lady Onlie, honest lucky.—
        Lady Onlie, &c.

179. Song.—Composed at Auchtertyre on Miss Euphemia Murray of Lentrose—

Tune, Andrew an' his cutty gun

Lady Onlie. *Text from the Hastie MS, f. 35, collated with SMM, 1788 (156; signed Z). The MS opens with the chorus*

Song. *Text from the Alloway MS, 1787, collated with SMM, 1788 (180; signed B), and SC, 1799 (61). First-line title in SMM and SC. In SMM and SC the chorus, as the air requires, precedes the first stanza*

B^Y Oughtertyre grows the aik,
   On Yarrow banks the birken shaw;
But Phemie was a bonier lass
   Than braes o' Yarrow ever saw.—

Chorus

Blythe, blythe and merry was she,   5
   Blythe was she but and ben:
Blythe by the banks of Ern,
   And blythe in Glenturit glen.—

2

Her looks were like a flower in May,
   Her smile was like a simmer morn,   10
She tripped by the banks of Ern
   As light's a bird upon a thorn.—

3

Her bony face it was as meek
   As ony lamb upon a lee;
The evening sun was ne'er sae sweet   15
   As was the blink o' Phemie's e'e.—

4

The Highland hills I've wander'd wide,
   And o'er the lawlands I hae been;
But Phemie was the blythest lass
   That ever trode the dewy green.—   20

---

1 Oughtertyre] *correcting* Auchtertyre *in MS*   3, 16, 19 Phemie] *correcting*
Effie *in MS*   7, 11 Ern] *correcting* Earne *in MS*   8 Glenturit] *correcting*
Glentorat *in MS*   14 a] *correcting* the *in MS*: the *SC*

180. On scaring some Water-Fowl in Loch-Turit, a wild scene among the Hills of Oughtertyre

WHY, ye tenants of the lake,
    For me your watry haunt forsake?
Tell me, fellow-creatures, why
At my presence thus you fly?
Why disturb your social joys,   5
Parent, filial, kindred ties?—
Common friend to you and me,
Nature's gifts to all are free:
Peaceful keep your dimpling wave,
Busy feed, or wanton lave;   10
Or, beneath the sheltering rock,
Bide the surging billow's shock.

Conscious, blushing for our race,
Soon, too soon, your fears I trace:
Man, your proud usurping foe,   15
Would be lord of all below:
Plumes himself in Freedom's pride,
Tyrant stern to all beside.

The eagle, from the cliffy brow,
Marking you his prey below,   20
In his breast no pity dwells,
Strong Necessity compels.
But Man, to whom alone is given
A ray direct from pitying Heaven,
Glories in his heart humane—   25
And creatures for his pleasure slain.

On scaring some Water-fowl. *Text from the Edinburgh edition, 1793, collated with MSS Lochryan (Loch), Alloway (Al), Glenriddell (Glen; pp. 74–76; transcript), the Huntington Library MS (HL; Geddes's copy of 87), and the edition of 1794. Title in Al and HL* ... Hills by Oughtertyre

12 Bide] Ride *MSS (alternative* Brave *in Al)*   13 our race] my kind *MSS*
14 Soon, too soon] *alternative* Just, too just *in Al*   trace] find *MSS*
18 Tyrant stern to] *alternative* And tyrannises *in Al*   19 the] his *Loch Glen*
23 to whom] *correcting* who boasts *in Loch Al*   alone is given] *correcting* the pitying
tear *in Al*   24 *Cancelled start* To boast *in Loch*   A ... Heaven,] *Al adds
(and ends with) cancelled lines:*
                Sympathy to sorrow dear,
                Vaunts his feelings and his parts—
                To improve the murdering arts;
26 pleasure] pleasures *Loch HL*

In these savage, liquid plains,
Only known to wandering swains,
Where the mossy riv'let strays,
Far from human haunts and ways;   30
All on Nature you depend,
And life's poor season peaceful spend.

Or, if man's superior might
Dare invade your native right,
On the lofty ether borne,   35
Man with all his powers you scorn;
Swiftly seek, on clanging wings,
Other lakes and other springs;
And the foe you cannot brave,
Scorn at least to be his slave.   40

181. My Peggy's face

Slowish

34 invade] *correcting* injure *in Loch*   39 the] that *Glen HL*   40 *Holograph
note added in Glen:* This was the production of a solitary forenoon's walk from
Oughtertyre-house.—I lived there, Sir William's guest, for two or three weeks, and
was much flattered by my hospitable reception.—What a pity that the mere
emotions of gratitude are so impotent in this world! 'Tis lucky that, as we are told,
they will be of some avail in the world to come.—

My Peggy's face. Text from SMM, 1803 (501; signed R. Burns), *collated with SC,
1803 (106). Holograph of ll. 1–4 on verso of the Hastie MS, f. 40 (206). Title in SC*
My Mary's Face, &c., *set to the air* The Ewie wi' the Crooked Horn *and reading*
Mary *for* Peggy *throughout*

MY Peggy's face, my Peggy's form,
The frost of hermit age might warm;
My Peggy's worth, my Peggy's mind,
Might charm the first of human kind.
I love my Peggy's angel air,   5
Her face so truly heav'nly fair,
Her native grace so void of art,
But I adore my Peggy's heart.

The lily's hue, the rose's die,
The kindling lustre of an eye;   10
Who but owns their magic sway,
Who but knows they all decay!
The tender thrill, the pitying tear,
The generous purpose nobly dear,
The gentle look that Rage disarms,   15
These are all Immortal charms.

182. Where braving angry Winter's storms

Tune, Neil Gow's lament for Abercairny

Slowish

Where braving angry Winter's storms. *Text from the Hastie MS, f. 39, collated with SMM, 1788 (195; signed R). Tune in SMM* N. Gow's Lamentation for Abercairny

WHERE braving angry Winter's storms
　　The lofty Ochels rise,
Far in their shade, my Peggy's charms
　　First blest my wondering eyes.—

As one who by some savage stream   5
　　A lonely gem surveys,
Astonish'd doubly marks it beam
　　With art's most polish'd blaze.—

Blest be the wild, sequester'd glade
　　And blest the day and hour,   10
Where Peggy's charms I first survey'd,
　　When first I felt their pow'r.—

The tyrant Death with grim controul
　　May seize my fleeting breath,
But tearing Peggy from my soul   15
　　Must be a stronger death.—

1 angry *SMM*: all the *correcting* wild the *in MS*　　　storms *SMM*: harms *MS*
5 As one who by some] *correcting* So when one by a *in MS*　　9 glade] *correcting* shade *in MS*　　10 day] *correcting* time *in MS*　　12 When *SMM*: Where *MS*

183. The banks of the Devon—

Tune, Bhannerach dhon na chri—

Slow

How pleasant the banks of the clear-winding Devon,
    With green-spreading bushes, and flowers blooming
    fair!
But the bonniest flower on the banks of the Devon
    Was once a sweet bud on the braes of the Ayr.
Mild be the sun on this sweet-blushing Flower,   5
    In the gay, rosy morn as it bathes in the dew;
And gentle the fall of the soft, vernal shower,
    That steals on the evening each leaf to renew!

O spare the dear blossom, ye orient breezes,
    With chill, hoary wing as ye usher the dawn!   10
And far be thou distant, thou reptile that seizest
    The verdure and pride of the garden or lawn!

The banks of the Devon. *Text from the Hastie MS, f. 37, collated with SMM, 1788*
(157; signed B), and SC, 1803 (134). First-line title in SC, with a note Written in
1787, on a young Lady, residing on the banks of the river Devon, in Clackmanan-
shire, but whose infant years were spent in Ayrshire. *Set in quatrains in SC*
    5 Mild] O mild *SC*   12 or] and *SC*

Let Bourbon exult in his gay, gilded Lillies,
  And England triumphant display her proud Rose,
A fairer than either adorns the green vallies   15
Where Devon, sweet Devon meandering flows.—

184. [Epitaph for William Nicol]

Y<small>E</small> maggots, feed on Willie's brains,
  For few sic feasts ye've gotten;
An' fix your claws into his heart,
  For fient a bit o't 's rotten.

185. Ca' the ewes— [A]

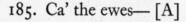

Slow

Chorus

C<small>A</small>' the ewes to the knowes,
  Ca' them whare the heather grows,
Ca' them whare the burnie rowes,
  My bonie Dearie.—

As I gaed down the water-side   5
There I met my Shepherd-lad,
He row'd me sweetly in his plaid,
  And he ca'd me his Dearie.—
      Ca' the &c.

Epitaph. *Text from Willison Glass,* Scenes of Gloamin': Original Scottish Songs, *1814 (p. 39). Title in Glass* Epitaph written by Burns, intended for his Friend, Mr. Wm. Nichol. *Later printings have* 1 Nicol's brain   3 in Nicol's heart   4 deil a bit. *H–H. record a manuscript (not holograph) with* Ye've got a prize o' Willie's heart *in l.* 3

Ca' the ewes. *Text from the Hastie MS, f. 56, collated with SMM, 1790 (264; unsigned). First-line title in SMM. For a later version of the song see* **456**

Will ye gang down the water-side
And see the waves sae sweetly glide   10
Beneath the hazels spreading wide,
　　The moon it shines fu' clearly.—
　　　　Ca' the &c.

I was bred up at nae sic school,
My Shepherd-lad, to play the fool;
And a' the day to sit in dool,   15
　　And naebody to see me.—
　　　　Ca' the &c.

Ye sall get gowns and ribbons meet,
Cauf-leather shoon upon your feet,
And in my arms ye'se lie and sleep,
　　And ye sall be my Dearie.—   20
　　　　Ca' the &c.

If ye'll but stand to what ye've said,
I'se gang wi' you, my Shepherd-lad,
And ye may rowe me in your plaid,
　　And I sall be your Dearie.—
　　　　Ca' the &c.

While waters wimple to the sea;   25
While Day blinks in the lift sae hie;
Till clay-cauld Death sall blin' my e'e,
　　Ye sall be my Dearie.—
　　　　Ca' the ewes &c.

186. On the death of the late Lord President Dundas—

Lone on the bleaky hills, the straying flocks
　Shun the fierce storms among the sheltering rocks;
Down foam the rivulets, red with dashing rains,
The gathering floods burst o'er the distant plains;
Beneath the blast the leafless forests groan,   5
The hollow caves return a sullen moan.—

17 meet, *SMM*: meet *MS*　　　22 I'se] *correcting* I'll *in MS*

On the death of the late Lord President Dundas. *Text from the Glenriddell MS (pp. 129–30), collated with the MS owned by Mr. Frank B. Bemis, Boston (Bemis; letter to*

Ye hills, ye plains, ye forests and ye caves,
Ye howling winds, and wintry-swelling waves,
Unheard, unseen, by human ear or eye,
Sad to your sympathetick glooms I fly;   10
Where to the whistling blast and waters' roar,
Pale Scotia's recent wound I may deplore.—

O heavy loss thy Country ill could bear!
A loss these evil days can ne'er repair!
Justice, the high vicegerent of her God,   15
Her doubtful balance ey'd and sway'd her rod;
Hearing the tidings of the fatal blow,
She sunk abandon'd to the wildest woe.—

Wrongs, Injuries, from many a darksome den,
Now gay in hope explore the paths of men: 20
See from his cavern grim Oppression rise,
And throw on Poverty his cruel eyes;
Keen on the helpless victim see him fly,
And stifle, dark, the feebly-bursting cry.—
Mark ruffian Violence, distain'd with crimes,   25
Rousing elate in these degenerate times;
View unsuspecting Innocence a prey,
As guileful Fraud points out the erring way:
While subtle Litigation's pliant tongue
The life-blood equal sucks of Right and Wrong.—   30
Hark, injur'd Want recounts th' unlisten'd tale,
And much-wrong'd Misery pours th' unpitied wail!

Ye dark, waste hills, ye brown, unsightly plains,
Congenial scenes! ye soothe my mournful strains:
Ye tempests, rage; ye turbid torrents, roll;   35
Ye suit the joyless tenor of my soul:

Charles Hay, ?24 December 1787), the Huntington Library MS (HL; in Geddes's copy of 87), and the MS owned by Admiral Sir F. Dalrymple-Hamilton of Bargany (Bar; transcript by the owner). Title in Bemis On . . . President; *in* HL On the death of Rob! Dundas of Arniston, Esq. late Lord President of the Court of Session; *in Bar* On the death of the R! Hon!! Robert Dundas Esq. late . . . College of Justice
   10 glooms] scenes *HL*   17–18 Hearing . . . She sunk] She heard . . . And sunk *Bemis Bar*   33 ye] and *Bemis HL Bar*   34 Congenial . . . mournful] Inspire and soothe my melancholly *Bemis*: To you I sing my grief-inspired *HL Bar* 35 rage] *correcting* sweep *in Bar*

Life's social haunts and pleasures I resign,
Be nameless wilds and lonely wanderings mine,
To mourn the woes my Country must endure,
That wound degenerate ages cannot cure.—   40

187. [Answer to Clarinda]

[From Clarinda on M.ʳ B——'s saying that he had 'nothing else to
do'.—

WHEN first you saw Clarinda's charms
        What raptures in your bosom grew!
Her heart was shut to love's alarms,
        But then—you'd nothing else to do.—

Apollo oft had lent his harp,   5
        But now 'twas strung from Cupid's bow;
You sung, it reach'd Clarinda's heart,
        She wish'd—you'd nothing else to do.—

Fair Venus smil'd, Minerva frown'd,
        Cupid observ'd, the arrow flew: 10
Indifference (ere a week went round)
        Shew'd—you'd had nothing else to do.—

Christmas eve   Clarinda—]

Answer to the foregoing—Extempore

WHEN dear Clarinda, matchless fair,
        First struck Sylvander's raptur'd view,
He gaz'd, he listen'd to despair,
        Alas! 'twas all he dar'd to do.—

40 *Foot-note in HL:* The foregoing Poem has some tolerable lines in it, but the
incurable wound of my pride will not suffer me to correct, or even peruse it.—I sent
a copy of it, with my best prose letter, to the Son of the Great Man the theme of
the Piece, by the hands too of one of the noblest men in God's world, Alex.ʳ Wood,
Surgeon—when behold, his Solicitorship took no more notice of my Poem or me
than I had been a strolling Fiddler who had made free with his lady's name over
the head of a silly new-reel! Did the gentleman think I look'd for any dirty gratuity!

Answer to Clarinda. *Texts from the Glenriddell MS (pp. 125–8).* From Clarinda *has
a note:* This Lady was the Authoress of two Songs, N.ᵒˢ 186 and 190, in the 2.ᵈ Vol.
of Johnson's Scots Musical Museum. *H–H. record another MS (not traced), reading*
stern command *in the* Answer, *l. 39*

Love, from Clarinda's heavenly eyes,   5
   Transfix'd his bosom thro' and thro';
But still in Friendship's guarded guise,
   For more the demon fear'd to do.—

That heart, already more than lost,
   The imp beleaguer'd all perdue;   10
For frowning Honor kept his post,
   To meet that frown he shrunk to do.—

His pangs the Bard refus'd to own,
   Tho' half he wish'd Clarinda knew:
But Anguish wrung th' unweeting groan—   15
   Who blames what frantic Pain must do?

That heart, where motely follies blend,
   Was sternly still to Honor true:
To prove Clarinda's fondest friend,
   Was what a Lover sure might do.—   20

The Muse his ready quill employ'd,
   No dearer bliss he could pursue;
That bliss Clarinda cold deny'd—
   'Send word by Charles how you do!'—

The chill behest disarm'd his muse,   25
   Till Passion all impatient grew:
He wrote, and hinted for excuse,
   'Twas 'cause he'd nothing else to do.'—

But by those hopes I have above!
   And by those faults I dearly rue!
The deed, the boldest mark of love,   30
   For thee that deed I dare to do!—

O, could the Fates but name the price,
   Would bless me with your charms and you!
With frantic joy I'd pay it thrice,   35
   If human art or power could do!

Then take, Clarinda, friendship's hand,
(Friendship, at least, I may avow;)
And lay no more your chill command,
I'll write, whatever I've to do.——   40
                    Sylvander——

188. Scots Ballad—

Tune—Mary weep no more for me—

M^Y heart is wae and unco wae,
    To think upon the raging sea,
That roars between her gardens green,
    And th' bonie lass of Albanie.——

Scots Ballad. *Text from the* Second Commonplace Book, *pp. 28–29 (2CPB).*
Chambers (1852) and H–H. used a MS (not traced) with these variants:

5 lovely] noble *MS*   8 They hae] They've *MS*   23 That] *om. MS*

This lovely maid's of noble blood,   5
　　That ruled Albion's kingdoms three;
But Oh, Alas! for her bonie face!
　　They hae wrang'd the lass of ALBANIE!—

In the rolling tide of spreading Clyde
　　There sits an isle of high degree;   10
And a town of fame whose princely name
　　Should grace the lass of ALBANIE.—

But there is a youth, a witless youth,
　　That fills the place where she should be,
We'll send him o'er to his native shore,   15
　　And bring our ain sweet ALBANIE.—

Alas the day, and woe the day,
　　A false Usurper wan the gree,
That now commands the towers and lands,
　　The royal right of ALBANIE.—   20

We'll daily pray, we'll nightly pray,
　　On bended knees most ferventlie,
That the time may come, with pipe and drum,
　　We'll welcome home fair ALBANIE.—

189. A Birth-day Ode. December 31ˢᵗ 1787.

AFAR th' illustrious Exile roams,
　　Whom kingdoms on this day should hail!
An Inmate of the casual shed;
　　On transient Pity's bounty fed;
Haunted by busy Mem'ry's bitter tale!   5
Beasts of the forest have their savage homes,
　　But He who should imperial purple wear
Owns not the lap of earth where rests his royal head:
　　His wretched refuge, dark Despair,

A Birth-day Ode. *Text from the Alloway MS (Al), collated with the transcript in the Glenriddell MS (pp. 106–8; Glen). Date 1787 in Glen: 1788 in Al*
　3 of] *in Glen*

While ravening Wrongs and Woes pursue,   10
    And distant far the faithful Few
        Who would his sorrows share!
        False flatterer, Hope, away!
Nor think to lure us as in days of yore:
    We solemnize this sorrowing natal day,   15
To prove our loyal truth—we can no more;
    And, owning Heaven's mysterious sway,
        Submissive, low adore.

        Ye honor'd, mighty Dead
    Who nobly perish'd in the glorious cause,   20
    Your King, your Country and her Laws;
From great Dundee who smiling Victory led,
    And fell a martyr in her arms,
    (What breast of northern ice but warms)
To bold Balmerino's undying name,   ⎫ 25
Whose soul of fire, lighted at Heaven's high flame, ⎬
Deserves the brightest wreath departed heroes claim; ⎭
    Not unreveng'd your fate shall lie;
        It only lags, the fatal hour:
        Your blood shall with incessant cry   30
        Awake at last th' unsparing Power!
As from the cliff with thundering course
        The snowy ruin smokes along,
With doubling speed and gathering force,
Till deep it crashing whelms the cottage in the vale; 35
    So Vengeance' arm, ensanguin'd, strong,
        Shall with resistless might assail:
Usurping Br—ns—ck's head shall lowly lay,
And St—rt's wrongs and yours with tenfold weight repay.

        Perdition, baleful child of Night,   40
        Rise and revenge the injur'd right
            Of St—rts' ROYAL RACE!
        Lead on th' unmuzzled hounds of Hell
        Till all the frighted Echoes tell
            The blood-notes of the chace!   45
        Full on the quarry point their view,
        Full on the base, usurping crew,

47 usurping] *correcting* degenerate *in A1*

The tools of Faction, and the Nation's curse:
    Hark! how the cry grows on the wind;
      They leave the lagging gale behind;   50
Their savage fury pitiless they pour,
With murdering eyes already they devour:
    See, Br—ns—ick spent, a wretched prey;
      His life, one poor, despairing day
Where each avenging hour still ushers in a worse!   55
    Such Havock, howling all abroad,
      Their utter ruin bring;
    The base Apostates to their God,
      Or Rebels to their KING!

190. Hunting Song

Tune—I rede you beware at the hunting

THE heather was blooming, the meadows were mawn,
   Our lads gaed a-hunting, ae day at the dawn,
O'er moors and o'er mosses and mony a glen,
At length they discovered a bonie moor-hen.

    I rede you beware at the hunting, young men;   5
    I rede you beware at the hunting, young men;
    Tak some on the wing, and some as they spring,
    But cannily steal on a bonie moor-hen.

Sweet brushing the dew from the brown heather bells,
Her colors betray'd her on yon mossy fells;   10
Her plumage outlustred the pride o' the spring,
And O! as she wantoned gay on the wing.

Auld Phœbus himsel, as he peep'd o'er the hill,
In spite at her plumage he tryed his skill;
He levell'd his rays where she bask'd on the brae—   15
His rays were outshone, and but mark'd where she lay.

Hunting Song. *Text from Cromek,* Reliques, *1808 (p. 450). H–H. record a MS (not traced) with these variants:*
  2 ae] one *MS*   5, 6 rede] red *Cromek*   16 His] But his *MS*

They hunted the valley, they hunted the hill;
The best of our lads wi' the best o' their skill;
But still as the fairest she sat in their sight,
Then, whirr! she was over, a mile at a flight.　　　20

191. [On Johnson's Opinion of Hampden]

FOR shame!
Let Folly and Knavery
Freedom oppose:
'Tis suicide, Genius,
To mix with her foes.

On Johnson's Opinion. *Text from a letter to the* Scotsman, *18 November 1882.*
Inscribed in a copy of Johnson's Lives *presented to Alexander Cunningham*

V

POEMS
1788

EDINBURGH AND ELLISLAND

192. Song

Bonny Mary

Slow

ANNA, thy charms my bosom fire,
And waste my soul with care;
But ah! how bootless to admire,
When fated to despair!

Yet in thy presence, lovely Fair,   5
To hope may be forgiven;
For sure 'twere impious to despair
So much in sight of Heaven.

Song. *Text from the Edinburgh edition, 1793, collated with the Lochryan MS (Loch; letter to Mrs Dunlop, 12 February 1788), MSS Glenriddell (p. 1) and Alloway, the* London Star, *18 April 1789, SMM, 1803 (530), SC, 1818 (218), and the edition of 1794. No title in Loch; first-line title in SMM, SC. Air in SMM* Bonny Mary; *in SC* Polwarth on the Green
1 Anna] Sweet Anne *SC*   2 waste] press *Loch*

193. An Extemporaneous Effusion on being appointed to the Excise

SEARCHING auld wives' barrels,
　　Ochon, the day!
That clarty barm should stain my laurels;
　　But—what 'll ye say!
These muvin' things ca'd wives and weans　　　5
Wad muve the very hearts o' stanes!

194. To the Weaver's gin ye go

MY heart was ance as blythe and free
　　As simmer days were lang,
But a bonie, westlin weaver lad
　　Has gart me change my sang.

An Extemporaneous Effusion. *Text from Cromek*, Reliques, *1808 (p. 411)*
　2 Ochon,] Och, ho! *Cromek*

To the Weaver's gin ye go. *Text from SMM, 1788 (103; signed X)*

Cho⁸

To the weaver's gin ye go, fair maids,   5
   To the weaver's gin ye go,
I rede you right, gang ne'er at night,
   To the weaver's gin ye go.

My mither sent me to the town
   To warp a plaiden wab;   10
But the weary, weary warpin o't
   Has gart me sigh and sab.
     To the weaver's &c.

A bonie, westlin weaver lad
   Sat working at his loom;
He took my heart as wi' a net   15
   In every knot and thrum.
     To the weaver's &c.

I sat beside my warpin-wheel,
   And ay I ca'd it roun';
But every shot and every knock,
   My heart it gae a stoun.   20
     To the weaver's &c.

The moon was sinking in the west
   Wi' visage pale and wan,
As my bonie, westlin weaver lad
   Convoy'd me thro' the glen.
     To the weaver's &c.

But what was said, or what was done,   25
   Shame fa' me gin I tell;
But Oh! I fear the kintra soon
   Will ken as weel's mysel!
     To the weaver's &c.

195. I'm o'er young to Marry Yet

Lively

I AM my mammy's ae bairn,
   Wi' unco folk I weary, Sir,
And lying in a man's bed,
   I'm fley'd it make me irie, Sir.
     I'm o'er young, I'm o'er young,   5
      I'm o'er young to marry yet;
     I'm o'er young, 'twad be a sin
      To tak me frae my mammy yet.

Hallowmass is come and gane,
   The nights are lang in winter, Sir;   10
And you an' I in ae bed,
   In trowth, I dare na venture, Sir.
     I'm o'er young &c.

Fu' loud and shill the frosty wind
   Blaws thro' the leafless timmer, Sir;
But if ye come this gate again,   15
   I'll aulder be gin simmer, Sir.
     I'm o'er young &c.

I'm o'er young to Marry Yet. *Text from SMM, 1788 (107; signed Z)*

196. McPherson's Farewell

Slowish

Chorus

FAREWELL, ye dungeons dark and strong,
    The wretch's destinie!
McPherson's time will not be long,
    On yonder gallows-tree.

Chorus

Sae rantingly, sae wantonly,   5
    Sae dauntingly gae'd he:
He play'd a spring, and danc'd it round
    Below the gallows-tree.

O what is death but parting breath?
    On many a bloody plain   10
I've dar'd his face, and in this place
    I scorn him yet again!
        Sae rantingly, &c.

Untie these bands from off my hands,
    And bring to me my sword;
And there's no a man in all Scotland,   15
    But I'll brave him at a word.
        Sae rantingly, &c.

McPherson's Farewell. *Text from SMM, 1788 (114; signed Z), collated with B.M.*
MS Egerton 1656 (f. 26)
    1 ye] you *MS*

I've liv'd a life of sturt and strife;
　　I die by treacherie:
It burns my heart I must depart
　　And not avenged be.   20
　　　　Sae rantingly, &c.

Now farewell, light, thou sunshine bright,
　　And all beneath the sky!
May coward shame distain his name,
　　The wretch that dares not die!
　　　　Sae rantingly, &c.

197. Stay, my Charmer, can you leave me?

Tune, An Gille dubh ciar dhubh

Slow

STAY, my Charmer, can you leave me;
　　Cruel, cruel to deceive me!
Well you know how much you grieve me:
　　Cruel Charmer, can you go!
　　Cruel Charmer, can you go!   5

By my love so ill requited;
By the faith you fondly plighted;
By the pangs of Lovers slighted;
　　Do not, do not leave me so!
　　Do not, do not leave me so!   10

24 dares] dare *MS*

Stay, my Charmer. *Text from the Hastie MS, f. 27, collated with SMM, 1788 (129; signed B). Title from SMM*

198. What will I do gin my Hoggie die

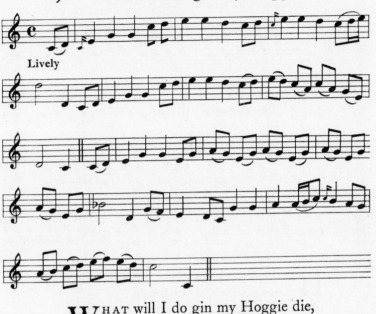

Lively

WHAT will I do gin my Hoggie die,
    My joy, my pride, my Hoggie;
My only beast, I had nae mae,
    And vow but I was vogie.—

The lee-lang night we watch'd the fauld,   5
    Me and my faithfu' doggie;
We heard nought but the roaring linn
    Amang the braes sae scroggie.—

But the houlet cry'd frae the Castle-wa',
    The blitter frae the boggie,   10
The tod reply'd upon the hill,
    I trembled for my Hoggie.—

When day did daw and cocks did craw,
    The morning it was foggie;
An unco tyke lap o'er the dyke   15
    And maist has kill'd my Hoggie.—

What will I do. *Text from the Hastie MS, f. 29, collated with SMM, 1788 (133, unsigned)*

199. Jumpin John

Lively

Chorus

HER Daddie forbad, her Minnie forbad;
   Forbidden she wadna be:
She wadna trow't, the browst she brew'd
   Wad taste sae bitterlie.

Chorus

The lang lad they ca' jumpin John   5
   Beguil'd the bonie lassie,
The lang lad they ca' jumpin John
   Beguil'd the bonie lassie.

A cow and a cauf, a yowe and a hauf,
   And thretty gude shillins and three;   10
A vera gude tocher, a cotter-man's dochter,
   The lass wi' the bonie black e'e.

Jumpin John. *Text from SMM, 1788 (138; unsigned)*
  7 jumpin] jumping *SMM*

200. Up in the Morning Early

Lively

CAULD blaws the wind frae east to west,
    The drift is driving sairly;
Sae loud and shill's I hear the blast,
    I'm sure it's winter fairly.
Up in the morning's no for me,   5
    Up in the morning early;
When a' the hills are cover'd wi' snaw,
    I'm sure it is winter fairly.

The birds sit chittering in the thorn,
    A' day they fare but sparely;   10
And lang's the night frae e'en to morn,
    I'm sure it's winter fairly.
        Up in the morning's, &c.

Up in the Morning Early. *Text from SMM, 1788 (140; signed Z)*
  4 it's] its *SMM*

201. Dusty Miller

Lively

H EY the dusty Miller,
  And his dusty coat;
He will win a shilling
  Or he spend a groat:
Dusty was the coat,   5
  Dusty was the colour;
Dusty was the kiss
  That I got frae the Miller.—

Hey the dusty Miller,
  And his dusty sack;   10
Leeze me on the calling
  Fills the dusty peck:
Fills the dusty peck,
  Brings the dusty siller;
I wad gie my coatie   15
  For the dusty Miller.

Dusty Miller. *Text from the Hastie MS, f. 31, collated with SMM, 1788 (144; unsigned)*

202. Duncan Davison

THERE was a lass, they ca'd her Meg,
 And she held o'er the moors to spin;
There was a lad that follow'd her,
 They ca'd him Duncan Davison.
The moor was driegh, and Meg was skiegh, 5
 Her favour Duncan could na win;
For wi' the rock she wad him knock,
 And ay she shook the temper-pin.

As o'er the moor they lightly foor,
 A burn was clear, a glen was green, 10
Upon the banks they eas'd their shanks,
 And ay she set the wheel between:
But Duncan swoor a haly aith
 That Meg should be a bride the morn,
Then Meg took up her spinnin-graith, 15
 And flang them a' out o'er the burn.

We will big a wee, wee house,
 And we will live like king and queen;
Sae blythe and merry's we will be,
 When ye set by the wheel at e'en. 20
A man may drink and no be drunk,
 A man may fight and no be slain:
A man may kiss a bony lass,
 And ay be welcome back again.

Duncan Davison. *Text from SMM, 1788 (149; signed Z). Burns's journal of his Border tour (1787) contains a fragment (p. 46):*

Tune, Duncan Davison

There was a lass they ca'd her Meg
The brawest lass in a' the town
And mony a lad her love did beg
Thro' a' the country round and round

18 queen;] queen *SMM*

203. Where Helen Lies

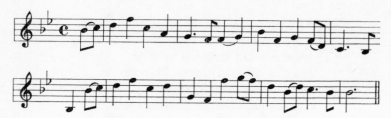

O THAT I were where Helen lies,
　Night and day on me she cries;
O that I were where Helen lies
　　In fair Kirkconnel lee.—
O Helen fair beyond compare,   5
A ringlet of thy flowing hair,
I'll wear it still for ever mair
　　Untill the day I die.—

Curs'd be the hand that shot the shot,
And curs'd the gun that gave the crack!   10
Into my arms bird Helen lap,
　　And died for sake o' me!
O think na ye but my heart was sair;
My Love fell down and spake nae mair;
There did she swoon wi' meikle care   15
　　On fair Kirkconnel lee.—

I lighted down, my sword did draw,
I cutted him in pieces sma';
I cutted him in pieces sma'
　　On fair Kirkconnel lee.—   20
O Helen chaste, thou wert modest,
If I were with thee I were blest
Where thou lies low and takes thy rest
　　On fair Kirkconnel lee.—

Where Helen Lies. *Text from the Hastie MS, f. 34, collated with SMM, 1788 (155; unsigned). Title from SMM*
　5 Helen] Helen, *SMM*   7 still] *correcting thus in MS*   21 thou wert modest] thou'rt now at rest *SMM*

I wish my grave was growing green,   25
A winding sheet put o'er my e'en,
And I in Helen's arms lying
        In fair Kirkconnel lee!
I wish I were where Helen lies!
Night and day on me she cries: 30
O that I were where Helen lies
        On fair Kirkconnel lee.

204. Duncan Gray—

WEARY fa' you, Duncan Gray,
        Ha, ha the girdin o't,
Wae gae by you, Duncan Gray,
        Ha, ha the girdin o't;
When a' the lave gae to their play,   5
Then I maun sit the lee-lang day,
And jeeg the cradle wi' my tae
        And a' for the bad girdin o't.—

Bonie was the lammas moon,
        Ha, &c.   10
Glowrin a' the hills aboon,
        Ha, &c.
The girdin brak, the beast cam down,
I tint my curch and baith my shoon,
And Duncan ye're an unco loon;   15
        Wae on the bad girdin o't.—

But Duncan gin ye'll keep your aith,
        Ha, &c.
I'se bless you wi' my hindmost breath,
        Ha, &c.   20
Duncan gin ye'll keep your aith,
The beast again can bear us baith,
And auld Mess John will mend the skaith
        And clout the bad girdin o't.—

Duncan Gray. *Text from the Hastie MS, f. 38, collated with SMM, 1788 (160; signed Z)*
    8 bad] *om. SMM*

205. The Ploughman

Lively

Chorus

THE Ploughman he's a bony lad,
  His mind is ever true, jo,
His garters knit below his knee,
  His bonnet it is blue, jo.

Chorus
Then up wi't a', my Ploughman lad,   5
  And hey, my merry Ploughman;
Of a' the trades that I do ken,
  Commend me to the Ploughman.

My Ploughman he comes hame at e'en,
  He's aften wat and weary: 10
Cast off the wat, put on the dry,
  And gae to bed, my Dearie.
    Up wi't a' &c.

I will wash my Ploughman's hose,
  And I will dress his o'erlay;
I will mak my Ploughman's bed,   15
  And chear him late and early.
    Up wi't a' &c.

I hae been east, I hae been west,
  I hae been at Saint Johnston,
The boniest sight that e'er I saw
  Was th' Ploughman laddie dancin.   20
    Up wi't a' &c.

The Ploughman. *Text from SMM, 1788 (165; unsigned)*

Snaw-white stockins on his legs,
  And siller buckles glancin;
A gude blue bannet on his head,
  And O but he was handsome!
    Up wi't a' &c.

Commend me to the Barn yard,   25
  And the Corn-mou, man;
I never gat my Coggie fou
  Till I met wi' the Ploughman.
    Up wi't a' &c.

206. Hey tuti tatey—

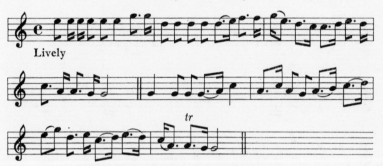

Lively

LANDLADY count the lawin,
  The day is near the dawin,
Ye're a' blind drunk, boys,
  And I'm jolly fou.—

        Chorus—
Hey tuti tatey, How tuti taiti,   5
Hey tuti taiti, wha's fou now.—

Cog an ye were ay fou,
Cog an ye were ay fou;
I wad sit and sing to you,
  If ye were ay fou.—   10
    Hey tuti &c.

Hey tuti tatey. *Text from the Hastie MS, f. 40, collated with SMM, 1788 (170; unsigned). Title in SMM* Hey Tutti Taiti
  4 I'm jolly] I'm but jolly *SMM*

Weel may we a' be,
Ill may we never see!
God bless the king
And the Companie!
Hey tuti &c.

207. Raving winds around her blowing

Tune, McGrigor of Roro's Lament

Very slow

RAVING winds around her blowing,
Yellow leaves the woodlands strowing,
By a river hoarsely roaring
Isabella stray'd deploring.
Farewell, hours that late did measure   5
Sunshine days of joy and pleasure;
Hail, thou gloomy night of sorrow,
Cheerless night that knows no morrow.

O'er the Past too fondly wandering,
On the hopeless Future pondering;   10
Chilly Grief my life-blood freezes,
Fell Despair my fancy seizes.

Raving winds around her blowing. *Text from SMM, 1788 (173; signed B), collated
with Currie (iv. 277–8)*

Life, thou soul of every blessing,
Load to Misery most distressing,
Gladly how would I resign thee,   15
And to dark Oblivion join thee!

208. Musing on the roaring Ocean

Tune, Druimionn dubh

MUSING on the roaring ocean
Which divides my Love and me,
Wearying Heaven in warm devotion
For his weal where'er he be;
Hope and Fear's alternate billow   5
Yielding late to Nature's law,
Whisp'ring spirits round my pillow
Talk of him that's far awa.—

15 Gladly . . . resign] O how gladly I'd resign *Currie*

Musing on the roaring Ocean. *Text from the Hastie MS, f. 41, collated with SMM, 1788 (179; signed R). Title from SMM. The Hastie MS contains (f. 27ᵛ) a fragment:*

Musing on the oceans roaring
Which divide my Love and me,
Every Power above imploring
For his weal where'er he be,
Hope and Fear's alternate billow

1 ocean] *correcting* oceans *in MS*   2 divides] *correcting* divide *in MS*   3 in]
correcting with *in MS*

Ye whom Sorrow never wounded,
   Ye who never shed a tear,   10
Care-untroubled, joy-surrounded,
   Gaudy Day to you is dear:
Gentle Night do thou befriend me;
   Downy Sleep the curtain draw;
Spirits kind again attend me,   15
   Talk of him that's far awa!

209. To daunton me—

THE blude-red rose at Yule may blaw,
   The simmer lilies bloom in snaw,
The frost may freeze the deepest sea,
But an auld man shall never daunton me.—

Chorus—
To daunton me, to daunton me,   5
   An auld man shall never daunton me.—

To daunton me. *Text from the Hastie MS, f. 42, collated with SMM, 1788 (182; unsigned). The Hastie MS contains (f. 33ᵛ) a fragment consisting of the chorus and ll. 11–14, 7–10, numbered as stanzas 1 and 2. The first stanza and chorus are included, without variation, in a fragmentary letter laid into Burns's copy of Oswald's* Caledonian Pocket Companion *(Letter 111)*
   5 me, to] me, an' to *MS (fgt.)*   5–6 om. *SMM*

2

To daunton me, and me sae young,
Wi' his fause heart and his flattering tongue,
That is the thing you shall never see
For an auld man shall never daunton me.—   10
  To daunton me, &c.

3

For a' his meal and a' his maut,
For a' his fresh beef and his saut,
For a' his gold and white monie,
An auld man shall never daunton me.—
  To daunton me, &c.

4

His gear may buy him kye and yowes,   15
His gear may buy him glens and knowes,
But me he shall not buy nor fee,
For an auld man shall never daunton me.—
  To daunton me, &c.

5

He hirples twa-fauld as he dow,
Wi' his teethless gab and his auld beld pow,   20
And the rain rins down frae his red-blear'd e'e,
That auld man shall never daunton me.—
  To daunton me, &c.

210. [Interpolation]

Your friendship much can make me blest,
  Oh, why that bliss destroy!
Why urge the only, one request
  You know I will deny!

8 and his flattering] and flattering *MS (fgt.) SMM*   9 shall never] ne'er shall
SMM   21 rins] rains *SMM*

Interpolation. *Verses added to 'Clarinda's' Talk not of love. Text from SMM, 1788
(186; signed M). Burns's letter to Clarinda, 4 January 1788 (Letter 170), offers her
ll. 1–4 with only as an alternative to odious (l. 3) and will as an alternative to must
(l. 4), and adds ll. 5–8 as a postscript (now missing from the MS)*

Your thought, if love must harbour there, 5
    Conceal it in that thought;
Nor cause me from my bosom tear
    The very friend I sought.

211. O'er the water to Charlie—

COME boat me o'er, come row me o'er,
    Come boat me o'er to Charlie;
I'll gie John Ross anither bawbee
To boat me o'er to Charlie.—

Chorus

We'll o'er the water, we'll o'er the sea, 5
    We'll o'er the water to Charlie;
Come weal, come woe, we'll gather and go,
    And live or die wi' Charlie.—

I lo'e weel my Charlie's name,
    Tho' some there be abhor him: 10
But O, to see auld Nick gaun hame,
    And Charlie's faes before him!
        We'll o'er &c.

I swear and vow by moon and stars,
    And sun that shines so early!
If I had twenty thousand lives, 15
    I'd die as aft for Charlie.—
        We'll o'er &c.

O'er the water to Charlie. *Text from the Hastie MS, f. 44, collated with SMM, 1788*
(187; unsigned)

212. Up and warn a' Willie—

U P and warn a' Willie,
 Warn, warn a';
To hear my cantie Highland sang,
 Relate the thing I saw, Willie.—

When we gaed to the braes o' Mar,   5
 And to the wapon-shaw, Willie,
Wi' true design to serve the king
 And banish whigs awa, Willie.—
Up and warn a', Willie,
 Warn, warn a';   10
For Lords and lairds came there bedeen
 And wow but they were braw, Willie.—

But when the standard was set up
 Right fierce the wind did blaw, Willie;
The royal nit upon the tap   15
 Down to the ground did fa', Willie.—
Up and warn a', Willie,
 Warn, warn a';
Then second-sighted Sandie said
 We'd do nae gude at a', Willie.—   20

Up and warn a' Willie. *Text from the Hastie MS, ff. 45–46, collated with SMM,
1788 (188; unsigned)*

 3 Highland] *later autograph insertion in MS*   6 wapon-shaw] *correcting*
weapon-shaw *in MS*   11 For] *marginal addition in MS*

But when the army join'd at Perth,
   The bravest ere ye saw, Willie,
We didna doubt the rogues to rout,
   Restore our king and a', Willie.
Up and warn a' Willie,   25
   Warn, warn a';
The pipers play'd frae right to left
   O whirry whigs awa, Willie.—

But when we march'd to Sherramuir
   And there the rebels saw, Willie;   30
Brave Argyle attack'd our right,
   Our flank and front and a', Willie.—
Up and warn a', Willie,
   Warn, warn a';
Traitor Huntly soon gave way   35
   Seaforth, St Clair and a' Willie.—

But brave Glengary on our right,
   The rebel's left did claw, Willie,
He there the greatest slaughter made
   That ever Donald saw, Willie.—   40
Up and warn a', Willie,
   Warn, warn a',
And Whittam sh–t his breeks for fear
   And fast did rin awa', Willie.—

For he ca'd us a Highland mob   45
   And soon he'd slay us a', Willie;
But we chas'd him back to Stirling brig
   Dragoons and foot and a', Willie.—
Up and warn a' Willie,
   Warn, warn a',   50
At length we rallied on a hill
   And briskly up did draw, Willie.—

But when Argyle did view our line,
   And them in order saw, Willie,
He streight gaed to Dumblane again   55
   And back his left did draw, Willie.—

Up and warn a' Willie,
  Warn warn a',
Then we to Auchterairder march'd
  To wait a better fa' Willie.—   60

Now if ye spier wha wan the day,
  I've tell'd you what I saw, Willie,
We baith did fight and baith did beat
  And baith did rin awa, Willie.
Up and warn a', Willie,   65
  Warn, warn a' Willie,
For second sighted Sandie said
  We'd do nae gude at a', Willie.—

213. The Rosebud—

Slow

62 I've tell'd] *correcting* I'll tell *in MS*   66 Willie] *om. SMM*

The Rosebud. *Text from the Hastie MS, f. 47, collated with SMM, 1788 (189; signed B). First-line title in SMM, which repeats ll. 5–8, 13–16, 21–24*

A ROSEBUD by my early walk,
  Adown a corn-enclosed bawk,
Sae gently bent its thorny stalk
    All on a dewy morning.—

Ere twice the shades o' dawn are fled,   5
In a' its crimson glory spread,
And drooping rich the dewy head,
    It scents the early morning.—

Within the bush her covert nest
A little linnet fondly prest,   10
The dew sat chilly on her breast
    Sae early in the morning.—

She soon shall see her tender brood
The pride, the pleasure o' the wood,
Amang the fresh green leaves bedew'd,   15
    Awauk the early morning.—

So thou, dear bird, young Jeany fair,
On trembling string or vocal air,
Shalt sweetly pay the tender care
    That tents thy early morning.—   20

So thou, sweet Rosebud, young and gay,
Shalt beauteous blaze upon the day,
And bless the Parent's evening ray
    That watch'd thy early morning.—

7 drooping] *corrects* hanging *in MS*   9 covert] *corrects* little *in MS*
10 A] *corrects* The *in MS*

214. [Revision for Clarinda]

Go on, sweet bird, and soothe my care,
   Thy tuneful notes will hush Despair;
Thy plaintive warblings void of art
Thrill sweetly thro' my aching heart.
Now chuse thy mate, and fondly love,   5
And all the charming transport prove;
While I a lovelorn exile live,
Nor transport or receive or give.

For thee is laughing Nature gay;
For thee she pours the vernal day: 10
For me in vain is Nature drest,
While joy's a stranger to my breast!
These sweet emotions all enjoy;
Let love and song thy hours employ!
Go on, sweet bird, and soothe my care;   15
Thy tuneful notes will hush Despair.

Revision for Clarinda. *Text from the Hastie MS, f. 48, collated with SMM, 1788 (190, signed M; title* To a Blackbird. By a Lady). *Revised by Burns (cf. Letter 183; 21 January 1788) from Clarinda's copy,* the first fruits of my muse, *sent to him on 19 January 1788 (Scott Douglas, v. 50):*

> To a Blackbird singing on a Tree.
>   Morningside, 1784.
>
> Go on, sweet bird, and soothe my care,
> Thy cheerful notes will hush despair;
> Thy tuneful warblings, void of art,
> Thrill sweetly thro' my aching heart.
> Now choose thy mate and fondly love,
> And all the charming transport prove—
> Those sweet emotions all enjoy,
> Let Love and Song thy hours employ;
> Whilst I, a love-lorn exile, live,
> And rapture nor receive nor give.
> Go on, sweet bird, and soothe my care,
> Thy cheerful notes will hush despair.

Line 9 is repeated in the Hastie MS and SMM

215. And I'll kiss thee yet, yet

Tune, Braes o' Balquhidder

Slowish

A<small>N</small> I'll kiss thee yet, yet,
    An I'll kiss thee o'er again;
An I'll kiss thee yet, yet,
    My bony Peggy Alison.
[Ilk Care and Fear, when thou art near,   5
    I ever mair defy them, O;
Young kings upon their hansel throne
    Are no sae blest as I am, O!]

And I'll kiss thee yet, yet. *Text from SMM, 1788 (193; signed Z), collated with Cromek*, Reliques, 1808 (*p. 441*) *and the Hastie (Ha) and Huntington Library (HL) MSS. No title in MSS. Autograph note in Ha (f. 49):* The chorus is the first, or lowest part of the tune—Each verse must be repeated twice to go through the high, or 2^d part—*Arrangement in Ha, ll. 9–12 and 1–4 (chorus), 13–16 and chorus; in SMM, ll. 1–4, 9–12 (repeated), 1–4, 13–16 (repeated). Lines 5–8 in Cromek and HL only*
  2 An] *om. in Ha*   5 *cancelled start* When thou art near *in HL*   8 no correcting *not in HL*

When in my arms, wi' a' thy charms,
   I clasp my countless treasure, O!   10
I seek nae mair o' Heav'n to share,
   Than sic a moment's pleasure, O!

And by thy een sae bony blue,
   I swear I'm thine forever O!
And on thy lips I seal my vow,   15
   And break it shall I never O!

216. Rattlin, roarin Willie

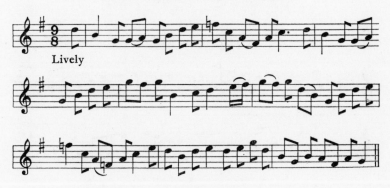

Lively

O RATTLIN, roarin Willie,
   O he held to the fair,
An' for to sell his fiddle
   And buy some other ware;
But parting wi' his fiddle,   5
   The saut tear blin't his e'e;
And Rattlin, roarin Willie,
   Ye're welcome hame to me.

O Willie, come sell your fiddle,
   O sell your fiddle sae fine;   10
O Willie, come sell your fiddle,
   And buy a pint o' wine;

12 moment's *Ha*: moments *SMM*

Rattlin, roarin Willie. *Text from SMM, 1788 (194; signed Z)*

If I should sell my fiddle,
    The warl' would think I was mad,
For mony a rantin day   15
    My fiddle and I hae had.

As I cam by Crochallan
    I cannily keekit ben,
Rattlin, roarin Willie
    Was sitting at yon boord-en',   20
Sitting at yon boord-en',
    And amang guid companie;
Rattlin, roarin Willie,
    Ye're welcome hame to me!

217. Clarinda

Slow and expressive

CLARINDA, mistress of my soul,
    The measur'd time is run!
The wretch beneath the dreary pole,
    So marks his latest sun.

To what dark cave of frozen night   5
    Shall poor Sylvander hie;
Depriv'd of thee, his life and light,
    The Sun of all his joy.

Clarinda. *Text from SMM, 1788 (198; signed B), collated with the Lochryan MS
(letter to Mrs Dunlop, 12 February 1788) and SC, 1810 (96). Dewar collated a MS
(not traced) with So eyes in l. 4*
    1 Clarinda,] Farewell, dear *SC*   6 Shall poor Sylvander] Alas! shall thy
poor wand'rer *SC*

We part—but by these precious drops,
      That fill thy lovely eyes!   10
No other light shall guide my steps,
      Till thy bright beams arise.

She, the fair Sun of all her sex,
      Has blest my glorious day:
And shall a glimmering Planet fix   15
      My worship to its ray?

218. The Winter it is Past

Very slow

THE winter it is past, and the summer's come at last,
      And the small birds sing on ev'ry tree;
The hearts of these are glad, but mine is very sad,
      For my Lover has parted from me.

The rose upon the brier, by the waters running clear,   5
      May have charms for the linnet or the bee;
Their little loves are blest and their little hearts at rest,
      But my Lover is parted from me.

15 shall a] ne'er shall *SC*

The Winter it is Past. *Text from SMM, 1788 (200; unsigned), collated with Cromek,*
Reliques, *1808 (p. 446; ll. 1–8 only)*
   1 summer's come] simmer comes *Cromek*   3 The . . . mine is] Now every
thing is glad while I am *Cromek*   4 For my Lover has] Since my true love is
Cromek

My love is like the sun, in the firmament does run,
    For ever constant and true;   10
But his is like the moon that wanders up and down,
    And every month it is new.

All you that are in love and cannot it remove,
    I pity the pains you endure:
For experience makes me know that your hearts are full of
            woe,   15
    A woe that no mortal can cure.

219. [To Clarinda]

Fair Empress of the Poet's soul,
    And Queen of Poetesses;
Clarinda, take this little boon,
    This humble pair of Glasses.

And fill them high with generous juice,   5
    As generous as your mind;
And pledge me in the generous toast—
    'The whole of Humankind!'

'To those who love us!'—second fill;
    But not to those whom we love,   10
Lest we love those who love not us:—
    A third—'to thee and me, Love!'

Long may we live! Long may we love!
    And long may we be happy!!!
And may we never want a Glass,   15
    Well charg'd with generous Nappy!!!!

9 the] *om. SMM*

To Clarinda. *Text from the Esty MS (dated* Edin^r March 17th 1788 *and signed*
Sylvander; *Dewar's transcript), collated with Cromek,* Reliques, *1808 (p. 404;
ll. 1–12 only). Title in Cromek* To a Lady, with a present of a pair of drinking glasses.

220. Song—

Tune—Captain Okean—

Slow

I

THE small birds rejoice in the green leaves returning,
  The murmuring streamlet winds clear thro' the vale;
The primroses blow in the dews of the morning,
  And wild-scattered cowslips bedeck the green dale:
But what can give pleasure, or what can seem fair,   5
  When the lingering moments are numbered by Care?
No birds sweetly singing, nor flowers gayly springing,
  Can sooth the sad bosom of joyless Despair.—

Song. *Text from the* Second Commonplace Book (*2CPB; p. 29*), *collated with the*
Lenox MS (*draft of ll. 1–8 in letter to Cleghorn, 31 March 1788*), *the* Lochryan MS
(*Loch; ll. 1–8 only*), SC, *1799 (97*), *and* Currie (*ii. 131*). *Title in* Loch A Stanza
composed for the Air, Captain Okain; *in* Currie The Chevalier's Lament. *First-line
title in* SC
    1 in] on *SC*   3 primroses] hawthorn trees *Currie*   blow] blush *Lenox Loch*
6 When] While *Lenox Currie*   by] wi' *SC*

2

The deed that I dared, could it merit their malice,
    A KING and a FATHER to place on his throne;   10
His right are these hills, and his right are these vallies,
    Where wild beasts find shelter but I can find none:
But 'tis not my sufferings, thus wretched, forlorn,
    My brave, gallant friends, 'tis your ruin I mourn;
Your faith proved so loyal in hot, bloody trial,   15
    Alas, can I make it no sweeter return!

221. Epitaph on R. Muir—

WHAT Man could esteem, or what Woman could
    love,
    Was He who lies under this sod:
If Such Thou refusest admittance above,
    Then whom wilt thou favor, Good God!

222. Epistle to Hugh Parker

IN this strange land, this uncouth clime,
    A land unknown to prose or rhyme;
Where words ne'er crost the muse's heckles,
Nor limpet in poetic shackles;
A land that prose did never view it,   5
Except when drunk he stacher't thro' it;
Here, ambush'd by the chimla cheek,
Hid in an atmosphere of reek,
I hear a wheel thrum i' the neuk,
I hear it—for in vain I leuk.—   10

12 wild] *following* ~~the~~ *in 2CPB*   but] tho' *SC*   15 faith] deeds *Currie*
16 it] you *Currie*   sweeter] better *SC*

Epitaph on R. Muir. *Text from the Bixby MS (letter to Mrs Dunlop, 13 December 1789)*

Epistle to Hugh Parker. *Text from Cunningham, 1834 (iii. 91–92; dated June 1788)*

The red peat gleams, a fiery kernel,
Enhusked by a fog infernal:
Here, for my wonted rhyming raptures,
I sit and count my sins by chapters;
For life and spunk like ither Christians,   15
I'm dwindled down to mere existence,
Wi' nae converse but Gallowa' bodies,
Wi' nae kend face but Jenny Geddes.
Jenny, my Pegasean pride!
Dowie she saunters down Nithside,   20
And ay a westlin leuk she throws,
While tears hap o'er her auld brown nose!
Was it for this, wi' canny care,
Thou bure the Bard through many a shire?
At howes or hillocks never stumbled,   25
And late or early never grumbled?—
O, had I power like inclination,
I'd heeze thee up a constellation,
To canter with the Sagitarre,
Or loup the ecliptic like a bar;   30
Or turn the pole like any arrow;
Or, when auld Phebus bids good-morrow,
Down the zodiac urge the race,
And cast dirt on his godship's face;
For I could lay my bread and kail   35
He'd ne'er cast saut upo' thy tail.—
Wi' a' this care and a' this grief,
And sma', sma' prospect of relief,
And nought but peat reek i' my head,
How can I write what ye can read?—   40
Tarbolton, twenty-fourth o' June,
Ye'll find me in a better tune;
But till we meet and weet our whistle,
Tak this excuse for nae epistle.

ROBERT BURNS.

223. [A] Written in Friar's Carse Hermitage
on the banks of Nith— June—1788

THOU whom chance may hither lead,
   Be thou clad in russet weed,
Be thou deckt in silken stole,
Grave these maxims on thy soul.—

Life is but a day at most,   5
Sprung from night, in darkness lost;
Hope not sunshine every hour,
Fear not clouds will always lour.—
Happiness is but a name,
Make CONTENT and EASE thy aim.—   10
Ambition is a meteor gleam,
Fame a restless, airy dream;
Pleasures, insects on the wing
Round Peace, the tenderest flower of spring;
Those that sip the dew alone,   15
Make the butterflies thy own;
Those that would the bloom devour,
Crush the locusts, save the flower.—
For the FUTURE be prepar'd,
Guard, wherever thou canst guard,   20
But thy utmost duly done,
Welcome what thou canst not shun:—

---

*Written in Friar's Carse Hermitage. Text from the Afton Lodge MS (ff. 18ᵛ–19ʳ and
27ᵛ–28ᵛ), collated with the* Second Commonplace Book (2CPB; pp. 16–17 and
20–21), Wallace, *Correspondence, p. 80 (Version A in letter to Mrs Dunlop, 2 August
1788; MS not traced), the Dumfries MSS (Version B only: Dum A, ll. 1–26 in letter to
Mrs Dunlop, 7 December 1788; Dum B, complete), the Huntington Library MS (HL;
Geddes's copy of 87), MSS Don, Adam (letter to William Dunbar, c. February 1789)
and Glenriddell (Glen; pp. 6–7 and 15–17), an undated print of Version B c. 1791
(91; collated Dewar), the Edinburgh editions of 1793, 1794 (Version B), and Currie,
1801 (ii. 157–8; Version A; the letter transcribed by Wallace, p. 80). Titles from HL;
slight variations in title in other MSS. See Commentary*

Version A. 8 always] ever *2CPB Wallace Currie*   12 a] *correcting* an *in Adam*
restless, airy] restless idle *other MSS Wallace*: idle restless *Currie*
13–14 Pleasures . . . spring;] *correcting*
               Peace, the tenderest flower of Spring;
               Pleasures, insects on the wing;
in 2CPB. Currie has the earlier version   18 save] *correcting* spare *in 2CPB*

Follies past, give thou to air;
Make their consequence thy care:
Keep the name of MAN in mind,   25
And dishonor not thy kind.——
Reverence with lowly heart
Him whose wondrous work thou art;
Keep his Goodness still in view,
Thy trust——and thy example too.——   30

Stranger, go! Heaven be thy guide!
Quod, the BEADSMAN ON NID-SIDE.——

223. [B] Altered from the foregoing—Dec— 1788

Thou whom chance may hither lead,
   Be thou clad in russet-weed,
Be thou deckt in silken stole,
Grave these counsels on thy soul.——

   Life is but a day at most,   5
Sprung from Night, in darkness lost,
Hope not sunshine every hour,
Fear not clouds will always lour.——

   As Youth and Love with sprightly dance
Beneath thy morning star advance,   10
Pleasure with her siren air
May delude the thoughtless pair;
Let Prudence bless Enjoyment's cup,
Then, raptur'd, sip and sip it up.——

23–24 Follies . . . care:] *accidentally om. Afton, where there is a cancellation of
ll. 27–28*   32 ON] OF *2CPB Wallace Glen Currie*

Version B. 6 *Additional couplet in 2CPB HL Adam Glen Don (following a cancellation of ll. 7–8):*
                        Day, how rapid in its flight!
                        Day, how few must see the night!
9 As 93 94: When *Dum A–B Adam Afton 91*   10 star] *alternative to* sun *in
2CPB*: sun *HL Don Adam*

As thy day grows warm and high,
Life's meridian flaming nigh,
Dost thou spurn the humble vale?
Life's proud summits would'st thou scale?
Check thy climbing step elate,
Evils lurk in felon-wait;   20
Dangers, eagle-pinion'd, bold,
Soar around each cliffy hold,
While chearful Peace, with linnet-song,
Chants the lowly dells among.—

As the shades of evening close,   25
Beckoning thee to long repose,
As life itself becomes disease,
Seek the chimney-nook of Ease:
There, ruminate with sober thought
On all thou'st seen, and heard, and wrought;   30
And teach the sportive Younkers round,
Saws of Experience, sage and sound.—
Say, Man's true, genuine estimate,
The grand criterion of his fate,
Is not, art thou High, or Low?   35
Did thy fortune ebb or flow?
Did many talents gild thy span?
Or frugal Nature grudge thee, One?
Tell them, and press it on their mind,
As thou thyself must shortly find,   40

18 summits] summit *91*   24 dells] dales *91*   25 As] When *2CPB Dum
A–B HL Don Adam 91*   the *94*: thy *MSS 91 93*   26 *Dum A ends*
31 Younkers round] *altered to* Younker train *in 2CPB*: Younker-train *Glen*
32 Saws . . . sound] Experience' lore, oft bought with pain *2CPB (alteration), Glen*
31–32 And . . . sound.] *in margin in Glen, marked* Altered   33 Man's . . .
estimate] *correcting* the criterion of their fate *in 2CPB*: the criterion of their fate
Dum B HL Don Adam 91   34 The grand criterion *Glen 93 94*: Th' important
query *2CPB Dum B HL Don Adam Afton 91*   34 his fate] their ~~state~~ fate
2CPB: their fate *Glen*: their state *Dum B HL Don Adam 91*   37–38 Did . . .
One?] *correcting*

Wast thou Cottager or King?
Peer or Peasant? No such thing!

in 2CPB. Dum B HL Don Adam and 91 have the earlier reading   39 and] *om. 91*

The smile, or frown, of awful Heaven,
To Virtue, or to Vice, is given:
Say, to be just, and kind, and wise,
There solid Self-enjoyment lies;
That foolish, selfish, faithless ways,   45
Lead to be wretched, vile and base.—

Thus, resigned and quiet, creep
To thy bed of lasting sleep:
Sleep, whence thou shalt ne'er awake,
Night, where dawn shall never break,   50
Till Future Life, future no more, ⎫
To light and joy the Good restore, ⎬
To light and joy unknown before.— ⎭

Stranger, go! Heaven be thy guide!
Quod, the BEADSMAN OF NITH-SIDE.—   55

224. The Fête Champetre—
Tune, Gillicrankie—

I

O WHA will to Saint Stephen's house,
    To do our errands there, man;
O wha will to Saint Stephen's house,
    O' th' merry lads of Ayr, man?
Or will we send a Man-o'-law,   5
    Or will we send a Sodger?
Or him wha led o'er Scotland a'
    The meikle URSA MAJOR?

2

Come, will ye court a noble Lord,
    Or buy a score o' Lairds, man?   10
For Worth and Honor pawn their word
    Their vote shall be Glencaird's, man?
Ane gies them coin, ane gies them wine,
    Anither gies them clatter;

55 OF 93 94: ON MSS 91

The Fête Champetre. *Text from Dewar's transcript of the Esty MS; letter to John
Ballantine, ? late July 1788. First words of ll. 33, 35, 53–54, where the MS is
defective, supplied from Gilbert Burns's edition, 1820 (iv. 402–5)*
    14 Anither] *correcting* And Jamie *in MS*

Anbank, wha guess'd the ladies' taste,   15
   He gies a Fête Champetre.—

3

When Love and Beauty heard the news,
   The gay green-woods amang, man,
Where gathering flowers and busking bowers
   They heard the blackbird's sang, man;   20
A vow they seal'd it with a kiss
   Sir Politicks to fetter,
As their's alone, the Patent-bliss,
   To hold a Fête Champetre.—

4

Then mounted Mirth, on gleesome wing,   25
   O'er hill and dale she flew, man;
Ilk wimpling burn, ilk chrystal spring,
   Ilk glen and shaw she knew, man:
She summonn'd every SOCIAL SPRITE,
   That sports by wood or water,   30
On th' bony Banks of Ayr to meet,
   And keep this Fête Champetre.—

5

Cauld Boreas, wi' his boisterous crew,
   Were bound to stakes like kye, man;
And Cynthia's car, o' silver fu',   35
   Clamb up the starry sky, man:
Reflected beams dwell in the streams,
   Or down the current shatter;
The western breeze steals thro' the trees,
   To view this Fête Champetre.—   40

6

How many a robe sae gayly floats!
   What sparkling jewels glance, man!
To HARMONY's enchanting notes
   As moves the mazy dance, man!
The echoing wood, the winding flood,   45
   Like Paradise did glitter,

When Angels met, at Adam's yett,
  To hold their Fête Champetre.—

7

When Politics cam there, to mix
  And make his ether-stane, man,   50
He circl'd round the magic ground,
  But entrance found he nane, man:
He blush'd for shame, he quat his name,
  Forswore it every letter,
Wi' humble prayer to join and share   55
  This festive Fête Champetre.—

225. [To Alexander Cunningham]

M^Y godlike Friend—nay do not stare,
  You think the phrase is odd like;
But, 'God is love,' the Saints declare,
  Then surely thou art Godlike.

And is thy Ardour still the same?   5
  And kindled still at Anna?
Others may boast a partial flame,
  But thou art a Volcano.—

Even Wedlock asks not Love beyond
  Death's tie-dissolving Portal;   10
But thou, omnipotently fond,
  May'st promise Love Immortal.—

Prudence, the Bottle and the Stew
  Are fam'd for Lovers' curing:
Thy Passion nothing can subdue,   15
  Nor Wisdom, Wine, nor Whoring.—

Thy Wounds such healing powers defy;
  Such Symptoms dire attend them;
That last, great Antihectic try,
  Marriage, perhaps, may mend them.—   20

To Alexander Cunningham. *Text from the Cunningham MS, Alloway (opening a letter dated* Ellisland in Nithsdale July 27th 1788). *Lines 13-16 are heavily deleted in the MS*

Sweet Anna has an air, a grace,
　　Divine magnetic touching!
She takes, she charms—but who can trace
　　The process of BEWITCHING?

226. O Mally's meek, Mally's sweet

Chorus

O MALLY's meek, Mally's sweet,
　　Mally's modest and discreet,
Mally's rare, Mally's fair,
　　Mally's ev'ry way compleat.

As I was walking up the street,   5
　　A barefit maid I chanc'd to meet,
But O, the road was very hard
　　For that fair maiden's tender feet.
　　　　Chorus, Mally's meek &c.

It were mair meet, that those fine feet
　　Were weel lac'd up in silken shoon,   10
And twere more fit that she should sit
　　Within yon chariot gilt aboon.
　　　　Chorus, Mally's meek &c.

O Mally's meek, Mally's sweet. *Text from SMM, 1803 (597; Written for this Work
by Robert Burns), collated with the Law MS sent to Johnson (transcript in the Burns
Chronicle, 1926, p, 63). Tune in MS Deil flee o'er the water wi' her. The song is
arranged as four stanzas in the MS, without chorus, in the sequence: ll. 5–12, 1–4,
13–16*
　　1 O] *not in MS*　　　　7 O, . . . hard] O . . . hard, *SMM:* the road seem'd hard
MS　　　8 fair maiden's] maid's *MS*　　　9 It were mair] 'Twere more *MS*
10 weel] *not in MS*　　11 And] *not in MS*　　12 Within] In *MS*

Her yellow hair, beyond compare,
  Comes trinkling down her swan white neck,
And her two eyes like stars in skies 15
  Would keep a sinking ship frae wreck.

227. I love my Jean

Tune—Miss admiral Gordon's Strathspey—

O^F a' the airts the wind can blaw,
    I dearly like the West;
For there the bony Lassie lives,
    The Lassie I lo'e best:

15 And] *not in MS*
I love my Jean. *Text from the Hastie MS, f. 55, collated with SMM, 1790 (235;
signed R), Stewart and Meikle, Stewart (S; 1802, pp. 204–5), and SC, 1805 (159).
Title from SMM. Tune in SC entitled* The Poet's ain Jean. *SC has two stanzas Added
by Mr. Richardson for this Work. First-line title in S*
    4 Lassie] lass that *S*

There's wild-woods grow, and rivers row,   5
    And mony a hill between;
But day and night my fancy's flight
    Is ever wi' my Jean.—

I see her in the dewy flowers,
    I see her sweet and fair;   10
I hear her in the tunefu' birds,
    I hear her charm the air:
There's not a bony flower, that springs
    By fountain, shaw, or green;
There's not a bony bird that sings   15
    But minds me o' my Jean.—

228. O, were I on Parnassus Hill

Tune, My love is lost to me

Moderately quick

5 There's] Tho' *S*: There *SC*   6 And] Wi' *S*   7 But] Baith *S*
10 I see her] sae lovely, *S*   11 in the tunefu'] voice in ilka *S*   12 I hear
her] wi' music *S*   15 There's not] Nor yet *S*

O, were I on Parnassus Hill. *Text from SMM, 1790 (255; signed R), collated with*

O WERE I on Parnassus hill;
Or had o' Helicon my fill;
That I might catch poetic skill,
    To sing how dear I love thee.
But Nith maun be my Muses well,   5
My Muse maun be thy bonie sell;
On Corsincon I'll glowr and spell,
    And write how dear I love thee.

Then come, sweet Muse, inspire my lay!
For a' the lee-lang simmer's day,   10
I coudna sing, I coudna say,
    How much, how dear, I love thee.
I see thee dancing o'er the green,
Thy waist sae jimp, thy limbs sae clean,
Thy tempting lips, thy roguish een—   15
    By Heaven and Earth I love thee.

By night, by day, a-field, at hame,
The thoughts o' thee my breast inflame;
And ay I muse and sing thy name,
    I only live to love thee.   20
Tho' I were doom'd to wander on,
Beyond the sea, beyond the sun,
Till my last, weary sand was run;
    Till then—and then I love thee.

SC, 1798 (29). Tune entitled O Jean I love thee *in SC. The Law MS (see* Burns Chronicle, *1926, pp. 63–64) has these variants:*
  8 dear] weel *MS*   24 I] I'd *MS*

229. The Banks of Nith

Tune, Robie donna gorach

Slow

T HE Thames flows proudly to the sea,
    Where royal cities stately stand;
But sweeter flows the Nith, to me,
    Where Cummins ance had high command:
When shall I see that honor'd Land,   5
    That winding Stream I love so dear!
Must wayward Fortune's adverse hand
    For ever, ever keep me here.

How lovely, Nith, thy fruitful vales,
    Where bounding hawthorns gayly bloom;   10
And sweetly spread thy sloping dales
    Where lambkins wanton through the broom!
Tho' wandering, now, must be my doom,
    Far from thy bonie banks and braes,
May there my latest hours consume,   15
    Amang the friends of early days!

The Banks of Nith. *Text from SMM, 1790 (295; signed B), collated with the Lochryan MS (letter to Mrs. Dunlop, 21 August 1788). Footnote to l. 4 in the MS* My Landlord, Mr Miller, is building a house by the banks of the Nith, just on the ruins of the Cummins' Castle.—

    5 honor'd] distant *MS*   9–12 How . . . broom!]
MS has

            Fair spread, O Nith, thy flowery dales,
                Where rove the flocks amang the broom;
            And richly wave thy fruitful vales,
                Surrounded by the hawthorns' bloom:

15 May there] There may *MS*   16 Amang the] With those my *MS*

230. To Robt Graham of Fintry Esqr., with a request for an Excise Division—

Ellisland—Sept. 8th 1788

WHEN Nature her great Masterpiece designed,
And framed her last, best Work, The Human
    Mind,
Her eye intent on all the mazy Plan,
She forms of various stuff the various Man.—
The USEFUL MANY first, she calls them forth,   5
Plain, plodding Industry, and sober Worth:
Thence Peasants, Farmers, native sons of earth,
And Merchandise' whole genus take their birth:
Each prudent Cit a warm existence finds,
And all Mechanics' many-aproned kinds.—   10
Some other, rarer Sorts are wanted yet,
The lead and buoy are needful to the net.—
The caput mortuum of Gross Desires,
Makes a material for mere knights and squires:
The Martial Phosphorus is taught to flow;   15
She kneads the lumpish Philosophic dough;
Then marks th' unyielding mass with grave Designs,
Law, Physics, Politics and deep Divines:
Last, she sublimes th' Aurora of the Poles,
The flashing elements of Female Souls.—   20

To Robt Graham of Fintry. *Text from the* Second Commonplace Book (*2CPB;
pp. 17–20*), *collated with Letter 260 (Dunlop 1; draft of ll. 49–65 in letter to Mrs.
Dunlop, 2 August 1788*), *the Adam MS (Adam 1, Sketch), the Watson MS (1123*),
*letter to Mrs. Dunlop, 5 September 1788 (Dunlop 2; Dewar's transcript), MS Adam 2
(probably one of the numerous copies sent out in January 1789), the Don MS (sent to
Lady Don? January 1789), the Huntington Library MS (HL; Bishop Geddes's copy
of 87, sent 3 February 1789), the Cowie MS, the transcript in the Glenriddell MS
(Glen; pp. 118–23), and Currie (ii. 168–71; from the copy for Graham). Title in MSS
Watson, Adam 2, Don Cowie and Glen* To R— G— Esq. requesting a favor*: in HL*
To Robert Graham of Fintry Esquire—accompanying a request—
    3 mazy] *correcting* various *in 2CPB*: various *Watson*   4 stuff] *correcting* parts
in 2CPB: parts *Adam 1 Watson Dunlop 2 Adam 2 Don HL Cowie Currie*   5 The
. . . forth] *correcting* Then first, she calls the USEFUL MANY forth *in 2CPB*: Then
first . . . forth *Adam 1* (calls *corrects* call'd), *Watson Dunlop 2 Currie*   9 pru-
dent] *correcting* wealthy *in Adam 1*   11 Sorts] *correcting* Speciesen *in Adam 1*:
Speciesen *Dunlop 2*   wanted] *correcting* needed *in Adam 1*   12 needful]
alternative to useful *in Adam 1*   13 Gross] Strong *Watson*   17 mass]
correcting stuff *in Adam 1*   18 Law, Physics, Politics] *correcting* Law, Politics,
Physics *in Adam 1*   Physics] physic *Currie*

The ordered System fair before her stood,
Nature, well-pleased, pronounced it very good;
Yet, ere she gave creating labor o'er,
Half-jest, she tryed one curious labor more.——
Some spumy, fiery, ignisfatuus matter,   25
Such as the slightest breath of air might scatter,
With arch-alacrity, and conscious glee,
(Nature may have her whim as well as we;
Her Hogarth-art perhaps she meant to show it)
She forms the Thing, and christens it——A POET.—— 30
Creature, tho' oft the prey of Care and Sorrow,
When blest today, unmindful of tomorrow;
A being formed t' amuse his graver friends,
Admired and praised——and there the wages ends;
A mortal quite unfit for Fortune's strife,   35
Yet oft the sport of all the ills of life;
Prone to enjoy each pleasure riches give,
Yet haply wanting wherewithall to live;
Longing to wipe each tear, to heal each groan,
Yet frequent all-unheeded in his own.——   40

But honest Nature is not quite a Turk;
She laught at, first, then felt for her poor Work:
Viewing the propless Climber of mankind,
She cast about a Standard-tree to find;
In pity for his helpless woodbine-state,   45
She clasp'd his tendrils round THE TRULY GREAT:
A title, and the only one I claim,
To lay strong hold for help on generous GRAHAM.——

23 Yet] But *Adam 1 Watson Dunlop 2 Adam 2 Don HL Cowie Currie*
28 whim] whims *Adam 2*   30 forms . . . christens] form'd . . . christen'd
Adam 1   34 wages] homage *Currie*   35 quite] *correcting* all *in Adam 1*
Fortune's] mortal *Adam 2*   38 haply] *correcting* frequent *in Adam 1 Watson*
39 Longing] *correcting* Wishing *in Adam 1*   40 frequent all] *correcting* oft
unseen *in Adam 1*   42 at,] at *Adam 1 Adam 2 Glen Currie*   43 Viewing]
correcting Pitying *in 2 CPB:* Pitying *Adam 1 Watson Dunlop 2 Adam 2 Don HL
Cowie Currie*   45 In pity for] *correcting* And to support *in 2 CPB:* And to
support *Adam 1 Watson Dunlop 2 Adam 2 Don HL Cowie Currie*   46 She . . .
TRULY] *correcting* Attached him to the GENEROUS, TRULY *in 2CPB:* Attached . . .
GENEROUS, TRULY *Adam 1 Watson Dunlop 2 Adam 2 HL Cowie Currie:*
Attached . . . bounteous truly *Don*   48 generous] *correcting* bounteous *in
2CPB:* bounteous *Adam 1 Watson Dunlop 2 Adam 2 HL Cowie Currie*

Pity the tuneful Muses' hapless train,
Weak, timid Landsmen on life's stormy main! 50
Their hearts no selfish, stern, absorbent stuff
That never gives—tho' humbly takes enough;
The little Fate allows they share as soon,
Unlike sage, proverbed Wisdom's hard-wrung boon:
The world were blest, did bliss on them depend, 55
Ah, that the FRIENDLY e'er should want a FRIEND!

Let Prudence number o'er each sturdy son
Who life and wisdom at one race begun,
Who feel by reason and who give by rule,
(Instinct's a brute, and Sentiment a fool!) 60
Who make poor, 'Will do,' wait upon, 'I should,'
We own they're prudent—but who owns they're
    good?
Ye Wise Ones, hence! ye hurt the social eye;
God's image rudely etch'd on base alloy!
But come, ye who the godlike pleasure know, 65
Heaven's attribute distinguished,—to bestow,
Whose arms of love would grasp all human-race;
Come, thou who givest with all a courtier's grace,
Friend of my life! (true Patron of my rhymes)
Prop of my dearest hopes for future times.— 70

Why shrinks my soul, half-blushing, half-afraid,
Backward, abashed, to ask thy friendly aid?
I know my need, I know thy giving hand,
I tax thy friendship at thy kind command:
But, there are such, who court the tuneful Nine, 75
Heavens, should the branded character be mine!

49 tuneful . . . hapless] hapless . . . tuneful *Adam 2 Don* hapless] helpless *Dunlop 1: correcting* helpless *in Adam 1, 2CPB* 51–52 Their . . . enough;] *not in Dunlop 1* 51–56 *Sequence in Adam 1:* 55–56 *(deleted),* 51–52, *part of 55 (deleted),* 53–56 53–54, 55–56 *Transposed in Dunlop 1* 53 The] Their *Dunlop 1 Adam 1 Adam 2 Don HL Cowie* allows] bestows *Dunlop 1* 57 Prudence] *correcting* Wisdom *in Adam 1* 61 'Will do,'] I will do *Adam 1* 72 ask] *correcting* seek *in 2CPB* 73 thy giving hand,] thy bounteous hand; *correcting* thou canst bestow *in Adam 1* 74 I tax . . . command] I crave . . . command *Adam 1 (correcting* Thy giving hand, experienced, well I know) *Dunlop 2 Currie* 74–78 I . . . prose.] *not in Watson; MS defective*

Whose verse in manhood's pride sublimely flows,
Yet vilest reptiles in their begging prose.
Mark, how their lofty, independant spirit
Soars on the spurning wing of injured Merit!   80
Seek you the proofs in private life to find?—
Pity, the best of words should be but wind!
So to heaven's gates the lark's shrill song ascends,
But grovelling on the earth the carol ends.—
In all the clamorous cry of starving Want   85
They dun Benevolence with shameless front:
Oblidge them, patronize their tinsel lays,
They persecute you all your future days.—

    E'er my poor soul such deep damnation stain,
My horny fist, assume the Plough again;   90
The pie-bald jacket, let me patch once more;
On eighteenpence a week I've lived before.—
Tho', thanks to Heaven! I dare even that last shift,
I trust, meantime, my boon is in thy gift:
That, placed by thee upon the wished-for height,⎫   95
Where Man and Nature fairer in her sight,   ⎬
My Muse may imp her wing for some sublimer ⎭
    flight.

78 vilest] meanest *Dunlop 2*   81 you . . . find?—] *correcting* not . . . find—
in 2CPB: not . . . find— *Adam 1 Dunlop 2 Currie*: not *and* you *alternatives in Watson*
84 But] *correcting* Till *in Adam 1*   85 In] *correcting* With *in Adam 1*
87 tinsel] *correcting* worthless *in Watson*   94 I trust, meantime] *correcting*
Meantime, I trust *in Adam 1*   96 Where] With *Don*

231. The seventh of November—

T<small>HE</small> day returns, my bosom burns,
    The blissful day we twa did meet:
Tho' Winter wild, in tempest toil'd,
    Ne'er simmer-sun was half sae sweet.
Than a' the pride that loads the tide,   5
    And crosses o'er the sultry Line;
Than kingly robes, than crowns and globes,
    Heaven gave me more—it made thee mine.—

While day and night can bring delight,
    Or Nature aught of pleasure give;   10
While Joys Above, my mind can move,
    For Thee and Thee alone I live!

The day returns. *Text from the Hastie MS, f. 54ᵛ, collated with the Huntington Library MS (HL; letter of 16 September 1788), SMM, 1790 (224; signed R), and SC, 1798 (28). The signature has failed to print in some copies of SMM. Title in HL* The Wedding-Day. A Song
  5 Than] Then *SMM*   10 Or] *correcting* While *in HL*   12 For . . . alone] Only for Love and Thee *HL*

When that grim foe of life below
Comes in between to make us part;
The iron hand that breaks our Band,   15
It breaks my bliss—it breaks my heart!

232. The blue-eyed Lassie

I GAED a waefu' gate, yestreen,
  A gate, I fear, I'll dearly rue;
I gat my death frae twa sweet een,
  Twa lovely e'en o' bonie blue.

14 Comes] *correcting* Steps *in HL*   15–16 *HL defective*

The blue-eyed Lassie. *Text from SMM, 1790 (294; Written for this Work by
Robert Burns), collated with the Lochryan MS (letter to Mrs. Dunlop, 29 October
1788), the Alloway (formerly Adam) and Mauchline MSS, SC, 1803 (119), and
Stewart, 1802 (S). Title in Alloway MS* Song.—The blue-eyed lass—Air by Capt[n]
R—; *subscription* To Capt[n] Riddel with the Author's grateful Compl. *The Mauch-
line MS is headed* Sent to Mr. Johnson. Lines written to Miss Jeffrey, Lochmaben.
The blue-eyed lassie *and subscribed* Written at Lochmaben.—Ellisland December
1789

'Twas not her golden ringlets bright, 5
  Her lips like roses, wat wi' dew,
Her heaving bosom, lily-white,
  It was her een sae bonie blue.

She talk'd, she smil'd, my heart she wyl'd,
  She charm'd my soul I wist na how; 10
And ay the stound, the deadly wound,
  Cam frae her een sae bonie blue.
But spare to speak, and spare to speed;
  She'll aiblins listen to my vow:
Should she refuse, I'll lay my dead 15
  To her twa een sae bonie blue.

233. A Mother's Lament for the loss of her only Son—

Finlayston House

5 golden] *correcting* bonnie *in Mauchline MS* 10 wist] wat *S* 13 to ...to]
I'd ...I'd *S* 15 dead] deed *S* 16 sae] o' *S*

A Mother's Lament. *Text from the Afton Lodge MS, 1791, f. 3, collated with the*

'F ATE gave the word, the arrow sped,'
  And pierc'd my Darling's heart;
And with him all the joys are fled,
  Life can to me impart.—

By cruel hands the Sapling drops,   5
  In dust dishonor'd laid:
So fell the pride of all my hopes,
  My age's future shade.—

The mother-linnet in the brake
  Bewails her ravish'd young;   10
So I, for my lost Darling's sake,
  Lament the live day long.—

Death! oft, I've fear'd thy fatal blow;
  Now, fond, I bare my breast;
O, do thou come and lay me low,   15
  With him I love at rest!

Dunlop MS (letter to Mrs. Dunlop, 27 September *1788), SMM, 1790 (271; signed B), and SC, 1798 (45). Title in SMM* A Mother's . . . her son. Tune, Finlayston House; *first-line title in SC, to the air* Gil Morris. *Title in Dunlop MS* Mʳˢ F— of C—'s lamentation for the death of her son; an uncommonly promising Youth of 18 or 19 years of age—
  5 cruel] savage *Dunlop*   15 come and] kindly *Dunlop SMM SC*

234. The lazy mist

T HE lazy mist hangs from the brow of the hill,
  Concealing the course of the dark winding rill;
How languid the scenes, late so sprightly, appear,
As Autumn to Winter resigns the pale year.
The forests are leafless, the meadows are brown,   5
And all the gay foppery of Summer is flown:
Apart let me wander, apart let me muse,
How quick Time is flying, how keen Fate pursues.

The lazy mist. Text from SMM, 1790 (232; signed B), collated with SC, 1798 (50).
Tune in SC Here's a health to my true Love
  2 the course] yᵉ course *SMM*   6 Summer] summer *SMM*

How long I have liv'd—but how much liv'd in vain;
How little of life's scanty span may remain: 10
What aspects, old Time, in his progress, has worn;
What ties, cruel Fate, in my bosom has torn.
How foolish, or worse, till our summit is gain'd!
And downward, how weaken'd, how darken'd, how pain'd!
Life is not worth having with all it can give,   15
For something beyond it poor man sure must live.

235. Whistle o'er the lave o't—

F‌IRST when Maggy was my care,
    Heaven, I thought, was in her air;
Now we're married—spier nae mair—
    Whistle o'er the lave o't.—

Meg was meek, and Meg was mild,   5
Sweet and harmless as a child—
Wiser men than me's beguil'd;
    Whistle o'er the lave o't.—

14 weaken'd,] weaken'd *SMM*

Whistle o'er the lave o't. *Text from the Philadelphia MS (letter to Johnson, 15
November 1788), collated with SMM, 1790 (249; signed X), and SC, 1805 (169).
First-line title in SC*
    4 Whistle] But whistle *SMM SC*   5 meek] *correcting* sweet *in MS*
8 Whistle] So whistle *SMM SC*

How we live, my Meg and me,
How we love and how we gree; 10
I carena by how few may see,
  Whistle o'er the lave o't.—

Wha I wish were maggots' meat,
Dish'd up in her winding-sheet;
I could write—but Meg maun see 't— 15
  Whistle o'er the lave o't.—

236. Tam Glen—

Tune, Merry beggars—

M<small>Y</small> heart is a breaking, dear Tittie,
  Some counsel unto me come len';
To anger them a' is a pity,
  But what will I do wi' Tam Glen?—

I'm thinking, wi' sic a braw fellow, 5
  In poortith I might mak a fen':
What care I in riches to wallow,
  If I mauna marry Tam Glen.—

There's Lowrie the laird o' Dumeller,
  'Gude day to you brute' he comes ben: 10
He brags and he blaws o' his siller,
  But when will he dance like Tam Glen.—

10 we gree] agree *SC*

Tam Glen. *Text from the Philadelphia MS (letter to Johnson, 15 November 1788),
collated with the Lochryan MS (letter to Mrs. Dunlop, 7 December 1788), SMM,
1790 (296; Written for this Work by Robert Burns), and SC, 1799 (66). First-line
title in SC, set to the air* The Mucking o' Geordie's Byre
  1 Tittie] *glossed* Sister *in Loch* 10 you brute'] you,' (coof) *SC*

My Minnie does constantly deave me,
　And bids me beware o' young men;
They flatter, she says, to deceive me,　　　　15
　But wha can think sae o' Tam Glen.—

My Daddie says, gin I'll forsake him,
　He'll gie me gude hunder marks ten:
But, if it's ordain'd I maun take him,
　O wha will I get but Tam Glen?　　　　20

Yestreen at the Valentines' dealing,
　My heart to my mou gied a sten;
For thrice I drew ane without failing,
　And thrice it was written, Tam Glen.—

The last Halloween I was waukin　　　　25
　My droukit sark-sleeve, as ye ken;
His likeness cam up the house staukin,
　And the very grey breeks o' Tam Glen!

Come counsel, dear Tittie, don't tarry;
　I'll gie you my bonie black hen,　　　　30
Gif ye will advise me to Marry
　The lad I lo'e dearly, Tam Glen.—

237. To the beautiful Miss Eliza J——n, on her principles of Liberty and Equality—

How Liberty, girl, can it be by thee
　　nam'd?
Equality too! hussey, art not asham'd:
Free and Equal indeed; while mankind
　　thou enchainest,
And over their hearts a proud Despot
　　so reignest.—

To ... Eliza J——n. *Text from the Huntington Library MS (letter to Creech, 30 May 1795), collated with the Esty MS (Dewar's transcript). Title in Esty* To Miss —— on her doctrines of Liberty and Equality.—
　4 proud] fair *Esty*

238. [Sketch for an Elegy]

CRAIGDARROCH, fam'd for speaking art
  And every virtue of the heart,
Stops short, nor can a word impart
    To end his sentence,
When mem'ry strikes him like a dart   5
    With auld acquaintance.

Black James—whase wit was never laith,
But, like a sword had tint the sheath,
Ay ready for the work o' death—
    He turns aside,   10
And strains wi' suffocating breath
    His grief to hide.

Even Philosophic Smellie tries
To choak the stream that floods his eyes:
So Moses wi' a hazel-rice   15
    Came o'er the stane;
But, tho' it cost him speaking twice,
    It gush'd amain.

Go to your marble graffs, ye great,
In a' the tinkler-trash of state!   20
But by thy honest turf I'll wait,
    Thou man of worth,
And weep the ae best fallow's fate
    E'er lay in earth!

Sketch for an Elegy. *Text from H–H., ii. 236–7 (MS not traced). See Commentary*

239. Elegy on Capt M—— H——, A *Gentleman* who held the Patent for his Honours immediately from Almighty God!

But now his radiant course is run,
For Matthew's course was bright;
His soul was like the glorious sun,
A matchless Heavenly Light!

O DEATH! thou tyrant fell and bloody!
  The meikle devil wi' a woodie
Haurl thee hame to his black smiddie,
    O'er hurcheon hides,
And like stock-fish come o'er his studdie   5
    Wi' thy auld sides!

He's gane! he's gane! he's frae us torn,
The ae best fellow e'er was born!
Thee, Matthew, Nature's sel shall mourn
    By wood and wild,   10
Where, haply, Pity strays forlorn,
    Frae man exil'd.

Elegy on Capt M—— H——. *Text from the Edinburgh edition, 1793, collated with the* Second Commonplace Book (*2CPB*), *the Bixby MS, the Lochryan MS (Loch; letter to Mrs. Dunlop, 30 July 1790), the Fintry MS (4 September 1790), the Cowie and Afton Lodge MSS, the* Edinburgh Magazine, *August 1790, and the edition of 1794. See Commentary. The* Magazine *follows Loch in lines 9–12, 22–24, 39–41, 45, 48, 49–60, 56, 66. Title in Fintry* Elegy on the death of the late Captⁿ Matthew Henderson, Edin^r.

Epigraph *om. Bixby; added at the end of the poem in Fintry; replaced in Loch and Cowie by* 'Should the Poor be flattered?' Shakespear; *corrected in 2CPB from*

But now his radiant course is run,
  For Matthew was a bright man;
His soul was like the glorious Sun,
  A matchless

9–12 Thee . . . exil'd.] *MSS have*

Thee, Matthew, woods and wilds shall mourn,
  Wi' a' their birth;
For whunstane man to grieve wad scorn,
  For poor, plain Worth.

Ye hills, near neebors o' the starns,
That proudly cock your cresting cairns;
Ye cliffs, the haunts of sailing yearns,   15
                Where Echo slumbers;
Come join, ye Nature's sturdiest bairns,
                My wailing numbers.

Mourn, ilka grove the cushat kens;
Ye hazly shaws and briery dens;   20
Ye burnies, wimplin down your glens,
                Wi' toddlin din,
Or foaming, strang, wi' hasty stens,
                Frae lin to lin.

Mourn, little harebells o'er the lee;   25
Ye stately foxgloves fair to see;
Ye woodbines hanging bonnilie,
                In scented bowers;
Ye roses on your thorny tree,
                The first o' flowers.   30

At dawn, when every grassy blade
Droops with a diamond at his head,
At even, when beans their fragrance shed,
                I' th' rustling gale,
Ye maukins whiddin thro' the glade,   35
                Come join my wail.

Mourn, ye wee songsters o' the wood;
Ye grouss that crap the heather bud;
Ye curlews calling thro' a clud;
                Ye whistling plover;   40
And mourn, ye whirring paitrick brood;
                He 's gane for ever!

---

20 briery] breerie *2CPB Afton*   22–24 Wi' . . . lin.] *Bixby and Loch have*
                    At toddlin leisure,
                Or o'er the linns wi' hasty stens
                    Flinging your treasure.

23 hasty] rumbling *Fintry*   32 his] its *MSS*   37 songsters] sangsters *MSS*
39 calling] skirlin *MSS*   40 plover] pliver *MSS*   41 whirring] birrin
MSS

Mourn, sooty coots, and speckled teals;
Ye fisher herons, watching eels;
Ye duck and drake, wi' airy wheels   45
            Circling the lake:
Ye bitterns, till the quagmire reels,
            Rair for his sake.

Mourn, clamouring craiks at close o' day,
'Mang fields o' flowering claver gay;   50
And when ye wing your annual way
            Frae our cauld shore,
Tell thae far warlds, wha lies in clay,
            Wham we deplore.

Ye houlets, frae your ivy bower,   55
In some auld tree, or eldritch tower,
What time the moon, wi' silent glowr,
            Sets up her horn,
Wail thro' the dreary midnight hour
            Till waukrife morn.   60

O, rivers, forests, hills, and plains!
Oft have ye heard my canty strains:
But now, what else for me remains
            But tales of woe;
And frae my een the drapping rains   65
            Maun ever flow.

Mourn, Spring, thou darling of the year;
Ilk cowslip cup shall kep a tear:
Thou, Simmer, while each corny spear
            Shoots up its head,   70
Thy gay, green, flowery tresses shear,
            For him that's dead.

45 duck] deuk *MSS*   48 Rair] Rowt(e) *MSS*   49 clamouring] clam'-
ring *94*   49–60 *stanzas transposed in Bixby Loch Cowie*   56 eldritch] aulder
2CPB Bixby Loch Cowie Afton: tottering *Fintry*   61 hills] woods *Bixby*
62 canty] rustic MSS (*alternative* jocund *Cowie*)   66 Maun] Must *MSS*
69 while] when *Loch*

Thou, Autumn, wi' thy yellow hair,
In grief thy sallow mantle tear;
Thou, Winter, hurling thro' the air   75
   The roaring blast,
Wide o'er the naked world declare
   The worth we've lost.

Mourn him thou Sun, great source of light;
Mourn, Empress of the silent night: 80
And you, ye twinkling starnies bright,
   My Matthew mourn;
For through your orbs he's taen his flight,
   Ne'er to return.

O, H********! the man! the brother!   85
And art thou gone, and gone for ever!
And hast thou crost that unknown river,
   Life's dreary bound!
Like thee, where shall I find another,
   The world around!   90

Go to your sculptur'd tombs, ye Great,
In a' the tinsel trash o' state!
But by thy honest turf I'll wait,
   Thou man of worth!
And weep the ae best fellow's fate   95
   E'er lay in earth.

THE EPITAPH

Stop, passenger! my story's brief,
  And truth I shall relate, man;
I tell nae common tale o' grief,
  For Matthew was a great man.   100

If thou uncommon merit hast,
  Yet spurn'd at Fortune's door, man;
A look of pity hither cast,
  For Matthew was a poor man.

If thou a noble sodger art,   105
    That passest by this grave, man;
There moulders here a gallant heart,
    For Matthew was a brave man.

If thou on men, their works and ways,
    Canst throw uncommon light, man;   110
Here lies wha weel had won thy praise,
    For Matthew was a bright man.

If thou at Friendship's sacred ca'
    Wad life itself resign, man;
Thy sympathetic tear maun fa',   115
    For Matthew was a kind man.

If thou art staunch without a stain,
    Like the unchanging blue, man;
This was a kinsman o' thy ain,
    For Matthew was a true man.   120

If thou hast wit, and fun, and fire,
    And ne'er gude wine did fear, man;
This was thy billie, dam, and sire,
    For Matthew was a queer man.

If ony whiggish whingin sot,   125
    To blame poor Matthew dare, man;
May dool and sorrow be his lot,
    For Matthew was a rare man.

106–7 man; . . . heart, *MSS*: man, . . . heart; *93 94*   109–12 If . . . man.]
not in Fintry and Cowie   114 Wad] Wouldst *2CPB Cowie Bixby*: Would *Fintry*
115 tear] drap *Fintry*: drop *Cowie*   123 This . . . sire] These bones a brother's
tears require *Cowie*   125–8 If . . . rare man.] *not in Fintry and Cowie, which
have*

     But now his radiant course is run,
        For Matthew was a bright man;
     His soul was like the glorious sun,
        A matchless heavenly light, man.

240. Auld lang syne

Chorus

tr

S H O U L D auld acquaintance be forgot
And never brought to mind?
Should auld acquaintance be forgot,
And auld lang syne!

Chorus

For auld lang syne, my jo,   5
For auld lang syne,
We'll tak a *cup o' kindness yet
For auld lang syne.

* Some Sing, Kiss, in place of Cup.

Auld lang syne. *Text from SMM, 1796 (413; signed Z), collated with the Alloway
MS (Al), the Washington MS (W; letter to Mrs. Dunlop, 7 December, 1788), the
Dalhousie MS (Dal; letter to Thomson, September 1793), the holograph in the inter-
leaved copy of SMM (IM), and SC, 1799 (68). Al is headed* A Fragment—Auld
Lang syne—*and consists of ll. 9–24, the last stanza defective. Lines 9–12 follow
ll. 21–24 in Dal and SC. Heading in IM* The original and by much the best Set of
the words of this Song is as follows. *First-line title in SC: text* From an old MS. in the
editor's possession.
  2 brought to mind] thought upon *W*   3 Should . . . forgot] Let's hae a
waught o' Malaga *W*   4 And auld] For auld *W*: And days o' *Dal IM SC*
5 For] And for *IM*   jo] Dear *Dal SC*   7 We'll . . . yet] Let's hae a waught
o' Malaga *W. Footnote in SMM only*

And surely ye'll be your pint stowp!
   And surely I'll be mine!   10
And we'll tak a cup o' kindness yet,
   For auld lang syne.
      For auld, &c.

We twa hae run about the braes,
   And pou'd the gowans fine;
But we've wander'd mony a weary fitt,   15
   Sin auld lang syne.
      For auld, &c.

We twa hae paidl'd in the burn,
   Frae morning sun till dine;
But seas between us braid hae roar'd,
   Sin auld lang syne.   20
      For auld, &c.

And there's a hand, my trusty fiere!
   And gie's a hand o' thine!
And we'll tak a right gude-willie-waught,
   For auld lang syne.
      For auld, &c.

241. Epitaph for J. H. Writer in Ayr

HERE lies a Scots mile of a chiel,
  If he's in heaven, L—d, fill him weel!

14 pou'd] pou't *Al W Dal*   15 fitt] foot *W Dal IM SC*   17 paidl'd
in] paidl't in *Al*: paidl't i' *W*: paidlet i' *Dal SC*: paidl'd i' *IM*

Epitaph. *Text from the Lochryan MS (letter to Mrs. Dunlop, 7 December 1788)*

242. My bony Mary

The secret kiss

G o fetch to me a pint o' wine,
  And fill it in a silver tassie;
That I may drink, before I go,
  A service to my bonie lassie:
The boat rocks at the Pier o' Lieth,   5
  Fu' loud the wind blaws frae the Ferry,
The ship rides by the Berwick-law,
  And I maun leave my bony Mary.

My bony Mary. Text from the Hastie MS (Ha), f. 55ʳ, collated with the Dunlop MS (D), SMM, 1790 (231; unsigned), and SC, 1805 (189). Lines 1–4 of D (letter to Mrs. Dunlop, 7 December 1788) in the Library of Congress, Washington; the remainder at Dumfries. Tune in Ha The secret kiss. In SC the piece is an alternative to a song by Ramsay, to the tune The old Highland laddie. Title from SMM

A draft of ll. 1–8 formerly owned by the Earl of Lincoln (collated Dewar) ends

    Tho' far ayont yon southern sun,
      Amang the Indies I should wander;
    Still thou art mine and I am thine,
      Oh! waes my heart that we should sunder.

  1 Go] Come, *SC*   8 leave] lea'e *D*

The trumpets sound, the banners fly,
   The glittering spears are ranked ready,   10
The shouts o' war are heard afar,
   The battle closes deep and bloody.
It's not the roar o' sea or shore,
   Wad make me langer wish to tarry;
Nor shouts o' war that's heard afar—   15
   It's leaving thee, my bony Mary!

243. Ode, Sacred to the Memory of Mrs.
—— of ——

DWELLER in yon dungeon dark,
  Hangman of creation, mark!
Who in widow weeds appears,
Laden with unhonoured years,
Noosing with care a bursting purse,   5
Baited with many a deadly curse?

STROPHE

View the wither'd beldam's face—
Can thy keen inspection trace
Aught of Humanity's sweet melting grace?
Note that eye, 'tis rheum o'erflows,   10
Pity's flood there never rose.
See those hands, ne'er stretch'd to save,
Hands that took—but never gave.
Keeper of Mammon's iron chest,
Lo, there she goes, unpitied and unblest,   15
She goes, but not to realms of everlasting rest!

---

12 deep] thick *D*   13 It's] But it's *D*

Ode. *Text from the Edinburgh edition, 1793, collated with the Fintry and Don MSS,
the Lochryan MS (Loch; letter to Mrs. Dunlop, January 1789), the Glenriddell MS
(Glen; pp. 109–10; transcript), the Star, 7 May 1789, and the edition of 1794*
   12 those] these *Fintry Don Loch Glen*   13 *Additional couplet in Fintry Don
Loch:*

          The Great despised her and her wealth,
          The Poor-man breathed a curse by stealth.

15 unblest,] unblest *94*

ANTISTROPHE

Plunderer of Armies, lift thine eyes,
(A while forbear, ye torturing fiends),
Seest thou whose step, unwilling, hither bends?
No fallen angel, hurled from upper skies;   20
'Tis thy trusty *quondam Mate,*
Doomed to share thy fiery fate,
She, tardy, hell-ward plies.

EPODE

And are they of no more avail,
Ten thousand glittering pounds a year?   25
In other worlds can Mammon fail,
Omnipotent as he is here?
O, bitter mockery of the *pompous bier,*
While down the wretched *vital part* is driven!
The cave-lodged beggar, with a conscience clear,   30
Expires in rags, unknown, and goes to Heaven.

244. [Versicles on Sign-posts]

THE everlasting surliness of a lion, Saracen's head, &c. or the un-
changing blandness of the Landlord welcoming a Traveller, on some
Sign-posts, would be no bad similies of the constant, affected fierceness
of a Bully, or the eternal simper of a Frenchman or a Fiddler.—

HE looked
Just as your Sign-post lions do,
As fierce, and quite as harmless too—

———————

Patient Stupidity
So, heavy, passive to the tempest's shocks,
Dull on the Sign-post stands the stupid Ox—   5

———————

19 step,] steps *Don Loch*   20 hurled] kicked *Fintry Don Loch*   23 plies]
flies *Don*

Versicles on Sign-posts. *Text from the* Second Commonplace Book *(2CPB; p. 22)*
5 Dull] Strong *alternative in 2CPB*

His face with smile eternal drest
Just like the Landlord to his guest,
High as they hang with creaking din
To index out the country Inn—

___

A head pure, sinless quite of brain or soul,   10
The very image of a Barber's Poll;
Just shews a human face and wears a wig,
And looks when well-friseur'd, amazing big—

245. To Mʳ John Taylor

WITH Pegasus upon a day
  Apollo, weary flying,
(Thro' frosty hills the journey lay)
  On foot the way was plying.—

Poor, slip-shod, giddy Pegasus   5
  Was but a sorry walker,
To Vulcan then Apollo gaes
  To get a frosty calker.—

Oblidging Vulcan fell to wark,
  Threw by his coat and bonnet;   10
And did Sol's business in a crack,
  Sol pay'd him with a sonnet.—

Ye Vulcan's Sons of Wanlockhead,
  Pity my sad disaster,
My Pegasus is poorly shod,   15
  I'll pay you like my Master.—

___

7 Just] *correcting* It *in 2CPB* 13 well-friseur'd,] *correcting* well-dressed, too, *in 2CPB*

To Mʳ John Taylor. *Text from the Alloway MS* (*signed* Robᵗ Burns *and subscribed* Ramage's / 3 o'clock)

246. A Sonnet upon Sonnets

FOURTEEN, a sonneteer thy praises sings;
  What magic myst'ries in that number lie!
Your hen hath fourteen eggs beneath her wings
That fourteen chickens to the roost may fly.
Fourteen full pounds the jockey's stone must be;   5
His age fourteen—a horse's prime is past.
Fourteen long hours too oft the Bard must fast;
Fourteen bright bumpers—bliss he ne'er must see!
Before fourteen, a dozen yields the strife;
Before fourteen—e'en thirteen's strength is vain.   10
Fourteen good years—a woman gives us life;
Fourteen good men—we lose that life again.
What lucubrations can be more upon it?
Fourteen good measur'd verses make a sonnet.

247. The Cares o' Love

HE

THE cares o' Love are sweeter far
  Than onie other pleasure;
And if sae dear its sorrows are,
  Enjoyment, what a treasure!

SHE

I fear to try, I dare na try   5
  A passion sae ensnaring;
For light's her heart and blythe's
    her song
  That for nae man is caring.

A Sonnet upon Sonnets. *Text from H–H. (ii. 232). MS not traced*

The Cares o' Love. *Text from H–H. (ii. 239). MS not traced*

248. Louis what reck I by thee

L OUIS, what reck I by thee,
   Or Geordie on his ocean:
Dyvor, beggar louns to me,
   I reign in Jeanie's bosom.

Let her crown my love her law,
   And in her breast enthrone me: 5
Kings and nations, swith awa!
   Reif randies I disown ye!—

    *   *   *   *   *

Louis what reck I by thee. *Text from SMM, 1796 (414; signed R)*

VI

POEMS
1789

ELLISLAND

249. Sketch. New Year's Day. To Mrs. Dunlop

This day, Time winds th' exhausted chain,
 To run the twelvemonth's length again:—
I see the old, bald-pated fellow,
With ardent eyes, complexion sallow,
Adjust the unimpair'd machine,   5
To wheel the equal, dull routine.

The absent lover, minor heir,
In vain assail him with their prayer,
Deaf as my friend, he sees them press,
Nor makes the hour one moment less.   10
Will you (the Major's with the hounds,
The happy tenants share his rounds;
Coila's fair Rachel's care to day*,
And blooming Keith's engaged with Gray;)
From housewife cares a minute borrow—   15
—That grandchild's cap will do to-morrow—
And join with me a moralizing,
This day's propitious to be wise in.

First, what did yesternight deliver?
'Another year is gone for ever.'   20
And what is this day's strong suggestion?
'The passing moment's all we rest on!'
Rest on—for what? what do we here?
Or why regard the passing year?
Will time, amus'd with proverb'd lore,   25
Add to our date one minute more?
A few days may—a few years must—
Repose us in the silent dust.

* This young lady was drawing a picture of Coila from *The Vision*.

Sketch. *Text from Currie, iv. 363–5*
  19 *Editor's paragraph*

Then is it wise to damp our bliss?
Yes—all such reasonings are amiss!   30
The voice of nature loudly cries,   )
And many a message from the skies,   }
That something in us never dies:)
That on this frail, uncertain state,
Hang matters of eternal weight: 35
That future life in worlds unknown
Must take its hue from this alone;
Whether as heavenly glory bright,
Or dark as misery's woeful night—
Since then, my honor'd, first of friends,   40
On this poor being all depends;
Let us th' important *now* employ,
And live as those who never die.
Tho' you, with days and honors crown'd,
Witness that filial circle round,   45
(A sight life's sorrows to repulse,
A sight pale envy to convulse)
Others now claim your chief regard;
Yourself, you wait your bright reward.

250. Elegy on the Year 1788

FOR Lords or kings I dinna mourn,
    E'en let them die—for that they're born!
But oh! prodigious to reflect,
A *Towmont*, Sirs, is gane to wreck!
O *Eighty-eight*, in thy sma' space   5
What dire events ha'e taken place!
Of what enjoyments thou hast reft us!
In what a pickle thou hast left us!

    The Spanish empire's tint a head,
An' my auld teethless Bawtie's dead;   10
The toolzie's teugh 'tween Pitt an' Fox,
An' our gudewife's wee birdy cocks;

Elegy on the Year 1788. *Text from Stewart,* 1801 *(pp.* 55–56), *collated with the* Edinburgh Evening Courant, *10 January* 1789, *Stewart,* 1802 *(pp.* 248–9), *and* Cromek, Reliques, 1808 *(p.* 422)
    12 our . . . birdy] 'tween our Maggie's twa wee *Cromek*

The tane is game, a bluidy devil,
But to the *hen-birds* unco civil;
The tither's dour, has nae sic breedin',   15
But better stuff ne'er claw'd a midden!

Ye ministers, come mount the pupit,
An' cry till ye be haerse an' rupit;
For *Eighty-eight* he wish'd you weel,
An' gied you a' baith gear an' meal;   20
E'en mony a plack, an' mony a peck,
Ye ken yoursels, for little feck!

Ye bonny lasses, dight your een,
For some o' you ha'e tint a frien';
In *Eighty-eight*, ye ken, was ta'en   25
What ye'll ne'er ha'e to gi'e again.

Observe the very nowt an' sheep,
How dowff an' dowie now they creep;
Nay, even the yirth itsel' does cry,
For Embro' wells are grutten dry.   30

O *Eighty-nine*, thou's but a bairn,
An' no owre auld, I hope, to learn!
Thou beardless boy, I pray tak' care,
Thou now has got thy Daddy's chair,
Nae hand-cuff'd, mizl'd, haff-shackl'd *Regent*,   35
But, like himsel', a full free agent.
Be sure ye follow out the plan   ⎫
Nae war than he did, honest man!   ⎬
As muckle better as you can.   ⎭
    January 1, 1789.

15 dour . . . breedin'] something dour o' treadin' *Cromek*   28 dowie now]
daviely *Cromek*   35 haff-] hap- *Cromek*

251. Robin shure in hairst

Brisk

Chorus

ROBIN shure in hairst,
I shure wi' him;
Fint a heuk had I,
Yet I stack by him.

Song

I gaed up to Dunse,   5
To warp a wab o' plaiden;
At his daddie's yet,
Wha met me but Robin.
Robin shure &c.

Was na Robin bauld,
Tho' I was a cotter,   10
Play'd me sic a trick
And me the Eller's dochter?
Robin shure &c.

Robin promis'd me
A' my winter vittle;
Fient haet he had but three   15
Goos feathers and a whittle.
Robin shure &c.

Robin shure in hairst. *Text from SMM, 1803 (543;* Written for this Work by Robert
Burns), *collated with a MS owned by Mr. Lester Garland (letter to Ainslie, 6 January
1789). The MS sets the song in four stanzas with a chorus* Fal lal &c.
  1, 13 Robin] O Robin *MS*   3 Fint . . . had I,] Ne'er . . . I had *MS*
4 Yet] Still *MS*   14 winter vittle] winter-victual *MS*   16 a *MS:* om. *SMM*

252. [Come rede me, dame]

To its ain tune—

1

COME rede me, dame, come tell me, dame,
   'My dame come tell me truly,
'What length o' graith, when weel ca'd hame,
   'Will sair a woman duly?'
The carlin clew her wanton tail,   5
   Her wanton tail sae ready—
I learn'd a sang in Annandale,
   Nine inch will please a lady.—

2

But for a koontrie c—nt like mine,
   In sooth, we're nae sae gentle;   10
We'll tak tway thumb-bread to the nine,
   And that's a sonsy p—ntle:
O Leeze me on my Charlie lad,
   I'll ne'er forget my Charlie!
Tway roarin handfu's and a daud,   15
   He nidge't it in fu' rarely.—

3

But weary fa' the laithron doup,
   And may it ne'er be thrivin!
It's no the length that maks me loup,
   But it's the double drivin.—   20
Come nidge me, Tam, come nudge me, Tam,
   Come nidge me o'er the nyvel!
Come lowse and lug your battering ram,
   And thrash him at my gyvel!

Come rede me, dame. Text from the Esty MS (Dewar's transcript), collated with MMC (pp. 32–34). Lines 5–7 are in a holograph fragment in the Watson MSS (Letter 304). Tune in MMC The Quaker's wife
17 laithron] laithern *MMC*   18 be] ken *MMC*   19 maks] gars *MMC*

253. [Caledonia]

Tune—Caledonian Hunt's delight—

THERE was on a time, but old Time was then young,
    That brave Caledonia, the chief of her line,
From some of your northern deities sprung,
    (Who knows not that brave Caledonia's divine)
From Tweed to the Orcades was her domain,   5
    To hunt, or to pasture, or do what she would;
Her heavenly relations there fixed her reign,
    And pledged their godheads to warrant it good.—

A lambkin in peace, but a lion in war,
    The pride of her kindred the Heroine grew;   10
Her grandsire, old Odin, triumphantly swore,
    'Who e'er shall provoke thee th' encounter shall rue!'
With tillage or pasture at times she would sport,
    To feed her fair flocks by her green-rustling corn;
But chiefly the woods were her fav'rite resort,   15
    Her darling amusement the hounds and the horn.—

Long quiet she reigned, till thitherward steers
    A flight of bold eagles from Adria's strand;
Repeated, successive, for many long years,
    They darkened the air and they plunder'd the land.   20
Their pounces were murder, and horror their cry,
    They'd ravag'd and ruin'd a world beside;
She took to her hills and her arrows let fly,
    The daring invaders they fled or they di'd.—

Caledonia. *Text from the Watson MS (1124; letter to Johnson, 23 January 1789),
collated with the Alloway MS (Al) and Currie (iv. 352–4). Title from Currie; tune
only in MSS. In Al ll. 41–48 are written on f. 2ᵛ, though there is ample space on f. 2ʳ;
they are probably a later addition*
    1 on a time] once a day *Currie*   was then] then was *Al Currie*   8 pledged
their] pledg'd her their *Currie*   14 green-rustling] green rustling *Al Currie*
21 horror] terror *Al Currie*   22 ravag'd] conquer'd *Al Currie*

The Camelon Savage disturb'd her repose   25
  With tumult, disquiet, rebellion and strife;
Provok'd beyond bearing, at last she arose,
  And robb'd him at once of his hopes and his life.
The Anglian lion, the terror of France,
  Oft prowling ensanguin'd the Tweed's silver flood;   30
But taught by the bright Caledonian lance,
  He learned to fear in his own native wood.—

The fell Harpy-raven took wing from the North,
  The scourge of the seas and the dread of the shore;
The wild Scandinavian boar issu'd forth,   35
  To wanton in carnage and wallow in gore:
O'er countries and kingdoms their fury prevail'd,
  No arts could appease them, no arms could repel;
But brave Caledonia in vain they assail'd,
  As Largs well can witness, and Loncartie tell.—   40

Thus bold, independant, unconquer'd and free,
  Her bright course of glory for ever shall run;
For brave Caledonia immortal must be,
  I'll prove it from Euclid as clear as the sun:
Rectangle-triangle the figure we'll chuse,   45
  The Upright is Chance, and old Time is the Base;
But brave Caledonia's the Hypothenuse,
  Then, Ergo, she'll match them, and match them always.

254. [At Whigham's Inn, Sanquhar]

ENVY, if thy jaundiced eye,
  Through this window chance to spy,
To thy sorrow thou shalt find,
  All that's generous, all that's kind,
Friendship, virtue, every grace,
  Dwelling in this happy place.

25–32, 33–40 *Transposed in Al, Currie*   25 Camelon Savage] Cameleon-
Savage *Al*

At Whigham's Inn. *Text from the* Burns Chronicle, *1896, p. 93*

255. [To William Stewart]

Brownhill Monday even:
DEAR Sir,

> IN honest Bacon's ingle-neuk,
> Here maun I sit and think;
> Sick o' the warld and warld's fock,
> And sick, d–mn'd sick o' drink!
>
> I see, I see there is nae help,   5
> But still down I maun sink;
> Till some day, *laigh enough*, I yelp,
> 'Wae worth that cursed drink!'
>
> Yestreen, alas! I was sae fu',
> I could but yisk and wink;   10
> And now, this day, sair, sair I rue,
> The weary, weary drink.—
>
> Satan, I fear thy sooty claws,
> I hate thy brunstane stink,
> And ay I curse the luckless cause,   15
> The wicked soup o' drink.—
>
> In vain I would forget my woes
> In idle rhyming clink,
> For past redemption d–mn'd in Prose
> I can do nought but drink.—   20
>
> For you, my trusty, well-try'd friend,
> May Heaven still on you blink;
> And may your life flow to the end,
> Sweet as a dry man's drink!
>
>   ROBT. BURNS.

To William Stewart. *Text from the Cowie MS*
  2 Here maun] *correcting* Dowie *in MS*   14 hate] *correcting* fear *in MS*

256. [Lines written in the Kirk of Lamington]

As cauld a wind as ever blew;
A caulder kirk, and in 't but few;
As cauld a minister's ever spak;
Ye'se a' be het or I come back.

257. Afton Water

Slow and tender

Flow gently, sweet Afton, among thy green braes,
Flow gently, I'll sing thee a song in thy praise;
My Mary's asleep by thy murmuring stream,
Flow gently, sweet Afton, disturb not her dream.

Thou stock dove whose echo resounds thro' the glen,   5
Ye wild whistling blackbirds in yon thorny den,
Thou green crested lapwing thy screaming forbear,
I charge you disturb not my slumbering Fair.

Lines. *Text from Lockhart, 1830 (p. 220), collated with Cunningham (iii. 302)*
4 or] ere *Cunningham*

Afton Water. *Text from SMM, 1792 (386; signed B), collated with the Lochryan MS
(letter to Mrs. Dunlop, 5 February 1789), the Afton Lodge MS (1791), ff. 29ᵛ–30ʳ,
and the transcript in the Hastie MS, f. 173 (not holograph). Title in Afton and Hastie
MSS* Sweet Afton—A Song—

1, 4, 9, 21, 24 sweet] clear *Loch*   2 Flow gently] And grateful *Loch*
6 wild whistling blackbirds . . . thorny] blackbirds that sing . . . wild thorny *Loch*
7 lapwing] Plover *MSS*

How lofty, sweet Afton, thy neighbouring hills,
Far mark'd with the courses of clear, winding rills;   10
There daily I wander as noon rises high,
My flocks and my Mary's sweet Cot in my eye.

How pleasant thy banks and green vallies below,
Where wild in the woodlands the primroses blow;
There oft as mild ev'ning weeps over the lea,   15
The sweet scented birk shades my Mary and me.

Thy chrystal stream, Afton, how lovely it glides,
And winds by the cot where my Mary resides;
How wanton thy waters her snowy feet lave,
As gathering sweet flowerets she stems thy clear wave.   20

Flow gently, sweet Afton, among thy green braes,
Flow gently, sweet River, the theme of my lays;
My Mary's asleep by thy murmuring stream,
Flow gently, sweet Afton, disturb not her dream.

258. Ode to the departed Regency-bill—1789

DAUGHTER of Chaos' doting years,
  Nurse of ten thousand hopes and fears;
Whether thy airy, unsubstantial Shade
(The rites of sepulture now duly paid)
    Spread abroad its hideous form   5
    On the roaring Civil Storm,
    Deafening din and warring rage
    Factions wild with factions wage;
Or underground, deep-sunk, profound,
    Among the demons of the earth,   10
With groans that make the mountains shake,
    Thou mourn thy ill-starred, blighted birth;

Ode to the departed Regency-bill. *Text from the Glenriddell MS (pp. 11–14;
Glen), collated with the Adam MS (draft ending at l. 58), the Lochryan MS (Loch;
letter to Mrs. Dunlop, 3 April 1789), the Don MS (letter to Lady Elizabeth Cunningham, 23 December 1789), and the Star, 17 April 1789 (signed Agricola and dated
Edinburgh, April 7th.). See Commentary. Title in Don* Ode to the memory of the
Regency bill 1789
4 rites *Adam Loch Don*: rights *Glen*

Or in the uncreated Void,
   Where seeds of future-being fight,
With lightened step thou wander wide,   15
   To greet thy Mother—Ancient Night,
And as each jarring, monster mass is past,
Fond recollect what once thou wast:
In manner due, beneath this sacred oak,
Hear, Spirit hear! thy presence I invoke!   20
   By a Monarch's heaven-struck fate!
   By a disunited State!
   By a generous Prince's wrongs!
   By a Senate's strife of tongues!
   By a Premier's sullen pride,   25
   Louring on the changing tide!
   By dread Thurlow's powers to awe,
   Rhetoric, blasphemy and law!
      By the turbulent ocean,
      A Nation's commotion!   30
      By the harlot-caresses
      Of borough-addresses!
      By days few and evil!
      Thy portion, poor devil!
By Power, Wealth, Show! the gods by men adored! 35
By Nameless Poverty! their hell abhorred!
   By all they hope! By all they fear!
   Hear!!! And Appear!!!

Stare not on me, thou ghastly Power;
   Nor grim with chained defiance lour: 40
No Babel-structure would *I* build
   Where, Order exiled from his native sway,
Confusion may the REGENT-sceptre wield,
   While all would rule and none obey:
Go, to the world of Man relate   45
   The story of thy sad, eventful fate;

---

24 strife] *corrected to* war *in Adam*: war *Loch*   *Additional couplet in Adam*
Loch Star:

                By Opposition's eager hand,
                Grasping at an airy wand!

27–28 By . . . law!] *om. Star*   42 native] regal *Adam Loch Star Don*   43 may]
might *Don*   45 relate] relate, *Glen*   46 sad] strange *Adam Loch Don Star*

And call Presumptuous Hope to hear,
And bid him check his blind career;
And tell the sore-prest Sons of Care,
Never, never to despair.—   50

Paint CHARLES's speed on wings of fire,
The object of his fond desire,
Beyond his boldest hopes, at hand:
Paint all the triumph of the Portland Band:
Mark how they lift the joy-exulting voice;   55
And how their numerous Creditors rejoice:
But just as hopes to warm enjoyment rise,
Cry, CONVALESCENCE! and the vision flies.—

Then next pourtray a darkening twilight gloom
    Eclipsing, sad, a gay, rejoicing morn,   60
While proud Ambition to th' untimely tomb
    By gnashing, grim, despairing fiends is borne:
Paint ruin, in the shape of high D——
    Gaping with giddy terror o'er the brow;
In vain he struggles, the Fates behind him press,   65
    And clamorous hell yawns for her prey below:
How fallen That, whose pride late scaled the
        skies!
And This, like Lucifer, no more to rise!
    Again pronounce the powerful word;
See Day, triumphant from the night, restored.—   70

---

47 Presumptuous] *following cancellation* on proud *in Adam*   49 sore-prest]
sore-vex'd *Adam Loch Don Star*   of Care] *correcting* of Grief and Care *in Adam*
51 CHARLES's speed] P–t's keen flight *Star*   on] with *Don*   52 his fond]
his longing, fond *Adam*   53 boldest] *om. Adam*   54 Portland] Tory *Star*
55–56 Mark . . . rejoice:] *om. Don Star*   55 Mark] Hark! *Adam*   they lift]
they seem to lift *Loch*   the joy-exulting] the joy-elated *Adam*: th' elated *Loch*
56 And . . . rejoice:] And who are these that in their joy rejoice? *Adam* (in their
joy *correcting* equality), *Loch*   56 *Additional lines in Adam and Loch:*

> Jews, Gentiles, what a [numerous *Adam*] motely crew!
> Their iron tears of joy their flinty cheeks bedew;
> See, how unfurled their parchment ensigns fly,
> And, PRINCIPAL AND INTEREST! all the cry.—

Adam has now unfurled *in the third line*   58 *Adam ends*   67–68 How . . .
rise!] *om. Don*

Then know this truth, ye Sons of Men!
(Thus end thy moral tale)
Your darkest terrors may be vain,
Your brightest hopes may fail.—

259. On Seeing a Wounded Hare limp by me, which a Fellow had just shot at

INHUMAN man! curse on thy barb'rous art,
And blasted be thy murder-aiming eye;
May never pity soothe thee with a sigh,
Nor ever pleasure glad thy cruel heart!

Go live, poor wanderer of the wood and field,   5
The bitter little that of life remains:
No more the thickening brakes and verdant plains
To thee shall home, or food, or pastime yield.

Seek, mangled wretch, some place of wonted rest,
No more of rest, but now thy dying bed!   10
The sheltering rushes whistling o'er thy head,
The cold earth with thy bloody bosom prest.

71 this truth] these truths *Loch Don Star*

On Seeing a Wounded Hare. *Text from the Edinburgh edition, 1793, collated with the Lochryan MS (Loch; letter to Mrs Dunlop, 21 April 1789), the Dumfries MS (Dum; letter to Cunningham, 4 May 1789), MSS Don and Afton Lodge, the Second Common-place Book (2 CPB; p. 35), and the edition of 1794. Title in Loch* On seeing a fellow wound a hare with a shot; *in Don* On seeing . . . a shot—April—1789; *in 2CPB* On seeing a fellow wound a hare—Spring—89

1 barb'rous] *correcting* cruel *in Dum:* savage *Afton*   4 ever] never *94*
7 and] *correcting* or *in 2CPB:* or *Dum Afton*   8 home, or food] food, or home *Dum Afton*   9 wretch] innocent *Loch Dum Don*   place of wonted rest] haunt of wonted rest *Afton:* wonted form *Loch Dum Don*   10 No . . . but now] That wonted form, alas, *Loch Dum Don*   11 sheltering] *correcting* nether *in Loch*
12 bloody . . . prest] blood-stain'd . . . warm *Loch Dum Don*   12 *Additional stanza in Loch Dum Don (Loch has* little Nurslings):

Perhaps a mother's anguish adds its woe,
The playful pair croud fondly by thy side;
Ah, helpless nurslings! who will now provide
That life a mother only can bestow.

Additional stanza in 2CPB (see Commentary):

Perhaps a mother's anguish adds its ~~throes~~ woe,
The ~~helpless~~ hapless Pair espy thee o'er the plain;
Ah ~~haples~~ helpless nurslings! who will now sustain
Your little lives, or shield you from the foe!

Oft as by winding Nith I, musing, wait
The sober eve, or hail the chearful dawn,
I'll miss thee sporting o'er the dewy lawn,   15
And curse the ruffian's aim, and mourn thy hapless fate.

260. A new Psalm for the Chapel of Kilmarnock, on the thanksgiving-day for his Majesty's recovery—

O, SING a new Song to the L——!
   Make, all and every one,
A joyful noise, ev'n for the king
   His Restoration.—

The sons of Belial in the land   5
   Did set their heads together;
Come, let us sweep them off, said they,
   Like an o'erflowing river.—

They set their heads together, I say,
   They set their heads together: 10
On right, and left, and every hand,
   We saw none to deliver.—

Thou madest strong two chosen Ones,
   To quell the Wicked's pride:
That Young Man, great in Issachar   15
   The burden-bearing Tribe.—

And him, among the Princes chief
   In our Jerusalem,
The Judge that's mighty in thy law,
   The Man that fears thy name.—   20

16 ruffian's aim] *alternative to* ruffian's art *in* 2CPB: ruthless wretch *Loch Dum Don*

A new Psalm. *Text from the Glenriddell MS (pp. 136–8; Glen), collated with the Alloway MS (Al; letter to Mrs. Dunlop, 4 May 1789), the* Morning Star, *14 May 1789, and the Don MS (endorsed in another hand* Enclosed in letter to lady E. Cunningham 23.12.89). *Title in Don* A Piece of new Psalmody said to be composed for, and sung on the late joyful solemnity—the twenty third of April last, in a certain chapel of ease somewhere in the meridian of K–lm–rn–ck.—
Dewar collated a fragment (ll. 9–15) inserted in a copy of 86, with only accidental variants (MS not traced)

Yet they, even they, with all their might,
  Began to faint and fail;
Even as two howling, ravening wolves
  To dogs do turn their tail:—

Th' Ungodly o'er the Just prevail'd,   25
  For so thou hadst appointed,
That thou might'st greater glory give
  Unto thine own Annointed.—

And now thou hast restor'd our State,
  Pity our kirk also,   30
For she by tribulations
  Is now brought very low!—

Consume that High-Place, PATRONAGE,
  From off thine holy hill;
And in thy fury burn the book   35
  Even of that man, MᶜGILL.—

Now hear our Prayer, accept our Song,
  And fight thy Chosen's battle:
We seek but little, L——, from thee,
  Thou kens we get as little.—   40

261. To Mᴦ MᶜMurdo, with a pound of Lundiefoot Snuff—

O COULD I give thee India's wealth
  As I this trifle send!
Because thy joy in both would be—
  To share them with thy Friend.—

But Golden Sands, Alas, ne'er grace   5
  The Heliconian stream:
Then take, what Gold shall never buy—
  An honest Bard's esteem.—

21 might] strength *Al Star Don*   34 thine] thy *Al Star Don*

To Mᴦ McMurdo. *Text from the Huntington Library MS (signed* Robᵗ Burns),
collated with Cunningham (iii. 114; Cun). Title in Cun To John M'Murdo, Esq.
  4 thy] a *Cun*   5 Alas, ne'er] did never *Cun*   7 shall] could *Cun*

262. Sketch. Inscribed to The R⁺ Hon. Ch. J. Fox Esq.—

How Wisdom and Folly meet, mix and unite;
   How Virtue and Vice blend their black and their white;
How Genius, th' illustrious father of fiction,
Confounds rule and law, reconciles contradiction,
I sing; if these mortals, the Critics, should bustle,   5
I care not, not I, let the Critics go whistle!

But now for a Patron, whose name and whose glory
At once may illustrate and honour my story.—

Thou, first of our orators, first of our wits,
Yet whose parts and acquirements seem just lucky hits; 10
With knowledge so vast, and with judgement so strong,
No man, with the half of 'em, e'er could go wrong;
With passions so potent, and fancies so bright,
No man with the half of 'em e'er could go right;
A sorry, poor, misbegot son of the Muses,   15
For using thy name offers fifty excuses.—

Good l—d, what is man! for as simple he looks,
Do but try to develope his hooks and his crooks,
With his depths and his shallows, his good and his evil,
All in all, he's a problem must puzzle the devil.—   20

On his one ruling Passion Sir Pope warmly labours,
That, like th' old Hebrew walking switch, eats up its
   neighbours;
Human nature's his Show-box—your friend, would you
   know him?
Pull the string Ruling Passion, the picture will show him.—

Sketch. *Text from B.M. MS Egerton 1656 (Eg; f. 20), collated with the Alloway MS (Al; letter to Mrs. Dunlop, 4 May 1789) and Currie (ii. 221–3). Al and Currie end at l. 38*

   10 just] mere *Currie*   12 could go] went far *Currie*   14 could go] went quite *Currie*   21 warmly] hugely *Al Currie*   23 Human nature's . . . your] Mankind are . . . a *Al Currie*

What pity in rearing so beauteous a system,   25
One trifling particular, Truth, should have missed him!
For spite of his fine theoretic positions,
Mankind is a science defies definitions.—

Some sort all our qualities each to its tribe,
And think Human-nature they truly describe.   30
Have you found this or t'other? theres more in the wind,
As by one drunken fellow his comrades you'll find.—
But such is the flaw, or the depth of the plan
In the make of that wonderful creature called MAN,
No two virtues whatever relation they claim,   35
Nor even two different shades of the same,
Though like as was ever twin brother to brother,
Possessing the one must imply you've the other.—

But truce with abstraction, and truce with a muse,
Whose rhymes you'll perhaps, Sir, ne'er deign to peruse: 40
Will you leave your justings, your jars and your quarrels,
Contending with Billy for proud-nodding laurels?
(My much-honor'd Patron, believe your poor Poet,
Your courage much more than your prudence you show it;
In vain with Squire Billy for laurels you struggle,   45
He'll have them by fair trade, if not, he will smuggle;
Not cabinets even of kings would conceal 'em,
He'd up the back-stairs and by G— he would steal 'em!
Then feats like Squire Billy's you ne'er can atchieve 'em,
It is not, outdo him, the task is, outthieve him.)—   50

263. [To Peter Stuart]

Dear Peter, dear Peter,
        We poor sons of metre
Are often negleckit, ye ken;
        For instance, your sheet, man,
        (Tho' glad I'm to see 't, man),
I get it no ae day in ten.

R. B.

25 beauteous] *correcting* glorious *in Eg*   29 all our] *corrects* human *in Al*
38 must] shall *Currie*   38 *Al and Currie end*   42 laurels?] laurels *Eg*
48 'em!] 'em *Eg*
To Peter Stuart. *Text from Scott Douglas (ii. 291)*

264. The Kirk of Scotland's Garland—
a new Song

I

ORTHODOX, Orthodox, who believe in John Knox,
  Let me sound an alarm to your conscience;
A heretic blast has been blawn i' the West—
That what is not Sense must be Nonsense, Orthodox,
That what is not Sense must be Nonsense.—   5

2

Doctor Mac*, Doctor Mac, ye should streek on a rack,
  To strike Evildoers with terror;
To join FAITH and SENSE upon any pretence
Was heretic, damnable error, &c.

  * Doctor McGill, Ayr—

The Kirk of Scotland's Garland. *Text from the Don MS (letter to Lady Elizabeth Cunningham, 23 December 1789), collated with the Lochryan MS (Loch; letter to Mrs. Dunlop, 17 July 1789, with the first rough-draft), B.M. MS Egerton 1656, f. 17 (Eg 1; marked* Copy to Fintray, *with a draft of letter to Graham of Fintry, 31 July 1789, on verso) and f. 16 (Eg 2), the Huntington Library MS (HL), Dewar's transcript of the MS sent to Logan (letter of 7 August 1789), the MS at Lady Stair's House, Edinburgh (LSH; a copy sent to? John McMurdo), the Glenriddell MS (Glen; pp. 139–42), a broadside* The Ayrshire Garland. An Excellent New Song. Tune, The Vicar and Moses *(AG; ?1789), and Stewart, 1801 (pp. 20–24). Foot-notes mainly from Glen.*

Title The Kirk's Alarm—A Ballad *Loch* (Alarm *correcting* Lament), *HL Logan LSH*: The Kirk of Scotland's Alarm. A Ballad *Eg 1, 2*: A Ballad—On the heresy of Dr McGill in Ayr— *Glen*: The Kirk's Alarm: A Satire *Stewart*. *Tune* Push about the brisk bowl *Loch Eg 1 HL Logan*: The hounds are all out *Don*: Come rouse brother sportsmen *LSH. See Commentary.*

The sequence is variable: in Loch, stanzas 1–8, 16, 9, 12 only; in Eg 1, stanzas 1–6, 16, 8, 9 only; in Eg 2, stanzas 1–6, 8, 7, 9, 16, 12 only; in HL, stanzas 1–8, 10, 9, 11–12, 13–16, 18; in Logan, stanzas 1–8, 10, 9, 11–13, 15, 14, 16, 18 and post-script 19a; in LSH, stanzas 1–9, 11–15, 10, 16, 18 and postscript 19b; in Glen, stanzas 1–2, 4–7, 10, 9, 11–13, 16, 15, 14, 18; in Stewart, stanzas 1–4, 6–8, 16, 13, 12, 9–11, 14–15, 17, 5, 18; and in AG stanzas 1–8, 16, 13, 12, 9, 11 (cf. Stewart).

  1 Orthodox, Orthodox,] Brother Scots, Brother Scots, *Eg 1*   3 A *Glen*: There's a *other MSS, Stewart*   6 streek *Glen*: stretch *other MSS, Stewart*
7 Evildoers] wicked Writers *Eg 1*   9 Was] *correcting* Is *in Eg 1*: Is *Stewart*

3

Town of Ayr, Town of Ayr, it was rash, I declare,   10
  To meddle wi' mischief a brewing;
Provost John* is still deaf to the Church's relief,
  And Orator Bob† is its ruin, &c.

4

D'rymple mild‡, D'rymple mild, tho' your heart's like a
      child,
  And your life like the new-driven snaw;   15
Yet that winna save ye, auld Satan maun have ye,
  For preaching that three's ane and twa, &c.

5

Calvin's Sons, Calvin's Sons, seize your spiritual guns—
  Ammunition ye never can need;
Your HEARTS are the stuff will be POWDER enough,   20
  And your SCULLS are a storehouse o' LEAD, &c.

6

Rumble John§, Rumble John, mount the steps with a
      groan,
  Cry, the BOOK is with heresy cramm'd;
Then lug out your ladle, deal brimstone like aidle,
  And roar ev'ry note o' the D–MN'D, &c.   25

7

Simper James‖, Simper James, leave the fair Killie dames,
  There's a holier chase in your view:
I'll lay on your head that the PACK ye'll soon lead,
  For PUPPIES like you there's but few, &c.

---

* Provost Ballantine—   † Mr Aiken—   ‡ Dr Dalrymple, Ayr—
§ John Russel, Kilmarnock—   ‖ Jas McKindlay, Kilmck.—

---

10 rash] mad *AG Stewart*   11 wi'] in *AG*   12 Provost John is] Your Rulers
AG   13 Bob is] Scribes are *AG*   14 heart's] *correcting* life's *in Don*
15 life] life's *LSH*   16 auld Satan maun *Glen*: old Satan must *other MSS AG*
18 seize] scour *AG*   19–21 Ammunition . . . LEAD, &c.] *Eg 1 has*
And form your battalions wi' speed;
With zeal battle-powder, be sure, double-load her,
And the bullets, Divinity-lead, Calvin's sons,
And the &c.
21 a storehouse] storehouses *Stewart*   24 lug out] out wi' *Eg 1*

8

Singet Sawnie*, Singet Sawnie, are ye herding the PENNIE,   30
Unconscious what danger awaits?
With a jump, yell and howl, alarm ev'ry soul,
    For Hannibal's just at your gates, &c.

9

Poet Willie†, Poet Willie, gie the Doctor a volley
Wi' your 'liberty's chain' and your wit: 35
O'er Pegasus' side ye ne'er laid a stride,
    Ye only stood by where he sh—, &c.

10

Andrew Gowk‡, Andrew Gowk, ye may slander the BOOK,
And the BOOK nought the waur, let me tell ye:
Ye're rich and look big, but lay by hat and wig—   40
    And ye'll hae a CALF'S-HEAD o' sma' value, &c.

11

Barr Steenie§, Barr Steenie, what mean ye, what mean ye?
If ye'll meddle nae mair wi' the matter,
Ye may hae some pretence, man, to havins and sense, man,—
    Wi' people that ken you nae better, &c.   45

12

Jamie Goose‖, Jamie Goose, ye hae made but toom roose
O' hunting the wicked Lieutenant;
But the Doctor's your mark, for the L—d's holy ark
    He has couper'd and ca'd a wrang pin in, &c.

---

  * A. Moodie, Riccartoun—
  † Willm Peebles in Newton upon Ayr, a Poetaster, who, among many other things, published an Ode on the Centenary of the Revolution in which was this line—'And bound in liberty's endearing chain'—
  ‡ Dr Andrew Mitchel, Monkton—   § Stephen Young, Barr—
  ‖ Ja^s Young in New Cumnock, who had lately been foiled in an ecclesiastic prosecution against a Lieut^t Mitchel—

---

  31 danger awaits] evils await *Stewart*   33 Hannibal's] the foul thief is *Stewart*
gates] gate *Stewart*   37 Ye . . . by] Ye but smelt, man, the place *Stewart*
sh— *Glen: — Don*   39 nought] not *Stewart*   ye] you *HL Logan*
40 Ye're] Tho' ye're *HL LSH*   but] yet *HL LSH*   44 man, . . . man,] *om.*
Stewart   45 that] wha' *Stewart*   46 Jamie . . . Jamie] Billie . . . Billie *Eg 2*
but] a *AG*   47 O'] In *Loch Eg 2 AG Stewart*

13

Davie Rant*, Davie Rant, wi' a face like a saunt,   50
  And a heart that wad poison a hog;
Raise an impudent roar, like a breaker lee-shore,
  Or the KIRK will be tint in a bog, &c.

14

Cessnock-side†, Cessnock-side, wi' your turkey-cock pride,
  O' manhood but sma' is your share;   55
Ye've the figure, it's true, even your faes maun allow,
  And your friends dare na say ye hae mair, &c.

15

Muirland Jock‡, Muirland Jock, whom the L—d made a
    rock
  To crush Common sense for her sins;
If ill-manners were Wit, there's no mortal so fit   60
  To confound the poor Doctor at ance, &c.

16

Daddie Auld§, Daddie Auld, there's a tod i' the fauld,
  A tod meikle waur than the CLERK:

* Dav.ᵈ Grant, Ochiltree—   † George Smith, Galston—
‡ John Shepherd, Muirkirk—
§ Will.ᵐ Auld, Mauchlin; for the Clerk, See, Holy Willie's prayer—

50–53 Davie . . . bog, &c. *Glen. Other MSS and Stewart have* (*text from HL*)*:*
          Davie Bluster, Davie Bluster, for a Saunt if ye muster,
            It's a sign they're no nice o' RECRUITS:
          Yet to WORTH let's be just, Royal blood ye might boast,
            If the Ass were the king o' the BRUTES, &c.
AG has:
          Pauky Clark to George Gordon—gi'e the Doctor a Cord–on,
            And to grape for witch marks—gi'e it o'er;
          If ye pass for a Saint, it's a sign, we maun grant,
            That there's few gentlemen i' the cor'.
54 Cessnock-side, Cessnock-side *HL Logan LSH Glen*: Irwin-side, Irwin-side *Don
Stewart*   turkey–cock] *correcting* Bubly-Jock *in HL*   57 dare na . . . hae]
daur na . . . hae *Glen*: they dare grant you nae *Stewart*   58 Jock . . . Jock . . .
made a rock] George . . . George . . . made a scourge *HL Logan*: Jock . . . Jock
. . . gave a stock *LSH*: Jock . . . Jock, when the L—d makes a rock *Stewart*
59 To . . . sins] Would set up a tinkler in brass *LSH*   crush] claw *HL Logan*
61 To . . . ance, &c.] To prove the poor Doctor an ass, &c. *LSH*   63 *Note in
Loch* G. Hamilton, Writer

Tho' ye do little skaith ye'll be in at the death,
    For if ye canna bite ye can bark, &c.   65

17

Holy Will*, Holy Will, there was wit i' your skull,
    When ye pilfer'd the alms o' the poor;
The timmer is scant, when ye're ta'en for a saint,
    Wha should swing in a rape for an hour, &c.

18

Poet Burns, Poet Burns, wi' your priest-skelping turns,   70
    Why desert ye your auld native shire?
Tho' your Muse is a gipsey, yet were she even tipsey,
    She could ca' us nae waur than we are, Poet Burns,
    She could ca' us nae waur than we are.—

[19*a*]

[Afton's Laird, Afton's Laird, when your pen can be spar'd,
    A copy o' this I bequeath,
On the same sicker score as I mention'd before,
    To that trusty auld Worthy, Clackleith, Afton's Laird,
    To that trusty auld Worthy, Clackleith.]

[19*b*]

[Factor John, Factor John, whom the Lord made alone,
    And ne'er made another thy peer,
Thy poor servant, the Bard, in respectful regard,
    Presents thee this token sincere, Factor John,
    Presents thee this token sincere.]

   * An E[lder] in M[auchlin]e—

---

64 Tho' . . . death,] Douglas, Heron, & Co. has e'en laid [brought *Eg 1*] you
fu' low, *Eg 1 Eg 2 Loch* (*corrected in HL to* Tho' ye downa do skaith, ye'll be in at
the death,): Ye ance swat for whiskie—ye're now no sae friskie; *AG* ye do little] ye
downa do *Logan*: ye can do little *Stewart*   65 For if] But tho' *Eg 1 Eg 2 Loch
AG*: And if *HL* (*correcting* But tho'): And gif *Stewart*   canna] can't *AG*   can]
may *Eg 1 Eg 2 Loch AG* (*corrected in HL to* can)   66–69 Holy . . . hour, &c.]
in Stewart only   71 ye] you *Logan*   72 yet were she even] e'en tho' she
were *Stewart*   Stanza 19a] *Postscript in Logan only*   Stanza 19b] *Postscript in
LSH only*

265. To M͟r Graham of Fintry, On being appointed to my Excise Division—

I CALL no goddess to inspire my strains,
A fabled Muse may suit a Bard that feigns:
'Friend of my life!' my ardent spirit burns,
And all the tribute of my heart returns,
For boons accorded, goodness ever new,   5
The Gift still dearer, as the Giver You.—

Thou Orb of Day! Thou Other Paler Light!
And all ye many-sparkling Stars of Night!
If aught that Giver from my mind efface;
If I that Giver's bounty e'er disgrace;   10
Then roll, to me, along your wandering spheres,
Only to number out A VILLAIN'S YEARS!

I lay my hand upon my swelling breast,
And grateful would—but cannot speak the rest.—

266. A Grace before dinner, Extempore

O, THOU, who kindly dost provide
For every creature's want!
We bless thee, God of nature wide,
For all thy goodness lent:
And, if it please thee heavenly guide,   5
May never worse be sent;
But whether granted or denied,
Lord bless us with content!
Amen!!!

To M͟r Graham of Fintry. *Text from the* Second Commonplace Book (p. 33), *collated with the* Lochryan MS (*letter to Mrs. Dunlop, 19 August 1789*), *the* Glenriddell MS (*p. 143*), *and* Currie (*iv. 400*). *Title in Glenriddell and Currie* To . . . Fintry on receiving a favor—
11 Then] Thou *Lochryan*   13–14 I . . . rest.] *om.* Glenriddell, Currie

A Grace before dinner. *Text from the* Glenriddell MS (*p. 159*), *collated with the* Edinburgh Evening Courant, *27 August 1789,* Currie (*iv. 402*), *and* Stewart, 1802 (*p. 256*)   4 all] this *Stewart*

267. Grace after Meat

O Thou, in whom we live and move,
　Who mad'st the sea and shore,
Thy goodness constantly we prove,
　And grateful would adore.

And if it please thee, Pow'r above,
　Still grant us with such store;
The *Friend* we *trust*; the *Fair* we *love*;
　And we desire no more.

268. Willie brew'd a peck o' maut

Chorus

Grace after Meat. *Text from Stewart, 1802 (p. 256), collated with the* Edinburgh
Evening Courant, *27 August 1789*

Willie brew'd a peck o' maut. *Text from SMM, 1790 (291; Written for this Work
by Robert Burns), collated with SC, 1805 (179). Title in SC* The happy Topers

O WILLIE brew'd a peck o' maut,
   And Rob and Allan cam to see;
Three blyther hearts, that lee lang night,
   Ye wad na found in Christendie.

                    Chorus
We are na fou, we're nae that fou,   5
   But just a drappie in our e'e;
The cock may craw, the day may daw,
   And ay we'll taste the barley bree.

Here are we met, three merry boys,
   Three merry boys I trow are we;   10
And mony a night we've merry been,
   And mony mae we hope to be!
      Cho:̱ We are na fou, &c.

It is the moon, I ken her horn,
   That's blinkin in the lift sae hie;
She shines sae bright to wyle us hame,   15
   But by my sooth she'll wait a wee!
      Cho:̱ We are na fou, &c.

Wha first shall rise to gang awa,
   A cuckold, coward loun is he!
Wha first beside his chair shall fa',
   He is the king amang us three!   20
      Cho:̱ We are na fou, &c.

269. The Five Carlins—A Ballad—Tune, Chevy chase

Written during the contested Election between Sir James Johnston and Capt. Miller for the Dumfries district of Boroughs.—

T HERE was five Carlins in the South,
    They fell upon a scheme,
To send a lad to London town
    To bring them tidings hame.—

Not only bring them tidings hame,   5
    But do their errands there;
And aiblins gowd and honor baith
    Might be that laddie's share.—

There was Maggy by the banks o' Nith*,
    A dame wi' pride enough;   10
And Marjory o' the mony lochs†,
    A Carlin auld and teugh:

And blinkin Bess of Annandale‡
    That dwelt on Solway-side;
And Brandy Jean that took her gill§   15
    In Galloway sae wide:

  * Dumfries   † Lochmaben   ‡ Annan   § Kircudbright

The Five Carlins. *Text from the Afton Lodge MS (ff. 20ʳ–22ᵛ), collated with MSS Lochryan (Loch; letter to Mrs. Dunlop, 2 October 1789), Cowie (letter to David Blair, December 1789) and Fintry (letter to Graham, 9 December 1789), B.M. MS Egerton 1656 (ff. 28–29; Eg), the Glenriddell MS (p. 89; Glen), Stewart, 1802, and Lockhart. Sequence in Loch, Eg: ll. 1–56, 81–88, 57–64, 73–80, 65–72 and 89–92. Sub-title in Afton Lodge MS only*
   1 was] were *Stewart*   4, 5 them] us *Stewart*   5 Not] Nor *Loch*
6 their] our *Stewart*   11 mony lochs] money Loch *Stewart*   14 dwelt]
dwells *Stewart*   on] near *Loch Cowie Fintry Eg Stewart*   15 Brandy] Whisky
Loch Cowie Fintry Eg Stewart

And black Jöan frae Crighton-peel*
    O' gipsey kith and kin:
Five wighter Carlins were na found
    The South Coontrie within.—   20

To send a lad to London town,
    They met upon a day;
And mony a knight and mony a laird
    That errand fain wad gae.—

O mony a knight and mony a laird   25
    That errand fain wad gae;
But nae ane could their fancy please,
    O ne'er a ane but tway.—

The first ane was a belted knight,
    Bred of a Border band,   30
And he wad gae to London town,
    Might nae man him withstand.—

And he wad do their errands weel,
    And meikle he wad say;
And ilka ane at London Court   35
    Wad bid to him, Gude-day!

The niest came in a Sodger-boy
    And spak wi' modest grace,
And he wad gang to London town,
    If sae their pleasure was.—   40

He wad na hecht them courtly gifts,
    Nor meikle speech pretend;
But he wad hecht an honest heart
    Wad ne'er desert his friend.—

* Sanquhar (Crighton old Castle, or, Peel—

17 And black Jöan] And auld black Joan *Stewart*   19 wighter] wightier
Stewart   24, 26 That] This *Loch Eg Stewart* (26)   30–32 band ... withstand]
clan ... withstan' *Lockhart*   35 ilka ... Court] ilka ane about the court *Loch Eg*
37 The] Then *Stewart*   Sodger-boy] sodger youth *Loch Cowie Fintry Eg Stewart*
came in] ane was *Glen*   38 And] *corrected to* Wha *in Glen*   39 gang] gae
Loch Cowie Fintry Eg Glen Stewart   41 gifts] gift *Stewart*

Now wham to chuse, and wham refuse,   45
  At strife thir Carlins fell;
For some had Gentle Folk to please,
  And some wad please themsel.—

Then up spak mim-mou'd Meg o' Nith,
  And she spak up wi' pride,   50
And she wad send the Sodger-lad
  Whatever might betide.—

For the Auld Gudeman o' London Court,
  She didna care a pin;
But she wad send the Sodger-lad,   55
  To greet his eldest son.—

Then started Bess of Annandale,
  A deadly aith she's taen,
That she wad vote the Border-knight,
  Tho' she should vote her lane.—   60

'For far-off fowls hae feathers fair,
  'And fools o' change are fain;
'But I hae try'd this Border-knight,
  'I'll try him yet again.'—

Says black Jöan frae Crighton-peel,   65
  A Carlin stoor and grim;
'The Auld Gudeman, or the Young Gudeman,
  'For me may sink or swim.

46 At . . . thir] To . . . thae *Stewart*   47 Folk] folks *Loch Cowie Fintry Eg*
49 up] out *Loch Cowie Fintry Eg* (*correcting* up) *Glen Stewart*   50 up] out
Fintry Glen Stewart   51, 55 lad] youth *Loch Eg Stewart:* boy *Glen*   54 didna]
did not *Stewart*   57 started] up sprang *Loch Cowie Fintry Eg* (*correcting* blinkin) *Glen Stewart*   58–60 A . . . lane.] *Loch, Eg have* (border knight *in Eg*)

         And swore a deadly aith,
      Says, 'I will send the belted knight
        'Spite o' you carlins baith.

61 For] Your *Fintry*   63 this] the *Stewart*   65 frae] o' *Eg*   66 stoor]
stout *Stewart*   67 the] om. *Stewart*

'For fools will prate o' Right, and Wrang,
   'While knaves laugh them to scorn;   70
'But the Sodger's friends hae blawn the best,
   'So he shall bear the horn.'—

Then Brandy Jean spak o'er her drink,
   'Ye weel ken, kimmers a',
'The Auld Gudeman o' London Court,   75
   'His back's been at the wa':

'And mony a friend that kiss'd his caup,
   'Is now a fremit wight;
'But it's ne'er be sae wi' Brandy Jean,
   'We'll send the Border-knight.'—   80

Then slaw rase Marjory o' the lochs,
   And wrinkled was her brow;
Her ancient weed was russet-grey,
   Her auld Scots heart was true.—

'There's some Great Folk set light by me,   85
   'I set as light by them;
'But I will send to London town
   'Whom I lo'e best at hame.'—

So how this weighty plea may end,
   Nae mortal wight can tell: 90
God grant the king, and ilka man,
   May look weel to themsel.—

69 will] may *Stewart*   70 them to scorn] in their sleeve *Loch Eg*   71–72
But . . . horn.] *Loch, Eg have*

            But wha blaws best the horn shall win,
              I'll spier nae courtier's leave.

73, 79 Brandy] Whisky *Loch Cowie Fintry Eg Stewart*   79 be] *om. Stewart*
sae wi'] said o' *edd.*   84 heart] blude *Lockhart*   85 There's . . . Folk] The
London court *Loch Eg*   87 But . . . to London town] And . . . the sodger
lad *Eg*: The Sodger shall to London gang *Loch*   88 Whom] Wha *Stewart*
Whom . . . hame.] To shaw that Court the same. *Loch Eg*   89 So] Then
Glen   weighty plea] sturt and strife *Loch*   may] will *Stewart*   90 Nae
mortal wight] There's naebodie *Loch Eg*   92 themsel] himsel *Cowie*

270. The Laddies by the Banks o' Nith

Tune, Up and waur them a', Willie

THE Laddies by the banks o' Nith
  Wad trust his Grace wi' a', Jamie;
But he'll sair them, as he sair'd the King—
  Turn tail and rin awa, Jamie.

  Up and waur them a', Jamie,   5
    Up and waur them a';
  The Johnstones hae the guidin o't,
    Ye turncoat Whigs awa!

The day he stude his country's friend,
  Or gied her faes a claw, Jamie,   10
Or frae puir man a blessin wan,
  That day the Duke ne'er saw, Jamie.
    Up and waur them, &c.

But wha is he, his country's boast?
  Like him there is na twa, Jamie;
There's no a callant tents the kye,   15
  But kens o' Westerha', Jamie.
    Up and waur them, &c.

The Laddies by the Banks o' Nith. *Text from Scott Douglas (ii. 281). First published
in John Goldie,* The Spirit of British Song (1826), *ii. 53. H–H. print another version
from the Rosebery collection (holograph; ii. 398):*

As I cam doon the banks o' Nith
  And by Glenriddell's ha', man,
There I heard a piper play
  Turn-coat Whigs awa, man.

Drumlanrig's towers hae tint the powers
  That kept the lands in awe, man:
The eagle's dead, and in his stead
  We've gotten a hoodie-craw, man.

The turn-coat Duke his King forsook,
  When his back was at the wa', man:
The rattan ran wi' a' his clan
  For fear the house should fa', man.

The lads about the banks o' Nith,
  They trust his Grace for a', man:
But he'll sair them as he sair't his King,
  Turn tail and rin awa, man.

To end the wark, here's Whistlebirk,
Lang may his whistle blaw, Jamie;
And Maxwell true, o' sterling blue;
And we'll be Johnstones a', Jamie.   20
Up and waur them, &c.

271. To Miss C*********, a very young Lady

Written on the blank leaf of a Book, presented to her by the Author.

BEAUTEOUS rose-bud, young and gay,
Blooming on thy early May,
Never may'st thou, lovely Flower,
Chilly shrink in sleety shower!
Never Boreas' hoary path,   5
Never Eurus' pois'nous breath,
Never baleful stellar lights,
Taint thee with untimely blights!
Never, never reptile thief
Riot on thy virgin leaf!   10
Nor even Sol too fiercely view
Thy bosom blushing still with dew!

Mayst thou long, sweet crimson gem,
Richly deck thy native stem;
Till some evening, sober, calm,   15
Dropping dews, and breathing balm,
While all around the woodland rings,
And every bird thy requiem sings;

To Miss C*********. *Text from the Edinburgh edition, 1793, collated with the Huntington Library MS (HL), MSS Adam, Alloway (Al), and Glenriddell (pp. 4–5; Glen), and the edition of 1794. A holograph version accompanying Burns's letter to Dr. Moore (28 February 1791; Alloway) agrees with the other MSS in line 2, transposes ll. 5–6, and lacks ll. 19–22. It is headed* Written on the blank leaf of a book, which I presented to a very young lady, whom I had formerly characterised under the denomination of The Rose-bud. *Title in Adam* Verses written on . . . presented to a very young lady; *in Glen* To Miss Jeany Cruikshank, a very young lady, only child of my much-esteemed friend, Mͬ Cruikshank of the High-School, Edinͬ— Written on the blank leaf of a book presented to her by the Author.—*Title in HL as in Glen, omitting* my much-esteemed friend
  2 thy . . . May] the . . . day HL Adam Al Glen   13 *No paragraph in Adam*

Thou, amid the dirgeful sound,
Shed thy dying honours round,　　　　20
And resign to Parent Earth
The loveliest form she e'er gave birth.

272. The Whistle. A Ballad

As the authentic *Prose* history of the WHISTLE is curious, I
shall here give it.—In the train of Anne of Denmark, when
she came to Scotland with our James the Sixth, there came
over also a Danish gentleman of gigantic stature and great
prowess, and a matchless champion of Bacchus. He had a　　5
little ebony Whistle, which, at the commencement of the
orgies, he laid on the table; and whoever was last able to

The Whistle. *Text from the Edinburgh edition, 1793, collated with the Huntington
Library MS (HL), MSS Watson (1126), Fintry, Alloway (Al), Glenriddell (Glen;
pp. 131–4), Dumfries (Dum); the London Star, 2 November 1791, the Edinburgh
Evening Courant, 5 November 1791, the Edinburgh Herald, 6 November 1791, the
Edinburgh Magazine, November 1791; SMM, 1792 (314); an undated print (see
Commentary), and the edition of 1794*

Prose note at the end of HL: The Prose story of the Whistle is this.—In the train of
James the sixth of Scotland's Queen, who was a princess of the House of Denmark,
there came over a Danish nobleman famous for his exploits at the Bottle.—He had
a little ebony Call or Whistle which he laid on the table, and whoever was last able
to blow the Whistle for sheer intoxication was acknowledged victor.—He challenged
the Bacchanalians of the Scotish Court, producing Vouchers of his victories at the
Courts of Copenhagen, Stockholm, Warsaw and Moscow; and threw down his
Whistle, his gage of defiance. When every other Scotish gentleman was routed,
Robert Lowrie Esq: of Maxwelton, ancestor to the present Sir Robert Lowrie, after
three days and nights hard contest, compleatly vanquished the Dane—
　　　　'And blew on the Whistle his requiem shrill—'
The Whistle was afterwards lost to a Walter Riddel of Glenriddel by the then laird
of Maxwelton, and continued in the House of Glenriddel untill it was lost as related
in the Ballad.—

Prose note at the end of Fintry: The Prose history of the Whistle is this.—In the train
of James the sixth's queen, there came over a Danish Nobleman famous for his feats
at the bottle.—He used to lay a little ebony call, or whistle, on the table, and the
man that was last able to blow the whistle for sheer intoxication, carried it off as a
trophy of victory.—He produced vouchers of his exploits, never conquered, at the
courts of Copenhagen, Stockholm, Moscow and Warsaw; and challenged the Scots
Bacchanalians to the field.—After routing every other Scotsman that opposed him,
he was at last completely vanquished, after three days and nights hard contest, by
Robṭ Lowrie of Maxwelton, ancestor to the present Sir Robert Lowrie of Maxwelton,
—A descendant of the great Robert, lost the Whistle afterwards to a son-in-law of
his own, a Walter Riddel of Glenriddel, ancestor to the present Robert Riddel Esqʳ
of Glenriddel; who again lost it, as related in the ballad, to Alexʳ Ferguson Esqʳ of
Craigdaroch.—

blow it, every body else being disabled by the potency of the
bottle, was to carry off the Whistle as a trophy of victory.——
The Dane produced credentials of his victories, without   10
a single defeat, at the courts of Copenhagen, Stockholm,
Moscow, Warsaw, and several of the petty courts in Ger-
many; and challenged the Scots Bacchanalians to the alternative of trying his prowess, or else of acknowledging their
inferiority.——After many overthrows on the part of the   15
Scots, the Dane was encountered by Sir Robert Lowrie of
Maxwelton, ancestor to the present worthy baronet of that
name; who, after three days and three nights' hard contest,
left the Scandinavian under the table, 'And blew on the
Whistle his requiem shrill.'   20

Sir Walter, son to Sir Robert before mentioned, afterwards lost
the Whistle to Walter Riddel of Glenriddel, who had
married a sister of Sir Walter's.——On Friday, the 16th
October 1789, at Friars-Carse, the Whistle was once more
contended for, as related in the Ballad, by the present Sir   25
Robert Lowrie of Maxwelton; Robert Riddel, Esq. of
Glenriddel, lineal descendant and representative of Walter
Riddel, who won the Whistle, and in whose family it had continued; and Alexander Ferguson, Esq. of Craigdarroch, likewise descended of the great Sir Robert, which last gentleman   30
carried off the hard-won honours of the field.

Slowish

Fal de   dal lal lal lay   and

long &c.

24 1789] 1790 93 94

I SING of a Whistle, a Whistle of worth,
    I sing of a Whistle, the pride of the North,
Was brought to the court of our good Scottish king,
And long with this Whistle all Scotland shall ring.

Old Loda*, still rueing the arm of Fingal,   5
The god of the bottle sends down from his hall—
'This Whistle's your challenge, to Scotland get o'er,
'And drink them to hell, Sir! or ne'er see me more!'

Old poets have sung, and old chronicles tell,
What champions ventured, what champions fell;   10
The son of great Loda was conqueror still,
And blew on the Whistle their requiem shrill.

Till Robert, the lord of the Cairn and the Scaur,
Unmatched at the bottle, unconquered in war,
He drank his poor god-ship as deep as the sea,   15
No tide of the Baltic e'er drunker than he.

Thus Robert, victorious, the trophy has gained,
Which now in his house has for ages remained;
Till three noble chieftains, and all of his blood,
The jovial contest again have renewed.   20

Three joyous good fellows with hearts clear of flaw;
Craigdarroch so famous for wit, worth, and law;
And trusty Glenriddel, so skilled in old coins;
And gallant Sir Robert, deep-read in old wines.

* See Ossian's Caric-thura.

---

3 Was] Which was *print*   4 *SMM adds chorus* Fal de dal lal lal lay *followed
by last line of the stanza*   5 Old . . . Fingal] *correcting* Old Loda of Tren-
mor's great grandson still sore *in Watson*   7-8 'This . . . more!'] *Watson has*
        'This Whistle's your challenge—blow till their last breath,
        'And since we can't fight 'em, let's drink 'em to death.'
9-10 *transposed in Watson*   11 son] *correcting* blood *in Watson*   13 *cancelled false start* And the Whistle still sounded *in Watson*   13, 17 Robert]
Walter *Watson*   18 Which] That *Watson*   20 The . . . have] Have lately
the jovial contest *Watson*   20 *Watson ends*   23 skilled] vers'd *HL Fintry
Al Glen*

Craigdarroch began with a tongue smooth as oil,   25
Desiring Glenriddel to yield up the spoil;
Or else he would muster the heads of the clan,
And once more, in claret, try which was the man.

'By the gods of the ancients!' Glenriddel replies,
'Before I surrender so glorious a prize,   30
'I'll conjure the ghost of the great Rorie More*,
'And bumper his horn with him twenty times o'er.'

Sir Robert, a soldier, no speech would pretend,
But he ne'er turned his back on his foe—or his friend,
Said, toss down the Whistle, the prize of the field,   35
And knee-deep in claret he'd die or he'd yield.

To the board of Glenriddel our heroes repair,
So noted for drowning of sorrow and care;
But for wine and for welcome not more known to fame,
Than the sense, wit, and taste of a sweet lovely dame.   40

A bard was selected to witness the fray,
And tell future ages the feats of the day;
A bard who detested all sadness and spleen,
And wished that Parnassus a vineyard had been.

The dinner being over, the claret they ply,   45
And every new cork is a new spring of joy;
In the bands of old friendship and kindred so set,
And the bands grew the tighter the more they were wet.

Gay Pleasure ran riot as bumpers ran o'er;
Bright Phoebus ne'er witnessed so joyous a corps,   50
And vowed that to leave them he was quite forlorn,
Till Cynthia hinted he'd see them next morn.

* See Johnson's tour to the Hebrides.

---

32 o'er] more *print*   33 would] could *print*   35 Whistle, the prize]
Whistle prize *SMM*   46 is] *correcting* was *in HL*: was *Glen*   47 so] well
print   49 as] till *print*   50 corps] core *94*   52 see] find *Fintry Al Glen
HL print*

Six bottles a-piece had well wore out the night,
When gallant Sir Robert, to finish the fight,
Turned o'er in one bumper a bottle of red,   55
And swore 'twas the way that their ancestor did.

Then worthy Glenriddel, so cautious and sage,
No longer the warfare, ungodly, would wage;
A high ruling elder to wallow in wine!
He left the foul business to folks less divine.   60

The gallant Sir Robert fought hard to the end;
But who can with Fate and Quart Bumpers contend?
Though Fate said, a hero should perish in light;
So uprose bright Phoebus—and down fell the knight.

Next uprose our Bard, like a prophet in drink:—   65
'Craigdarroch, thou'lt soar when creation shall sink!
'But if thou would flourish immortal in rhyme,
'Come—one bottle more—and have at the sublime!

'Thy line, that have struggled for freedom with Bruce,
'Shall heroes and patriots ever produce: 70
'So thine be the laurel, and mine be the bay;
'The field thou hast won, by yon bright god of day!'

272A. [Answer to an Invitation]

THE King's most humble servant, I
    Can scarcely spare a minute;
But I'll be wi' you by an' bye,
    Or else the deil's be in it.

55 in] at *print*   56 ancestor] ancestors *print*   62 can] *correcting* 'gainst
in Dum   63 should] shall *print*   64 down fell] downfell *Fintry Al*   65 our]
the *Dum print*   67 would] wouldst *Fintry Al Glen HL Dum print*   69 have]
has *print*   71 laurel] Whistle *print*   72 *additional stanza in Al, presenting
the poem to* Mr Cairns, Junr, *of Torr, Dumfries:*

> But one sorry quill, and that worn to the core;
>   No Paper, but such as I shew it:
> But such as it is, will the good laird of TORE
>   Accept, & excuse the poor POET.—

Answer. *Text from Duncan's edition, 1801 (p. 307), collated with Chambers–Wallace,
iii. 105*

1 most humble servant,] poor blackguard slave am *Ch–W.*   2 Can scarcely]
And scarce dow *Ch–W.*   4 deil's be] devil's *Ch–W.*

273A. [From Dr. Blacklock]

Edinburgh, 24th August, 1789.

[D]EAR Burns, thou brother of my heart,
Both for thy virtues and thy art;
If art it may be call'd in thee,
Which Nature's bounty large and free,
With pleasure on thy breast diffuses,
And warms thy soul with all the Muses.
Whether to laugh with easy grace,
Thy numbers move the sage's face,
Or bid the softer passions rise,
And ruthless souls with grief surprise,
'Tis Nature's voice distinctly felt,
Thro' thee her organ, thus to melt.

Most anxiously I wish to know,
With thee of late how matters go;
How keeps thy much lov'd Jean her health?
What promises thy farm of wealth?
Whether the Muse persists to smile,
And all thy anxious cares beguile?
Whether bright fancy keeps alive?
And how thy darling infants thrive?

For me with grief and sickness spent,
Since I my journey homeward bent,
Spirits depress'd no more I mourn,
But vigour, life and health return.
No more to gloomy thoughts a prey,
I sleep all night, and live all day;
By turns my book and friend[s] enjoy,
And thus my circling hours employ;
Happy while yet these hours remain,
If Burns could join the cheerful train,
With wonted zeal, sincere and fervent,
Salute once more his humble servant,
                THO. BLACKLOCK.]

From Dr. Blacklock. *Text from Currie, ii.* 257-8

273B. [To Dr. Blacklock]

My Rev^d and dear Friend

Wow, but your letter made me vauntie!
    And are ye hale, and weel, and cantie?
I kend it still your wee bit jauntie
      Wad bring ye to:
Lord send you ay as weel's I want ye,   5
      And then ye'll do.—

The *Ill-thief* blaw the *Heron* south!
And never drink be near his drouth!
He tald mysel, by word o' mouth,
      He'd tak my letter;   10
I lippen'd to the chiel in trouth,
      And bade nae better.—

But aiblins honest Master Heron
Had at the time some dainty *Fair One*,
To ware his theologic care on,   15
      And holy study:
And tired o' *Sauls* to waste his lear on,
      E'en tried the *Body*.—

But what d'ye think, my trusty Fier,
I'm turn'd a Gauger—Peace be here!   20
Parnassian *Quines* I fear, I fear,
      Ye'll now disdain me,
And then my fifty pounds a year
      Will little gain me.—

Ye glaiket, gleesome, dainty Damies,   25
Wha by Castalia's wimplin streamies
Lowp, sing, and lave your pretty limbies,
      Ye ken, Ye ken,
That strang Necessity supreme is
      'Mang sons o' Men.—   30

To Dr. Blacklock. *Text from the Alloway MS, collated with Currie* (ii. 259–62)
  21 *Quines*] queens *Currie*

I hae a wife and twa wee laddies,
They maun hae brose and brats o' duddies;
Ye ken yoursels my heart right proud is,
   I need na vaunt;
But I'll sned boosoms and thraw saugh-woodies 35
  Before they want.—

Lord help me thro' this warld o' care!
I'm weary sick o't late and air!
Not but I hae a richer share
   Than mony ithers;   40
But why should ae man better fare,
  And a' Men brithers!

Come, *Firm Resolve* take thou the van,
Thou stalk o' carl-hemp in man!
And let us mind, faint heart ne'er wan   45
   A lady fair:
Wha does the utmost that he can,
  Will whyles do mair.—

But to conclude my silly rhyme,
(I'm scant o' verse and scant o' time,) 50
To make a happy fireside clime
   To weans and wife,
That's the true *Pathos* and *Sublime*
  Of Human life.—

My Compliments to Sister Beckie;   55
And eke the same to honest Lucky,
I wat she is a dainty Chuckie
   As e'er tread clay!
And gratefully my gude auld Cockie
  I'm yours for ay.—   60
   Robt Burns

Ellisland
21st Oct. 1789

35 boosoms and] besoms— *Currie*

274. A Song—

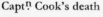

I

Tʜᴏᴜ lingering Star with lessening ray
  That lovest to greet the early morn,
Again thou usherest in the day
  My Mary from my Soul was torn—
O Mary! dear, departed Shade!   5
  Where is thy place of blissful rest?
Seest thou thy Lover lowly laid?
  Hearest thou the groans that rend his breast?

A Song. *Text from the Huntington Library MS, collated with the Lochryan MS (letter to Mrs. Dunlop, 8 November 1789), SMM, 1790 (279; Written for this Work by R. Burns), and SC, 1803 (114). Tune in SMM* Captⁿ Cook's death &c.; *in SC entitled* Highland Mary. *The Aldine editor (1839) records a MS with these variants:* 6, 30 blissful] heavenly *MS*   27 stronger] deeper *MS. The quotation (ll. 29–32) in Burns's letter to Mrs. Dunlop, 13 December 1789, has* heavenly *in l. 30*

2

That sacred hour can I forget,
    Can I forget the hallowed grove,   10
Where by the winding Ayr we met,
    To live one day of Parting Love?
Eternity can not efface
    Those records dear of transports past;
Thy image at our last embrace,   15
    Ah, little thought we 'twas our last!

3

Ayr gurgling kissed his pebbled shore,
    O'erhung with wild-woods, thick'ning, green;
The fragrant birch, and hawthorn hoar,
    Twined, am'rous, round the raptured scene: 20
The flowers sprang wanton to be prest,
    The birds sang love on ev'ry spray;
Till too, too soon the glowing west
    Proclaimed the speed of winged day.—

4

Still o'er these scenes my mem'ry wakes,   25
    And fondly broods with miser-care;
Time but th' impression stronger makes,
    As streams their channels deeper wear:
My Mary, dear, departed Shade!
    Where is thy place of blissful rest!   30
Seest thou thy Lover lowly laid!
    Hearest thou the groans that rend his breast!

18 wild-woods, thick'ning,] wild-woods thickening *SMM SC*   green] *om. SC*

275. On the Late Captain Grose's Peregrinations thro' Scotland, collecting the Antiquities of that Kingdom

Hear, Land o' Cakes, and brither Scots,
　Frae Maidenkirk to Johny Groats!—
If there's a hole in a' your coats,
　　I rede you tent it:
A chield's amang you, taking notes,　　　　　　5
　　And, faith, he'll prent it.

If in your bounds ye chance to light
Upon a fine, fat, fodgel wight,
O' stature short, but genius bright,
　　That's he, mark weel—　　　　　　10
And wow! he has an unco slight
　　O' cauk and keel.

By some auld, houlet-haunted, biggin*,
Or kirk deserted by its riggin,
It's ten to ane ye'll find him snug in　　　　15
　　Some eldritch part,
Wi' deils, they say, L——d safe's! colleaguin
　　At some black art.—

Ilk ghaist that haunts auld ha' or chamer,
Ye gipsy-gang that deal in glamor,　　　　　20
And you, deep-read in hell's black grammar,
　　Warlocks and witches;
Ye'll quake at his conjuring hammer,
　　Ye midnight b——es.

* Vide his Antiquities of Scotland.

On the Late Captain Grose's Peregrinations. *Text from the Edinburgh edition, 1793, collated with the Huntington Library MS (HL), the Fintry MS (letter to Graham, 9 December 1789), MSS Lochryan (Loch; see Commentary), Alloway (Al) and Glenriddell (pp. 8–10; Glen), the* Edinburgh Evening Courant, *27 August 1789 (EEC) and the edition of 1794. An undated and incorrect print entitled* Address to the People of Scotland, respecting Francis Grose, Esq. *follows EEC. Title in HL Fintry Glen* On Captn Grose's present peregrinations . . . kingdom
　3 If] *correcting* Gif *in HL*　　12 O'] At *HL*　　13 By] *corrected to* At *in HL:* At *Fintry*　　auld, houlet-haunted] *correcting* lane tower, or ancient *in HL*

It's tauld he was a sodger bred,   25
And ane wad rather fa'n than fled;
But now he's quat the spurtle-blade,
    And dog-skin wallet,
And taen the—*Antiquarian trade*,
    I think they call it.   30

He has a fouth o' auld nick-nackets:
Rusty airn caps and jinglin jackets*,
Wad haud the Lothians three in tackets,
    A towmont gude;
And parritch-pats, and auld saut-backets,   35
    Before the Flood.

Of Eve's first fire he has a cinder;
Auld Tubalcain's fire-shool and fender;
That which distinguished the gender
    O' Balaam's ass;   40
A broom-stick o' the witch of Endor,
    Weel shod wi' brass.

Forbye, he'll shape you aff fu' gleg
The cut of Adam's philibeg;
The knife that nicket Abel's craig   45
    He'll prove you fully,
It was a faulding jocteleg,
    Or lang-kail gullie.—

But wad ye see him in his glee,
For meikle glee and fun has he,   50
Then set him down, and twa or three
    Gude fellows wi' him;
And *port, O port!* shine thou a wee,
    And THEN ye'll see him!

---

* Vide his treatise on ancient armour and weapons.

---

27 quat] *correcting* left *in HL* 35 parritch-pats] pirratch-pats *HL Fintry Loch Glen*: pitcher-pats *EEC* saut-backets] san-backets *EEC* 36 Before] Afore *HL Fintry EEC* 39 That which] *correcting* And what *in HL* 43 Forbye] Besides *HL Fintry Loch EEC* shape] cut *HL Fintry EEC* 44 cut] shape *HL Fintry EEC* 45 nicket] cutted *HL EEC* 47 It was] If 'twas *MSS* 50 and] *correcting* or *in Glen*

Now, by the Powers o' Verse and Prose!   55
Thou art a dainty chield, O Grose!—
Whae'er o' thee shall ill suppose,
    They sair misca' thee;
I'd take the rascal by the nose,
    Wad say, Shame fa' thee.   60

276. Written under the picture of the celebrated Miss Burns

CEASE, ye prudes, your envious railing,
  Lovely Burns has charms—*confess;*
True it is, she had one failing,
  Had ae woman ever less?

277. Song—

Tune—Auld Sir Symon

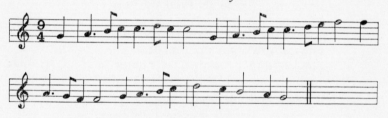

I'LL tell you a tale of a Wife,
  And she was a Whig and a Saunt;
She liv'd a most sanctify'd life,
  But whyles she was fash'd wi' her—.—
    Fal lal &c.

Written under the picture of . . . Miss Burns. *Text from Stewart, 1802 (p. 303)*

Song. *Text from a transcript of Burns's letter to Maxwell, 20 December 1789 (MS formerly in the collection of Mr. L. Wilmerding, New York), collated with MMC (pp. 23–25), which lacks stanzas 3, 6, and 7. A stanza quoted casually in a letter to Ainslie, 29 July 1787, is apparently an alternative to ll. 41–44 (transcript from Messrs Maggs):*

    Then hey, for a merry good fellow,
      And hey, for a glass of good strunt;
    May never WE SONS OF APOLLO
      E'er want a good friend and a —.

2

Poor woman! she gaed to the Priest,   5
  And till him she made her complaint;
'There's naething that troubles my breast
  'Sae sair as the sins o' my —.—

3

'Sin that I was herdin at hame,
  'Till now I'm three score and ayont,   10
'I own it wi' sin and wi' shame
  'I've led a sad life wi' my —.—

4

He bade her to clear up her brow,
  And no be discourag'd upon 't;
For holy gude women enow   15
  Were mony times waur't wi' their —.—

5

It's naught but Beelzebub's art,
  But that's the mair sign of a saunt,
He kens that ye're pure at the heart,
  Sae levels his darts at your —.—   20

6

What signifies Morals and Works,
  Our works are no wordy a runt!
It's Faith that is sound, orthodox,
  That covers the fauts o' your —.—

7

Were ye o' the Reprobate race   25
  Created to sin and be brunt,
O then it would alter the case
  If ye should gae wrang wi' your —.—

6 till] to *MMC*   15 holy] haly *MMC*   16 Were] Are *MMC*   18 But] And *MMC*   20 Sae levels] So he levels *MMC*

8

But you that is Called and Free
　Elekit and chosen a saunt,　　　　　　　　30
Will't break the Eternal Decree
　Whatever ye do wi' your —?—

9

And now with a sanctify'd kiss
　Let's kneel and renew covenant:
It's this—and it's this—and it's this—　　　35
　That settles the pride o' your —.—

10

Devotion blew up to a flame;
　No words can do justice upon 't;
The honest auld woman gaed hame
　Rejoicing and clawin her —.—　　　　　　40

11

Then high to her memory charge;
　And may he who takes it affront,
Still ride in Love's channel at large,
　And never make port in a —!!!

278. Prologue—

No song nor dance I bring from yon great city,
　That queens it o'er our taste—the more's the
　　pity:
Tho' by the bye, abroad why will you roam?
Good sense and taste are natives here at home;
But not for panegyric I appear,　　　　　　　5
I come to wish you all a good new year!

34 covenant] the cov'nant *MMC*　　39 woman] carlin *MMC*　　42 who
takes] wha taks *MMC*　　44 And] But *MMC*

Prologue. *Text from Currie (ii. 280–1; letter to Gilbert Burns, 11 January 1790),
collated with MSS Dumfries (Dum) and Alloway (Al; letter to George Sutherland, 31
December 1789). Title from Dum. Al is a draft of ll. 7–14 only*
　1 nor] no *Dum*

Old Father Time deputes me here before ye,
Not for to preach, but tell his simple story:
The sage grave ancient cough'd, and bade me say,
'You're one year older this important day,'   10
If *wiser too*—he hinted some suggestion,
But 'twould be rude, you know, to ask the question;
And with a would-be-roguish leer and wink,
He bade me on you press this one word—'THINK!'

Ye sprightly youths, quite flush with hope and spirit, 15
Who think to storm the world by dint of merit,
To you the dotard has a deal to say,
In his sly, dry, sententious, proverb way!
He bids you mind, amid your thoughtless rattle
That the first blow is ever half the battle;   20
That tho' some by the skirt may try to snatch him,
Yet by the forelock is the hold to catch him;
That whether doing, suffering, or forbearing,
You may do miracles by persevering.

Last, tho' not least in love, ye youthful fair,   25
Angelic forms, high Heaven's peculiar care!
To you old Bald-pate smooths his wrinkled brow,
And humbly begs you'll mind the important—Now!
To crown your happiness he asks your leave,
And offers, bliss to give and to receive.   30

For our sincere, tho' haply weak endeavours,
With grateful pride we own your many favors;
And howsoe'er our tongues may ill reveal it,
Believe our glowing bosoms truly feel it.

9 sage grave] sage good *Dum* (*correcting* reverend), *Al*   13-14 And . . .
THINK!'] *not in Dum*   14 He . . . word] Said, Sutherland, in one word, bid
them *Al*   16 think to storm the world] trust to win your way *Dum*
17 dotard has a deal] Sage has ever much *Dum*   20 ever] *corrected to* more
than *in Dum*   23-24 That . . . persevering.] *not in Dum*   26 Angelic
forms,] Ye angel forms *Dum*   27 old] the *Dum*   30 offers, bliss] offers
bliss, *Dum*   31 weak endeavours] poor endeavor *Dum*   32 With . . .
favors;] *Dum has*
                    To try at least to win your honor'd favor,
                    For Gratitude, and other *weighty* reasons
                    To please you be our task all times and seasons,
34 glowing bosoms truly] glowing grateful bosoms *Dnm*

279. Nithsdale's welcome hame—

Slowish

THE noble Maxwels and their powers
   Are coming o'er the border,
And they'll gae big Terreagles' towers
   And set them a' in order:
And they declare, Terreagles fair,   5
   For their abode they chuse it;
There's no a heart in a' the land
   But's lighter at the news o't.—

Tho' stars in skies may disappear,
   And angry tempests gather;   10
The happy hour may soon be near
   That brings us pleasant weather:

Nithsdale's welcome hame. *Text from the Hastie MS, f. 88, collated with the Alloway
MS (Al) and SMM, 1792 (364; signed R). SMM repeats ll. 5–8 to suit the air. Title
in Al* Nithsdale's Welcome to Terreagles—
   9 stars in skies] moon and stars *Al*   11 The . . . be] We wat na when the
hour is *Al*

The weary night o' care and grief
    May hae a joyfu' morrow,
So dawning day has brought relief,   15
    Fareweel our night o' sorrow.—

280. Green Sleeves—

G REEN sleeves and tartan ties
    Mark my truelove where she lies;
I'll be at her or she rise,
    My fiddle and I thegither.—

Be it by the chrystal burn,   5
Be it by the milk-white thorn,
I shall rouse her in the morn,
    My fiddle and I thegither.—

13 night o' care and] winter night o' *Al*

Green Sleeves. *Text from the Alloway MS, collated with the Huntington Library MS*

281. [To Alexander Findlater]

Ellisland Saturday morning

D<small>EAR</small> Sir,
　　　　　our Lucky humbly begs
Ye'll prie her caller, new-laid eggs:
L—d grant the Cock may keep his legs,
　　　　　Aboon the Chuckies;
And wi' his kittle, forket clegs,　　　　　5
　　　　　Claw weel their dockies!

Had Fate that curst me in her ledger,
A Poet poor, and poorer Gager,
Created me that feather'd Sodger,
　　　　　A generous Cock,　　　　　10
How I wad craw and strut and r—ger
　　　　　My kecklin Flock!

Buskit wi' mony a bien, braw feather,
I wad defied the warst o' weather:
When corn or bear I could na gather　　　　　15
　　　　　To gie my burdies;
I'd treated them wi' caller heather,
　　　　　And weel-knooz'd hurdies.

Nae cursed C<small>LERICAL</small> E<small>XCISE</small>
On honest Nature's laws and ties;　　　　　20
Free as the vernal breeze that flies
　　　　　At early day,
We'd tasted Nature's richest joys,
　　　　　But stint or stay.—

But as this subject's something kittle,　　　　　25
Our wisest way's to say but little;
And while my Muse is at her mettle,
　　　　　I am, most fervent,
Or may I die upon a whittle!
　　　　　Your Friend and Servant—　　　　　30
　　　　　　　Rob.ᵗ Burns.

To Alexander Findlater. *Text from the Rosebery MS (Dewar)*

PRINTED IN GREAT BRITAIN
AT THE UNIVERSITY PRESS, OXFORD
BY VIVIAN RIDLER
PRINTER TO THE UNIVERSITY